Into 3D with form·Z

Into 3D with form•Z

Modeling, Rendering, and Animation

Lachmi Khemlani

Foreword by **Dr. Mark Gross**

McGraw-Hill

New York San Francisco Washington, D.C. Auckland Bogotá
Caracas Lisbon London Madrid Mexico City Milan
Montreal New Delhi San Juan Singapore
Sydney Tokyo Toronto

Library of Congress Cataloging-in-Publication Data

Khemlani, Lachmi.
     Into 3D with form•Z : modeling, rendering, and animation / Lachmi
Khemlani.
       p.   cm.
     Includes index.
     ISBN 0-07-034933-9
Computer graphics. 2. form•Z. I. Title.
   T385.K484   1999
   006.6'93—dc21   99-25561
                                         CIP

McGraw-Hill

A Division of The McGraw·Hill Companies

    4 5 6 7 8 9 0 DOC/DOC   0 4 3 2 1

P/N 134570-1
PART OF
ISBN 0-07-034933-9

The sponsoring editor for this book was Wendy Lochner, the editing supervisor was David E. Fogarty, and the production supervisor was Pamela A. Pelton.

Printed and bound by R. R. Donnelley & Sons Company.

This book was printed on recycled, acid-free paper containing a minimum of 50% recycled de-inked fiber.

To Pran and Sarisha

Contents

Personalizing Your Environment .... WORKSHOP 3 115

Enhancing Your Modeling Capabilities .... WORKSHOP 4 175

Illuminating and Texturing Your World

WORKSHOP 6

Becoming Enmeshed in Your Creations 305

Foreword

In 1990, I visited a research lab in the Architecture department at Ohio State University, where Chris Yessios and his students were developing and working with a collection of computer graphics routines for modeling and visualizing three dimensional solids, surfaces, and voids. Some years earlier, I had run across Yessios's Ph.D. thesis from the early 1970s, on computer aided tools for site planning* when I was doing research for my own Ph.D. work. Chris Yessios and Yehuda Kalay had been the first students of Chuck Eastman, who was then heading a research effort in computer aided architectural design at Carnegie Mellon University. More recently, Yessios had developed a concept he called "void modeling," which recognizes the importance—in architectural design—not only of three dimensional solids and surfaces, but also of the *spaces* made by the arrangement of forms.

A year later, Yessios and his student David Kropp started a company, auto•des•sys, which developed and began to market a new three-dimensional modeling package for architects, under the name form•Z. The company offered an attractive joint-study program for schools that were willing to provide feedback and examples of the best student work for publication in auto•des•sys's magazine. Like many universities, we began to use it in teaching computer-aided design. It was an instant success: Students loved it, and teachers began to accept that from now on, three dimensional drawings "made on computer" would augment hand-made basswood and foam core models and sketches in design studio reviews. And as students moved out into the world of professional design, they began to introduce the software into the firms they joined. Today, form•Z is widely used in architecture firms as well as in urban planning, industrial and product design, and in the entertainment industry.

As with all new technologies, at first there was some resistance. Some effects you can only obtain with a pencil, or a rapidograph pen. But, once students and teachers began to see that digital media can augment, and need not replace, the traditional hand-made drawings and models, they began to enthusiastically adopt form•Z in their design and presentation work.

form•Z proved to be a winner, partly because Yessios and his development team had good ideas about how modeling software should serve designers, and partly because they listened to their clients. They responded to bug reports and they added features that their users requested. As a result, form•Z has grown from a simple surface and solid modeler to a sophisticated instrument, with advanced features for simulating textures and lighting, modeling meshes and terrain, and producing animated walk-throughs. You can use it to do amazing things.

That is why you need this book. form•Z is a rich piece of software and it takes time and effort to master it. There's a lot to learn. You can shorten your learning curve by getting started with an expert. Lachmi Khemlani has been teaching form•Z to architecture students at the University of California at Berkeley for several years. Based on this experience, she has developed this sequence of workshops that guides you through the basic structure of the program, and shows you by example how to create various forms and achieve desired effects.

---

* "Syntactic Structures and Procedures for Computable Site Planning," Ph.D. dissertation, Carnegie Mellon University, 1973.

Powerful programs like form•Z don't grow on trees. They arise—often out of university research labs—from a combination of experience with real world needs and knowledge of the capabilities of emerging technologies. By the time this book is published, Khemlani will have completed her own Ph.D. in computer aided design, working under the direction of Yehuda Kalay at Berkeley. And so we come full circle: the next generation of digital design media is already in the works. Meanwhile, you can get started mastering today's cutting edge technology, with this well crafted introduction to modeling, rendering, and animating in form•Z.

Mark D. Gross

Associate Professor
Department of Planning and Design
University of Colorado

Preface

Welcome to the world of 3D modeling, rendering, and animation! Imagine yourself as a sculptor, a carpenter, an architect, an interior designer, a product designer, or any kind of form-giver. You have visions of forms that you want to create and you would like to visualize them accurately in all their three-dimensional reality. You could build small-scale physical models for each of them, but you find that to be not only a cumbersome and time-consuming process, but limiting in several ways. Different shapes need vastly different materials to be modeled, and not all forms can be created with wood and paper. Also, you are frustrated by the lack of malleability of a physical model which makes it so difficult to change as your design ideas develop; you find yourself having to start from scratch every time. You would like a tool that enables you to create three-dimensional forms just as easily as your pencil moves across a piece of paper sketching them, and which can make changes and revisions to these forms as quickly as your mind goes through them. Welcome to form•Z!

form•Z is rapidly becoming one of the most popular programs for 3D design available today. Its sophistication and versatility coupled with ease of use has attracted a lot of users, both in schools as well as in the industry. No longer are designers content to use the computer to merely draft out their designs while doing their conceptualizing solely on paper; they are taking advantage of the tremendous potential offered by 3D modeling software to enhance their designing capabilities. They are discovering that being able to actually visualize their creations interactively in 3D while designing them, becomes an incentive to explore so many more alternative solutions than is possible to do using the traditional paper-and-pencil or physical model-building methods.

3D modeling motivates you to begin conceptualizing your design as you would do in real life, complete in all dimensions, rather than with projections like plans, elevations, and sections. If you want a sphere, you create a sphere. If you want a cylindrical hole punched into the sphere, that is exactly what you do. You do not try and imagine how it would look like from a particular direction and orientation. You simply build it as it would be, apply appropriate textures and simulate the desired lighting conditions, and then you have the choice to look at it from any angle, any perspective that you want. Therein lies the real power of 3D modeling. It is the closest that you can get to visualizing your design short of actually going out and creating it in real life, without having to resort to the unwieldy and inflexible process of physical model-building. What's more, form•Z provides all these powerful capabilities while still being "a lot of fun to work with"—as most designers comment when they are introduced to the program.

This book aims to give you a comprehensive understanding of how to use form•Z for 3D modeling, rendering, and animation. It comes directly from my several years of experience as an instructor in the Architecture department at University of California, Berkeley, teaching courses in which students learn how to use form•Z to explore diverse shapes and forms for their studio design projects.

The Approach

The content of this book is primarily organized into seven chapters—I refer to these as *workshops*. They are structured according to the way I teach the program to students at Berkeley, in a seven-week module. Each workshop follows a similar format—it contains a series of exercises, designed and grouped together according to the "theme" of that workshop, as reflected in its title. Each exercise consists of a sequence of steps which are described in detail. Performing these exercises as illustrated will enable you to learn about each and every one of the tools in the program and the operations that you can perform with it. Every workshop concludes with a suggested assignment, incorporating the tools learned in that session. Along with this, a demonstration of a sample design problem, based on the suggested assignment, is also provided—the main steps in the modeling process to achieve the desired form are described in detail.

This strategy has been devised to help you learn the different ways in which a design can be modeled, involving a certain sequence of operations. In the course of my teaching, I have found that many students, even after learning the use of the various tools, find the most difficult aspect of 3D modeling to be this: What approach should they take to arrive at a particular form? In form•Z, there is invariably more than one way to model something. One approach may be slow, arduous, and involved. Another may be faster, more logical, and more accurate. How can you identify which is the "better way" to model something? Undoubtedly, this is something which comes with practice. But for now, I anticipate that by observing the sequence of operations *I* choose to arrive at a particular form (which comes from many teaching sessions and solving the umpteen modeling problems students come up with!), you can begin to identify for yourself, the easier, faster, and more efficient way to model various kinds of objects. I often have students coming to me with an overall form and asking—"Where do I start for something like this?" Some of the examples I present here come straight from such modeling problems I was asked to help with.

The content of each workshop has evolved considerably from the time I first taught the course, based on my assessment of the manner in which students responded to it, and their direct feedback and evaluation of the course after each session. In fact, I consider the sequence in which the material is presented and the manner in which the exercises are designed as two of the main strengths of this book. Without this carefully thought-out and organized sequence, one might just as well go through the manuals of the program and try and learn how to use form•Z from them.

It is important to understand the difference between a book and a manual. A manual is indispensable as a source of reference for a program. However, by virtue of its very nature, it is not the best way to learn to *use* a program. A manual has to describe everything, all the features that exist in a program, equally well in full detail—even those features that you might rarely or never ever have to use. A manual does not discriminate between important and unimportant features—it must tell you everything. Moreover, a manual describes all the tools and their operations in the sequence in which they appear in the program, rather than in the manner in which the tools are most likely to be used and need to be learned by the user.

The intent of this book is not to replace the use of the manuals altogether, for those of you who have access to them. You might need to consult them occasionally for more detailed information about certain tools and operations. What this book will do is guide you in learning to use the program easily. You will start with the more elementary tools and create simple forms and compositions, build up your understanding of the program gradually, and learn to create more complex shapes and carry out more complicated operations as the workshops progress. By the end of the book, you will have worked with all the tools and should be well on your way towards using form•Z comfortably, confidently, with a clear understanding of what tool to use to create, render, and animate the forms you envision.

This book does not require you to have had prior experience with either 3D modeling or 2D drafting programs. However, basic familiarity with your operating system is assumed. This includes opening, closing, and saving files; working with windows; using the shortcut keys that appear on the pulldown menus; performing basic operations such as cut, copy, and paste that are found in almost any application; doing a page setup before printing; and so on. Refer to the manuals that came with your operating system if you need help with any of these tasks.

Overview of the Book

form•Z gives you the option of working in two different environments—*modeling* and *drafting*—each of which has its own set of tools and its own windows. The modeling environment is for working in 3D, while drafting is exclusively 2D. Although they are not synchronized, i.e., the drafting module does not automatically generate plans and sections of modeling objects, communicating between the two environments is fairly straightforward. Since the objective of this book is 3D design, we will concentrate primarily on the modeling environment in all the workshops. An Appendix is provided at the end of the book, however, that will give you an overview of the drafting module, which provides you with tools and capabilities similar to what you can find in other conventional drafting programs.

The book starts with an introductory chapter which will give you a basic understanding of the form•Z interface, starting with launching the program, to learning to exchange files with other CAD and graphics programs. Then come the actual workshops, a brief overview of which is given in the following paragraphs.

Workshop 1 will introduce you to the basic modeling operations of form•Z. You will learn how to create simple 2D and 3D objects, along with some elementary transformations and boolean operations. You will also learn how to interact with the program through the various palettes and dialogs associated with different tools.

In Workshop 2, you will learn how to create models that are "to scale." This includes setting up the units of measurement, using the coordinate displays effectively, and specifying values using the mouse as well as the keyboard. You will also see how to restrain the cursor movement in various ways, create new objects with reference to existing ones, work at multiple levels ranging from points to groups, apply transformations and make copies of objects in different ways, and finally, work with the insertion tools which can be used to perform some boolean operations more simply and elegantly.

Workshop 3 will teach you how to customize your working environment. You will learn to modify the default colors used by the system, create new colors or surface styles, change the way the various display options work, use multiple layers, and create and save your own reference planes and views of the modeling world. Finally, you will learn how to save the modified settings as "preference files," which you can then recall for use in other projects when needed.

In Workshop 4, you will be introduced to several new modeling tools for creating more complex forms. You will see how to revolve simple 2D shapes about an axis or "sweep" and "skin" them along various paths, derive new objects from existing ones in various ways, work with powerful sectioning tools, model undulating landforms and terrains, round object edges and corners, and transform objects using draft angles. You will also learn how to build up sophisticated configurations by attaching objects to each other in various ways, align and distribute objects, extend and trim them with respect to other objects, and position them along a path to generate interesting forms.

Workshop 5 is devoted to imaging, lights, and textures. You will study the extensive set of options available to you for rendering your models, learn how to light up your objects in various ways using multiple light types, and explore the radiosity-based rendering feature which enhances lighting effects considerably. You will also see how to map textures to objects more precisely, apply multiple textures to the same surface using decals, and look at some other object attributes that can be manipulated to achieve interesting rendering effects.

Workshop 6 covers all various mesh-related tools of form•Z which can greatly enhance your ability to do organic modeling, i.e., modeling of non-rectilinear forms. This includes creating plain and smooth meshes on the surfaces of objects, and applying movements, disturbances, various kinds of deformations, and image-based displacements to meshed objects, all of which can be used to mold objects in various ways. You will also work with various parametric curves and meshed objects including "nurbz" and "patches," and learn how to carry out boolean operations on meshed objects.

In Workshop 7, you will be introduced to the amazing realm of 3D text with which you can populate your models. You will learn to create and use "symbols" or object libraries, and venture further into the realm of organic modeling using the sophisticated capabilities of "metaformz." Finally, you will see how to generate QuickTime VR movies as well as animation sequences of your modeling world.

The book concludes with an Appendix that provides a brief overview of the drafting module of form•Z.

About form•Z

This book incorporates the latest release of form•Z—version 3.0. This version is a major overhaul from the earlier versions, with a change in interface as well as the introduction of many new features and tools. As far as the older tools are concerned, some of them are now located differently within the tool palettes, and in many cases, what were previously options within a tool are now separate tools in their own right. Keep this in mind if you are using a version of form•Z prior to 3.0, and you will be able to use this book just as gainfully. You will also have a head start with version 3.0, whenever you decide to upgrade.

form•Z is available as three separate programs: form•Z, form•Z RenderZone, and form•Z RadioZity. The first includes just the modeling functions; the second includes lighting, texture mapping, and rendering capabilities; while the third adds radiosity-based rendering, which simulates the lighting conditions in a scene more accurately and realistically. This book covers the features available in all three programs.

form•Z comes on both the Macintosh and Windows platforms, and using popular terminology, I will refer to these as *Mac* and *PC* respectively. The window snapshots and dialog boxes that are illustrated in this book come from both platforms. As far as usage is concerned, there are only minor differences between the two which I will mention as and when they appear. The reader of this book is by no means limited to either platform—it can be used by both the Mac and PC users of form•Z.

Starting with version 3.0, form•Z is no longer supported on 68K Mac and Windows 3.1. For the Mac platform, you need a Power Macintosh with MacOS version 7.1.2 or later, at least 16 MB RAM, and 20 MB hard disk space. The minimum system requirements on the PC side are a 486 processor, Microsoft Windows NT v.3.5 or later, Windows 95, or Windows 98, 16 MB RAM, and 20 MB hard disk space. A Windows NT version of form•Z is also available for D.E.C's Alpha processor, which requires 32 MB RAM and 30 MB hard disk space.

Acknowledgments

I owe this book to my husband, Pran Kurup. It was he who suggested I write it in the first place, and has continued to provide tremendous support and motivation throughout this endeavor, not to mention tons of firsthand advice coming from his own book-writing experiences. It has been great having such a sounding board for ideas right in my own home.

Long-term credit for this venture goes all the way back to my parents, Rita and Shyam Khemlani, who never told me there was anything I could not do in life.

My heartfelt gratitude goes to Wendy Lochner, Senior Editor for Architecture at McGraw-Hill, who responded to my book proposal with such enthusiasm and did everything it took to turn it into an actual book.

Special thanks to Chris Yessios, President of auto•des•sys Inc., for heading the development of a splendid program like form•Z, and for his support of this book ever since its inception. His feedback on the manuscript was invaluable, coming from a source who knows the subject so well.

I would like to thank Mark Gross, who shares my enthusiasm for form•Z, and kindly agreed to write the Foreword for this book.

I could not have written this book if I had not been given the continued opportunity to teach form•Z at Berkeley by Yehuda Kalay, Professor of Architecture. I thank him also for reviewing my book proposal for McGraw-Hill.

I am grateful to all the students at Berkeley who have, over the years, enrolled in my form•Z workshops. Their endless barrage of questions taught me more than I could have ever hoped to learn on my own.

It has been a real pleasure working with Margaret Webster-Shapiro, Assistant Art Director at McGraw-Hill, on the cover design of this book.

I appreciate the efforts of all the people at McGraw-Hill whom I interacted with during the course of this project: David Fogarty, Editing Supervisor; Robin Gardner, Editorial Assistant; Cathy Markoff, Associate Marketing Manager; Thomas Kowalczyk, E.D.P. manager; and Pamela Pelton, Production Supervisor. Special thanks to Handel Low, Senior Designer, for the original design of the CD face.

Thanks are also due to the folks at auto•des•sys Inc. for their help and support: in particular, David Kropp, Vice President for Development, who supervised the production of the master CD, and Bill Robinson, Art Director, who finished the design of the CD face.

Many thanks to the artists who contributed their images for the back cover: Pedro Bonta, Michael Llewellyn, Chris Lockwood, and Kenneth Stolls.

On a more personal note, I would like to thank my mother-in-law, Saroja Kurup, who was around at a crucial phase and helped take care of my newborn daughter, giving me much-needed time to wrap up this book.

Above all, I'd like to acknowledge my baby daughter, Sarisha, who not only has peacefully endured my book-writing stress all this time, but on the contrary, has been my greatest stress-reducer since she was born.

Getting Acquainted

This introductory chapter starts with an overview of the different kinds of objects, both 2D and 3D, that can be created in form•Z, giving you a snapshot of the entire program and its repertoire. Keep this broad picture in mind when you proceed to the workshops and start exploring the individual tools. You will find yourself working with greater clarity and a lot less confusion than you would if you just plunged into the details right away.

After the overview of objects, the rest of the Introduction focuses on some of the key features of the form•Z interface which you should be comfortable with before proceeding to the workshops. You will start by launching the program, then move on to look at the different component windows which make up the interface. You will learn how to work with the various tool palettes, get online help when you need it, and enhance your speed and efficiency with the program by creating your own shortcut keys for various tools and operations. Finally, you will learn how to communicate between form•Z and other CAD and graphics programs.

1. Overview of form•Z Objects

form•Z is both a solid and surface modeler. Unlike some other modeling programs which simulate the modeling of solids by actually manipulating only surfaces, form•Z is a "true" solid modeler. As a result, it has a large number of tools that let you model even complex solids in relatively simple ways.

Figure I.1 shows a simplified chart categorizing the various object types you will find in form•Z. There are dedicated modeling tools for each of these objects. In addition, there are several other tools that can manipulate these objects in various ways; for instance, there is a Sweep tool that can convert a 2D open surface into a 3D solid object by simply "sweeping" it along a 2D path. You will learn more about this tool in Workshop 4.

As shown in Figure I.1, there are three basic categories of objects: surfaces, surface solids, and solids. A *surface* object can be further divided into two subtypes: *open* surfaces whose endpoints do not meet, therefore these objects have no area; and *closed* surfaces whose endpoints do meet, which therefore have an area. Each of these object categories comprises several different kinds of objects.

Notice that the *closed surface object* category looks almost identical to the *surface solid* category. Both have no thickness and therefore no volume. The only visible difference seems to be that closed surfaces have directions (just like open surfaces), whereas surface solids have no directionality. The underlying difference is that a closed surface object is *one-sided*: it has a single surface that has an area. The directions indicated are the directions of the edges that make up this single surface, which in turn are determined by how these edges are drawn. In contrast, a surface solid is *two-sided*: it is actually a solid with two equal, coincident, and opposite surfaces, but no thickness. You will learn more about the operational differences between these two kinds of objects once you proceed to the workshops.

Figure I.1

Objects in form•Z.

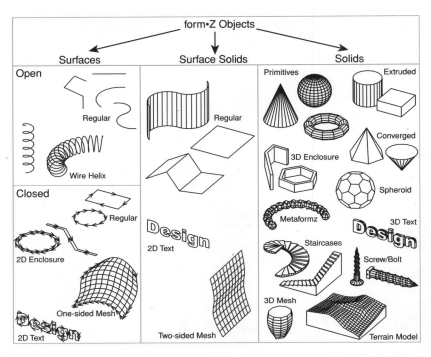

Notice also the objects referred to as *enclosures*, both in 2D as well as in 3D. Mathematically, these are no different from the regular objects in their respective categories. The distinction is made because form•Z has dedicated tools for creating both 2D and 3D enclosures, which is of great convenience, especially in architectural modeling.

By far the largest variety of objects is in the *solids* category, reinforcing the emphasis of form•Z on simplifying the complicated process of solid modeling as much as possible. Some of these objects are shown in Figure I.1; a complete listing would take up too much space. All the objects shown are mathematically true solids with a definite volume, but it helps a great deal to have separate tools devoted exclusively towards creating basic primitives, simple extrusions, converged solids, spheroids, terrain models, staircases, and so on.

Objects in form•Z have an additional attribute of "personality," which is not illustrated here to avoid confusion. We will study the different personalities an object can assume in Section 2.3 of Workshop 1.

Now that we have a basic understanding of the different kinds of objects that can be created in form•Z, let us proceed towards getting acquainted with the actual form•Z interface.

2. Launching form•Z

The form•Z folder on your desktop should look like the one shown in Figure I.2 if you are using a PC. The Mac icons are similar. Go ahead and launch form•Z by double-clicking on the main application icon, which is circled in the illustration. It takes a few moments for the program to go through the initialization routines, after which you will be asked to click or press the return (Mac) or Enter (PC) key to continue. Do so.

Figure I.2

The form•Z folder with its various icons. The main application icon is circled.

Much of the form•Z interface is visible to you as soon as you start the application—the main graphics window, several other floating windows, and rows and columns of various tools for different functions. At first sight, it might seem overwhelming, making you wonder how you are ever going to be able to find your way around the program without getting confused or lost. The rest of this chapter is aimed at alleviating precisely this fear—it will help you navigate through the program easily and understand how to work with the various components that make up the form•Z program. You should come away from it with an appreciation of what is, in fact, a very lucid, easy-to-use, and elegant user interface.

3. Exploring the Basic Interface

As soon as you launch the form•Z application, you are presented with the screen layout shown in Figure I.3. The basic interface is made up of several different items; these are annotated in the illustration and briefly described below. Some of the items are referred to by an abbreviation which is given in parentheses beside the name. Keep a careful note of this—the same abbreviation will be used in referring to these items throughout the book.

Menu Bar

This is the standard menu bar located at the top of the screen. In form•Z, it consists of nine pulldown menus for different functions, including Help. (If you are using Version 8.0 or higher of the Mac OS, you will see an additional Help menu at the end which provides help with the Mac OS functions. Be careful not to confuse this with the form•Z Help menu.) In this book, menu items will be referenced in the format, *main menu > submenu*. So, for instance, Display > Wire Frame refers to the Wire Frame item under the Display menu.

Glance through the menus and you will find that some of the menu items have an asterisk * sign associated with them. This indicates that there is a dialogue box (called *dialog* for short) associated with the operation performed by that item, containing various options. This dialog can be accessed by selecting that menu item with the option key (Mac) or Ctrl+Shift keys (PC) pressed. You will learn more about working with dialogs in Workshop 1.

Figure I.3

The different components making up the form•Z interface.

Window Name

form•Z is organized in projects. A "project" essentially corresponds to a file. By default, form•Z presents you with a new Untitled1 project when it is launched. The word Model in square brackets in the window title bar indicates that you are in the modeling environment. Of course, you also know this from the fact that all the three coordinate axes—X, Y, and Z—are visible in the window. In the drafting environment, the word [Model] in the window title would be replaced by [Draft], and you would see only the X and Y axes. This makes it possible to easily distinguish between the two window types. For most of this book, we will be dealing with the modeling environment, and consequently, with modeling windows.

One project can have many windows associated with it, hence the window is named Untitled1-1, indicating that it is the first window of the Untitled1 project. Even though multiple windows can be opened for a particular project, only one can be "active" at any given time. Essentially, this means that you can work in only one window at a time. A window is made active by clicking on it. When a project is saved, all the windows "associated" with that project are saved. Further discussion on associated windows will appear in Workshop 3.

Graphics Window

The graphics window is where all the modeling and visualization activities take place. Initially, this is blank except for the default display of the XY reference plane grid colored in teal (a bluish-green color), and the three coordinate axes—X, Y, and Z—colored in red. The black line with the arrow at one end represents the direction of the sun.

The graphics window can be divided into a number of frames, each of which can be set to a different view of the modeling world. It is possible to continue drawing from one frame to another; this provides additional flexibility and convenience in modeling. By default, the graphics window consists of a single frame, as you can see. It is indicated by the name, frame 1-1(Axon), appearing at the top of the window, just below the window title bar. The two numbers stand for the window number and frame number respectively, while the word Axon in parentheses is the name of the view to which the frame is set. We will learn more about frames and how to work with them in Workshop 3.

Modeling Tools (M-Tool)

One of the most user-friendly aspects of the form•Z interface, in contrast to other modeling and drafting programs, is that you never have to type in any commands! You simply click on the icon of whatever operation it is that you wish to perform. All the hassles associated with typing, including typing mistakes, are avoided altogether. Moreover, the icons of all the tools can be readily seen and consequently easily accessed, rather than being buried under layers of menu hierarchies.

All the tools in form•Z are divided into two categories: those that deal with the creation and editing of entities, grouped under the *modeling tool palette*; and those that deal with manipulating some aspect of the window display, grouped under the *window tool palette*. The modeling tool palette is the vertical palette positioned on the left side of the graphics window. It consists of 14 rows of tools, arranged in two columns, used to carry out the various modeling operations. Each row in turn has many tool icons. The complete modeling tool palette is shown in Figure I.4.

Figure I.4

All the tools in the modeling tool palette.

In this book, any tool from the modeling palette will be referred to by its row number, accompanied by an "a" or a "b" to indicate whether it is in the left column or the right column respectively, then followed by its order in that row. Thus, for example, M-Tool:5b,1 refers to the first tool, Revolve, located in the right column of the fifth row. Check it out and verify that this is indeed the case. A more comprehensive discussion on the use of the palettes appears a little later in Section 4.

Window Tools (W-Tool)

The window tool palette is the horizontal palette positioned in the lower left margin of the graphics window. It consists of eight vertically arranged columns of tools. As mentioned earlier, the tools here control the graphic environment of the window, so every window of the project will have its own set of window tools located at its base. The complete window tool palette is shown in Figure I.9. Just as with the modeling tools, the window tools will be referred to by their position in the columns. So, for instance, W-Tool:6,4 refers to the fourth tool from the bottom, Midpoint Snap, in the sixth column. Again, check it out.

When you work with multiple windows and find it inconvenient to access each one of their window tool palettes individually, the same set of tools is also available as a "floating palette" (described next) from the Palettes main menu. You can open this and position it anywhere on the screen for easy access. The tools activated in this floating palette will change depending upon which window is activated, keeping in sync with that window's own tool palette.

Floating Palettes

These are small floating windows that can be positioned anywhere on the screen—there are thirteen in all. Of these, nine are opened by default when you open a new project, and positioned as shown in Figure I.3. Each of them can be closed if not required by clicking on the close button in the upper left corner, and can be reopened, when required, by going to the Palettes menu and selecting the required palette.

4. Working with the Tool Palettes

You have seen that there are two kinds of tool palettes—modeling and window. Each one of these comprises many tools grouped together in related rows (as in the case of modeling tools) or in related columns (as in the case of window tools). Both these palettes work on similar principles, which are briefly discussed below.

All the tools in a row (or column) are not immediately visible. To see the entire set, you need to click on the first tool in that row, keeping the mouse down. This brings up the complete set of tools from which the desired one can be selected by moving to it (see Figure I.5). The selected tool will now be positioned in the beginning of the row, and it will remain there until another tool from that set is selected. This avoids the tedium of having to go over the same process again when working with a particular tool repeatedly. The selected tool will be highlighted to indicate that it is the currently active tool from the entire palette. Only one such tool can be active at any given time.

Figure I.5

Taking a look at all the tools belonging to one row of the modeling tool palette.

While most of the tools in both the modeling and window tool palettes are colored in black, you can see that some tools in three particular rows—2, 4, and 11—of the modeling palette are colored in teal or magenta. These tools function differently from the other tools—they *set a mode* for the black-colored tools to operate in, rather than *perform an operation*. You will learn more about each of these tools as the workshops progress.

Any particular row or column of tools from either palette can be "torn off" by clicking on it and dragging to position it anywhere on the screen (see Figure I.6) Subsequently, all the regular window operations—moving, closing, and so on—can be applied to it. This is particularly useful when you work with a certain set of tools very frequently and require them to be constantly visible to you.

Figure I.6

Two tool palettes "torn off" the screen.

Figure I.7

The dialog invoked by the Customize Tools command.

Once you have gained expertise with the program and use it extensively, you might also like to "customize" the tool palettes, based on your style of working and the project at hand. Customization basically involves reorganizing the tools in the palettes, deleting some of them if necessary. To undertake this process, select the last command from the Palettes menu, Customize Tools. This invokes the dialog shown in Figure I.7. The Category popup menu at the top of the dialog lets you select which tool palette you want to customize: drafting, modeling, or window. The default, as you can see, is the modeling tool palette.

The Icons Customization dialog contains three separate windows showing the icons of the tool palette that is selected for customization. All three windows have different functions. The Tool Bar window shows the first icon of each set of tools (row or column) in the palette, as it appears in the toolbar on the screen. An icon is selected by clicking on it; this actually selects the entire set of tools represented by that icon. Multiple icons can be selected using the Shift key. Once an icon is selected, it can be deleted by clicking on the accompanying Remove button, or it can be dragged to another location in the toolbar. If you double-click on an icon, a dialog is invoked in which you can change the default name assigned to that tool set. You can also create new tool sets using the accompanying New button; these are placed by default at the bottom of the toolbar. Thus, in the Tool Bar window, you are essentially working with *entire tool sets*.

To "fill" new tool sets that you have created with tools, you have to use the second window in the Icons Customization dialog, Tool Palettes. This window shows the individual tools in each tool set whose first icon is depicted in the Tool Bar window. Here again, icons can be selected for repositioning or deletion by clicking on them. You can move an icon to a different location in the same palette, or move it to a different palette. Once selected, an icon can be deleted using the accompanying Remove button. Thus, you are actually working with *individual tools* here rather than with entire tool sets.

There is a third window in the dialog called Tool Set, which also displays the individual tool icons of the palette selected for customization. Unlike the Tool Palettes window which gets updated to show the customized toolbar of that palette, the contents of the Tool Set window do not change. It retains all the available tools in their default positions in the palette; the tools cannot be deleted or repositioned. However, they *can* be copied across to the tool sets in the Tool Palettes window above by clicking and dragging. Thus, if you delete some tools in the Tool Palettes window and find out at a later stage that you need to include them again, you can always copy them across from the "permanent" collection in the Tool Set window.

The few remaining options located at the base of the Icons Customization dialog serve various functions. The Defaults button is used to reset the selected palette to the default form•Z layout. Reset, on the other hand, resets the layout to what it was when the dialog was invoked, eliminating all the subsequent changes. You can save your customized layout to a menu file, automatically given the ".mnu" extension, using the Save command. Many such menu files can be created. Any menu file can be loaded for use in subsequent sessions of form•Z using Load. The last option, Icon Style, lets you choose between three different types of looks for the various icons. The default of Gray gives them a 3D appearance, as shown in Figure I.7. In all the other illustrations, the Original style has been used.

 Throughout this book, the tool icons will mostly be shown in the Original form•Z style as it is clearer in print.

Since there are so many tools in both the modeling and window tool palettes put together, it can be a somewhat daunting task, as a beginner to the program, to remember what each tool is used for. Although by the end of this book you will have learned about each tool in depth, you can get a "sneak preview" right away by using the Help option, which is discussed in detail next.

5. Getting Help

form•Z has a comprehensive, well-organized and user-friendly help system built into its interface. Instead of the conventional Help menus found in other applications in which you have to traverse a series of hyperlinks to ultimately get to the information you want, form•Z tells you directly what any tool or menu item is used for. Say, for instance, you want more information about the Mesh tool, which is the first tool in the left column of the sixth row of the modeling palette. Simply select it and then go to Help > General. This invokes a dialog which provides a brief synopsis about the selected tool (Figure I.8).

Figure I.8

The Help dialog for the Mesh tool.

Figure I.9

The Help dialog for the window tool palette. Information is being displayed about W-Tool:7,1.

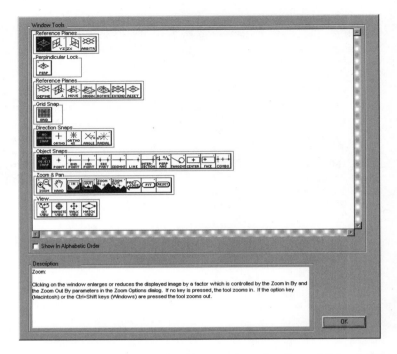

You can see that the Help dialog also gives you the option to branch off to additional information about each one of the tools and menus that make up the form•Z environment. If you click on the Window Tools button, for instance, a dialog displaying all the window tools is invoked (see Figure I.9). Information about any tool can now be obtained by simply highlighting it with the cursor. You don't need to click on a tool, merely move the mouse over it. Similarly, information about all the modeling tools can be obtained in an identical fashion by invoking the Modeling Tools option in the Help dialog.

Each one of the options shown in the Help dialog in Figure I.8 is also directly accessible from the Help menu. So, for instance, you can directly access the Window Tools dialog shown in Figure I.9 by going to Help > Window Tools. Spend some time at this stage browsing through the descriptions of some of the tools in both the modeling as well as the window tool palettes. It will give you a good feel for what the different kinds of tools are and how they are organized.

Check out also the Keyboard and Menus options in the Help menu; you will find them very useful. The Drafting Tools option can be explored when you go through the brief overview of the drafting module in the Appendix. The Error Messages option lets you view a log of the errors you ran into during your work, while the Project Info dialog provides you with useful information about the objects in the project

6. Creating Your Own Shortcut Keys

Many of the commands that appear in the form•Z pulldown menus have their associated shortcut keys, which appear beside the name of the command, just like in any other program. Thus, the default shortcut key for File > Quit, as you would expect, is command+Q on the Mac and Ctrl+Q on the PC. However, as you will see from browsing through the various menus, not all commands have such shortcut keys associated with them. When you start working with the tool palettes, you will find that the various tools they contain also do not have shortcut keys associated with them by default. In versions prior to 2.9, you had no choice but to select these menu commands and tools using the mouse in the regular fashion, without any shortcut keys.

form•Z now has an added utility that lets you create and store your own shortcut keys. With this utility, you can assign your own key combinations to the tools and commands that you use very frequently, bringing them literally to your fingertips. If a shortcut key already exists for a particular command, you can also choose to overwrite it with your own combination. Different users can create their own sets of shortcut keys and save them in files, which they can readily access even when they move to a different computer. The convenience of this utility can greatly enhance your speed and efficiency with the program, taking it to an altogether new level of user-friendliness!

The process of creating shortcut keys is carried out in the Key Shortcuts Manager dialog (Figure I.10-a), which is accessed by going to Edit > Key Shortcuts. The window on the left lists all the menu items and tools, hierarchically grouped under the menu or tool palette name. There are 15 main categories to begin with. Any category can be opened or closed by clicking on the arrows (Mac) or the plus/minus signs (PC) beside its name. Figure I.10-a shows the Help menu expanded in this fashion, the contents of which you are already acquainted with from the previous section. Any item from the expanded list can be selected by clicking on it. If a shortcut key is associated with that item by default, it will appear in the Shortcuts window on the right side of the dialog.

Figure I.10

The Key Shortcuts Manager dialog, showing the expanded list of items under the Help menu, and the Add Shortcut dialog (Mac), showing the shortcut created for the selected item.

As you can see, there is no shortcut key associated with the Modeling Tools item that is selected in Figure I.10-a. To create your own shortcut key for this command, simply click on the Add button. This will open up the Add Shortcut dialog (Figure I.10-b), the contents of which will differ slightly depending upon which platform you are using. The idea, however, is the same: you can make up a combination of *keys* (such as Control, Option, and so on), and *key strokes* (such as A, B, 1, 2, etc.) or *mouse clicks* (single, double, etc.) that will function as the shortcut key for the selected item. Note that you can use either a key stroke or a mouse click in a shortcut, but not both.

Figure I.10-b shows that the combination of Control+1 on the Mac has been selected as the shortcut for the Modeling Tools Help item. To see if it actually works, exit both dialogs by clicking on their OK buttons and test this key combination; you should find that it opens up the Modeling Tools Help dialog without requiring you to go and select it from the menu. Convenient, isn't it?

The Key Shortcuts Manager dialog has some additional options for managing shortcuts. You can Edit or Delete a particular shortcut, Clear all of them, or Reset them to what they were when you last entered the dialog. You can Save your set of created shortcuts to a file, which is automatically given the ".sct" extension. You can use the Load button to load this shortcut file in future working sessions of form•Z. The Load Defaults button will load all the default shortcuts, while the List Shortcuts button will list the current set of shortcuts in an organized fashion. It also gives you the option to print the list for easy reference.

While you may not need to create your own shortcuts while you are learning the program, you will find this a very convenient utility once you become proficient with form•Z and start using it extensively. Be aware, therefore, that such a utility exists, so that you know how to use it once the time comes.

7. Communicating with Other Programs

form•Z allows you to read from and write to a large variety of file formats used by other CAD and graphics programs. These include DXF, DWG, 3D Studio, EPS, Lightscape, BMP, EPS, TIFF, Illustrator, JPEG, and so on. The complete list can be seen by going to the Open, Save As or Import commands under the File pulldown menu and opening the File Format popup list located at the base of the dialog that is invoked (see Figure I.11). Exporting animation files is handled differently, and we will look at that process in Workshop 7.

Figure I.11

The Save Project As dialog, showing the list of different file formats that a form•Z project can be saved in.

Figure I.11 shows the Save Project As dialog, which enables you to *export* a form•Z file to a different file format. Depending upon the format chosen, a dialog containing various options is invoked, allowing you to specify the translation parameters. In this dialog, the options common to all file formats are located at the top, while the options specific to the chosen file format are located at the bottom. This is clearly visible in the dialog for the DXF file format, shown in Figure I.12. Many of the translation options contained in these dialogs may not be comprehensible now, but will be self-explanatory once you master form•Z. Of course, you must also have a good understanding of the programs you want to export the form•Z files to. You might have to make a few trial runs of different export parameters, until you can pinpoint the exact combination which serves your purpose.

Figure I.12

The Export Options dialog for the DXF file format, invoked from the Save Project As dialog.

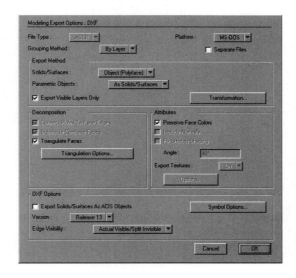

There are two ways of *importing* a file of a different format into form•Z. You can simply open the file itself by going to File > Open and selecting the file. Needless to say, it has to match one of the formats contained in the accompanying File Format popup list. After the file is selected, an Import Options dialog for that file format will open up, similar in content and organization to the Export Options dialog. Here, you can modify the default import parameters, if required. These again will be largely self-explanatory once you master the program. After the import parameters have been specified, the file opens up in a new form•Z window, that is, as a new form•Z project.

The other way of importing a file of a different format is to use File > Import. It works exactly like Open, except that the contents of the imported file are placed in the currently active form•Z project. This is useful because very often you need to add an object or element created using another program into an existing form•Z file, rather than open it as a separate project.

Finally, note that the file formats of programs creating 2D elements or images—for instance, Illustrator, TIFF, Targa, JPEG, and so on—can be imported either as modeling elements or as drafting elements, into the modeling and drafting environments respectively. So make the appropriate selection in the Import Options dialog, depending upon what you wish to achieve.

With this brief introduction to the form•Z interface, we are now ready to take our first plunge into the world of 3D modeling, rendering, and animation, starting with Workshop 1.

Letting Yourself Go

This workshop will introduce you to the basic modeling operations of form•Z. It comprises four exercises, covering a wide range of both modeling and window tools. You will learn how to create simple 2D and 3D objects, along with some elementary transformations and boolean operations. You will also learn how to interact with the program through the various palettes and dialogs associated with different tools.

In this workshop, the concern will not be with aspects such as working units, drawing scale, creating objects of specific dimensions, and so on. The idea, instead, is to simply let yourself loose and create any forms you want, of any size and scale you want.

WORKSHOP 1

Beginning with 2D: A Complete Session

In this exercise, we will run through an entire session of form•Z, starting with launching the program, creating simple 2D elements, performing basic operations such as moving and deleting objects, changing viewpoints as well as the display mode, deriving 3D objects from 2D elements, and finally, printing what we have. This exercise is slightly atypical, since it deals with such a broad range of tools and functions. Most of the other exercises, particularly in succeeding workshops, will focus on a single tool or a group of related tools. It is important, however, to start with as large a picture as possible.

1.1   Setting the Stage: Starting form•Z

▣ Launch form•Z. A default modeling window will appear on the screen, as you saw in Figure I.3 of the Introduction. Save it as a new project using **File > Save As** and specify a suitable file name. The file is saved by default in the form•Z format and an extension of ".fmz" is automatically given to the file name. Although you have a choice of deleting this extension, it is advisable to retain it in order to be able to differentiate between the various file types that can be generated in form•Z alone.

Once you start working on actual projects, make it a habit to keep saving at regular intervals so that you don't lose your work in the event of a computer crash. form•Z does have an "automatic save" option like many other programs, and we will look at this feature in Workshop 3. (However, it may not always be advisable to use such an option, for reasons we shall soon see.) At any point of time, you can choose to go back to the last saved version of the project using **File > Revert to Saved**.

▣ The default view is axonometric. Change it to a plan view by selecting **View > Top**. The graphics window will now resemble a graph sheet.

▣ Turn off the palettes for **Coordinates, Tool Options, Lights, Objects, Layers, Views**, and **Animation** by clicking on their close buttons. You will not be using these in most of the exercises in this workshop. Make sure that the **Prompts** palette is open—this is where you will interface with the program, give your input, and receive messages from the system.

▣ Let the **Surface Styles** palette (or the **Colors** palette in the non-RenderZone version of form•Z) also be open, so that you can create objects with different colors. The color that is highlighted in this palette is the *active* color; all objects are created using the active color. To designate another color from the palette as the active color, simply click on it and it will be highlighted. Change the active color frequently in this manner as you work on the rest of the exercise—having a large variety of colors on your screen will make it a lot more fun.

1.2   Single-line 2D Mode

▣ Select **M-Tool:2a,1**. Recall from the Introduction that this notation refers to the first tool in the left column of the second row of the modeling tool palette. Make sure you have selected the icon shown on the right.

The entire second left row consists of the *object generation modes*—the mode that is selected from here will determine what kinds of objects the tools in the third row will create: 2D single or double lines, or 3D extruded, converged, or enclosed solids. The first tool on this row, which you have just selected, sets the object generation mode to 2D Surface Object.

1.3   Creating Closed Shapes

▣ Select the Rectangle tool, the first of the drawing tools in the left column of the third row. Use it to draw a rectangle anywhere on the screen. The first click of the mouse picks one end, the second click completes the figure. Don't worry about the dimensions of the shape at this stage.

Notice that you do not have to keep the mouse down and drag to draw the rectangle, as in many other drawing programs—form•Z considers the multiple-click method more user-friendly than the click-and-drag method. The same concept applies to all the other drawing operators as well.

▣ Now select M-Tool:3a,2—the 3 Point Rectangle tool—and draw another rectangle on the screen. Notice the difference in method. Three clicks are required here, and the rectangle does not have to be aligned parallel to the X and Y axes, as with M-Tool:3a,1 (see Figure 1.1 to clarify the difference). The first two mouse clicks determine the alignment of the rectangle; the third determines its dimensions. Remember that your mode is still set to 2D Surface Object, so that is exactly the kind of object you are creating.

Figure 1.1

2D single-line shapes created using the first two tools in the left column of the third row.

▣ Continue to use all the other tools in the third left row to create different shapes: polygons, circles, and ellipses. You will notice that there are multiple tools for drawing circles as well as ellipses, depending upon how you want the operation to be executed. Explore all of them and see how they differ. The icons of these tools do a good job of indicating how they operate, so use them as your guide.

  All the objects you are creating now are one-sided surfaces, not two-sided surface solids.

▣ Remember to work with different colors by frequently changing the active color in the Surface Styles palette. Avoid choosing red for now as it is the color used by the program for highlighting selected objects, so it can be confusing to have objects colored in red as well. For all those of you who love red—don't despair! You will learn to change the system default colors in Workshop 3 and then be able to use all the red you want.

WORKSHOP 1

1.4 Working with Dialogs and the Tool Options Palette

You will have noticed that the Polygon operator (M-Tool:3a,3) creates only six-sided shapes. Obviously, you might need to change that specification at times to be able to create polygons of other shapes. This can be done very easily:

◻ Double-click on the Polygon tool icon. Alternately, click on it while holding down the option key (Mac) or Ctrl+Shift keys (PC). On the PC, you can also simply click on the icon with the right mouse button.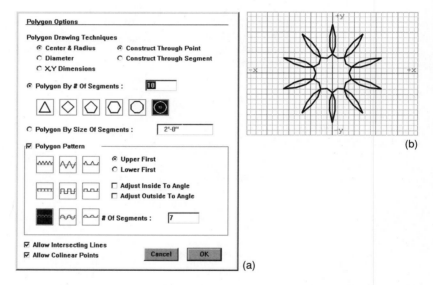

◻ In response to one of these techniques, a dialog pops up in which you can specify the number of sides you want your polygon to have (see Figure 1.2-a). You can also choose to create a polygon by specifying a fixed length for its side instead of the number of sides. For this you would select the Polygon By Size Of Segments option and specify the required value. Following the conventional software interface, radio buttons in the dialog denote exclusive either/or choices, whereas checkboxes are for additional non-exclusive options.

Figure 1.2

Exploring polygon-creation options. (a) The dialog of the Polygon tool. (b) A patterned polygon, created with the specifications shown in the dialog.

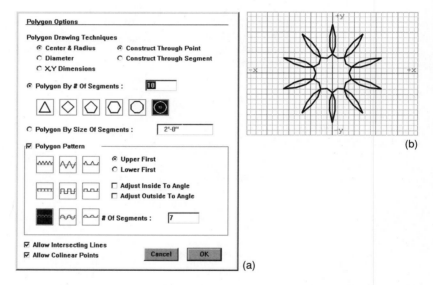

Keep in mind that once you create a polygon with a certain number of sides or a specific segment length, you cannot go back and change its number of sides or segment length to some other value using the Polygon Options dialog. This is a very common misconception in the early stages. It is important to realize that all the drawing tools you are working with now are for *creating* new objects rather than *editing* existing ones. In the same sense, most of the tool dialogs are meant to be used *before* rather than *after* the event. As far as editing existing objects is concerned, there are various means to do so, and we shall be looking at them in due course.

◻ The Polygon Options dialog has a number of additional options that you should explore. Start by experimenting with the different Polygon Drawing Techniques that are listed, and find one that is best suited to your modeling needs and style.

◻ You can also choose to create patterned polygons by checking the Polygon Pattern option and selecting one of the nine choices it contains. Figure 1.2-b shows the polygon created by the pattern selection depicted in Figure 1.2-a. You will find that when you create patterned polygons, additional mouse clicks are required to define the pattern in addition to the polygon. There are some other options associated with patterned polygons available in the dialog, which will lead to additional variations of each of the nine main patterns. You can explore these in detail at leisure.

■ The last two options appearing at the bottom of the Polygon Options dialog, Allow Intersecting Lines and Allow Collinear Points, are self-explanatory. You can let them remain selected, unless you have specific reasons for disallowing intersecting lines or coincident points in the polygons you create.

■ Move on to any one of the Circle tools. Draw a few circles with large diameters and you will find that they are actually created using a sequence of segments, almost like a many-sided polygon. In fact, all the curved shapes created using the drawing tools on that row are faceted in the same manner. The number of segments or facets is referred to as the *resolution* of the curve. If you want to create large circles, you should increase the resolution so as to get a smoother curve. This, again, requires accessing the dialog of the Circle tools.

■ Double-click on any one of the Circle tools to open its dialog (Figure 1.3-a). You can choose to increase the number of segments from the default value of 24. Alternately, you can specify a maximum segment size, which will automatically adjust the resolution of the curve so that the size of a facet does not exceed the specified length. Experiment with both options and see how they affect the circles that you create.

Notice that the dialog shown in Figure 1.3-a is entitled Arc/Circle/Ellipse Resolution, indicating that the resolution specified here will apply to *all* the tools that create arcs, circles, and ellipses. Thus, the same dialog will be invoked when you double-click on any of the tools that create these curves. This means that if you change the resolution for one type of curve, you do not have to repeat the process for the other types of curves, unless you want to specify a different resolution.

The last word on resolution: be careful not to increase it too much. The higher the number of facets or the smaller the maximum segment size, the smoother the curve will be; but it will also make all future operations involving that object much more complex and memory intensive. Settle for the minimum resolution you can get away with. form•Z has sophisticated display options which can make a curved object look smooth even though it is faceted, so don't worry too much about the facets hampering the quality of your final renderings noticeably.

Figure 1.3

Specifying the resolution of arcs, circles, and ellipses. (a) In the tool dialog. (b) In the Tool Options palette.

■ The options that are contained in the dialog of a tool are also available continuously in the floating palette called Tool Options, which you had closed in the beginning of this exercise. Go ahead and reopen this palette from the Palettes menu. Then select any one of the Circle or Ellipse tools from the third left row. You will find that the resolution options you accessed earlier by invoking the dialog of the tool (Figure 1.3-a) are now also visible in the Tool Options palette (Figure 1.3-b), and can be modified in the same fashion. The Tool Options palette additionally shows the option associated with the active 2D Surface Object mode, Construct Parametric Object, which is discussed in the next section.

▪ Select the Polygon tool once again, and turn your attention to the Tool Options palette. The number of options is now considerably larger compared to the resolution options shown in Figure 1.3-b, with the result that they do not "fit" within the palette. If you still want to use the Tool Options palette, you have to either resize it so that all the options are visible, or else, navigate through it in the following manner. Place the cursor within the palette, and click and drag in the vertical direction—this will scroll the contents of the palette upwards or downwards, letting you access all the sections. You can also close and open individual sections by clicking on the arrows (Mac) or the plus/minus signs (PC) accompanying each section.

The Tool Options palette thus provides you with an alternative to accessing the dialog of a tool by the double-click or another method. However, it is recommended that while using each tool in form•Z for the first time, you invoke its dialog rather than rely on the palette. This is because the dialog shows you all the options associated with the operation of that tool at a glance and in a nicely organized fashion, so they are easier to study than they would be if you were using the palette. Also, keep in mind that the options for the window tools do not appear in the Tool Options palette, so you always have to invoke their dialogs to work with the options of these tools.

To conclude this section, here is some additional information on dialogs. In general, the dialog for any tool contains various options that determine how that tool will function. If a dialog *is* associated with a tool, it is indicated by a tiny red mark on the top right corner of that tool's icon. As you will see by browsing through the tools in both the modeling as well as the window tool palettes, most of the tools do have dialogs associated with them.

While this book discusses the dialog options for most of the tools, it does not cover every single dialog and every single option contained in it. Such an undertaking is beyond the scope of a single book. Therefore, you should do a certain amount of exploration and discovery on your own, and determine how the dialog options that are not covered here affect the behavior of their respective tools.

1.5   Creating Open Shapes

We will now proceed to work with the tools in the right column of the third row of the modeling tool palette. From their icons, it will be obvious that these are tools which let you draw *open* shapes, in contrast to the tools in the left column which let you create *closed* shapes only. Remember that your object generation mode is still set to 2D Surface Object, so you will be continuing to create single-line 2D objects.

▪ Use the first and second tools in the row to create points and single lines respectively. The Point tool requires the selection of a single point in the graphics window, while the Single Line tool requires the selection of two points. Keep in mind that a single point object is not a "true" object; however, it can be useful as a reference for creating other kinds of objects by means of snapping, which we will look at in Workshop 2.

▪ Next, draw a sequence of lines, referred to as a *polyline*, using M-Tool:3b,3—the Vector Lines tool. To end the polyline, double-click at the last point. To close the shape instead of simply ending it, use a triple-click. The last one is a little tricky; you will learn an easier way to close shapes in the next workshop.

■ If you disabled the Allow Intersecting Lines and Allow Collinear Points options in the Polygon Options dialog you worked with earlier, you will find that the Vector Lines tool also does not let you create intersecting lines or have collinear points. This shows how the dialogs of all the tools are interrelated, ensuring that the different tools behave consistently, according to the same specifications. You can access the dialog of the Vector Lines tool in the usual manner to enable or disable these two options.

■ Continue working with the remaining tools in the third right row to create various elements. The four tools located immediately after the Vector Lines tool let you draw various kinds of spline curves in different ways. Try them all out. The smoothness of the curves is determined by their resolution, specified by a value called Smooth Interval in a dialog which is accessible from all these curve tools.

■ The following tool, Stream Lines, works a little differently—you hold the mouse down and use it like a pencil to do a freehand sketch in the window. The smoothness of the sketch, as you would by now have learned to expect, is governed by a value called the Stream Distance which you can change in the dialog of this tool. Its value is defaulted to 2'-0", which is why the sketching might not feel very smooth to begin with.

■ The third right row ends with six different Arc tools which enable you to create arcs in various ways. Experiment with each one of them. Here again, the icons do a good job of explaining how the tools work. So, for instance, M-Tool:3b,9 is the clockwise Arc tool for which you first select a point on the arc, then the center of the arc, and finally the endpoint of the arc. You will find yourself relying on different arc tools for modeling different objects, depending upon what the configuration of the object is.

Figure 1.4

Various shapes created individually with some of the tools in the right column of the third row.

Figure 1.4 gives you a sampling of shapes that can be created using some of the tools in the third right row individually. These tools can also be used in *combination* with one another to create a single shape of the type shown in Figure 1.5. The process is described next.

■ Select any one of the tools in the third right row and create a shape. Then, instead of double-clicking to end the shape, simply choose another tool from that row—the last point of the previous shape will act as the first point for the operation of the new tool you just selected. This process can be repeated for as long as necessary. When you are finally ready to end the process, double-click at the last point or triple-click to close. Try this out a few times, creating various shapes. It is important to learn how to do this, as you will find yourself using it frequently.

Figure 1.5

A single element created by combining the use of many tools in the right column of Row 3. A triple-click was used at the end to close the figure.

Of all the single-line 2D shapes that can be created with the drawing tools in the current row, some of them behave a little differently. These are the spline curves, the arcs, and any shape which combines vector lines, spline curves, and arcs. By default, they are created as parametric objects called *polycurves*. A parametric object, as you will study in more detail in Section 2.3, stores its creation parameters with it, which can be edited at a later stage to modify the object. Different types of parametric objects can be created in form•Z, and there are different kinds of tools to edit them. Polycurves, in particular, are edited using the Edit Controls tool (M-Tool:4b,2), and we will study that process in Section 4.7 of Workshop 2. If you do *not* wish to create parametric polycurves every time you draw spline curves and arcs, simply invoke the dialog of the 2D Surface Object mode and deselect the Construct Parametric Object option.

1.6   Double-line 2D Mode

In this section, you will be dealing with double-line rather than with single-line 2D shapes.

▣   Go back to the second left row of the modeling tool palette and select the second tool in this row (M-Tool:2a,2) instead of the first which you were using so far. This sets the object generation mode to 2D Enclosure. Recall from Section 1 of the Introduction that 2D enclosures are double-line 2D elements.

▣   Now repeat the entire sequence of steps (Section 1.3 to Section 1.5) that you have done so far, and observe the differences in the 2D elements that are created. Note that you will still be using the drawing tools located on Row 3 to actually create the objects—the only difference is the change of mode.

▣   If you need to change the width of the enclosure from its default value, access the dialog for M-Tool:2a,2—a procedure you should be familiar with by now. You can change the Enclosure Wall Width here to any specified value. You can also change the Justification option which determines where the double-line will be drawn with respect to the points you select. The default selection of Center, which distributes the width of the enclosure equally on both sides of the selection point, might not be the best option in all cases.

Figure 1.6 shows some 2D enclosures with varied widths and justification options, created using various drawing tools from Row 3. By this time, you should be well on your way towards mastering these tools, since you would have gone over each one of them twice so far.

Figure 1.6

Various kinds of 2D enclosures.

1.7   Cleaning Up: Moving and Deleting

Very soon, you will use the 2D shapes that you have created as base shapes for the generation of 3D objects. Before moving on to that, you might want to rearrange your objects in a more pleasing composition by moving them around on the gridded reference plane in the graphics window. If you have too much clutter, you may even want to delete some objects. Let us see how to perform these operations.

▣   Turn your attention to the left column of Row 11 of the modeling tool palette. This special teal-colored row determines the *self-copy mode* and is set to Self by default. If it is not, do so by clicking on M-Tool:11a,1, the Self tool, now. This ensures that any subsequent transformations—move, rotate, mirror, scale, etc.—that you perform are applied *to* the object selected, rather than in making a copy of it.

▣   Select Move (M-Tool:12a,1) and click on any object. You will now be able to move the selected object around the screen—it will be rubber-banded as you move the mouse. (Note, again, that you do *not* have to keep the mouse down and *drag* the element.) When you have found an appropriate position, click a second time to establish the move. Continue using the Move tool in this manner to reorganize your collection of objects as desired.

▣   To delete objects, simply select the Delete tool—the only tool located in the left column of the last row. Any object that you now click on will be deleted. Continue to apply the tool in this manner to all the objects you want to delete.

The Move and Delete operators can also be applied to many objects at a time rather than on each object individually as we have done. We will see how to do this in Section 3.4. For now, let us concentrate on completing our full session of form•Z.

1.8   Changing Views

So far, we have been working in the Top view which lets us see the X and Y dimensions only. This was fine as long as we were working with 2D objects alone. But to prepare for the generation of 3D objects, let us switch to a view in which all three dimensions are visible. Such a view is referred to as a *non-planar* view, as opposed to a *planar* view which lets you see two dimensions only. A planar view is also technically referred to as a *projection* view.

■ Open up the View menu. You will find a √ mark against Top as well as Axonometric, indicating that the current view is looking straight down on the XY plane. There are a total of six groups of options under the View menu; concentrate only on the first three of these for now. The first group consists of five predefined non-planar views, along with a Custom View Angles option that lets you define your own viewing angles. The second group has the six planar views possible with respect to the coordinate system you see in the window; Top is the first of these. The third group gives you an additional five options that determine how the chosen view appears.

■ We will look at all these options in detail in Workshop 3. For now, settle for any of the non-planar Axonometric views so that you can see all the three coordinate axes, X, Y, and Z. The first two, [z=30° x=60°] and [z=45° x=45°], are very common and are used for most of the illustrations in this book.

1.9 Specifying Heights

Let us move to a different dimension. After all, it *is* the 3D aspect that we are most interested in, is it not? What you will proceed to do next is convert the 2D shapes you have created into various kinds of 3D objects. Before you do this, however, you need to specify what the heights of these blocks are going to be.

■ Go to the Heights pulldown menu. By default, the height is set to a preset value—usually 10'-0" in the English measurement system—indicated by a √ mark against it in the Heights menu. You can preselect another height from among the values listed here, or go to the Custom option for defining your own values. This selected value—whether preset or customized—will set the heights of objects for all subsequent 3D modeling.

■ If heights need to be constantly varied and you would like to indicate them graphically as you go along, the first option from the Heights menu, Graphic/Keyed, needs to be activated. Select this option for now, as shown in Figure 1.7. This lets you specify the height of a 3D object interactively, either with a mouse click or by typing the required value in the Prompts palette using the keyboard. In this workshop, we will deal with the first method only, leaving numeric input through the keyboard for Workshop 2.

Figure 1.7

The Heights menu, with the option set to Graphic/Keyed.

1.10   Deriving 3D Objects from 2D Shapes

Now that the heights aspect has also been settled, we are finally ready to move into the third dimension. To derive 3D objects from 2D elements, look at the left column of the fifth row of the modeling tool palette. It contains all the *derivative object* tools, used to derive new objects from existing ones in various ways. We will work with only three of these tools for now.

■ Select M-Tool:5a,3. This is the Extrusion tool, used to derive simple extruded objects from 2D shapes. Click on any element and watch the extrusion being rubber-banded as you drag the mouse in the Z direction to indicate the height of the object. Click when you get to the height you want, and your 3D object is complete. You can also go in for *negative* heights by moving in the − Z direction. Repeat this process with some more of the 2D elements that you have; however, leave some for deriving other kinds of objects as well. Keep an eye on the instructions that appear in the Prompts palette and follow them. In general, you will find this a useful habit to cultivate.

■ Repeat the same procedure using the Convergence tool (M-Tool:5a,4) as well as the 3D Enclosure tool (M-Tool:5a,5), and observe the differences in the forms that are generated (see Figure 1.8). Convergence creates conical or pyramidal objects, while 3D Enclosure creates the 3D equivalent of a 2D enclosure from any kind of 2D shape. Notice also that if the base shape is a 2D enclosure, there is no difference between the kind of object derived by the Extrusion tool or the 3D Enclosure tool.

Figure 1.8

Extruded, converged, and enclosed 3D objects derived from existing 2D shapes, using the first three tools in the left column of Row 5.

■ Invoke the dialogs of these three tools in turn to explore the options they contain. The Extrusion and Convergence tool dialogs are identical. By default, the extrusion or convergence happens in a direction perpendicular to the reference plane. Thus in Figure 1.8 where XY is the reference plane, the heights are defined in the Z direction. You can also choose to extrude or converge in a direction perpendicular to the *surface* of the object, an option that is relevant only when the base 2D object is inclined with respect to the reference plane. We have no such objects yet but will be creating them soon in Workshop 2 (see Figure 2.11), so keep this option in mind for later use. When an open 2D shape is extruded or converged, the type of object that is created is a surface solid by default. If you would like this to be a surface object instead, you should check the Make Surface Object From Open Source Shape box in the dialog. Finally, there is a Status Of Objects button which we will explore in Section 3.7, so don't worry about it for now.

■ The dialog of the 3D Enclosure tool is a little different. It contains a number of options related to the justification, thickness, and configuration of the enclosure, which we will study while working with the 3D Enclosed Solid tool (M-Tool:2a,5) in Section 2.2. The remaining options are identical to those in the Extrusion and Convergence tool dialogs we just discussed. Notice that the 3D Enclosure operation can never produce a surface object since it converts an open shape to an enclosed shape before extrusion.

1.11 Changing the Display

Let us move on to briefly discuss how the objects in the graphics window are shown to us. The kind of display that you see in Figure 1.8 is called a *wireframe* display. In this mode, all the lines of the object are shown, even those which would not be visible to your eye from the position in which you are viewing it. This kind of display can get a little confusing to visualize, as you can see. Also, it may not be the most attractive mode of presentation. You therefore have the option of switching to a different display.

▦ Go to the Display menu. The second group of items in this menu comprises the various kinds of displays available in form•Z. Concentrate on the first six of these for now. Switch to each one of them in turn and observe the differences. Compare what you see to Figure 1.9, which shows a relative comparison of these six modes for the same configuration of objects.

Figure 1.9

Various display modes for the same set of objects. The display of the grid and axes has been turned off in these illustrations.

Wire Frame

Hidden Line

Quick Paint

Surface Render

Shaded Render

RenderZone

Displays can be broadly divided into two categories: *line* and *paint*. Wire Frame is one example of a line display; Hidden Line is the other. A Wire Frame display is the only mode which displays open surfaces by default, as you can see in Figure 1.9. Thus, if your window appears blank even though you are confident you had drawn *something* (open shapes) on it, you can be sure you are no longer in the Wire Frame mode. A Hidden Line mode is similar to Wire Frame except that it hides lines that would not be visible to you from your current viewpoint. It is therefore more realistic.

All the other display modes are paint displays. Quick Paint is the fastest of these but is also the least accurate, especially for complex shapes and configurations, so don't rely on it too often. You can see the inaccuracy right away in Figure 1.9. Surface Render, Shaded Render, and RenderZone are progressively more sophisticated and accurate displays which take a long time to execute, particularly for complex models. RenderZone, especially, is best left for final presentations.

Recent versions of form•Z have two additional display modes called QuickDraw 3D and OpenGL. Both of these are available on the Mac, whereas the PC supports only OpenGL. (If you have a recent version of form•Z but find that these modes are deactivated on your computer, it means that your operating system has not been updated to include the necessary extensions. Get some technical help to make the needed changes.) These two display modes enable you to carry out interactive modeling of objects using shaded surfaces rather than lines. To get a feel for this, create some objects, first using the Surface Render display mode and then the QuickDraw 3D or OpenGL mode. The difference should be obvious at once. These display modes work faster when the window size is smaller, so keep this in mind if you use them frequently. Also, these modes are meant for interactive modeling only and cannot be used for printing.

Each one of the display modes in form•Z comes with its own options, which we will explore in detail in Workshops 3 and 5.

1.12 Ending the Show: Printing and Closing

We are approaching the end of our first complete form•Z session. Save the project, if you like, using File > Save. Let us see how we would go about printing what we have.

◼ First, make sure that your display is set to a suitable mode, depending upon the desired quality of the output. Hidden Line or Surface Render displays print well and take less time than the higher modes, so you can settle for either of these. Also, the current view is what gets printed, so make sure you switch to an appropriate view before printing.

◼ Go to File > Page Setup to set the size and orientation of your paper. This is the standard Page Setup dialog found in most programs, and the options it contains will depend upon the printer you have selected.

◼ Next, go to Plot/Print Setup in the same menu. This is the key dialog for determining what will print and how, so let us look at it in some detail. It is shown in Figure 1.10. To begin with, you can specify the Plot Scale in which the file is to be printed. But since we haven't been modeling using proper dimensions yet, a plotting scale is of little consequence and will be rather arbitrary. Therefore, check the Scale to Fit Media option for now. This will fit all the objects within the specified paper size (Figure 1.11-a). Use the Page Preview command to contrast the results, before and after selecting this option.

Figure 1.10

The Plot/Print Setup dialog.

Plot/Print Setup

| Plot Scale | 1/16" | = 1'-0" | ☑ Scale To Fit Media |

Plot/Print Type :   X Justification   Y Justification

- ◉ Extents   ○ Left Edge   ○ Top Edge
- ○ Window Contents   ◉ Center   ◉ Center
- ○ Dump Window   ○ Right Edge   ○ Bottom Edge
- ○ Dump Screen

- ☐ Plot Grid   ☐ Crop Marks
- ☐ Plot Axis   ☐ File Name & Date
- ☐ Print Text As Paths   ☐ Overlap Pages
- ☐ Include Background   ☐ Frame : [_____]
- ☐ Solid Color Printing   Image Detail : [High Resolution]

[Page Preview...]

[Page Setup...] [Print...]   [Cancel] [OK]

□ Turn your attention to the other options in the Plot/Print Setup dialog. By default, the Plot/Print Type is set to Extents, which means that all the objects you created will be printed. However, you could also print out only a part of the project by first zooming in to that section of the window, then selecting Window Contents as the Plot/Print Type. (You will learn how to use the Zoom tools a little later in Section 3.8.) The remaining two Plot/Print Type options simply create screen dumps of the window and the screen respectively, at a low resolution but faster than the first two options, and should be used for rough drafts only.

Figure 1.11

Different plot scales for printing. (a) Choosing the Scale To Fit Media option fits the plot within the specified paper size. (b) Not selecting this option uses the Plot Scale value to determine the size of the plot. A large value (1/2"=1'-0") was specified to generate this illustration, leading to a plot extending over several pages, as indicated by the dashed lines.

(a)

(b)

▣ The X and Y Justification options are used to determine the alignment of the plot with respect to the page. The most commonly used Center options are selected by default.

▣ Once you begin modeling to scale and specify a value for Plot Scale rather than use Scale To Fit Media, the plotting may take place on several sheets of paper (as shown in Figure 1.11-b) if it cannot fit on a single sheet in the specified scale. In this case, you will find it useful to check both the Overlap Pages and Crop Marks options. The first will provide some overlap between neighboring pages, while the second will mark the corners of the plots on each page. This will enable you to easily collate the individual sheets into the full plot.

▣ The remaining options in the Plot/Print Setup dialog are fairly self-explanatory, and you can explore them on your own. For instance, you can check the Frame option and choose a frame thickness which will be used to border your plot. Activate the Solid Color Printing option to see if it yields better results, but most often it will not, in which case it is better to keep it turned off. Don't worry about the Print Text As Paths option for now—we will come back to it when working with text objects in Workshop 7.

▣ A note of caution: you should *always* do a Page Preview of your plot before you issue the Print command to check if the plot is satisfactory. By a simple oversight, you might forget to select the Scale To Fit Media option, making the plot extend over several sheets of paper in the default scale. And before you realize it, the printer will be spurting out loads of paper with not more than a few lines on each! Therefore, use the environmentally friendly Page Preview option generously.

▣ This marks the end of Exercise 1. You can close the current project using File > Close and exit form•Z using File > Quit. However, if you would like to continue working, don't quit now. Just move on to Exercise 2.

Direct 3D

EXERCISE 2

So far, we have been working with 2D shapes and creating 3D objects by applying certain operations to them. This is rather a roundabout way, though, to go about 3D modeling, isn't it? Therefore, without any further delay, let us proceed to learn how to generate 3D objects directly. This can be done in two ways. We will first look at the traditional form•Z method which involves the use of the third, fourth, and fifth object generation modes located in the left column of Row 2 of the modeling tool palette. Just like the first two modes you worked with in the last exercise, these are used in conjunction with the drawings tools on Row 3. The second method of directly generating 3D objects was introduced in version 3.0. It gives you the ability to create five different kinds of primitive objects which are parametric in nature, which means that they can be easily modified after they have been created, simply by changing any of their creation parameters.

Additionally in this exercise, we will take a brief look at the different object personalities in form•Z, learn how to model various kinds of spheroids for which there is a dedicated tool, and use different reference planes for the creation of objects. Let us start, however, by looking at how to use the Clear command, which we might need at this point.

2.1   Clearing the Project of All Objects

If you did not quit form•Z at the end of the last exercise but moved on directly to this exercise, do the following:

▣ If you saved Exercise 1 and closed that file, open a new modeling project by going to File > New[Model].

▣ If you did not close the Exercise 1 file and do not wish to save it, start with a clean slate by going to Edit > Clear, located in the third group of the menu. This will clear all the visible objects in your graphics window.

▣ If you went through Section 1.10 on deriving 3D objects in the last exercise, you will find all the original 2D shapes from which 3D objects were derived still remaining in the window, even after executing Clear. These objects are colored in gray and cannot be moved or deleted. In fact, they cannot even be selected with the Pick tool (M-Tool:4b,1). Try it. Such objects are called *ghosted* objects. How and why were these objects created? You shall have the answer to that question later in Section 3.7. For now, simply clear these objects as well by going to Edit > Clear All Ghosted, located just below Clear.

2.2   3D Object Generation Modes

▣ Select M-Tool:2a,3. This sets the object generation mode to 3D Extruded Solid. You can now create a 3D extrusion directly by drawing a base shape with any of the tools on Row 3 and specifying the height with an additional mouse click. If you started a new session of form•Z for this exercise, don't forget to set the Heights menu to Graphic/Keyed so that you can specify the extrusion height interactively with the mouse, rather than letting it acquire a default preset value.

▣ Use all the tools on Row 3 to create different kinds of solids and surfaces directly in 3D. A *solid* will be created when the base shape is closed, as with the tools in the left column of Row 3; a *surface solid* will be created when the base shape is open, as with the tools in the right column. The Extrusion/Convergence Options dialog, which we studied in Section 1.10, is also applicable to the 3D Extruded Solid tool and you can use it to specify that a *surface object* be created from an open source shape, if required. Again, refer back to Section 1 of the Introduction describing the basic objects in form•Z to clarify the difference between solids, surface solids, and surface objects.

 A surface object can be converted to a surface solid and vice versa by using the One Sided/ Two Sided tool (M-Tool:10b,3). The conversion choice is made in the dialog of the tool.

▣ Experiment with different colors and shapes. You can change the display mode to Quick Paint to visualize the objects better as you are creating them, or to QuickDraw 3D or OpenGL, which can be slower but more fun.

▣ Repeat the previous steps with the object generation mode set to 3D Converged Solid (M-Tool:2a,4), and finally with it set to 3D Enclosed Solid (M-Tool:2a,5). You will find that you are generating the same kinds of solids that you created in Exercise 1, but now directly instead of operating on 2D shapes.

▣ For 3D enclosures, you can change the enclosure thickness by accessing the dialog of the 3D Enclosed Solid tool (shown in Figure 1.12-a). There are also the same Justification options in this dialog that you encountered for the 2D Enclosure tool in Section 1.6. For 3D enclosures, whether generated directly (by setting the mode to M-Tool:2a,5) or from 2D shapes (using M-Tool:5a,5), there are additional options in the tool dialog that control the resultant object. You can choose to have enclosures with either the top, or the bottom, or both enclosed, and specify the corresponding thicknesses. In effect, you can create a hollow volume, bounded on all sides by slabs, directly in one step by selecting the appropriate options. Such volumes are illustrated in Figure 1.12-b.

Figure 1.12

The dialog for the 3D Enclosed Solid tool, and the enclosed objects created with the set of options specified in it.

(a)

(b)

2.3 Different Object Personalities

You have seen how the object generation modes located in the left column of Row 2 can be used in combination with the drawing tools on Row 3 to create a large variety of objects. All of these, except for the polycurves you learnt about in Section 1.5, are non-parametric objects—their creation parameters are not stored with them, so they cannot be accessed and modified at a later stage to make changes to the objects. Moreover, these objects have what is known as the *facetted* personality. This is the simplest kind of object in which the surface is made up of a series of polygonal facets. These facets are visible when the object is rendered, even in the high-end Shaded Render and RenderZone display modes. For a curved facetted object to appear smoothly rendered, its resolution has to be high when it is created. Even then, you will see the facets if you zoom in close enough.

Both the geometry and topology of a facetted object are structured in a definite hierarchy: point, segment, outline, face, volume, and object. Each of these parts can be selected and modified by setting the appropriate topological level (which you will learn to do in Section 3.1 of Workshop 3). This alters the configuration of the object, and is thus a means to edit it. Of course, basic transformations such as move, rotate, scale, and so on can also be applied to the object.

In contrast to the objects created using the object generation modes, the primitive objects that we will learn to create next are truly parametric—their creation parameters are stored with them, and can be accessed and modified at a later stage to edit the object. These objects are created with the *analytic* personality, so called because their generation is based on classic analytic geometric equations. We will refer to them as "analytic primitives."

One of the main advantages of non-facetted objects such as the primitives, in addition to the fact that they can be edited by modifying their creation parameters, lies in how they are rendered. A curved primitive object will render perfectly smooth in the Shaded Render and RenderZone display modes, even if you zoom in very close. The parameters that are stored with the object enable its "true" curvature to be derived on-the-fly while rendering, accounting for the "perfect" smoothness. This is not the case with a facetted object. The contrast is remarkable, as you can see in Figure 1.13.

Figure 1.13

The contrast in smoothness between the rendering of two spheres of the same size but with different personalities: analytic and facetted.

Primitive Sphere   Facetted Sphere

Once an analytic primitive has been created, it can be converted to a facetted, nurbz, or patch object, using the Drop Controls tool (M-Tool:10b,5). The conversion from primitive to nurbz or patch can also be accomplished with the Edit Controls tool (M-Tool:4b,2) or the Edit Surface tool (M-Tool:4b,3). We will learn more about all these tools in Workshop 6.

Both *nurbz* and *patch* objects are again parametric in nature, but it is possible to derive objects with these personalities from non-parametric objects as well. We will study this process later in Workshop 6. For now, let us simply understand what these personalities mean. A nurbz object internally has a NURBS (Non-Uniform Rational B-Splines) based representation, consisting of control lines with parameters such as degree, knots, and weights from which curved surfaces can be generated. These control parameters can be modified to smoothly reshape the object.

In contrast, an object with the patch personality is internally represented by a set of patches. A single patch is a rectangular or triangular tile, whose sides are control lines from which curved surfaces can be generated. The patches which make up an object do not have to be all of the same size, enabling them to effectively model curved objects with widely varying surface detail. Just like nurbz objects, patch objects are also reshaped by manipulating their control lines, a process we shall look at in Workshop 6.

There is a fifth object personality available in form•Z, also parametric in nature, called *metaformz*. There are dedicated tools for deriving and modifying objects with this personality, all of which we will explore in Workshop 7.

 A parametric object is also known as a "controlled" object, as it is stored with the control parameters that can be accessed and modified to reshape the object.

Now that we have some idea of the different kinds of personalities that an object in form•Z can assume, let us proceed to look at how to create the analytic primitives we just discussed.

2.4   Modeling Primitive 3D Objects

form•Z gives you the ability to directly create five different types of primitive 3D objects: cube, cone, cylinder, sphere, and torus. The tools for generating these primitives are grouped together in the left column of the first row of the modeling tool palette.

■ Select the first tool in the row, Cube, and invoke its dialog. You will find that you have three different options for creating a cube: Preset, Diagonal, and Axial. Try them all out. The Preset option lets you specify the Width, Depth, and Height of the cube in the accompanying fields. A single click of the mouse in the graphics window is then used to place the cube of the specified dimensions in the desired location. In contrast, for the Diagonal and Axial options, all three dimensions of the cube are specified graphically using the mouse. The Diagonal option, like the Rectangle tool (M-Tool:3a,1) you encountered in Section 1.3, lets you only model a cube that is aligned parallel to the coordinate axes. With the Axial option there is no such limitation, and an additional mouse click is needed to determine the alignment of the cube, just as with the 3 Point Rectangle tool (M-Tool:3a,2).

■ Move on to the next tool in the left column of the first row, Cone, and explore all its options (see Figure 1.14). Switch to the Surface Render mode to see the results better. There are five basic means to model a cone: the Preset option is similar to that for the Cube tool you just explored, while the other four options simply give you different ways of modeling the base of the cone. If you activate the Truncated Cone option, the graphical modeling process gets slightly modified to enable you to specify how the truncation happens. The Partial option, when checked, lets you create partial cones with the specified Start and End angles for the circumference of the base.

■ The Cone tool also has three different types of Closure options which determine whether the resulting cone becomes a solid or surface object. The default option of Plane, as you can see, creates a solid object for both complete and partial cones by closing both the base and side surfaces. The None option does not close any surfaces, so the cone remains a surface object. The final option, Center, generates a solid cone like the Plane option, but in a slightly different fashion for partial cones. Rather than using a single face to close the side of the cone, two faces are used that extend to the axis of the cone. The difference is illustrated in Figure 1.14.

Figure 1.14

The Cone Options dialog, and the different types of conical objects that can be created using the various options.

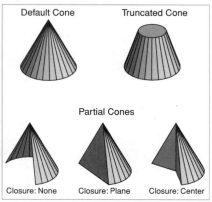

The Cone Options dialog contains a Wires And Facets option at the base that we haven't yet explored. The same option also applies to the remaining three analytic primitives, so let us finish working with these before we examine what the Wires And Facets option is all about.

■ Proceed to work with the remaining three primitive tools in a manner similar to the first two tools. The options for the Cylinder tool are identical to those for the Cone tool, except that there is no truncation option. The Sphere tool, again, has the same Closure and Partial options, with the latter ability being provided for both the horizontal and the vertical directions. The last primitive tool, Torus, lets you model a ring or donut-like shape. It has options similar to those of the other primitives, so exploring them should be easy. The only thing to note is the meaning of the three parametric terms, Major Radius, Minor Radius X, and Minor Radius Z, all of which are illustrated in Figure 1.15.

Figure 1.15

The meaning of the three parametric terms used to define a torus object.

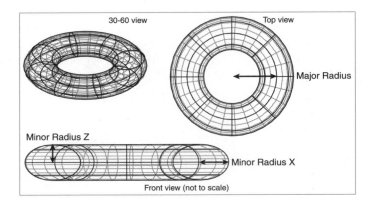

Let us now study the Wires And Facets option which is accessible in the form of a button from the dialogs of four out of the five analytic primitives: cone, cylinder, sphere, and torus. Click on this button from any of the dialogs and the Wires And Facets Options dialog will be invoked (see Figure 1.16-a). Here, you can control how the primitive object that is created will be displayed in the first four display modes. This display involves two different components: *wires* and *facets*. Both of these can be seen in the Wire Frame display, with the facets shown in a lighter shade of the object color than the wires. In contrast, the Quick Paint, Hidden Line, and Surface Render displays show only the facets (see Figure 1.16-b). You have already seen how parametric objects are smoothly rendered in Shaded Render and RenderZone, so the settings in the Wires And Facets Options dialog do not affect these displays.

The wires displayed for a primitive object are affected by the two settings in the Wires section of the dialog. The Density determines how many wires are drawn, while the Smoothness slider bar lets you set the smoothness with which the wires are drawn. Experiment with different values for both parameters, with the display mode set to Wire Frame so that you can see the changes.

The options for the display of facets are much more extensive. We can explore the effect of each option by setting it to different values and creating the same primitive for comparison (see Figure 1.17). Start with the default values under Facets and create a sphere. Use the Preset option with the default value of 4'-0" for the three radii, so that you are guaranteed the same dimensions for the sphere each time. Change the display to Surface Render in order to see the facets clearly.

Figure 1.16

The Wires And Facets Options dialog, and the Wire Frame and Surface Render displays of a primitive sphere.

(a)

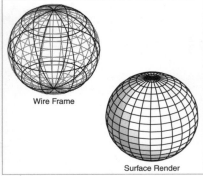

(b)

- Reduce the Max # Of Facets values for both Length and Depth from the default of 24 to 12. (The checked lock icon ensures that both values remain identical, so you have to change only one field. If you ever need different values, simply deselect the lock icon.) The sphere now created will have exactly half the resolution of the first sphere.

- Next, activate the Max Facet Segment Length option and leave it to the default value of 2'-0". Create a third sphere, but you will find that its resolution is identical to that of the second sphere. Delete the sphere you just created, get back to the Wires And Facets Options dialog, and deselect the Max # Of Facets option. The sphere you now create will follow the Max Facet Segment Length specification—it is facetted until the side length of each facet is not larger than the specified value of 2'-0". Thus, you can see that if multiple facetting criteria are selected, the one which produces the least facets takes precedence, so watch your criteria selection carefully.

- Explore the remaining four Facets options in the same fashion, creating new spheres to compare the results of each change in setting. The Max Normal Deviation option facets the sphere until the angle between the normals of two adjacent facets is not greater than the angle specified alongside. The Max Surface Deviation option, on the other hand, ensures that the distance between the center of a facet and the true point on the curved surface of the sphere is not greater than the accompanying value. The Triangulate option triangulates each facet, the importance of which we will see in Section 5.6 of Workshop 2. And finally, the Optimize option reduces the number of facets in highly dense areas such as the poles of the sphere, instead of letting the facetting criteria be uniformly applied throughout its surface.

Figure 1.17

Spherical primitives produced with the various facetting options in the Wires And Facets Options dialog.

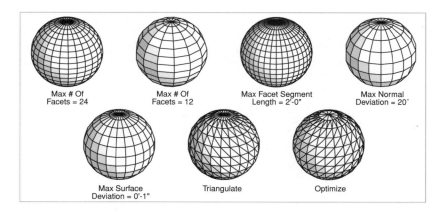

2.5 Creating Spheroids

In addition to the Sphere tool you just saw which lets you create primitive spheres, form•Z has a second tool for modeling various kinds of spheroids. These are also parametric in nature, and can be edited after they have been created. They are, however, created as facetted objects rather than as the analytic ones created by the Sphere tool.

- Select the Spheroid tool from the right column of the first row, and invoke its dialog. It is somewhat similar to the dialogs of the primitive tools, in that it has a Preset option along with a number of other methods for modeling the spheroid (Figure 1.18-a). Try them all out. The icons do a good job of explaining how each method works.

WORKSHOP 1

Figure 1.18

The eight different types of spheroids that can be created with the Spheroid tool, shown along with the tool dialog.

(a)

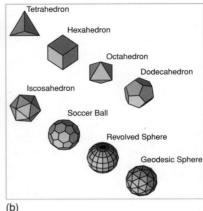

(b)

◼ Turn your attention to the Shape popup list in the Spheroid Options dialog. The default selection is Geodesic Sphere, the spheroid type you just created. There are seven other types. Activate each of them in turn and create the corresponding spheroids. Compare your results with those illustrated in Figure 1.18-b.

◼ Explore also the sub-options for Revolved Sphere and Geodesic Sphere, experimenting with different values that determine the resolution, and consequently, the smoothness of the solid. Geodesic spheres can be created at four levels of resolution, indicated by the # Of Levels value. Alternately, you can specify an Edge Size, just as you did for 2D curves. In general, geodesic spheres give you the smoothest rendering of all the spheroids, so you can use them by default. Just as with 2D curves, settle for the smallest resolution (lower levels or larger edge sizes) that you can get away with, so that subsequent operations are faster and less memory-intensive.

2.6   Using Predefined Reference Planes

All modeling activity takes place with reference to a plane. So far, you have been working entirely on the predefined XY plane, indicated by the teal-colored reference grid. All 2D drawing activity took place on this plane. All extrusions (i.e., defining the heights of objects) took place in the direction perpendicular to this plane, along the Z axis.

It is, of course, conceivable that using the XY plane alone may be sufficient for all your modeling activity. However, at times, it might be faster and more convenient to use some other reference plane for modeling certain objects. In addition to the XY plane, form•Z has two other predefined planes—the YZ and the ZX planes—that are defined by the three red-colored coordinate axes and are orthogonal (i.e., perpendicular) to the XY plane. We will work with these two planes right now.

form•Z also lets you create your own customized reference planes, which can be non-orthogonal, passing through any set of lines in 3D space. We will work with such planes in Workshop 3.

◼ Turn your attention to the first column of window tools at the base of the graphics window. If you like, you can "pull it out" and position it as a floating palette on the screen (Figure 1.19-a). This palette is where the selection of the active reference plane is made, and it contains four options: XY, YZ, ZX, and ARBITR (which stands for Arbitrary). XY is active by default which is why you have been using it all this time. Let us see what it is like working with the other two planes. Ignore the

Arbitrary option for now—you will use it when you create customized reference planes in Workshop 3.

■ Select the YZ option by clicking on it. The grid will change from spanning the X and Y axes to spanning the Y and Z axes. Proceed to create any 3D object. You will see that the base shape is now created on the active YZ plane, while the height of the object is given in the direction of the perpendicular X axis. Continue to create more objects on this plane. You should have something similar to what is shown in Figure 1.19-b.

■ Finally, switch to ZX, the last of the three predefined planes, and create some 3D objects. The heights will now be defined along the Y axis, as shown in Figure 1.19-c.

Figure 1.19

Working with predefined reference planes. (a) The window tool palette of the reference planes. XY is highlighted, indicating that it is the active plane. (b) Modeling using the YZ plane. (c) Modeling using the ZX plane.

(a)

(b) YZ plane   (c) ZX plane

You can see right away the flexibility and convenience afforded by being able to use additional planes for modeling. Of course, you can create simple compositions such as those shown in Figure 1.19 by using only the XY plane, and then moving or rotating the objects to the desired position. (You will learn to use the Rotate tool in Workshop 2.) However, it is faster, and more intuitive and elegant, to use the other two planes for modeling objects that relate to them better than to the XY plane. For more complex objects and configurations that you will model later, you will find the use of multiple reference planes absolutely indispensable.

EXERCISE 3

Some Basic Functions

Now that we have learned to create various kinds of 2D and 3D objects, it is time to look at some frequently used functions, without which we would not be able to proceed very far with our modeling. These functions include changing the color of objects after they have been created, moving objects perpendicular to the reference plane, undoing and redoing operations, making multiple selections using the Pick tool, selecting and deselecting objects, ghosting and unghosting objects, and finally, zooming and scrolling through the graphics window. Let us start with the aspect of color.

3.1   Changing Colors

You already know from Section 1.1 how to create an object in a desired color. What if you want to change the color of an object *after* it has been created? Here is how you can do that.

■ Select the Color tool from the modeling palette—the first icon in the left column of the thirteenth row. Then highlight the required color in the Surface Styles palette and simply "apply" it to the object whose color you wish to change. The selected object gets colored in the new color.

■ You can repeat the same color for many objects or choose different colors. The Color command remains active until you select some other tool.

3.2   Using the Perpendicular Lock

So far, you have been executing only planar moves with the Move tool—moving objects horizontally on a plane. You will often need to execute moves *perpendicular* to the active plane. Let us see how to do this.

■ Make sure you are in a non-planar view, seeing all three axes, X, Y, and Z. Select the Move tool (M-Tool:12a,1) and apply it to an object. Try moving the object in a direction vertical to the currently active plane. You may think you have succeeded in doing so, but if you check the exact position of the object by switching to some of the planar views—Top, Right, Front, etc.—from the View menu, you will find that you have only moved the object *along* the plane rather than perpendicular to it. If your display mode is set to QuickDraw 3D or OpenGL, you should be able to spot the error at once. Try it.

■ Now click on the single tool located in the second column of the window tool palette. This is called the Perpendicular Lock. When selected, it gets highlighted in black, indicating that it is active. Use the Move tool again. You will find that now you can move objects only in a direction perpendicular to the plane.

■ When you do not want to restrict movement to the vertical direction only, deselect the Perpendicular Lock tool by clicking on it again. It will no longer be highlighted, indicating that it is not active. (Such a tool is referred to as a *toggle switch*.) Don't forget to turn it off in this manner when not needed, otherwise your regular planar moves will not be performed correctly, leaving you wondering what is going wrong!

 The Perpendicular Lock is relevant only to non-planar views. When you see your project in a planar view, you will be able to move objects along that plane only. In such views, the Perpendicular Lock automatically switches itself off.

3.3   Undoing and Redoing

form•Z does not have merely the two standard Undo and Redo commands that you find in most programs. Instead, it has six commands related to undoing and redoing, located in the first group of the Edit menu. Let us see how they work.

■ Keep selecting the first command, Undo, to keep undoing in reverse order the operations you have just performed. You may find it more convenient to use the shortcut key for Undo, listed beside the command name in the menu.

Notice that Undo applies *only* to operations that cause *changes to the objects* (such as object creation, move, color, etc.), but not to operations which make changes to the graphic environment (such as switching reference planes) or modify options in the various dialogs (such as changing the number of sides of a polygon). Such changes cannot be reversed using the Undo tool. Keep this in mind, as it often tends to be a source of some confusion.

■ You can also conveniently undo multiple operations in one step. Notice the * sign next to the Undo command in the Edit menu—this indicates that a dialog containing options is associated with that command. To access this dialog, select Undo while holding down the option key (Mac) or Ctrl+Shift keys (PC). This brings up an Undo List from which you can select multiple consecutive operations to be undone, starting with the most recent operation (see Figure 1.20-a). By default, only the last 10 operations are listed. To undo more operations, open up the Undo List again after undoing the last set.

 Don't expect to be able to undo only specific operations from the Undo List, for instance, only the third and sixth operations. That is an impossible demand!

■ The second command in the Edit menu, Redo, simply redoes the operation you have last undone. It can be executed repeatedly to redo a sequence of undo operations, but it works only if selected immediately after an Undo command. If you did a multiple series of Undo commands, you can use the third command, Redo All, to reverse all of them in one step and restore the project to what it was before the Undo commands were performed.

■ The Undo and Redo commands also work while you are in the middle of an operation. Use the Vector Lines tool (M-Tool:3b,3) to draw a continuous sequence of lines, but don't double-click or triple-click to end. Select Undo instead, and you will find that the last point which you selected gets deselected, without affecting any of the points selected before it. Any number of points can be repeatedly deselected in this manner by continuing to use Undo; thereafter, selection of new points can be resumed. If, after the command has been executed fully (i.e., you have double-clicked or triple-clicked) and you select Undo, the complete object will be undone rather than just a single segment.

■ Proceed to select the fifth command from the Edit menu, Reset Undo/Redo. Now try and Undo the last operation you performed and you will find that you can no longer do so. The Reset Undo/ Redo option sets a new starting point beyond which an Undo cannot be executed. It does this by erasing all the earlier records of the model at its various stages.

With the help of all these Undo and Redo commands, you can experiment with various modeling alternatives without the fear of making an unredeemable error. It will always be possible to go back and undo operations that were not done right. The Reset Undo/Redo command can be used to mark the end of an experimentation phase—in fact, you should make it a point to do so, whenever you feel confident that you no longer need to return to any earlier stage of your modeling. This will help to free up valuable disk space, particularly for large projects

■ Carry out a few more modeling operations and then select Replay, the fourth command in the Edit menu. This clears the window and plays back in sequence all the operations you just performed since the Reset Undo/Redo option was selected. You can pause the playback at any time for visual inspection by holding the mouse down, and release it for resuming the replay. It is a nifty little feature which can be often useful.

◻ The last item in the Undo/Redo group under the Edit menu is Undo Options. Select this command, and it will open up a dialog in which you can make various changes to how the Undo operation will work (Figure 1.20-b).

Figure 1.20

Using Undo. (a) The Undo List, showing multiple operations selected for undoing. (b) The Undo Options dialog.

(a)

(b)

◻ As you can see, it is possible to completely turn off the Undo feature if disk space happens to be at a premium. Fortunately, a less drastic option is also available—you can simply choose to limit, in three different ways, the number of Undo records that will be stored, rather than have an unlimited number. You can also change the number of Undo operations that are displayed in the Undo List from the default value of 10.

◻ Selecting the Save Undos In Project option will save all the undo records along with a project file. This means that when you open the file again, you can also Undo operations executed in previous sessions of working on that project. However, be careful with this option as it could increase your file size substantially.

◻ The last option in the Undo Options dialog, Reset After Saving Project, erases the undo records every time a project is saved. It may be checked by default, in which case you should be careful not to use the auto-save option (which you will study in Workshop 3)—this might save your file at some arbitrary point of time while you are still in the process of experimentation, and prevent you from using Undo to reverse something you didn't do right. If you must use the auto-save feature, remember to deselect this option and you should be fine.

3.4 Prepicking and Postpicking

All this time, we have been moving, coloring, or deleting objects by selecting them *after* choosing the Move, Color, or Delete tools respectively. This is referred to as *postpicking*, and here, the operation is executed only on one object at a time. If, however, you want to move, color, delete, or carry out any other operation on many objects at the same time, it is more convenient to use what is known as the *prepicking* method.

◻ Go to the Pick tool (M-Tool:4b,1) and keep selecting all the objects on which a certain operation is to be performed. The selected objects get highlighted in red.

■ Once all the desired objects have been selected, go to the tool you wish to use: Move, Color, Delete, etc. Execution of the operation will now make the required change in *all* the objects selected—they will be moved together, or colored in the selected color, or deleted—in one single step.

■ Using the Delete tool in the prepicking mode can be a little confusing at first. After you finish making the selection of objects and activate the Delete tool, the Prompts palette will instruct you to "Click to Delete Picked Objects." You *must* execute this click for the deletion to happen. You can click *anywhere* in the graphics window, even on blank space; you do not necessarily have to click on an object. Alternately, you can also use the Delete key (Mac) or Backspace key (PC) on your keyboard instead of the Delete tool to carry out the deletion operation after prepicking.

■ Keep in mind that you can use the prepicking method for many other operations as well. For instance, you can select a number of 2D shapes with the Pick tool, and then derive extruded 3D objects of the same height from all of them at the same time by using the Extrusion tool (M-Tool:5a,3). Try it!

3.5 Area Picking

Prepicking objects individually, as you did in the last section, can get quite tedious if you have many objects to select. If the targeted objects lie close together, it might be more convenient to select them by enclosing them in a boundary which is demarcated with the mouse. This is known as *area picking*.

■ Make sure you have a number of objects in the graphics window; if required, create some more. Select the Pick tool. You will now use it to draw a rectangular boundary that encloses all the objects you need to select. Click on one corner of this boundary, keep the mouse down, drag it until you define the opposite corner, and then release the mouse. All the objects that lie completely within this boundary will get selected. Keep in mind that the first click should always be on blank space rather than on an object, otherwise only that object will get selected.

The rectangular boundary you just defined is referred to as a *frame*. You can also use a different kind of bounding area for selecting objects, known as a *lasso*, by choosing this option in the dialog of the Pick tool.

■ Double-click on the Pick tool to open its dialog. It contains a large number of options which we will explore in depth in Workshop 2. For now, simply look at the two Area Pick options located at the base of the dialog. Frame is selected by default. Change the selection to Lasso and exit the dialog.

■ Back in the graphics window, first deselect any objects that are selected by clicking on blank space. Now click and drag to select objects using area picking as you did earlier. Notice that you are no longer restricted to defining a rectangle as the bounding area—you can draw out any freehand enclosure with the mouse, as if you were sketching. Once you have released the mouse button, all the objects lying within this freehand enclosure get selected.

■ Get back to the Pick Options dialog and activate the remaining Pick Crossing option in the Area Pick section. If you now use area picking, you will find that objects crossing the bounding frame or lasso also get selected, in addition to the objects lying completely inside it.

■ When area picking is used, notice that any previously selected entities get deselected automatically, since you have to start by clicking on a blank area of the window. To select additional entities while still maintaining the current selection, press the Shift key on your keyboard while area picking.

▣ Area picking is only available when using the Pick tool for prepicking—it cannot be used for postpicking. Thus, for instance, if you have already selected the Move tool, you cannot use area picking to select the objects you want to move. Instead, you first need to activate the Pick tool, draw a bounding area to enclose the objects you wish to select, and *after* the objects have been selected, use the Move tool to carry out the desired transformation.

3.6 Other Methods of Selection...and Deselection

In addition to the Pick tool, there are a few other commands that can be employed for making selections. These are located in the third group of the Edit menu. Let us try them all out.

▣ Start with Select Previous. This repicks the last round of selected entities and is useful when a number of selections are accidentally deselected. Very often while making multiple selections, it happens that you don't click close enough to an object to select it, resulting in the deselection of objects you have already selected. It can be quite tedious to make the selection all over again, so Select Previous comes in really handy in such a situation.

▣ Select All Unghosted will select all the visible elements in your project, as opposed to Select All Ghosted which will select the ghosted elements only. The concept of ghosting, and the difference between visible and ghosted objects is explained in detail in the next section.

▣ Next, go to the Select By command. This opens up a dialog in which you can select objects by various categories such as Object Type, Surface Style, Layer, and so on. In subsequent workshops, you will learn more about many of the object attributes that appear in this dialog, which will be unfamiliar to you right now. Figure 1.21 shows the Select By dialog in which all objects colored in two different surface styles have been targeted for selection. You can also have multiple selection criteria by activating more than one category. This kind of selection ability can be extremely convenient. It also motivates you to draw your entities systematically, differentiating them by layers, colors, and so on, to make full use of this option.

Figure 1.21

Using the Select By command to select objects that are colored in the two highlighted surface styles.

■ Let us move on to deselection, the inverse process of selection. The Deselect option, located immediately after the Select By option, lets you deselect all the objects that are currently selected. But you have already seen how you can achieve the same result by simply clicking on a blank area of the window, away from any object.

■ To deselect only one object from a number of selected objects, click on that object itself rather than on a blank portion of the window.

3.7 Ghosting and Unghosting Objects, and the Status of Objects Option

The concept of ghosting is unique to form•Z—you will not find this utility in other CAD programs. Ghosting is an alternative attribute to visibility that objects in form•Z can have. Visible objects are those that you see in your window in the color which was assigned to them. These can be selected and operated upon in the usual manner. Another name for visible objects is "unghosted" objects. Ghosted objects, in contrast, have the default color of gray; also, they are inactive and cannot be selected for the execution of any operation. Unghosted objects can be ghosted by the Ghost command (M-Tool:13b,1) and ghosted objects can be unghosted by the Unghost command (M-Tool:13b,2). Unghosting is, thus, the inverse process of ghosting.

But how are ghosted objects created in the first place and what are they used for? You have already worked with three of the derivative object tools in the left column of Row 5, which derived 3D objects from 2D shapes. What happened to the original 2D elements? They were ghosted by default, and therefore, retained in the project, making it possible to retrieve them at a later stage, if needed. Let us see how this can be done.

Figure 1.22

Creating ghosted objects. (a) The Status Of Objects dialog, showing the status set to Ghost. (b) Generating 3D objects with the Extrusion operation. (c) Moving the objects aside to reveal the original 2D objects in ghosted mode.

■ Select any of the three derivative tools you worked with in Section 1.10, say Extrusion (M-Tool:5a,3), and invoke its dialog. Click on the Status Of Objects button that you had previously ignored. The Status Of Objects dialog is invoked, giving you three choices of what to do with the original objects from which new objects will be derived. This Status Of Operand Objects is set to Ghost by default (Figure 1.22-a), which is why ghosted objects were created when you had used this tool earlier. You can choose right away to retain (Keep) or throw away (Delete) the original objects, but stick with Ghost for now. The Status Of New Objects options are more relevant to the boolean operations which will be covered in Exercise 4, so ignore them at present.

■ Notice the checkbox called Global at the top of the dialog, which is selected by default. This means that the current settings of the dialog will be applied to all the tools to which the Status Of Objects option is relevant. To make the change in settings only for the tool you are invoking this dialog from, click on the checkbox and it will change to reflect the current tool.

■ Now go ahead and apply the Extrusion tool to some 2D objects (Figure 1.22-b). Then delete the 3D objects you just derived or move them aside. If you are not in the Wire Frame display mode, switch to it. You will see your original 2D objects in ghosted form (Figure 1.22-c).

Suppose that you have performed a large number of subsequent operations, and you suddenly realize you want to retrieve one or more of these 2D objects. You cannot go back all the way using Undo without losing what you have subsequently done, and you would rather not have to recreate the objects. This is what you can do:

■ To retrieve only one or a few ghosted objects, apply the Unghost tool (M-Tool:13b,2) to them directly. They will come back as regular objects, with their original colors, and you can now operate on them just like any other visible objects.

■ When a large number of ghosted objects needs to be unghosted, it would be tedious to apply the Unghost tool to each one of them individually. It is better to apply the prepicking method. However, you cannot select them in the normal fashion by using the Pick tool. Instead, go to Edit > Select All Ghosted. All the ghosted objects get highlighted in red, indicating that they are selected. Then select the Unghost tool and click in the graphics window to unghost all the selected objects. You can reghost the ones you did not wish to retrieve by using the Ghost tool (M-Tool:13b,1).

■ As emphasized, ghosted objects can only be seen in the Wire Frame display mode. If you tend to use this mode of display very often and don't want these objects cluttering up your screen, but also do not want to get rid of them irrevocably, you can hide them by choosing Edit > Hide Ghosted.

■ If, on the other hand, you are confident that you will never need them again, you can delete all ghosted objects by going to Edit > Clear All Ghosted. They will now be permanently erased from the database of your project, reducing the size of the project file. It is a good practice to periodically clear ghosted objects, particularly if the file is getting too large.

3.8 Zooming And Scrolling

In all this time that you have been working, you may have, on occasion, inadvertently moved some objects out of view in the graphics window. It is time to learn how to use the zoom and scroll commands so that you can bring them back.

■ Go to the seventh column of the window tool palette at the base of the graphics window. This is the Zoom & Pan palette. Drag it out and position it on one side of the graphics window, and explore each one of the tools in turn.

■ The first tool, Zoom, is the familiar "magnifying glass" that you find in most programs. It lets you zoom in or out of a specified area of the window by clicking in the center of that area. By default it zooms in, indicated by the + sign. Use it with the option key (Mac) or Ctrl+Shift keys (PC) to zoom out. The extent of the zooming in or zooming out is determined by percentage factors that you can modify in the dialog of this tool. This dialog actually contains options for all the zoom tools and can be accessed by going to any one of them.

■ The second tool, Hand, is again the familiar tool used for scrolling through a window. Click and drag to move the displayed image in any desired direction.

■ The next two tools, Zoom In By Frame and Zoom Out By Frame, allow you to zoom in and out of any part of the window by drawing a rectangular frame. By default, zoom frames are drawn from the center out. If you prefer to draw frames by demarcating their corners, select that option in the Zoom Options dialog. Keep in mind that you have to *click and drag* to indicate a frame. If you simply click, the program assumes that your frame is fully defined by that single point and will naturally protest with a warning message.

■ With all these four tools, you will notice that once selected, each remains active even after it has been applied, enabling it to be repeatedly applied any number of times. Thus, you can keep zooming in and out or scrolling without having to reselect the tool each time—you only need to do it once. During this process, all other tools become deactivated, as shown in Figure 1.23. When you have finished using the tool, simply click on it or on any one of the other grayed out tools, or press the Esc key, and the tool palette display will be restored to normal. This is referred to as *continuous window tool control*. If you find this feature annoying or difficult to get used to, you can disable it by going to Edit > Preferences and deselecting the checkbox for this option. Thereafter, these tools will function in the regular fashion you are accustomed to. (We will be looking at the Preferences dialog in detail in Workshop 3.)

■ The next two tools, Zoom In Incrementally and Zoom Out Incrementally, do so by the same preset percentage factors specified in the Zoom Options dialog that you saw for the first Zoom tool. The difference is that these tools always zoom in or out from the center of the window. Thus, you don't need to click in the window at all for these tools to work.

■ The Previous tool takes you one step back to the previous zoom/scroll view, if any.

Figure 1.23

All other tools are deactivated when the Zoom In By Frame tool is selected.

◼ The Fit tool automatically adjusts the zoom level so that all the objects in the project fit within the graphics window. It is thus a frequently used tool. It has a few associated options in the Zoom Options dialog which you should explore. You can choose to fit selected entities only within the window rather than all the objects in the project, as well as change the default border size between the "fitted" objects and the edge of the window. The options related to lights and camera views will be clear once you study these topics in Workshop 3.

◼ The last tool, Reset, takes you to the default viewing size of the reference plane and coordinate axes, the one you see when you first open a new project. You can change this default viewing size, if necessary, by going to the Display menu and choosing a different display scale from the first group of menu items. A Custom Display Scale can also be specified. This display scale is the viewing size you will return to whenever you select the Reset tool.

 Changing the display scale is an alternate way of zooming in or out, but unlike the regular Zoom tools, it also has the effect of resetting the display. Therefore, use it for the latter purpose only, and rely on the Zoom tools in the window tool palette for the regular zooming in and out operations.

◼ Finally, turn your attention to the percentage value displayed in the box at the right end of the window tool palette. This shows the current zoom level of the graphics window relative to the current display scale. If you click on this box, the Zoom Percentage popup menu is invoked, from which a different zoom percentage can be selected to zoom in or zoom out. It's a convenient alternative to the other Zoom tools—try it.

This marks the end of Exercise 3. You should now feel much better equipped to move on to some more complex operations, such as the booleans.

EXERCISE 4

Combining Objects in Various Ways: The Booleans

Very often, the objects that you will need to model will be quite complex, impossible to generate directly from the various 2D and 3D modeling tools that you have learned so far. You might need to create several objects and then combine them in various ways to finally achieve the configuration you are looking for. If you are familiar with set theory, you know that there are three basic operations that can be performed on two sets: addition, subtraction, and intersection. Such operations are referred to as *boolean operations*. Objects that have an area (such as closed surfaces) or a volume (such as solids) can also be thought of as sets, and the same boolean operations can be applied to them to generate interesting and infinitely varying forms.

form•Z not only has the three basic boolean operators corresponding to addition, subtraction, and intersection—in the form of the Union, Difference, and Intersection tools respectively—but has two additional operators that are a convenient variation on the booleans—the Split and Trim & Stitch tools. All these tools are located in the left column of the eighth row of the modeling tool palette. In this concluding exercise for Workshop 1, we will look at the first four of the boolean tools, along with the related Join and Separate tools which are located in the right column of the same row. The Trim

WORKSHOP 1

& Stitch tool is a little more involved, targeted primarily towards complex objects called meshes, so we shall leave it for Workshop 6 which is devoted to meshed objects.

 If a boolean operation is applied to an analytic primitive, it gets converted to a facetted object and loses its parametric nature.

As a rule, the boolean tools should only be applied to two or more objects which intersect each other in some manner. Let us, therefore, do some preparation before we start working with them.

▣ Rearrange the objects in your window with the Move tool to get some intersecting groups. To position objects more accurately along the horizontal plane, change to Plan view. Then go to the Back/Front or Right/Left views to do the same in the vertical direction. Also, bring together objects of various colors within a group—this will yield very interesting and colorful results. It will also serve to demonstrate a key concept in coloring that we will look at later on in this exercise.

▣ After you have finished collecting all the objects in intersecting groups, switch back to a non-planar view. This will afford a better view of the boolean operations.

4.1 Union

▣ Activate the Union tool (M-Tool:8a,1) and follow the instructions that appear in the Prompts palette. You will be asked to select two objects for a union. If you now select any two objects that intersect or at least touch each other (see Figure 1.24-a), the boolean operation of addition is performed and they are united into one object. Any further transformation such as moving, changing colors, and so on, will now be performed on the unioned entity rather than the individual objects.

 Union is the only boolean tool which works even if the objects only touch each other. All the others require them to actually intersect.

▣ In a Wire Frame mode, you will still be able to see the two original objects in ghosted mode (see Figure 1.24-b). The booleans are another instance of tools which operate on existing objects to create new ones, so the Status Of Objects options we discussed earlier are applicable to them as well. These options appear in the Tool Options palette when the Union tool is activated. You can set the Operand Status to Keep or Delete instead of Ghosted, if necessary. Alternately, you can go to Edit > Hide Ghosted or switch to another form of display to make the ghosted objects invisible to you. You also know how to retrieve the original objects (from Section 3.7), should you require to do that later.

▣ If you want to unite more than two objects at a time, use the prepicking method: select all the objects you wish to unite using the Pick tool first, then apply the Union tool. Keep in mind that the operation is actually executed on two consecutively selected objects at a time—in other words, you must ensure that the objects selected first and second actually intersect or touch, the object selected third intersects or touches the union of the first two, the object selected fourth intersects or touches the union of the first three, and so on.

▣ The Union tool, along with the other booleans, also works on 2D closed surfaces with the same results and under the same conditions. Try it out. Don't expect, however, to be able to unite a surface and a solid—that is mathematically impossible and will not work.

4.2 Intersection

▣ Repeat the same sequence of operations you just performed, now with the Intersection tool and using the postpicking method. The Intersection operation will create an object that is common to both the objects involved in the operation. Using the prepicking method will be quite tricky since you have to ensure that each object has some common area or volume with the intersection of the previously selected objects, otherwise the result of the operation will be a null object. It is safer to always use the postpicking method for this tool.

▣ An Intersection operation is illustrated in Figure 1.24-c. Notice that two separate volumes are created as a result of the operation, since a solid cylinder is being intersected with a 3D enclosure. Should these separate volumes be one object, or should each volume be a separate object? This is where the Status Of New Objects item under Status Of Objects becomes relevant. It has two options, one for each of these two cases. Select the one that is appropriate to the situation. Even if you select the Single Object option for now, you can later separate the volumes, if required, by using the Separate tool (M-Tool:8b,2) which you will soon learn about.

Figure 1.24

The Union, Intersection, and Difference tools applied to a pair of objects. The original objects are shown, along with the Wire Frame and Surface Render displays of the resultant objects.

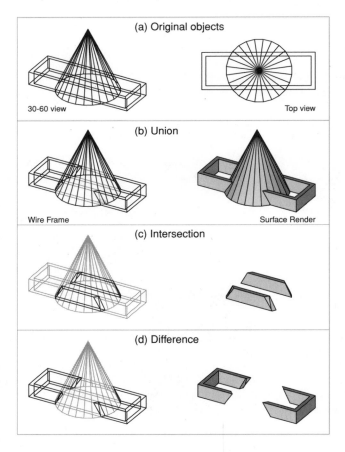

(a) Original objects

30-60 view   Top view

(b) Union

Wire Frame   Surface Render

(c) Intersection

(d) Difference

4.3   Difference

▣ Move on to explore the Difference tool in the same manner. It works just like subtraction—it returns the first object minus the second object. Thus the sequence of selection is important here, even when the post-picking method is used. If you use the pre-picking method, each subsequent volume starting with the second object will be subtracted from the first object, so make the selection carefully.

▣ A useful "architectural" implementation of the Difference tool is to create different kinds of openings in enclosures. Try it.

▣ In the Difference operation illustrated in Figure 1.24-d, notice again that two separate volumes result from the operation. You already know now how to deal with such a situation.

4.4   Split

▣ The final boolean operator is the Split tool, used for splitting objects against one another. Apply it to two intersecting objects. You will find that the second object disappears, but not before it has split up the first object along their mutual lines of intersection. Figure 1.25-a shows the result of a Split operation by moving away some of the newly created objects to reveal the original ones in ghosted mode. You can see that this operation is actually equivalent to the combination of both Difference and Intersection applied to the same set of objects—you get the first object minus the second, as well as their intersection.

▣ What you just performed was a One Way Split operation. There is a second kind of Split operation called Two Way Split. Open the dialog of the Split tool and set the option to Two Way. Apply it to a pair of intersecting objects, and you will find that it gives you *both* the objects trimmed against each other, rather than just the first object trimmed against the second. It is illustrated in Figure 1.25-b, again by moving away the newly created objects from the originals.

Figure 1.25

One Way and Two Way Split operations, applied to the same set of objects shown in Figure 1.24-a. The split pieces have been moved aside to reveal the original objects in ghosted mode.

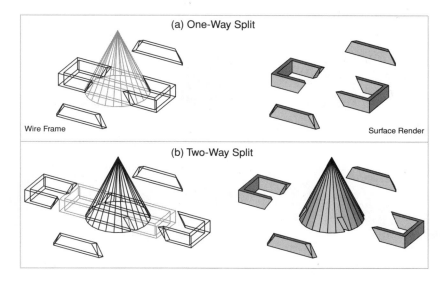

(a) One-Way Split

Wire Frame   Surface Render

(b) Two-Way Split

4.5   The Color Tool Revisited

Now that you have worked with the boolean tools, let us look at an important concept related to object colors that tends to be extremely frustrating if you don't know what is going on.

◾ Perform any of the boolean operations on two objects with different colors (Figure 1.26-a). Look at the result in the Wire Frame display mode. You will find that the new object appears fully colored in the color of the first operand object (i.e., the object which was selected first while executing the boolean operation). Now switch to the Surface Render display, and surprisingly, you will find that some faces of the new object, those that were derived from the second operand object, have the color of that object (see Figure 1.26-b).

◾ Select a new color from the Surface Styles palette, different from those already visible in the object, and use the Color tool (M-Tool:13a,1) to change the color of the object to the selected color. If you are still in the Surface Render mode, you will find that there are no visible effects of this operation—the object continues to have the same colors as before. But if you switch to the Wire Frame display, the object has indeed acquired the new color. Keep trying to do this, and you will find that the Wire Frame display shows the new color but the Surface Render display continues to show the original colors.

What is going on? You will be tempted to believe it is a bug in the program and throw up your hands in exasperation! This is indeed a confusing and vexing problem until you know how to fix it.

The crux of the problem is this—an object of the kind you have created acquires separate color attributes, one for the object itself and others for its faces. What you see in Wire Frame display is the *object* color, whereas what you see in the paint display modes are the *face* colors. This happens whenever an object is created by combining other objects, which means that all the booleans will produce such objects. Even if the original objects were of the same color, the new object and its faces will still acquire separate color attributes. Try it!

So what do we do when we need such objects to go back to being single-colored objects, in which the faces have the color of the object itself rather than their own colors? The solution is actually very simple.

Figure 1.26

Working with multiple object colors. (a) Two intersecting objects in different colors. (b) Applying the Difference tool to create an object with faces of different colors. (c) Setting the Color tool option to Clear All Face Surface Styles. (d) Applying the Color tool to the object to color all its faces in the same surface style.

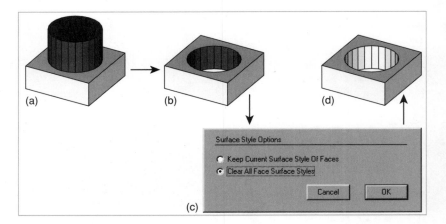

■ Invoke the dialog of the Color tool and choose the second option, Clear All Face Surface Styles (Figure 1.26-c), instead of the first option which is selected by default. Now reapply the Color tool to the object which has multiple surface colors. You will find all faces of the object seamlessly taking on the color that is currently active in the Surface Styles palette (Figure 1.26-d). There will be no further discrepancy between what you see in the Wire Frame display and what you see in the Surface Render display.

In short, whenever you find that you are not able to change the color of an object as seen in a paint display mode, you should remember to apply the Color tool to it with the Clear All Face Surface Styles option activated.

4.6 Joining and Separating Volumes

You have seen that when you apply the Union tool to objects which intersect or touch each other, their individual volumes are combined into a single volume which makes for the resultant object. The Union tool cannot be applied to non-intersecting objects, since their volumes cannot be combined. form•Z, however, provides you with another tool that enables you to treat several non-intersecting objects as a single object, on which desired modeling operations can then be performed. This is the Join tool, and it is accompanied by a related but opposite tool, Separate.

■ Select two or more non-intersecting objects with the Pick tool. Then apply the Join tool (M-Tool:8b,1) to them. Select one of them again with the Pick tool—you will find that all the objects you had applied the Join tool to get highlighted. What you have effectively done is joined them into a single object.

■ Next, apply the Join tool in the same fashion to two or more intersecting objects. You will find that unlike the Union operation, the individual volumes of the objects are *retained* rather than combined. Essentially, the Join tool operates in the same way, irrespective of whether the selected objects intersect or not.

■ One advantage of the Join tool over the Union tool is that the joined objects can be separated at any time using the Separate tool (M-Tool:8b,2). Apply Separate to the joined objects you just created and you will find that you have retrieved the original objects, just as they were before the Join operation was applied to them.

■ You have already seen how the Separate tool can be applied to separate noncontiguous volumes of the same object, created by boolean tools such as Intersection and Difference. Thus, the scope of the Separate tool is not restricted to objects joined with the Join tool. Moreover, the Separate tool can also be used to separate objects along selected segments or faces. The choice of operation is made in the tool dialog. You will be able to apply it in these other modes once you learn to work with the Segment and Face topological levels in Section 3.1 of Workshop 2.

Figure 1.27

The use of the Join tool. (a) Initial configuration of objects. (b) Desired configuration, achieved by using the Join tool and then the Difference tool.

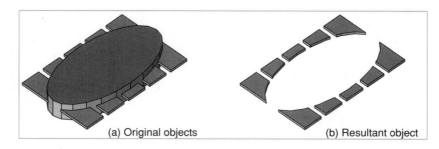

(a) Original objects   (b) Resultant object

With the Join tool, any number of objects, located anywhere with respect to each other, can be temporarily or permanently joined. Any modeling operation will then be performed on all of them collectively. Figure 1.27 shows a situation where the use of the Join tool is indispensable. An elliptical extrusion needs to be subtracted from a series of non-intersecting slabs. Rather than performing the Difference operation individually for each slab and unghosting the extrusion each time for use with the next slab—an incredibly tedious process!—we can simply join all the slabs with the Join tool and subtract the elliptical extrusion from the collective volume.

This concludes the exercises for Workshop 1. You have covered a lot of ground and learned enough to be able to create fairly complex configurations. You will be guided through one such project in the suggested assignment for this workshop. Attempt at least one such modeling exercise yourself before moving on to the next workshop.

ASSIGNMENT 1

A Simple Pavilion

Create a simple pavilion using all the tools you have learned so far. Don't worry about scale, dimensions, or accuracy for now. You need not necessarily have a concept in mind before you start this exercise. You can use the medium itself to generate ideas for you as you are modeling.

The actual exercise of modeling the pavilion shown here will now be demonstrated step by step. How your graphics window should look at the end of each step is illustrated alongside, along with the modeling tools that need to be used. The CD-ROM accompanying this book has a separate form•Z file for each step of this exercise in the Assignments > Workshop1 folder, and you can always use them for reference if you get stuck. A color rendering of the completed project is in the Assignment1.tif file in the same folder.

◀ **Step 1**

Open a new form•Z project. Change to the Top view by going to View > Top. Set the Heights menu to Custom and specify the height as 5'-0". Set the object generation mode in the left column of the second row to 3D Extruded Solid.

Use Rectangle (M-Tool:3a,1) to draw four squares as shown. Use the grid lines for reference, but don't worry about perfect accuracy for now.

Step 2

Set Heights to 2'-0". While still in the Top view and 3D Extruded Solid mode, draw another square which intersects all the first four blocks at their corners.

Switch to a non-planar view and Union each of the four smaller blocks with the larger slab. This becomes the base of the pavilion. (You can add the steps to climb to the base later. Let us complete the basic structure for now.)

◁ Step 3

Switch back to the Top view. Set the object generation mode to 2D Enclosure by selecting M-Tool:2a,2. Change the width of the enclosure to 2'-0" by accessing the tool dialog.

Select M-Tool:3a,2 and draw a square inclined at an angle of 45° as shown.

Step 4

Switch to a non-planar view. Set Heights to Graphic/Keyed. Select the Convergence tool (M-Tool:5a,4) and generate a 3D pyramid from the 2D enclosure, specifying an appropriate height interactively with the mouse. This object will be the roof of the pavilion.

WORKSHOP 1

Step 5

Highlight the Perpendicular Lock tool (W-Tool:2,1) to activate it. Then use the Move tool to displace the pyramid vertically upwards by an appropriate distance.

Step 6

Switch back to the Top view and set the object generation mode to 2D Surface Object. In the dialog of any one of the Circle tools, reduce the resolution value from 24 to 8 segments. Then draw four small circles at the four corners of the pyramid.

Change to a non-planar view and extrude each circle by the same height, up to the base of the pyramidal roof. These circular extrusions will serve as the supports for the roof.

Step 7

Create an extruded solid, aligned diagonally like the pyramid and passing through its center. By now, it should be easy for you to figure out how to do this.

WORKSHOP 1

Step 8

Use the central solid to carry out a One Way Split of the pyramidal roof. Remember—the roof should be selected first!

Step 9

Now use the Move tool, with the Perpendicular Lock activated, to displace the split top portion of the roof vertically upwards by a small distance.

Step 10

Finally, add circular supports for this displaced portion of the roof as well. When you are done, you should have a simple, structurally stable pavilion as shown.

You now have the basic structure of a pavilion which you can build upon and embellish, as per your creative visions. As you can see, you were able to create a 3D model of some complexity in a relatively short sequence of steps. The process was simple and quite intuitive, and will become more so as you continue to work with the program.

Creating objects of specific dimensions, undoubtedly a more complicated task than what we have been doing so far, will be our next challenge, and we will take it up in Workshop 2.

Bringing a Sense of Scale

In this workshop, you will learn how to create models that are of specific dimensions. The process involves setting up the units of measurement, using the coordinate displays effectively, and specifying values using the mouse as well as the keyboard. All these aspects will be covered in Exercise 1. Exercises 2 and 3 will show you how to restrain the cursor movement in your window in various ways, create new objects with reference to existing ones, and work at multiple levels ranging from points to groups.

Some additional key functions in modeling will be covered in Exercises 4 and 5. You will learn how to apply transformations and make copies of objects in different ways, as well as use the extensive set of dedicated line editing functions. Finally in Exercise 6, you will work with the Insertion tools which can be used to perform, more simply and elegantly, some of the boolean operations you mastered in Workshop 1. In the concluding assignment for this workshop, you will apply all that you have learned in creating the block model (i.e., the massing model) of a building.

Sizing Up Your World

WORKSHOP 2

Throughout the last workshop, you worked without worrying about dimensions, scale, units, and so on. This may be fine in the early stages of a design when you are exploring various shapes and forms, but sooner or later, you will have to bring scale into your modeling world. Exercise 1 will guide you through this process. You will start by learning how to specify the measurement unit according to the requirements of the project, which may be different from the default unit settings. Then, you will see how to track the cursor coordinates in the graphics window, using both the Coordinates and the Prompts palettes. Finally, you will master a crucial aspect of accurate modeling—using the keyboard to specify object positions and dimensions, both in relative as well as absolute terms.

▣ Launch form•Z and save the default modeling window that appears as a new project. Close all palettes except Prompts, Coordinates, and Surface Styles. As usual, also set the Heights menu to Graphic/Keyed so that you can specify object heights interactively.

1.1 Specifying the Working Units

▣ Go to Options > Working Units. A dialog is invoked containing various options for selecting the type of measurement unit and its accuracy (Figure 2.1).

▣ Select the Unit Type—English or Metric—you want to work with, and the Base Unit for that type. (Throughout this book, the English system has been used, with the Base Unit set to Feet. If you are using the Metric system, simply substitute the appropriate metric values for feet and inches.)

▣ Key in also, in the same dialog, the desired values for both Numeric Accuracy and Angle Accuracy if they differ from the defaults. In general, you should try and set these to *not less than the minimum levels of accuracy* you need in a project. Thus, if you are modeling small objects like furniture, you will need a numeric accuracy of at least 1/8" and an angle accuracy of 0.1°. On the other hand, if you are modeling large objects such as a city block, you can probably get away with a numeric accuracy of 1" and an angle accuracy of 1°, which are the specifications shown in Figure 2.1.

▣ Before you close the Project Working Units dialog, check out also the Numeric Options and Angle Options and set them as required. Numeric Options lets you select one of four different formats to see the coordinate display in, along with some decimal formatting options (Figure 2.2-a). Angle Options similarly lets you specify the format of the angle display, along with the direction of the 0° angle and the measurement method. Stick with the defaults for now, if you don't quite know what to settle for.

Figure 2.1

The dialog for setting the working units of the project.

█ Don't worry about the Coordinates Palette Unit Type and the Prompts Palette Unit Type in the Project Working Units dialog for now. These options can be set directly from the Coordinates and Prompts palettes respectively, and we shall see in due course what they are used for.

1.2 Tracking Coordinates

█ Let us assume you've set the Unit Type to English, the Base Unit to Feet, the Numeric Accuracy to 0'-1", and the Numeric Display to Architectural. Notice that as you now move the cursor in the graphics window, the coordinates of the current position are interactively displayed in the Coordinates palette in the specified format (Figure 2.2-b). Carry out any modeling operation, and you will find that the same format is also followed for the coordinate display in the Prompts palette (Figure 2.2-c).

Figure 2.2

The Numeric Display Options dialog used for specifying the format of the coordinate display, which is reflected in both the Coordinates and the Prompts palette.

(a)

(b)

You will be closely following the coordinate displays in both these palettes when you create models that are to scale. It is important to remember that in a CAD system like form•Z, *all modeling is done to true scale*, i.e., in the actual size of the object. So, for example, if a box is 20' long, 15' wide, and 10' high, you are going to create it in these very dimensions: 20' by 15' by 10'. It is only when you want to *print* your project that you need to specify a scale. Thus, confusion about the best or the most appropriate scale for creating a particular drawing, usually encountered when doing drawings manually, is completely done away with in form•Z.

Moving on to the actual modeling process, suppose that we really want to create the box specified above. Let us see if we can accomplish this task by tracking coordinates alone.

█ Choose the appropriate combination of tools from the toolbox—the Rectangle tool (M-Tool:3a,1) in 3D Extruded Solid mode (M-Tool:2a,3), or the Cube tool (M-Tool:1a,1). Let's assume you have selected the first combination. Click on a point anywhere in the window to get the first point of the box, and keep a mental note of its coordinates by reading them off the Coordinates palette.

█ Then, move the cursor to a point which is approximately 20' away on the X axis and 15' away on the Y axis, again by keeping track of the coordinate display and doing a quick calculation. This will be the diagonal point of the base of our box. Click to record it as such.

▣ Finally (since you haven't preset a height in the Heights menu), drag the cursor to specify the height of the box following the same procedure. This time it is easier as the z coordinate was initially 0.

Incredibly tedious, wasn't it? And this for just a single entity. How much more tedious it would be if you had to model many more such entities, all related to one another dimensionally, you can well imagine! Obviously, this is not the right way to go about creating scaled models.

Let us do it the proper way then, making a more intelligent use of the coordinate displays.

1.3 Direct Numeric Input

▣ Delete the box you just created; you will create another, more accurate one. Make sure the same tool or tool combination is selected as before.

▣ Let us start from the point [0,0,0] which is generally a good starting point and can be conveniently used to locate the "origin" of the model. Try moving the cursor exactly to this position with the help of the coordinate display in the Coordinates palette. Though not impossible, this can be difficult, particularly if your Numeric Accuracy is set to a very low value (which is why you were cautioned against making it needlessly small). It would be easier to just type the coordinates in. This is referred to as *direct numeric input*.

▣ Turn your attention from the Coordinates to the Prompts palette. You will find it prompting you for the *first corner point* of the extruded rectangle. Instead of clicking on a point in the window, type in the coordinate value 0',0',0' in the palette at the prompt line (see Figure 2.3) and press the return (Mac) or Enter (PC) key. The point [0,0,0] will be selected as the first point of the box. Make sure you do not move the mouse while inputting data numerically, as the new cursor position then overrides what has been typed in.

Figure 2.3

Specifying the point [0,0,0] as the first corner point of an extruded rectangle in the Prompts palette.

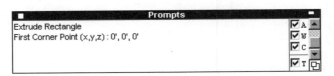

▣ Having specified the first point, the Prompts palette will prompt you for the *second corner point* of the extruded rectangle. This is the diagonal point of the base of the box, and it should be [20,15,0] to create a box with a base of 20' by 15'. Type in this value and hit return or Enter as before.

▣ Finally, you will be prompted for the height of the box. Key this in as 10'. Your box will be complete, created according to the required .

This is how direct numeric input can be used to create precise models with accurate measurements. Practice this technique some more with other kinds of objects until you are comfortable with it, as it is a vital component of any serious modeling activity.

Something to note about direct numeric input: If the Base Unit is set to Feet and your coordinate input for a particular operation does not use inches, you can do away altogether with the quotes that you would normally use to indicate units in feet. Also, if the z coordinate is 0, it is enough to just input the x and y coordinates. So, for instance, the point [2'-0",10'-0",0'-0"] can be input simply as [2,10], the point [2'-6",5'-0",0'-0"] as [2'-6",5], and so on.

1.4   Absolute and Relative Coordinates

In the last section, it was easy to specify the second point of the box, since we made sure that the first point coincided with [0,0,0]. However, this will not always be the case. Let us see how to deal with the situation where the first point is *not* [0,0,0].

■ Start the procedure for creating a new box. Type in the values 18,15 for the first point in the Prompts palette.

To specify the second corner point of a 20' by 15' by 10' box starting at [18,15,0], we need to calculate its x and y coordinates by adding the distances of 20 and 15 to the first point coordinates of 18 and 15 respectively. Such coordinates are known as *absolute coordinates*, since they are specified with respect to the origin [0,0,0] of the coordinate system. As you can see, it can get very tedious specifying absolute coordinates in this manner, because most objects in our modeling world will *not* conveniently start at the origin. There should be a better way.

There is! We can avoid the whole "absolute coordinate" rigmarole by using *relative coordinates*. These are essentially coordinates relative to the point last selected, which is useful because once the first point for an object has been specified, subsequent points can be measured from the previous point only. You no longer have to bother with calculating distances from the origin. Let us see how this works.

■ By default, the entries you make in the Prompts palette are treated as absolute coordinates. You need to change this so that it works in relative mode. Moreover, you can make this change even while you are in the *middle* of an operation, like you are now. Click on the checkbox labeled A (which stands for "absolute") that is located on the right side of the Prompts palette. The box will be unchecked, indicating that all the entries will now be treated as relative coordinates (Figure 2.4).

■ Notice that for the second point of the box, you are now asked to input [Δx, Δy, Δz] (Mac) or [Æx, Æy, Æz] (PC), instead of [x, y, z]. These new inputs represent the distance of the desired point from the *point entered previously*. Simply input 20,15 as shown in Figure 2.4, and the relative point [20,15,0] will be selected as the diagonal point of the base of the box.

Figure 2.4

Using relative rather than absolute coordinates to specify the second corner point of the base of the box.

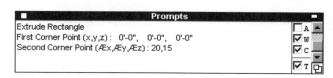

■ Complete the object by keying in the height of the box as 10.

■ In the same manner, use the other drawing tools on Row 3 as well as the primitives to create various kinds of scaled objects, using direct numeric input and relative coordinates. You might want to use absolute coordinates for specifying the first point of an object, in which case you need

to click on the A box as you did earlier. It will get checked, setting the Prompts palette mode back
to the default of absolute.

 *When you input values through the keyboard for the drawing tools in the right column of
Row 3 (which create open shapes), type the character "e" in the Prompts palette to "end"
the command. It thus equates a double-click of the mouse, as you learnt in Section 1.5 of
Workshop 1. Similarly, the character "c" can be typed to "close" the figure and is thus the
keyboard equivalent of a triple-click.*

1.5 Switching Between the Prompts and Coordinates Palettes

You have seen that while using direct numeric input, you often have to keep switching between the
absolute and relative modes while you model. The first point of a new object is usually specified using
absolute coordinates (since this determines the location of the object in the coordinate space), while
subsequent points are easier to specify using relative coordinates (since they determine the dimensions
of the object). Rather than being forced to select and deselect the A box in the Prompts palette
repeatedly as you did in the preceding section, you can follow the more convenient process described
here.

▣ Set the Prompts palette to relative mode, but let the Coordinates palette, which has the same A
checkbox, remain in absolute mode. Go through the process of creating a box again. Move the
cursor to the x field in the Coordinates palette and enter the absolute x coordinate of the first point
of the box. Press the Tab key (very important!) to move to the y field, and specify the absolute y
coordinate. Do the same for the z field; then press return or Enter. You will find that this point
specified in absolute coordinates has indeed been selected in the graphics window as the first
corner point of the box. Thus, you used the Coordinates palette rather than the Prompts palette
for numeric input this time, and absolute coordinates to position your box correctly.

▣ For the second point which you want to specify in relative coordinates, return to the Prompts
palette by clicking on it. Delete the values for this point that appear here automatically (based on
the cursor movement), and enter the values you want.

▣ Finally, specify the height in the Prompts palette itself, in relative mode. Your box will be created
accurately with the specified dimensions.

▣ You may occasionally find that in the process of switching back and forth between the two palettes,
the values you entered in the Prompts palette are lost if the cursor is accidentally moved out of the
palette. This happens because "tracking" the cursor position is on by default; therefore, whenever
the cursor is inside the graphics window, the Prompts palette will display its coordinate position.
If this is annoying and inconvenient, you can turn tracking off by deselecting the T checkbox in
the lower right corner of the Prompts palette. Your keyboard input values will no longer be
overridden if the cursor accidentally moves out of the palette on to the window. Tracking cannot
be turned off in the Coordinates palette, so you can still read the current cursor position off it.

1.6 Cartesian and Polar Coordinates

In addition to absolute and relative coordinates, you can also choose between cartesian and polar
coordinates. You have been using cartesian coordinates so far, which consist of three coordinate values:
x, y, and z. In contrast, polar coordinates are made up of three different values: the *distance* of the new

point from the origin point in absolute mode or the previous point in relative mode, the *angle* made by the line connecting these two points with the horizontal axis in the positive direction, and the *coordinate value* of the point in a direction perpendicular to the currently active plane.

- ▣ Deselect the box labeled C (standing for "cartesian") in the Prompts palette. This will set the coordinate mode to polar instead of the default of cartesian. The Coordinates palette can be set to polar mode in the same fashion; however, leave it as cartesian, so that you can easily switch between the two modes using both palettes.

- ▣ Switch to the Top view and select the Vector Lines tool (M-Tool:3b,3) in 2D Surface Object mode (M-Tool:2a,1). You will use polar coordinates to create an isosceles triangle with a base angle of 75° as shown in Figure 2.5, an operation which would be impossible to execute with precision using cartesian coordinates alone. (Try it if you're not convinced!)

- ▣ Click anywhere to select the first point of the triangle, or locate the origin using absolute cartesian coordinates in the Coordinates palette.

- ▣ Deselect the A box in the Prompts palette so that you can use *relative* polar coordinates. For Point #2 of the triangle, you will be prompted for [dist, ang, z]—standing for distance, angle with the +X axis, and the z coordinate (since you are using the XY plane). Delete the values that automatically appear in the Prompts palette (if tracking is on) and enter a value of say 40 for the distance, 75 for the angle, and 0 for the z coordinate.

- ▣ For Point #3, specify the same values, except that the angle value should be negative, i.e., –75. This gives us the two equal and opposite sides of our isosceles triangle, as shown in Figure 2.5.

- ▣ At the prompt for Point #4, enter c or triple-click to close the figure. The base of the triangle will be added, completing the shape.

Figure 2.5

Using relative polar co-ordinates in the Prompts palette to accurately create an isosceles triangle of specific dimensions.

1.7   Scaled Moves

Now that you know how to model properly dimensioned shapes and objects, it is also essential to be able to perform transformations like Move accurately. Let us see how this can be done.

◼ Suppose the triangle you just created needs to be moved from its current position to a point 10' away along both the X and Y axes. To carry out this operation, first select the C box in the Prompts palette to change the mode back from polar to cartesian. Ensure, however, that the A box is still deselected.

◼ Now highlight the Move tool (M-Tool:12a,1), select the triangle, and key in 10,10,0 (or simply 10,10) as the *relative coordinates* of the move. The triangle will be moved to the desired new location.

Now that we know how to use direct numeric input to create objects that are accurately dimensioned and positioned, let us move on to look at another set of utilities that will further assist us in this process.

EXERCISE *2*

Restraining the Cursor

If you are the kind of person who hates using the keyboard, direct numeric input would be something you would like to avoid as much as possible. You *can* rely on the mouse for much of your input; however, you should then learn to do it more efficiently by restraining the mouse so that it moves only in a specified manner and not anywhere in the graphics window. This is referred to as *snapping*, and it enables you to easily and accurately select the points that are needed for carrying out any operation. form•Z provides you with three kinds of snapping: *grid* snapping, *direction* snapping, and *object* snapping. Exercise 2 is devoted to exploring these three snapping methods.

Let us first see how to change the settings of the graphics window, since some of the snap options directly depend upon it.

2.1 Setting Up the Graphics Window

The graphics window setup involves aspects such as changing the size of the reference plane grid with respect to which objects are being created, turning off the grid and axes displays when they are not needed, changing the cursor display to an extended cursor, displaying a ruler along the edge of the window, and auto scrolling. All these options are available under the Windows pulldown menu. We will explore each one of them in turn.

◼ Select the Window Setup command, located in the fourth group of the Windows menu. (In versions prior to 2.9, this command was located under the Options menu.) A dialog will be invoked in which you can make various changes to the settings of the graphics window (Figure 2.6). Experiment with all the options, exiting the dialog to see the modified grid and axes displays each time You can turn off the grid and axes displays, turn on the display of axis marks that indicate the position of the cursor with respect to the axis, and opt for a dot grid instead of the default line grid. Ignore the Show Reference Plane Axis option for now—it will be clear once you start dealing with arbitrary reference planes in Workshop 3.

◼ The most important feature in the Window Setup dialog is the option to change the default size of the reference grid to values more suited to a particular project. There are two aspects to this grid:

a module along all three directions, X, Y, and Z; and the number of subdivisions for each module. You can see that the grid in the graphics window resembles a graph sheet, with the main modules in bold and the smaller subdivisions in fainter lines. To specify different grid settings, simply enter the new values in place of the defaults. Figure 2.6 shows the Window Setup dialog with grid settings of 10' modules and 10 subdivisions along all three directions. The resultant grid is also shown.

Keep in mind that the grid extends infinitely beyond what is actually displayed in the graphics window. You will learn to modify the default extent of the grid display in Workshop 3.

Figure 2.6

The Window Setup dialog with different settings from the defaults, and the resultant grid. The display of axis marks has been turned on.

▣ Notice that when you change the grid settings for one module, the other two modules get conveniently updated to have the same values automatically. If you need to have different module and subdivision settings along the X, Y, and Z directions, simply deselect the XYZ Grid Lock option and you will be able to do so.

▣ The Auto Grid Scaling option, when selected, automatically adjusts the grid settings when you make a change to the display scale under the Display menu (as you learnt in Section 3.8 of Workshop 1). The adjustment is made in such a way that the density of the grid in the window remains constant. Choosing a smaller display scale, for instance, increases the size of the main modules and vice versa. Try it.

▣ When you open up multiple associated windows for the same project (as you will in Workshop 3), the All Windows option in the Window Setup dialog will be activated, allowing you to apply the modified settings simultaneously to all open windows. You will encounter this option frequently in other dialogs as well, so keep this explanation in mind.

▣ Exit the Window Setup dialog after you have explored all the options. Notice that the options to turn the grid and axes displays on and off are also directly available in the fourth group of the Windows menu. This saves you from the hassle of opening the Window Setup dialog repeatedly to make these changes.

▣ Proceed to select the Extended Cursor command from the Windows menu. It gets activated, and the regular cursor switches to an extended mode that you might find more convenient to use at times (see Figure 2.7). Explore also the Extended Cursor Options item in the same menu. To turn the Extended Cursor off, simple select the command again, and it will switch back to regular mode.

■ Similarly, explore the Show Rulers command, located in the fifth group of the Windows menu, as well as the subsequent Ruler Options dialog. Here, you can make various changes to the default ruler display, such as the sides of the window on which it appears, the coordinate mode that is used, the text and markings on the ruler, the increments, origin, and so on. In particular, setting the Coordinate Mode to Relative is extremely useful, as it automatically repositions the origin at every currently selected point instead of leaving it fixed at [0,0,0]. This is illustrated in Figure 2.7, which also shows how the Show Ruler and Extended Cursor options work well together in planar views. Needless to say, having a ruler display around the edge of the window is most useful when you are working in a planar view rather than in a 3D view.

Figure 2.7

The Extended Cursor and Show Ruler options make an effective combination in a planar view. The ruler coordinate mode is set to Relative. The window settings are the same as those shown in Figure 2.6.

■ Finally, let us look at auto scrolling. This is the ability of the graphics window to scroll automatically when the cursor is moved beyond its edges in the middle of an operation. Turn this feature on by selecting Windows > Auto Scroll, and test it out by using any of the modeling tools you have learnt so far. Select a first point in the window, then move the cursor beyond one of its edges. It will scroll automatically, allowing you to select subsequent points in areas that were previously not visible to you. It thus saves you from the bother of using the Zoom or Hand tools in the middle of an operation and can be convenient once you get used to it.

Having finished the task of setting up the graphics window according to our desired specifications, let us move on to look at the various snapping options, starting with Grid Snap.

2.2 Grid Snapping

Grid snapping restricts the movement of the cursor in the window to the points of an invisible rectangular grid, based on the active reference plane. It will not move to points outside this grid. This kind of snapping is particularly useful for those projects in which some underlying grid is used as the basis for modeling.

▣ Click on the fourth window tool located at the base of the graphics window. This is the Grid Snap tool, and just like the Perpendicular Lock (W-Tool:2,1), it works like a toggle switch. On clicking, it gets highlighted, indicating that it is active. Now move the mouse around in the window, keeping an eye on the coordinate display in the Coordinates palette. You will find that the cursor movement is not very smooth and that you cannot move to points below a certain increment value.

▣ Deactivate the Grid Snap switch by clicking on it again, and notice that the cursor movement is much smoother. In the Coordinates palette, you will now see that the cursor moves to point increments equal to the Numeric Accuracy value specified in the Project Working Units dialog in Section 1.1.

▣ Double-click on the Grid Snap tool to open its dialog (Figure 2.8). Here, you can change the default X, Y, and Z snap values to suit the requirements of your project. Set these now to values much higher than the defaults. The XYZ Snap Lock option in the dialog is checked by default, constraining the three directions to the same snapping value, so it is enough to change it along one of the axes only. The remaining option, Match Grid Module, can be checked if you want the snapping modules to automatically match the grid divisions specified in the Window Setup dialog. Leave this option deselected for now, but keep it in mind for later use.

Figure 2.8

The Grid Snap Options dialog, with different settings from the defaults.

▣ Exit the dialog and perform any modeling operation. You will find that you can no longer graphically select points in the window which are located at intervals less than the new grid snap values along the three axes.

Although you cannot rely on Grid Snap completely for complex modeling operations and will have to fall back on direct numeric input occasionally, it is definitely better than letting your cursor move anywhere in the graphics window, even at those fractional points you will never want or need to select!

2.3 Direction Snapping

Direction Snap is the fifth set of window tools, located immediately after Grid Snap. Its task is to constrain the *directional position* of each input point, relative to its previous point. There are five different Direction Snap tools, of which only one can be active at any given time. We will activate each option in turn and see how it affects the movement of the cursor during a modeling operation.

▣ Select the Vector Lines tool—a good tool with which to explore direction snapping, as demonstrated in Figure 2.9. Turn the Grid Snap off, if it is active, so that it does not interfere with your understanding of the Direction Snap options.

▣ The default option for direction snapping is No Direction Snap (indicated by the icon displaying 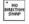 None), which means that the cursor movement is free and not constrained in any particular direction. You are therefore free to draw lines in any direction, as you can test.

Figure 2.9

Different shapes created using each of the five Direction Snap options.

▣ Select the next option, Ortho. This restricts the cursor movement to the horizontal and vertical directions only, relative to the active reference plane. Thus, if you are working on the XY plane, you can only draw lines that are parallel to the X axis or to the Y axis.

▣ Switch to Ortho 45. This sets the directional snapping to the vertical, horizontal, *and* diagonal directions, relative to the active reference plane. Thus, you can draw lines parallel to the axes or diagonal to them.

▣ The Angle option is next. This sets the directional snapping to a user-defined angle, set by default to 45°. Invoke the dialog of the Angle tool and change the Angle value to say, 30°. Alternately, you can specify the angle in terms of a Slope value. Exit the dialog. You will find that you can now move only at an angle of 30° with respect to any of the axes, as illustrated in Figure 2.9. This option is very useful when you are working on a part of the model which is tilted at a fixed angle with respect to the axes.

▣ Switch to the last option, Radial. The movement of the cursor will now be restricted to angular increments *centered* about the previous point. After the first point is selected, you can only move radially about that point at a certain angle. Invoke the dialog of the tool and change the By Angle Of value to 60° (which corresponds to 360 ÷ 30 = 12 Radial Divisions, if you prefer to do it that way). Activate also the Distance Snap option and set its value to say, 5'. Exit the dialog to get back to the graphics window. You will find that the cursor movement is now restricted to only those points which are located at 5' intervals, radiating out at an angle of 60° from the point last selected. Obviously, this a useful option in modeling certain objects, such as the example shown in Figure 2.9.

▣ Finally, try combining the use of all five Direction Snap options to create a single object. You can keep alternating between these different snaps, even in the middle of an operation. In general, this applies to most of the tools in form•Z.

2.4 Object Snapping

The third and final snapping mode—Object Snap—is used for selecting points *in relation to existing objects*. It is thus a crucial snapping mode, since new objects that you need to create will almost always be related in some manner to objects that you have already modeled. There are a large number of Object Snap options, located in the sixth set of window tools immediately after Direction Snap. The use of these options is illustrated in Figure 2.10. Let us look at each one of them in turn.

▣ Make sure you have at least a few objects on your screen with which to test object snapping. Turn off Grid Snap and set Direction Snap to None, so that they do not interfere in your understanding of object snapping. Then activate any of the 2D or 3D modeling tools to test the different Object Snap options.

■ The first option is No Object Snap, indicated by the icon displaying None in the sixth window tool position. It is selected by default when you launch form•Z and means that no object snapping is activated.

■ Select the second option, Point. Move the cursor near an object and watch it "snap" on to the nearest point of that object, highlighting it in green which is the default color for snapping. Move the cursor around and snap it to a few other points until you get a feel for how it works.

■ Select the next option, Endpoint. This snaps the cursor to the endpoint of the nearest segment. For all practical purposes, it works the same way as Point, except that it also highlights the segment whose endpoint it is snapping to. Endpoint is one of the most frequently used object snaps in any kind of modeling.

■ Try Midpoint next. This makes the cursor snap to the midpoint of the nearest segment, a facility that is often useful.

Figure 2.10

The use of each one of the Object Snap options.

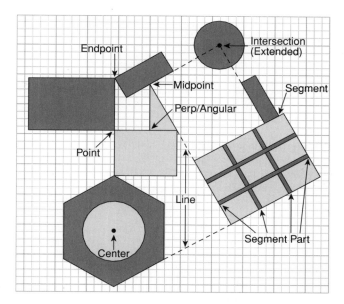

■ Move to the next option, Segment Part. This snaps not only to the endpoints but also to some intermediate points of a segment. Try it on a few segments and you will find that, by default, it snaps to points located at 1/3rd and 2/3rd distances along the segment, i.e., it divides a segment into 3 parts and then snaps to the resulting points. Naturally, you would expect to be able to modify this behavior through a dialog. Double-click on the Segment Part tool and it will bring up the Object Snaps dialog, which will be discussed in detail in the next section. For now, simply change the number of interval divisions in the Snap To Segment Part section to a value other than the default of 3, and test it out.

■ The next object snap, Segment, snaps to *any* point of a segment nearest to the cursor position, not just the endpoint, midpoint, or a particular division, as with the preceding options. Although you will have far less occasion to use this option compared to the other snaps, it can be useful sometimes, particularly when dimensional accuracy is not a prime concern (as in the initial stages of design conceptualization).

◻ Move to the Line snapping option. It is similar to the Segment snap just before it, except that the cursor also snaps to points located *beyond* the endpoints of the segment. In essence, an imaginary line of infinite length is constructed in place of the fixed-length segment, and the cursor snaps to the point on this imaginary line closest to it. Experiment with this option and see how it can be very effectively used for creating objects that are aligned with existing objects but not necessarily touching them, as illustrated in Figure 2.10.

◻ With the Intersection option, you can locate and snap to the intersection point of any two segments. Try it. Then invoke the Object Snaps dialog through any one of the object snap tools, and check the Extended Intersections option. You will find that you can now also locate intersection points lying *outside* the lengths of the segments, following the same principle as the Line snap tool. Such an intersection is illustrated in Figure 2.10. For Intersection, keep in mind that the two segments have to be in the same plane and should not be parallel to each other. In planar views, some segments might look as though they are in the same plane, but they are actually not, so Intersection will not work. Watch out for such situations—it is often a source of great vexation!

◻ Next, select the Perpendicular/Angular snap tool. This is slightly confusing, since it initially snaps to any point of a segment rather than a specific point. Once, however, the first point for a modeling operation is selected, subsequent point selections work differently—the cursor snaps only to those points on other segments which connect to the current point at a 90° angle, *if* any such points exist. By default, the Perpendicular/Angular snap works in Perpendicular mode. You can access the Object Snaps dialog and switch to the Angular mode, where you can specify any other angle value. Then, only points on other segments connecting at that angle to the specified point will be located.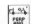

◻ The next option, Tangent, is applicable only to the drafting module and is therefore deactivated. Move to the option after it, Center Of Face, which is used for locating and snapping to the centroid of any closed 2D shape or any face of a 3D object. Try it, and notice that in a 3D view, you cannot use it on those 3D object faces that are hidden from you, even though you may be in the Wire Frame display mode.

◻ Try out also the Face option, which locates points that are within a closed 2D shape or a 3D face not hidden from you. It is similar to Center Of Face, except that it snaps to *all* points within the face and not just the centroid. It is particularly useful when you have to create an object on a surface that is not parallel to any of the three predefined reference planes, XY, YZ and ZX. This is illustrated in Figure 2.11, where a number of 3D objects are constructed on the inclined faces of a pyramid rather than on the current reference plane. Note that to generate the extrusion perpendicular to the inclined surface, you *must* open the dialog of the 3D Extruded Solid tool and select the Perpendicular To Surface option instead of the default Perpendicular To Reference Plane option (Figure 2.11-a). Recall that you learnt about this option in Section 1.10 of Workshop 1.

◻ Finally, move to the last option, Combination (phew!). This allows you to simultaneously use more than one of the ten object snap modes available in the modeling environment that you just covered. The choice of these snaps is made in the dialog of the Combination snap tool. Here, you will find the icons of all the snaps—simply highlight the ones you want to activate in your combination. The default selections are Point, Endpoint, and Midpoint. There is also a button to access the Object Snaps dialog, which is what we will be looking at next.

Figure 2.11

Using Face snap to create 3D objects on inclined surfaces. The right option for generating an extrusion perpendicular to the inclined surface rather than the active reference plane has to be specified first.

(a)

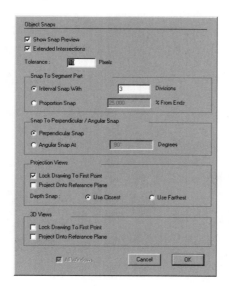

(b)

2.5   Options for Object Snapping

■ Double-click on any one of the first ten Object Snap tools, or click on the Object Snaps button in the dialog of the Combination tool. This will bring up the Object Snaps dialog, which contains options that apply to all the tools as well as options that apply only to specific tools (Figure 2.12). Let us see what these options are.

Figure 2.12

The Object Snaps dialog.

■ The Show Snap Preview and Tolerance options apply to all the tools. You can turn the snap preview off, if required, but it is generally useful to keep it turned on so that you can see what the cursor is snapping to. The tolerance value in pixels controls how close the cursor has to be to an entity to snap on to it. You can change the default tolerance value of 10 pixels to suit your requirements.

■ The Extended Intersections option affects not only the Intersection snap as you saw in the last section, but also the Perpendicular/Angular snap. Since infinite lines are superimposed on finite segments when this option is selected, the Perpendicular/Angular snap will now *always* find locations for subsequent points—which could lie beyond the endpoints of existing segments—that would connect to the current point at the specified angle.

■ The next two groups in the Object Snaps dialog are relevant only to specific snap options. Snap To Segment Part, as you have seen, applies to the Segment Part snap, allowing you to change the number of interval divisions that the segment will be divided and snapped to. You also have the option of choosing the Proportion Snap method, where you specify a proportionate distance from either endpoint at which the snapping will occur. As far as the Snap To Perpendicular/Angular Snap options concerned, you have already familiarized yourself with them in the last section.

The next two sections in the Object Snaps dialog apply to all the snaps. They are extremely important and you should take care to understand them well. Object snapping is not always straightforward, particularly in planar views such as Top, Front, etc., since you could have many points of 3D objects overlapping with one another. Moreover, points selected without snapping will always lie on the current reference plane, which further complicates matters. Try it.

Figure 2.13 illustrates such a scenario of erroneous object snapping. Item (a) shows the original set of 3D objects in 30-60 Axonometric view. In (b), the view is switched to Right, and Endpoint snap is used to create two 2D enclosures, spanning across the original objects. The intention was to create these in a single plane, and it seems as though the objective has been achieved. However, switching back to the 30-60 view shown in (c), the result is obviously erroneous. This is because the points selected without snapping lie on the YZ plane with an x coordinate of 0, as opposed to the snapped points which lie on a different plane.

▪ Coming back to the Object Snaps dialog, the Projection Views section gives you some options that let you control better how snapping will take place in planar views, thereby avoiding the problem we just saw. (Recall that a planar view is technically referred to as a "projection" view.) Turn to the Depth Snap option first. This determines which point will be snapped to in a planar view when there are overlapping points. You can simply choose to locate the point closest to you in the current view (which is the default and which is what happened in Figure 2.13), or the farthest.

Figure 2.13

An example showing how endpoint snapping, which looks correct in a planar view, turns out to be erroneous when seen in a 3D view. The correct solution, achieved by checking the Lock Drawing To First Point option, is shown in (d).

(a) Original configuration

(b) Endpoint snapping in Right view

(c) Incorrect solution

(d) Correct solution

▣   To avoid the problem shown in Figure 2.13, you can select either of the two remaining options under Projection Views. The Lock Drawing To First Point option will ensure that all the subsequent points selected for an operation lie on the same plane as the first point selected. As shown in Figure 2.13-d, this achieves the desired result. Alternately, you can choose the Project Onto Reference Plane option, which projects all the points that are selected, by snapping or otherwise, on to the current reference plane, thereby ensuring that the object lies on one plane. You can then switch to a non-planar view and move the object to where it should have been located.

▣   Keep in mind that both these two options, when selected, also affect regular modeling operations in planar views, even if snapping is not used. Therefore, you should turn them off when you are not consciously using them.

▣   The Lock Drawing To First Point and Project Onto Reference Plane options also appear separately under the 3D Views section of the Object Snaps dialog. They work identically to those under Projection Views, but are listed separately so that you can have different settings for planar and non-planar views, if necessary.

This marks the end of Exercise 2, by which time you should have mastered the art of snapping to perfection! Let us move on to learn how to work at levels both above and below that of the individual object.

Exercise 3

Transcending Objects: Working at Multiple Levels

So far, we have been working entirely at the level of the objects themselves—moving them around, coloring them, deleting them, and so on. As far as facetted objects are concerned, however, you can select and modify not just the objects, but also individual object parts such as points, segments, faces, and so on. The level with which you choose to work is referred to as the *topological level*. The ability to work with multiple topological levels provides us with enormous flexibility in modeling and shaping facetted objects, as we shall see in the course of this exercise. We will also work with groups, a topological level higher than that of the individual object.

Recall from Section 2.3 of Workshop 1 that all objects created using the object generation modes on Row 2 in conjunction with the drawing tools on Row 3 are facetted objects. Keep this in mind while working with topological levels lower than object.

3.1   Working with Points, Segments, Outlines, and Faces

▣   Open up the left column of Row 4 of the modeling tool palette, from where you can choose between eight different kinds of topological levels. You will work with all these levels now except the Hole/Volume level, which will be covered in Exercise 5. A topological level is made active by clicking on it, and it remains active until a new level is selected.

▣   Start by setting the topological level to Point. Then apply the Pick tool (M-Tool:4a,1) to any facetted object and you will find that you can only select the endpoints of the individual segments that make up the object. While you can *snap* on to midpoints and other points along segments (as you learnt in Section 2.4), you cannot *select* them with the Pick tool because such points are calculated on-the-fly rather than stored in the form•Z project database.

■ Now activate the Move tool and move the selected points. You will find that in the process, you have distorted the shape of the object itself to which the points belong. While this gives you enormous capability, make sure you use it wisely, else you might end up with objects having non-planar faces, as shown in Figure 2.14-a. (There is a way to fix this non-planarity problem, and we will look at it in Exercise 5.)

■ Repeat the process by setting the topological level to Segment, Outline, and thereafter to Face, and see how easily you can modify the size and shape of an object in any desired manner by moving its constituent parts (Figure 2.14). An outline, as you can see, is one level below a face—a face can have one or more outlines.

Figure 2.14

Modifying a facetted object by moving a point, segment, outline, and face, shown in (a), (b), (c), and (d) respectively. The original object is shown on the left, highlighting in bold the entities that were subsequently moved.

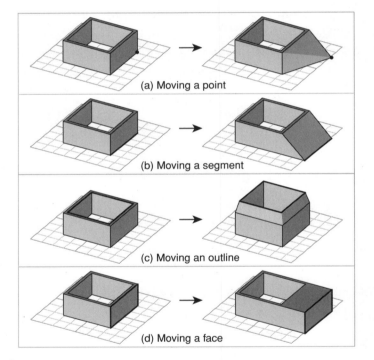

(a) Moving a point

(b) Moving a segment

(c) Moving an outline

(d) Moving a face

■ Try out also the Auto topological level, which automatically selects an entity at any level—point, segment, and so on—that is nearest to the cursor position. Depending upon the type of entity, the cursor changes its icon to indicate what will be selected. Auto is a convenient option when you are frequently working with entities at different topological levels.

Moving faces is the answer to one of the most frequently asked "beginner questions" in form•Z: "How do you change the height of an object?" While there is no fixed direction for measuring heights since objects can be drawn on any plane in space and extruded in any direction, you can simply select the appropriate face of the object and move it in the direction in which it is to be transformed.

■ By default, a face is selected by clicking on any two of its edges. If you prefer to select a face by clicking inside its boundary, invoke the Pick Options dialog by double-clicking either on the Pick tool or the Face topological level, and select the Clicking Inside Boundaries option. However, it might be wise to stick with the default of Clicking On Edges, since Clicking Inside Boundaries does not work for hidden faces, i.e., faces which are not in the line of sight from the current viewpoint. Try it.

■ It is also possible to apply the same transformation to many entities at different topological levels in one step. To do so, you have to resort to the *prepicking* method. Select some entities at one topological level, say Point, then switch to another level, say Segment, and make some more selections. Alternately, use the Auto level to select both the points and segments. Now apply the Move tool to the selection. All the entities—points as well as segments—are moved by the same distance and in the same direction.

■ The topological level specified on Row 4 determines what is selected even when you use *area picking* (as you learnt in Section 3.5 of Workshop 1). Thus, if the topological level has been set to Point, only the points within the bounding frame or lasso will be selected. Try this out.

■ All of the topological levels have a dialog associated with them, as you can see from the red marks on their icons. Invoke this dialog through any of the tools, and you will find that it is the same Pick Options dialog that is associated with the Pick tool. This shows how closely the Pick tool and the topological levels are related. You have already explored two options in this dialog that are related to the Face level. We will explore the other options in more detail in Exercise 4.

Although you will be using the Object level for most of your modeling activity, the other topological levels will come in very useful when you need to edit existing facetted objects, as you can see. You should always keep an eye on Row 4 and make sure that the topological level is set appropriately, depending upon the operation you wish to perform. A very common mistake is to forget this, and then wonder why some operations are not being performed at all. For instance, the Extrusion operation (M-Tool:5a,3) will not work with the topological level set to Point, since a point cannot, by its very nature, be extruded.

Similarly, it makes no sense to color a point or a segment. Different faces of an object, however, can have different colors, as you saw in Section 4.5 of Workshop 1.

3.2   Inserting Points and Segments

You saw in Figure 2.14 how facetted objects can be modified by moving constituent parts such as points, segments, and so on. To provide you with further flexibility in modeling, form•Z also lets you *insert* points and segments on existing objects, which can then be manipulated to transform the object in a desired manner. There are other kinds of insertions as well, which work as a convenient alternative to the boolean operations, and we will explore these later in Exercise 5. For now, let us focus on the Insert Point and Insert Segment tools, located in the left column of Row 10 of the modeling tool palette.

■ Select the Insert Point operator (M-Tool:10a,7) and apply it to any segment of a 2D or 3D object. The change will not be visible unless you activate the Show Points option in the Wire Frame Options dialog, which you will study in Section 2.1 of Workshop 3. However, you can snap to the inserted point using the Point or Endpoint snap tools. Then, with the topological level set to Point, you can apply the Move tool to it, or select it with the Pick tool for some other operation. Essentially, you can manipulate it just like any other existing point to modify the object it belongs to.

INTO 3D WITH FORM•Z

Figure 2.15

Use of the Insert Segment tool.

(a) Inserting a segment on the top face of a cube

(b) Moving the segment using Perpendicular Lock

(c) Moving the segment without using Perpendicular Lock

■ Move on to the Insert Segment operator (M-Tool:10a,8) which works in a similar fashion. Use it to insert a segment on a surface, which can either be a closed 2D object or the face of a 3D object; you cannot insert a segment on an open 2D shape. The endpoints of the inserted segment must lie on the edges or points of the surface. The various point and segment snapping options can come in useful here. Inserting a segment on a surface effectively divides it up into two parts, and you can manipulate the inserted segment or the new faces to modify the object. An example is illustrated in Figure 2.15. As always, be careful when you move the segments you insert, so that you don't end up with non-planar faces and undesired results (as in Figure 2.15-c).

3.3 Deleting Topological and Geometrical Entities

So far, you have deleted entities only at the object level. However, form•Z allows you to delete entities at all topological levels, ranging from points to groups. Objects and groups are deleted by using the familiar Delete tool (M-Tool:14a,1). But in order to delete entities at topological levels lower than Object, you must use either the Delete Topology or the Delete Geometry tool, depending upon the result you want to achieve. Both these tools are located in the right column of Row 14, just next to the Delete tool.

■ Set the topological level to Point. Select the Delete Topology tool and apply it to any point of a facetted object. You will find that all the segments connected to that point get deleted. If the faces connected to these segments are not coplanar, the object will acquire non-planar faces. Apply the same tool to a segment and then to a face by setting the topological level appropriately. You will find that deleting a segment again results in non-planar faces if the faces on both sides of the segment are not coplanar, while deleting a face simply removes it from the object it belongs to. All these Delete Topology operations are illustrated in Figure 2.16.

Figure 2.16

Applying the Delete Topology and Delete Geometry tools at different topological levels. The results are shown in Wire Frame as well as Surface Render.

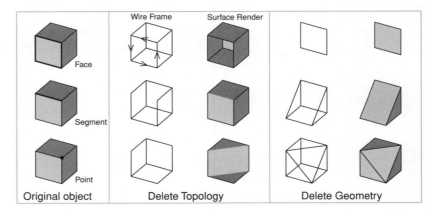

Original object | Delete Topology | Delete Geometry

▣ Now switch to the Delete Geometry tool and apply it to a point, a segment, and a face in the same manner. It operates very differently from the Delete Topology tool, as you can see in Figure 2.16. Deleting a point once again deletes all the segments connected to that point, but a new face is added to the object, ensuring planarity. Deletion of segments and faces operates on the same principle, sometimes leading to very interesting and unexpected results. In general, you will find yourself using the Delete Geometry tool a lot more than the Delete Topology tool.

3.4   Working with Groups

A group is a topological level higher than an individual object in the sense that multiple objects can be brought together into groups. It is also possible to have *multiple levels of hierarchy*, with several groups themselves forming a larger group. Any kind of operation can then be performed on the entire group rather than on individual objects. Let us see how groups work.

▣ Create some additional objects in the current project so that you have a total of at least five objects. Use Pick (M-Tool:4b,1) with the topological level set to Object (M-Tool:4a,5) to select any three of these objects. Then select the Group tool (M-Tool:8b,3) and following the instructions in the Prompts palette, click anywhere in the window. The selected objects will be collected together into a single group.

▣ However, there is no visible change in the window, so how do we know what really happened? Let us see if we can apply some operation to the entire group. Set the topological level to Group (M-Tool:4a,6) and choose a different color from the Surface Styles palette. Then activate the Color tool and select any one of the three objects that you had grouped. You will find that all the three objects in the group acquire the new color. In the same manner, you can apply any other transformation in one step to the entire group.

▣ Form a second group of the remaining objects in your project. Then set the topological level to Group and use the Pick tool to select both the groups. Finally, select the Group tool (M-Tool:8b,3) again and, as prompted, click anywhere in the graphics window. What you just did was create a higher level group containing the existing two groups, as illustrated in Figure 2.17. Any transformation such as Move or Color will now be applied at the level of the highest group (provided, of course, that the topological level is set to Group). Try it. You will find that all objects in both groups undergo the operation you apply.

But now, how can a transformation be applied to only a lower-level group, if necessary? This requires the use of the Objects palette, which we will look at in the next section. For now, let us see how to ungroup objects once they have been grouped.

▣ Select the Ungroup tool, located immediately after the Group tool in the right column of the eighth 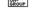 row. Make sure the topological level is still set to Group. Click on any one of the objects that was grouped. There is no visible change, but if you now use the Pick tool to select a group, you will find that you can select and transform the two original groups independently of each other. What you just did was break the highest level of the grouping hierarchy. Apply the Ungroup tool once again to each of the two remaining groups—this will break down all the groups and return you to your original modeling world, devoid of any groupings whatsoever.

▣ Undo all the ungrouping operations you just performed so that you get back to the state where you had two groups forming a larger group. This state can be used to explore some of the other options of the Ungroup tool. Open its dialog by double-clicking on it. The default selection is

Dismantle One Level, which is why you were ungrouping only one level of grouping at a time (Figure 2.17-a).

◼ Choose the second option, Dismantle All Levels, and reapply the Ungroup tool to one of the grouped objects. You will find that you have now broken down not only the higher level group but also all the groups contained within it—in a single step. This option thus destroys the grouping links at *all* levels, for the selected group and those below it (Figure 2.17-b).

◼ Once again, undo what you just did to get back to the grouped state. Now activate the third option in the dialog of the Ungroup tool, Remove Object From Group. Set the topological level to Object and apply the Ungroup tool to one of the grouped objects. You will find that the selected object is now removed from all the groups to which it belongs (Figure 2.17-c). This option is useful when you wish to extract only one or a few objects from a large group—it saves you from the tedious process of ungrouping the whole group and having to reassemble it.

Figure 2.17

The three different options of the Ungroup tool and how they work. The broken group links are indicated by dotted lines.

Working with groups can be very useful and convenient. For instance, in architectural modeling, you can group together similar elements of a building such as columns, beams, floor slabs, doors, windows, and so on in different categories, i.e., groups. At a higher level in the hierarchy could be a floor, so that all objects and groups on one floor could be part of that floor group. At a still higher level in the hierarchy could be the entire building, useful if the project consisted of a cluster of buildings. In this way, a hierarchical grouping relating the model to the real world scenario could be established. Thereafter, any geometric transformation could be applied to an entire group at any level, modifying all its objects as well as objects in the lower-level groups contained within it.

3.5   Using the Objects Palette

◼ form•Z automatically makes an entry in the Objects palette for each object that is created in the project. Since you had closed this palette at the beginning of the workshop, go to the Palettes menu and select the Objects palette to open it. Resize it so that you can see all the entries it contains. Based on the last section on groups, your palette should be similar to that shown in Figure 2.18-a.

◼ Notice that there are entries for objects as well as for groups. All the entries are automatically named in the sequence in which the corresponding objects and groups were created. Generate some new objects and use the Group and Ungroup tools on them; watch the changes being reflected in the Objects palette. The concept of groups within a larger group is really simple to comprehend by seeing the manner in which the group entries are listed in this palette.

■ Let us now solve the problem of selecting a lower-level group for an operation, once it has been made part of a larger group. Simply click in the first column of the Objects palette, next to the name of that group. A √ mark will appear beside the name of the group and the names of all the objects contained in it, as shown in Figure 2.18-b. At the same time, all these objects will be automatically selected in the window, enabling you to apply any desired operation to them.

■ In the same manner, if you click beside the name of the highest level group, all the groups it contains and the objects within these groups get selected. You can even select individual objects using the same method. The Objects palette is thus a convenient shortcut for making various kinds of selections.

■ You can change the default names that have been assigned to objects and groups in the Objects palette. This will help you easily identify a specific object or group when required, which would be a difficult task otherwise, particularly as the number of new objects and groups continues to increase. To change a name, simply click on it in the palette. It gets highlighted, and you can now write over it. Press Return or enter after you finish typing. It is best to assign a new name to an object or group as soon as it is created, allowing you to use the Objects palette more efficiently. Figure 2.18-c illustrates the same Objects palette shown earlier, but with modified object names.

Workshop 2

Figure 2.18

Working with the Objects palette. (a) All the entries for the objects and groups created in Section 3.4. (b) Selecting all the objects in a lower-level group. (c) Ghosting an entire group of objects.

Be warned, however, that as the size of your project expands by ever-increasing numbers of objects, keeping track of each one of them through the Objects palette by renaming them can get very tedious, and you might just abandon it after some time. Lots of form•Z users get by without using the Objects palette at all. So use it if it suits your style of working, but remember that it is not mandatory. In particular, once you learn to work with layers in Workshop 3, you will find that what you can do using the Group tool and the Object palette, you can just as easily do using layers. Still, it is important to be cognizant of these features of the program, should you need to use them at some point.

▣ Let us look at the other functionalities afforded by the Objects palette. Click on the shaded diamond icon in the third column of the palette, next to the name of an object. This icon, which indicates the attribute of *visibility*, gets unshaded. At the same time, the object will become ghosted in the window (Figure 2.18-c). You will see the ghosted object only if you are in the Wire Frame display mode and Edit > Hide Ghosted is not selected. This technique is thus a convenient shortcut to the Ghost tool (M-Tool:13b,1) you learned about in Section 3.7 of Workshop 1.

▣ Click once more on the same spot—in the third column next to the name. The object will become invisible. A third click restores it to its original state of visibility, and the diamond icon too will be shaded as before. Again, this is a convenient shortcut for the Unghost tool (M-Tool:13b,2); it can even be applied to retrieve ghosted objects that are created as a result of modeling operations such as Extrusion, Union, Difference, and so on, that you covered in Workshop 1.

▣ There are two more object attributes that can be manipulated using the Objects palette—*pickability* and *snapability*—indicated by the lock icon and the shaded circle respectively. Click next to an object name in the column to the right of visibility; a lock icon will appear there. Now try and select the object or perform any other operation on it, and you will find that you cannot. It is effectively "locked" against any possible action. This is useful when you are no longer working on an object and want to prevent any operation from accidentally being applied to it.

▣ Repeat the same process with the last column of the Objects palette. When you click on the shaded circle in the same line as an object, the circle disappears. Now try snapping on to that object using any of the Object Snap tools, and you will find that you cannot. This ability is useful when there are many objects spaced closely together, making it difficult to snap to the objects you need. You can turn off the snapability attribute of the other objects so that snapping to the required objects is made easier.

▣ You can also manipulate the visibility, pickability and snapability attributes of all the objects within a group simultaneously by using the corresponding icons next to the name of the group, as in Figure 2.18-c. Try it.

▣ The listing of object and group names in the Objects palette behaves in a manner similar to the listing of files and folders in the navigation windows of most operating systems, which should be familiar to you. Thus, if you click on the downward-pointing arrow next to a group name, the arrow will point sideways and the object listing for that group will be suppressed. Clicking on a sideways-pointing arrow has the reverse effect. The arrows thus work as toggle switches, allowing you to expand or compress the listing of names as desired.

▣ You can create new groups directly in the Objects palette by clicking in the blank space under the last name entry—such groups are empty to begin with. You can move an object to a group, or transfer it from one group to another, by simply "dragging and dropping" it in the targeted group. An object can be dropped out of all groups in a similar fashion. The same technique can also be used for rearranging the order in which the entries are listed in the palette. Multiple consecutive entries can be selected by clicking and dragging across their names. The Objects palette thus provides you with many convenient shortcuts, particularly for the Group and Ungroup tool operations.

▣ Let us conclude this section by looking at the Objects dialog (shown in Figure 2.19) that is associated with the Objects palette. There are three ways to invoke this dialog: one, go to Options > Objects; two, click anywhere in the Objects palette while holding down the option key (Mac) or Ctrl+Shift keys (PC); three, simply click in the top row of the Objects palette where the column title Name appears. Go ahead and open the dialog using one of these methods.

▣ In the Objects dialog, you can create new groups and sort all the existing entries. An individual object or group is selected by clicking on it (as shown in Figure 2.19), after which a variety of operations can be applied to it such as Delete, Copy, Edit, or moving it to the top or bottom of its list. Clicking on the Edit button will open up the Query Object Attributes dialog for an object, which will be covered in Section 5.4 of Workshop 5, or the Query Group dialog for a group, which you will learn about in the next section. (Double-clicking on the object or group name in the Objects palette itself also has the same effect.) The Purge button, if active, indicates that there are "empty" groups, i.e., groups without objects, which you can choose to delete from the project by clicking on this button. You can also choose to change the default object and group names, if you prefer something else.

You may not have realized that every object in form•Z comes with its own local origin and coordinate system, centroid, and bounding volume, all of which are stored along with the object. They can be displayed by setting the appropriate options in the Wire Frame Options dialog, which we will look at in Section 2.1 of Workshop 3. When displayed, it is possible to *snap* to the origin and centroid of an object using the point snapping options. The location of these points is determined when the object is created, based on choices made in the Objects dialog. These locations can subsequently be changed by using the Query tool, coming up in the next section.

▣ Turn your attention to the two groups of options located in the lower half of the Objects dialog. There are four choices for the Default Object Axes Location, which determines the initial placement and orientation of an object's axes when the object is created. Three of the same choices are available for locating the Object Centroid. All the options are self-explanatory, except perhaps the Per Object Type, which locates the origin and axes according to the type of object. With this option which is selected by default, the origin of a cube or a cylinder, for instance, will be placed at the center of its base, while that of a sphere will be placed at its center.

Figure 2.19

The Objects dialog that is associated with the Objects palette.

When you use the Preset option for generating analytic primitives, the single point in the window you click on is actually the origin of the object. The complete object gets positioned according to the selection for Default Object Axes Location in the Objects dialog.

3.6 Querying at Different Levels

Now that you know how to work with different topological levels ranging from points to groups, you will often need to obtain various kinds of information about an entity, such as the exact coordinate position of a point, the length of a segment, the circumference and area of a face, the volume of a solid object, the number of objects in a group, and so on. You can obtain all this information and more by using the Query tool, located in the right column of Row 11 of the modeling tool palette.

▣ Set the topological level on Row 4 to Point. Then activate the Query tool (M-Tool:11b,1) and apply it to any point of an object. This invokes a dialog which lists the coordinate values of the selected point. These values are also editable, enabling the position of the point to be changed by keying in different values (Figure 2.20-a). This technique is often useful for fixing a point precisely in an exact location when it cannot be done so graphically.

▣ Next, apply the Query tool to a segment by changing the topological level appropriately. A different dialog is now presented, showing the coordinate values of the endpoints of the segment and allowing them to be edited. The length of the segment is also calculated and displayed (Figure 2.20-b).

Figure 2.20

The Query dialog for a point, a segment, and an object.

▣ Apply the Query tool to an object in a similar fashion. The dialog that is invoked contains extensive information about the type, topology, and geometry of the object (Figure 2.20-c). It tells you whether the object is well formed or not, and how many non-planar faces it has, if any. The surface area is calculated and displayed, as well as the volume if it is a solid object. Keep in mind that the level of Numeric Accuracy you specified in your Working Units dialog (in Section 1.1) will be reflected in the calculation, so set this appropriately. The locations of the Center Of Gravity and the Object Axes are also given in the Query Object dialog and can be modified here, if required.

■ For a parametric object, the Edit button at the top of the Query Object dialog is active, leading you to a second dialog. Here, various changes can be made to the creation parameters of the object, so the dialog will be different depending upon its type. The dialog for a conical primitive is shown in Figure 2.21—you can see how similar it is to the Cone Options dialog that was illustrated in Figure 1.14. The Edit dialog, however, also displays the Dimensions of the object and allows them to be modified. The width, depth, and height are specified with respect to the local origin and axes orientation of the object, which can also be changed in the same dialog. Try modifying the dimensions, and you will find the change reflected in the preview window on the left. The set of tool icons located at the base of this window let you see the object from different directions, as well as zoom and scroll. From left to right, these tools are: Top, Right, Back, and Axonometric views; Fit; Zoom In/Out (use the option or Ctrl+Shift keys for zooming out); Scroll; and finally, Interactive Rotation of View.

Figure 2.21

Accessing the Edit dialog for a primitive cone from the Query Object dialog.

■ After exploring all aspects of the Query Object dialog, proceed to apply the Query tool to a face, an outline, and then to a group. The Query dialogs for a face and an outline provide information about these entities in a format similar to that provided for an object, although the scale of this information is much less. The Query dialog for a group, which you may have explored in the last section, gives you some additional information about a group that might come in useful.

There is an Attributes tool located immediately after the Query tool on Row 11, which can only be applied to objects and faces. It provides information about various attributes of these entities such as color, smooth shading, and so on. You will be learning about most of these attributes in the next three workshops, so we will postpone working with the Attributes tool till the end of Workshop 5. However, we can work now with the Measure tool, which follows right after the Attributes tool.

3.7 Measuring Distances Using Different Topological Levels

■ Invoke the dialog of the Measure tool (Figure 2.22-a). Here, you will find six distance-calculating options which are crucial in the process of creating scaled models. Let us select each one of them in turn and see what they do.

■ Activate the first option, Length Of Vector/Boundary Line. You can now apply the Measure tool to any segment, outline, face, open 2D object, or closed 2D object containing a single outline, and it will calculate and display the total length of all the segments that make up the selected entity.

You can also select multiple entities, at the same or at different topological levels, to obtain the combined segment length. Thus, it goes one step further than the Query tool, which provides these calculations for a single entity only.

■ With the Interactive Point To Point option, you first select a point. Then, as you move the cursor around in the window, the distance between the first point and the current position of the cursor gets interactively displayed in the Prompts palette (Figure 2.22-b). The T box must be checked to enable tracking. You can use the relevant Object Snap tools if you need to measure distances between specific points of objects. Keep in mind that if you *are* using object snapping, you can measure distances in 3D, e.g., across the diagonals of a box; but if you are not, you will only be measuring distances in 2D, along the current reference plane. If this is confusing, open up the Coordinates palette and keep track of the actual X, Y, and Z values of the cursor as you move it in the window.

Figure 2.22

The dialog of the Measure tool, and using its Interactive Point To Point option to measure the distance between two points.

(a)

(b)

■ Move on to the next option, Point/Segment To Point/Segment. The Measure tool now gives you the distance between any two points, two parallel segments, or a point and a segment. What is really convenient is that you don't have to bother with setting the topological level to Point or Segment—it just finds the nearest point or segment automatically.

■ The remaining three options are very similar to the one you just explored. Point To Surface lets you select first a point and then a face on an object, and gives you the shortest distance between them. Point To Reference Plane requires you to select just a point, and it will tell you its distance from the current reference plane. (Keep this in mind when you work with reference planes in Workshop 3.) And finally, Surface To Parallel Surface gives you the distance between any two parallel faces, belonging to the same object or to different objects.

EXERCISE 4

Executing Transformations and Making Copies

So far, we have worked with just one kind of geometric transformation—Move. In this exercise, we will work with the other elementary transformation tools located in the left column of Row 12 of the modeling tool palette. These are closely related to the Self/Copy modes on Row 11 which allow you to make copies of objects in various ways, so it will be a good time to study these as well. We will then explore alternative ways of executing transformations, learn to define and execute composite transformations in the form of macros, and work with the special tool that is exclusively devoted to editing lines. Finally, we will see how polycurves and analytic primitives can be graphically edited after they have been created.

4.1 Elementary Geometric Transformations

▣ Open a new project or clear the window of all its contents. Create some objects using the tools you are familiar with by now. You will apply some elementary transformations to these objects. Make sure that the left column of Row 11 of the tool palette is set to Self, so that all transformations at this stage are applied to the targeted object itself.

▣ You have already worked with Move. Therefore, proceed directly to Rotate, which is used for rotating any entity about a point. Activate this tool in the left column of Row 12 and follow the instructions in the Prompts palette. Select the object to be rotated; then enter a *center of rotation*, either by keying in its coordinates or by selecting a point graphically with the mouse. You can also select a point on the object itself or on any other object by using the appropriate Object Snap tool. The point selected as the center of rotation will affect how the rotated object will be positioned, as demonstrated in Figure 2.23, so pick it carefully.

▣ Next, you will be prompted for the *angle of rotation*. You can enter this value numerically in degrees—a positive value for the anticlockwise direction; a negative value for clockwise rotation (unless you changed the default Angle Settings in the Working Units dialog, in which case you should follow that specification). Alternately, you can indicate the angle graphically by selecting, first, a reference point, and second, a new position for that reference point. Direction snapping can be useful in doing this precisely. Switching to a planar view also helps in performing rotation more accurately.

Figure 2.23

Applying the Rotate transformation to an object. The rotated object is positioned differently (b and c), depending upon where the center of rotation is picked.

| (a) Original object | (b) Rotate +30˚ | (c) Rotate +30˚ |

▣ Just like the Move tool, the Rotate tool can be applied to the individual points, segments, outlines or faces of an object to produce interesting deformations. Try it. You can also apply the same rotation to many entities at a time by prepicking them with the Pick tool and then selecting the Rotate tool. However, a transformation like rotation, unlike translation, is usually applied to a single entity at a time because it is relative to the center of rotation, which would usually be different for different entities.

▣ Proceed to select the next transformation tool on Row 12, Scale. This tool is used to scale an entity *independently* in the X, Y, and Z directions. Select an object for scaling and then establish a *base of scale*—this can be any point selected, as in Rotate. Most often, you would choose either a vertex of the object or the center of one of its faces as the base of scale, using object snapping to

7

pick the point accurately (see Figure 2.24-a). Just like the center of rotation for the Rotate tool, the base of scale for the Scale tool affects the position of the resultant object, so select it with care.

■ After selecting the base of scale, you need to specify three *scaling factors* to indicate the amount of scaling along the X, Y, and Z axes. For instance, if you want to scale an object such that it is half the original size in the X direction, twice the original size in the Y direction, and unchanged in the Z direction, your scaling factors would be [0.5,2,1]. Figure 2.24-b shows an example of scaling with these factors. It is most common to key in these values in the Prompts palette, but you could also specify them graphically by selecting a reference point and dragging it until the desired scaling is achieved.

■ Move to the next tool, Uniform Scale, which is identical to Scale in all respects except that it applies a uniform scaling factor along the three axes (as shown in Figure 2.24-c). Thus, after you specify the base of scale, you are prompted for a single value rather than three separate values. Again, you can specify this through the keyboard or indicate it graphically with the mouse.

Figure 2.24

Applying the Scale and Uniform Scale tools to an object. The scaling factors were [0.5,2,1] for scaling and [1.5] for uniform scaling.

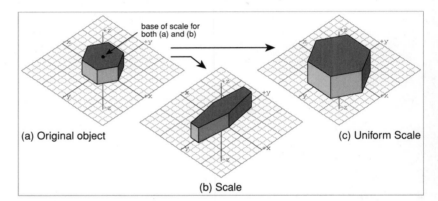

(a) Original object   (c) Uniform Scale

(b) Scale

■ Both the Scale and Uniform Scale tools have a dialog associated with them in which you can choose to Scale By Absolute Value rather than Scale By Percentage, which is the dynamic scaling you have been doing so far. Select this alternate option. You will find that when you now apply any of the Scale tools to a segment, face, outline, or object, a new dialog is invoked in which you can conveniently modify the actual dimensions of the selected entity. For Scale, you can modify all three direction values independently (by deselecting the lock icon in the dialog), whereas for Uniform Scale, you can modify only a single value which will be applied to all three directions. Although you can apply this scaling technique to multiple selections, it works best when applied to a single entity at a time.

■ Proceed to select the fifth transformation tool, Mirror. This tool mirrors the selected object or objects about an *axis of reflection*, indicated by two successive mouse clicks. Note that the axis of reflection is the perpendicular bisector of the line that connects the two selected points, rather than the line itself. For this transformation, it usually helps to have an existing object whose points can be used as reference points (as shown in Figure 2.25-a). If such an object does not exist, create one.

■ Mirroring an object by specifying the perpendicular bisector of the mirror line rather than the mirror line itself might seem counter-intuitive. In that case, you can choose to apply this transformation in a different way. Invoke the dialog of the Mirror tool and you will find that you can also choose to mirror about a point, segment, or surface, instead of specifying the axis of reflection dynamically as you just did. Explore all of these options. The most intuitive one seems to be About A Segment in which you simply select an existing segment as the axis of reflection. The About A Surface option makes it possible to perform the Mirror operation in actual 3D space (as shown in Figure 2.25-b) rather than only along a plane (as shown in Figure 2.25-a).

■ The next tool in the left column of Row 12, Repeat Last Transformation, repeats the most recently executed geometric transformation on a different object of your choice. In addition to the object, the base point for the transformation also has to specified. The remaining factors, such as the translation distance, or the angle of rotation, or the scaling factor, will be taken from the previous transformation. Try it out.

Figure 2.25

Two ways of applying the Mirror tool. (a) Dynamic option. The selected points and the resulting axis of reflection are indicated. (b) About A Surface option. The surface of reflection is indicated.

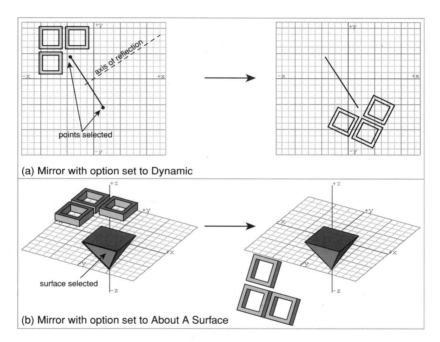

(a) Mirror with option set to Dynamic

(b) Mirror with option set to About A Surface

4.2   The Self-Copy Modifiers

All the transformations you executed in the last section were applied to the selected entity directly, i.e., you were moving the object itself, or rotating it, or scaling it. Even while using Mirror, you were relocating the object itself to its mirror image position. You must have found this quite annoying, since you would usually expect a Mirror command to produce a mirror image *copy* of an object while still retaining the original.

What controls the behavior of the transformation tools on Row 12 is the row of teal-colored tools located just above it. These tools are referred to as the *self-copy modifiers*, and they determine whether a transformation is applied to the object itself or in making copies of it. Let us look at each of them in turn.

▣ The Self mode (M-Tool:11a,1) is the default option to which the self-copy modifier is set, the mode you were working in all this time. It determines that any transformation executed is performed on the object itself. That is why even a transformation such as Mirror in Self mode did not make a copy of the object, but simply changed its position.

▣ Switch to the One Copy mode (M-Tool:11a,2) and apply one of the transformation tools, say Move, to an object. You will find that a copy of the object is now produced in the transformed state, leaving the original as it is.

▣ The next mode, Continuous Copy, is practically the same as the Copy mode, except that the copy-making process does not terminate after a single copy is made. You can make multiple copies of the object one after another, simply by selecting additional transformation points. To terminate the making of copies, double-click with the mouse in the graphics window or type an "e" in the Prompts palette. The copy-making process will also stop if you select another tool from the modeling palette.

▣ Try out the next self-copy mode, Repeat Copy, in the same manner. You can now make multiple copies of the object using the *same* transformation parameters that were established by the first execution of the operation, simply by clicking the mouse repeatedly. You do not have to specify new transformation values for additional copies, as you did for Continuous Copy. Thus, if you are using the Move tool in Repeat Copy mode, once you specify the distance of the first move, subsequent copies *at the same distance* can be generated by continuing to click the mouse anywhere in the window. The copy-making process is terminated in the same manner—double-click or type an "e." Figure 2.26 shows how a repetitive configuration is created by using the Rotate tool in Repeat Copy mode.

▣ Move on to the Multi Copy mode. It is similar to Repeat Copy except that it lets you make the desired number of copies in one step, rather than having to click for each additional copy. The number of copies needed is specified in the Copy Options dialog accessible from the Multi Copy tool; the default number is 6. The transformation values from one copy to the next are identical and are established by the first execution of the operation, just as for Repeat Copy. Thus, the configuration shown in Figure 2.26 could have been generated in one step by using the Multi Copy mode, with the number of copies specified as 6.

Figure 2.26

A repetitive configuration generated by rotating an object about the indicated point in the Repeat Copy mode. After the first rotated copy, five more identically rotated copies were generated using five mouse clicks.

(a) Original object

(b) Single rotated copy

(c) Multiple rotated copies

▣ Invoke the Copy Options dialog from any one of the Copy modes, and look at the Multi-Copy section. In addition to the # Of Copies, there are two alternate options that determine how the multi-copying operation is performed. You have been working with the default of Even Increment, in which you specified the first copy, and the remaining were generated based on its transformation parameters. For the Divide Distance option, on the other hand, you specify the *last* copy instead of the first. The desired number of copies is then evenly distributed between the original object and the last copy. Experiment with this mode of multi-copying as well. You might find it more useful than the default mode, since design is usually done from the "outside in"—a basic framework is first established which is then filled in.

■ The Copy Options dialog contains one more option, Return To Self After Copy, which applies to all the Copy modes. When selected, it automatically reverts the self-copy mode back to Self each time a Copy mode is used. It can be helpful if you keep forgetting to switch back to Self for applying transformations to objects without making copies. Basically, it ensures that Self is always selected by default.

■ Finally, try changing the topological level in Row 4 to Point, Segment, Outline, or Face, and watch what happens when you apply a transformation using a Copy mode. You will find that the transformation does *not* result in multiple copies of the selected point, segment, outline, or face. Essentially, you cannot make copies of object parts, but only of entire objects, groups, holes, and volumes (the last two will be covered in Exercise 5).

4.3 Copying and Duplicating

form•Z has two additional ways of making copies of objects. These involve the use of the Copy and Duplicate commands under the Edit menu.

■ You must be familiar with the Cut, Copy, and Paste commands found under the Edit menu of virtually any program. In form•Z, you can use these commands to transfer or copy objects from one project to another, as well as to transfer or copy objects from one layer to another *within* the same project. (Keep this in mind when you work with layers in Workshop 3.) Objects that are cut or copied are temporarily stored in the clipboard, the contents of which can be viewed by going to Edit > form•Z Clipboard.

■ If you Copy an object and simply Paste it (without changing layers), it will be pasted exactly on top of the original object. Thus, you will not be able to see the copy unless you apply a transformation such as Move to the object, in which case you will have the object in its original position and a copy of it in the transformed position. It is thus the equivalent of a Move using the Copy mode, but in a more roundabout manner; so there is no reason why you should ever use this option, except on the rare occasion when you want to make a copy of an object in exactly the same position.

■ The Duplicate command, however, is a viable alternative to the Move and Copy combination. Select an object using the Pick tool. Then go to Duplicate in the Edit menu. A copy of the selected object will be made at some distance away from the original, allowing you to see and work easily with both the original as well as the duplicated copy. Notice also that the duplicated copy remains highlighted, allowing you to continue the duplication process by simply selecting Duplicate again. Thus, you have the convenient equivalent of the Repeat Copy and Multi Copy modes as well.

■ Naturally, you would like to control the distance by which the duplication takes place. This distance is known as the *duplication offset*, and it can be specified by going to the Duplication Offset command, located just below Duplicate in the Edit menu. A dialog is invoked in which you can specify the required translation along all the three axes.

■ Note that the Duplicate command can only be applied to objects and groups, not to entities at any other topological level. But you can, of course, apply it to multiple selections of objects and groups, just as you did for a single object.

4.4 Defining and Using Macro Transformations

Coming back to the geometric transformations, form•Z allows you to record a sequence of frequently used transformations into a *macro*. Thereafter, the recorded macro can be applied to any entity to execute the entire sequence of transformations on it directly in one step, doing away with the tedium of performing each transformation individually. Such composite transformations are known as macro transformations, and they can save you a lot of time and effort in modeling. Let us see how macro transformations are recorded and executed.

▣ With the Pick tool, select an object on which you will carry out a certain sequence of transformations, say Move, Rotate, and Scale. Set the self-copy modifier on Row 11 to Define Macro. As soon as you select this mode, a dialog will be invoked asking you to name the macro transformation. Give it an appropriate name.

▣ You are now ready to begin recording your macro. Select the Move tool and translate the selected object by a certain distance. Since you used the Pick tool to select the object, it will remain selected even after the execution of the Move tool. Go ahead and apply a Rotate operation to it, and then a Scale or Uniform Scale operation. Let us assume that this is all we want to record in our macro. To stop the recording, simply go to the left column of Row 11 and select any one of the other self-copy modifiers instead of Define Macro; the macro definition will be automatically completed.

▣ You will now apply the macro you just recorded to another object. First, set the self-copy mode to Self. Then go to 1-Macro-T (M-Tool:12a,7), the first of the three Macro-T tools in the left column of Row 12, and watch the message in the Prompts palette. It gives you the name of the macro you just recorded and asks you to select an object for applying the macro to (assuming the topological level is still set to Object). Do so. You will then be prompted for the *macro origin*, which is the point relative to which the entire sequence of recorded transformations will take place. Select an appropriate point and watch the object being transformed according to all the operations you had previously recorded, but this time in a single step.

Figure 2.27

Using a macro transformation comprising Move, Rotate, and Uniform Scale in Multi Copy mode. The actual macro is shown in Figure 2.29.

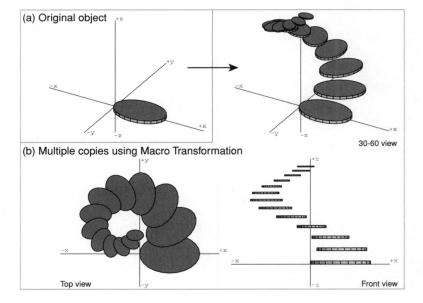

(a) Original object

30-60 view

(b) Multiple copies using Macro Transformation

Top view

Front view

Figure 2.28

The Macro Transformations dialog, showing how the recorded macros can be assigned to any of the three Macro-T tools.

■ Repeat the application of the macro on another object, this time in Multi Copy mode, and see how you can model complex configurations such as the one shown in Figure 2.27 in just one step.

■ Define at least three more macros using the Define Macro mode as you did earlier. How do you now choose from among the four macros you have defined so far? Notice that in the left column of Row 12, there are two more Macro-T tools labeled 2-Macro-T and 3-Macro-T, following 1-Macro-T. Select each one of these tools in turn. You will find that the first three recorded macros are stored sequentially in these three tools—you can apply them to an object by simply selecting the corresponding tool. Try it.

■ What about the fourth macro—or the fifth, sixth, and so on, if you have defined more? How do you access these for applying to other objects? For this, you need to invoke the Macro Transformations dialog from any of the three Macro-T tools. You will find that all the recorded macros are listed on the left, while the specific macros assigned to the three Macro-T tools appear on the right. Suppose you want to assign the fourth rather than the second macro to 2-Macro-T. To do so, simply highlight the fourth macro and then click on the 2-Macro-T icon (see Figure 2.28). The change will be registered, and once you return to the graphics window, you will find that selecting the 2-Macro-T tool selects the fourth macro for application to an object.

Figure 2.29

The Macro Definition dialog for the macro used in the example illustrated in Figure 2.27.

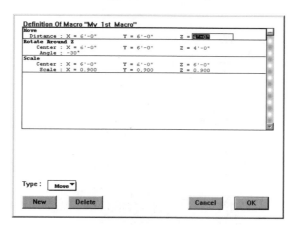

■ Invoke the Macro Transformations dialog once again, and highlight one of the macros. Notice that you have the option to Rename or Delete the highlighted macro, if necessary. There is also an Edit option which seems intriguing. Click on this button, and you will see another dialog which displays all the transformations recorded in that macro, along with their respective numeric values. These values can be edited by highlighting them and typing over them, as shown in Figure 2.29. This facility is useful when you want to make precise adjustments to the macro definitions. You can also delete a particular transformation from the macro, completely change its type (for instance, change Move to Rotate), or add a new transformation and numerically specify the corresponding values.

■   Back in the Macro Transformations dialog (Figure 2.28), notice that there is also a New button. If you click on this, it will take you to the same Macro Definition dialog you just saw, except that it will contain no transformations. These will have to be added using the options in this dialog, with the corresponding values specified numerically. As a designer, you might prefer the more intuitive graphical method for macro definition you used earlier, rather than this textual one.

■   To end this section, define a new macro using an *existing* macro as one of the component transformations. This can be done by simply using one of the Macro-T tools while recording the new macro, in the same way as you would use Move, Rotate, etc. Needless to say, you can have multiple macros recorded in another macro—try it!

     Macro transformations are independent of the topological level of the entity used for their definition. Thus, you can define a macro using an object, but you can apply it just as well to points, segments, faces, groups, etc.

4.5   Transformations Using the Pick Tool

In form•Z, basic transformations like translation, rotation, and scaling can also be carried out using the Pick tool, making it a convenient alternative at times to the dedicated transformation tools on Row 12. Exploring how this works involves taking a comprehensive look at the Pick Options dialog you first encountered in Section 3.5 of Workshop 1. In the process, let us also look at the other Pick tool options, in addition to those related to transformations, that we haven't yet covered.

■   Double-click on the Pick tool, or on any one of the topological levels on Row 4. The Pick Options dialog will be invoked (Figure 2.30). The first and last options in this dialog are already familiar to you.

Figure 2.30

The Pick Options dialog.

■   Breeze through the non-transformation related options first, which happen to be quite self-explanatory. You can turn off the Beep When Deselecting Picked Elements option if you find the beep annoying. If you are used to other programs in which the Shift key *has* to be pressed to make multiple selections, you have the option of retaining the habit by checking the Use Shift Key For Multiple Pick box. You can also choose to Auto Select New Objects which can be useful in some specific modeling situations, as you will see in the next workshop. To make the cursor behave for all topological levels like it does for Auto, turn on the Show Pick Cursor option—it will now change to a different icon when brought near a selectable entity, depending upon the active topological level.

▣ Turn your attention to the Return To Pick Tool option. By default, form•Z retains the selection of a tool until another tool is selected. However, if you usually do not apply the same operation repeatedly and find this aspect of the interface hindering your speed, you can check this option to automatically shift the selection to the Pick tool after the execution of an operation by another tool. Within this option, you can also, if necessary, choose to reselect the last tool applied by clicking in the window while holding down the control key (Mac) or Ctrl+Alt keys (PC).

▣ In Section 3.1, you saw how you could modify facetted objects in various ways by selecting and manipulating their individual points, segments, outlines, and faces. By default, you cannot work at these topological levels with parametric objects. However, if you activate the Pick Facets Of Controlled Objects option in the Pick Options dialog, you will be able to select and modify the points, segments, etc. of the facets of parametric objects (recall that these are made up of wires and facets). Such changes, however, are not permanent as the object is still governed by its creation parameters, so this option is not very useful. If you need to edit the facets of parametric objects, they first need to be converted to facetted objects using the Drop Controls tool (M-Tool:9b,5), which will be covered in Workshop 6.

▣ The first of the two options which gives the Pick tool the ability to carry out geometric transformations is Click And Drag. Select this option by checking the box and exit the Pick Options dialog. You will find that you can now use the Pick tool to transform an entity in various ways. For moving, simply click on the entity (which can be at any topological level) and drag. To rotate with respect to the active reference plane, click and drag while pressing the control key (Mac) or Ctrl+Alt keys (PC). To rotate with respect to the plane of the screen, use the command key (Mac) or Ctrl key (PC). To scale, click and drag while pressing the option key (Mac) or Ctrl+Shift keys (PC). Try out all these transformations.

▣ If you keep the Shift key pressed down during any of these operations, some additional constraints such as orthogonal movements, 45° rotation, and 5% scaling only are applied to the transformation. Check this out as well.

The Click And Drag method can be convenient, particularly if it is another interface characteristic you are used to. However, keep in mind that this method does not guarantee preciseness and accuracy since you cannot use direct numeric input—you have to rely only on the mouse. Also, you can transform only one entity at a time, not multiple entities. When you use Click And Drag therefore, keep Grid Snap (W-Tool:4,1) turned on for at least some degree of accuracy.

The last group of options in the Pick Options dialog are grouped under the Use Nudge Keys section. This feature is active by default. It lets you use the arrow keys on your keyboard, in combination with the Pick tool, to carry out the same transformations—move, rotate, and scale—you just saw. The difference between this and the Click And Drag method is that you can specify the *exact* values by which the transformation will occur, thereby guaranteeing accuracy. Also, you can apply the Nudge Keys method to multiple selections at a time. This makes it equivalent, both in scope as well as accuracy, to the actual geometric transformation tools and, therefore, of real value. Let us see how it works.

WORKSHOP 2

▣ Make sure the Use Nudge Keys option is selected. Take note of the values specified for Translate By, Rotate By, and Scale By, and change them if necessary.

▣ Back on the screen, select multiple entities at different topological levels with the Pick tool. Then keep pressing one of the four arrow keys on your keyboard, and watch your selection respond by moving along an axis by the amount specified in the Translate By field. For instance, the left arrow key ← will move the selection left with respect to the active reference plane. Experiment with all the arrow keys in this manner, and note the direction of movement. Then use the Shift key combined with the up ↑ or down ↓ arrow keys and watch the selection move in a direction perpendicular to the reference plane.

▣ Similarly, explore other key combinations for executing transformations. These are: control (Mac) or Ctrl+Alt (PC) for rotation, option (Mac) or Ctrl+Shift (PC) for uniform scale, and command (Mac) or Ctrl (PC) for independent scale. The extent of rotation and scaling will be determined by the Rotate By and Scale By values specified in the Pick Options dialog. When working with multiple selections, if the rotation and scaling needs to be applied for each element about its individual centroid rather than about the collective centroid of the entire selection, simply check the Apply To Each Selected Entity Individually option in the Use Nudge Keys section.

▣ By default, nudge key transformations are executed with respect to the active reference plane, which, as you will learn in Workshop 3, can also be user-defined. To always execute the transformations with respect to the original reference plane (referred to as the "world coordinate system"), deselect the Relative To Reference Plane option in the Pick Options dialog.

▣ To find out the exact nudge key combination for any transformation along a specific direction, go to Edit > Key Shortcuts. You are familiar with this dialog from Section 6 of the Introduction. Expand the Selection item, and within it, the Nudge Keys item, as shown in Figure 2.31. You can now highlight any of the direction-specific transformations contained in the list to see its shortcut key combination.

Figure 2.31

Finding the exact Nudge Key shortcut for a particular transformation in the Key Shortcuts dialog.

We will end this section by looking at a feature of the Pick tool that does not appear in its dialog, but is nevertheless very important. This is the *pick parade* feature, used for selecting entities that overlap or lie directly on top of other entities, making it difficult to select them in the regular fashion.

▣ Set the object generation mode on Row 2 to 2D Surface Object and create a 2D shape that coincides exactly with the face of a 3D object. Use Endpoint snapping for accuracy. Then activate the Pick tool and the Object topological level, and click on an edge of the newly created shape. As you would expect, the 2D shape gets selected since it was created more recently, not the 3D object overlapping with it.

▣ You could, of course, select the 3D object by clicking on one of its other edges. But suppose that, for some reason, all its edges were lying behind other objects. To go about selecting the object in such a situation (which is not uncommon, as you will discover in the course of your modeling), this is what you need to do: Click on the overlapping edge with the Pick tool while holding down the Shift key. The first object found at that point gets highlighted in black. Click again, still holding down the Shift key, and the next object found at that point gets highlighted. In this manner, all overlapping objects at that point get highlighted in turn (or "paraded") with each click. When the entity you are interested in gets highlighted, release the Shift key and click one last time—this will select it, highlighting it in the usual selection color which is red.

Experiment with the pick parade feature a little more before moving on to the next section.

4.6   Editing Lines

We will now look at a set of tools that are used for carrying out specific transformations on lines and other 2D surface objects. Very often, 2D objects are created as the base elements for generating 3D objects and they need to be manipulated in ways that 3D objects do not. The first six tools in the left column of Row 10 bundle together a large number of line-manipulation functions that you will find extremely helpful in certain situations. Let us see how they work.

▣ Clear the graphics window of all objects and switch to the Top view. Select the 2D Surface Object mode and create a number of lines and rectangles. Let some of the shapes intersect with each other.

▣ Let us start with the first tool, Break (M-Tool:10a,1), which is used for breaking a continuous line into two parts. Select this tool and apply it to a line, keeping track of where you click on the line to select it. There appears to be no visible change. But if you now apply the Move tool to the line, you will find that it has been broken into two parts at the point where you clicked on it. Thus, you can move one part of the line away from the other. Object snapping can be used to locate the break point more precisely—for instance, Intersection for breaking a line at the point where it intersects with another line, Endpoint for breaking up a rectangle at its endpoints, and so on. Note that you need to break at least two points in a closed shape like a rectangle to be able to separate the two broken parts.

▣ Let us now explore the options of the Break tool. Invoke its dialog (Figure 2.32) and you will find that the default option you were just using was Break At Click. It is accompanied by a tolerance distance, which you can change. If you click within this distance from a point, the break happens at the point rather than on the segment ending at that point. The second option, Break With Line, is used to break one or more lines at their points of intersection with another line. You can preselect any number of lines with the Pick tool, then select the break line after activating the Break tool. Try it.

▣ It is also possible to create a space before and after the break, which will make the break more visible. This can be done by activating the Break Distance option and choosing one of two methods. Try out both of them. The Offset method lets you specify a left and right offset distance independently, while the Length method requires you to specify a single value which is equally distributed on both sides of the break. Figure 2.32 illustrates both the Break At Click and Break With Line operations, applied with a break distance.

Figure 2.32

The two main operations of the Break tool, along with its dialog.

■ Move on to select the next line-editing tool, Close. This is used for converting an open line to a closed shape. The line must contain a minimum of two or three segments, depending upon which of the three options for Close is activated in its dialog. Trim and Join need at least three segments, while Connect needs at least two. Work with all three in turn. Trim connects the two end segments of the line by extending or trimming them at their point of intersection. In contrast, Join deletes the last point of the line and connects the point before it to the first point; thus, the direction of the line is important here. The last option, Connect, simply adds a new segment that connects the first and last points of the line. All three methods of closing lines are illustrated in Figure 2.33.

■ To see the direction of a surface object in the Wire Frame mode, select Display > Wire Frame while holding down the option key (Mac) or Ctrl+Shift keys (PC), and check the Show Direction option under 2D Surface Objects in the dialog that opens up. You will study this dialog in detail in Workshop 3.

Figure 2.33

The three options of the Close tool. The directions of the lines are also indicated.

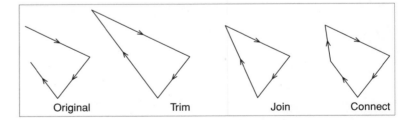

■ Select the next tool, Trim. This lets you trim segments of lines against each other, either by extending them or trimming them at their point of intersection. Obviously, the selected segments should not be parallel and must lie on the same plane. With this tool, only the individual segments of 2D shapes get selected, irrespective of what the currently active topological level is. Try it on some segment pairs until you understand how it works.

■ Invoke the dialog of the Trim tool (Figure 2.34-a), and you will find that it has three main options. The default is Trim Pairs Of Segments, which is the operation you just performed. This has four additional sub-options—Open, Join, Round, and Bevel. Explore each one of them. The default of

Open ensures that the trimmed elements are retained as separate entities. Thus, after trimming them, you can select and transform them independently of each other. Join, on the other hand, not only trims the segments against each other but also joins the separate lines into one continuous line. This could involve a change in the direction of one of the lines, as shown in Figure 2.34-b. Round goes a step further—not only does it join the lines into one object, it also rounds the point of intersection by the values listed for the # Of Edges (which determines the resolution of the curve) and Radius fields. The last sub-option, Bevel, works on the same principle, beveling the intersection point by a distance specified in terms of two Offset values or a single Length value. All these four sub-options are illustrated in Figure 2.34-b. Note that for the Join, Round, and Bevel sub-options, the original lines are ghosted by default, so the Status Of Objects option becomes applicable.

■ When using the Trim Pairs Of Segments option, if a segment extends beyond the intersection point, where you click to select it will determine which part of the segment will be retained (Figure 2.34-c). Therefore, make the selection carefully to get the desired results. Also, see how pairs of closed shapes can be transformed in interesting ways by trimming their segments against each other (Figure 2.34-d).

Figure 2.34

The various operations of the Trim tool, along with its dialog. The points where the selections for trimming were made are also indicated.

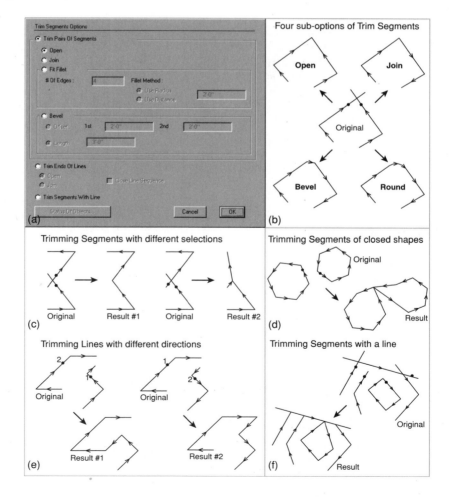

◼ Move to the second option of the Trim tool, Trim Ends Of Lines. This is very similar to the first option, except that the operation is applied to entire lines rather than to individual segments of lines. Because of this, the directions of the lines play an important role in determining how they get trimmed, as illustrated in Figure 2.34-e. Again, you have the choice of letting the trimmed lines remain as independent objects (the Open sub-option), or merging them into a single line object (the Join sub-option). Additionally, you can check the Close Line Sequence box if you want to close the resultant shape. The prepicking method can be used to advantage here if a large number of lines is to be trimmed or joined. Of course, you must first ensure that the lines have the appropriate directions, otherwise the operation will give you unexpected results.

◼ The last option of the Trim tool, Trim Segments With Line, is used to trim one or more segments against a trim line. The trim line itself does not get modified in any way. A large number of segments can be prepicked, using the Segment topological level, to be trimmed against the same line, as shown in Figure 2.34-f.

◼ Move to the fourth line-editing tool in the left column of Row 10, Connect. This has two options in its dialog, Connect Segments and Connect Lines. With the first option, the Connect tool can be used to join two segments by connecting their open ends with a new segment. One end of each segment, therefore, has to be open. The selected segments can belong to the same line or to different lines. In the first case, which is identical to the Connect sub-option of the Close tool, the open line will get transformed to a closed surface. In the second case, which is illustrated in Figure 2.35-a, the lines will be combined into one open surface. Notice that this may involve a change in the direction of the second line, as shown.

◼ The second option, Connect Lines, is similar to the first except that it operates on lines instead of segments. The line directions play an important part here. As you can see in Figure 2.35-b, the last point of the first line is connected to the first point of the second line. Additionally, if the Close Line Sequence box is checked, the first and last points of the combined line are also connected, resulting in a closed shape as shown. Unlike the Connect Segments option, the directions of the lines being connected never change when Connect Lines is used, and the point of selection *on* the line also does not matter. Using the prepick method, many lines can be connected at a time by selecting them in the desired sequence.

Figure 2.35

The two operations of the Connect tool.

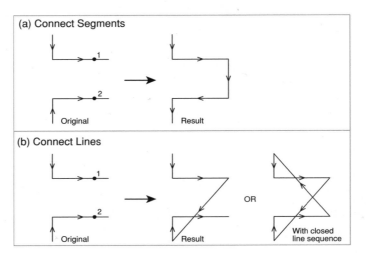

Figure 2.36

Using the Join tool.

▪ Move on to the next tool, Join. This is used for joining lines whose endpoints coincide or are located closer than the distance specified in the accompanying Tolerance field. More than two lines can be selected by prepicking. Needless to say, this is a very convenient tool because you will often end up creating separate lines for what should have been a single line. Since you are dealing with lines, direction is again important. The direction of the first line will be applied to the joined object, as shown in Figure 2.36, so make sure you select the appropriate line first.

▪ Check the Close Line Sequence box in the dialog of the Join tool and reapply it to a set of lines. You will find that if the distance between the first and last points of the joined line sequence is less than the specified Tolerance value, the line will be converted to a closed shape (Figure 2.36).

▪ The Join tool has an additional option, Join All. It is similar to Join except that you need to select just one line. This line will then automatically be joined to all the lines with compatible directions whose endpoints are coincident or closer than the Tolerance value. Alternately, just click in the graphics window, away from any object, and all the line sequences that can potentially be joined are done so in a single step. Once you learn about layers, you can choose to restrict the joining to visible layers only.

▪ The last of the line-editing tools, Fillet/Bevel, can be used to round and bevel the endpoints of a segment. The corresponding options in the dialog of the tool are Fit Fillet and Bevel respectively. You are already familiar with the round and bevel concepts from the Trim tool you saw earlier, including the parameters that control the extent of rounding and beveling. The topological level plays an important role for both functions. If Point is selected, a single point is rounded or beveled. If Segment is selected, the operation is applied to both endpoints of the segment. For the other topological levels, all points are affected, leading to potentially interesting shapes as shown in Figure 2.37. Watch out for segment lengths that are too small to permit a fillet of the specified radius, or a bevel of the specified distance.

Figure 2.37

The Fit Fillet and Bevel operations applied to a patterned polygon, with the topological level set to Object.

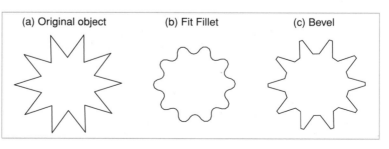

4.7   Editing Polycurves and Analytic Primitives

Recall that polycurves are parametric 2D shapes created when the 2D Surface Object mode is used to generate spline curves, arcs, or any shape which combines vector lines, spline curves, and arcs. Polycurves are edited using the Edit Controls tool, located immediately after the Pick tool on Row 4. Let us see how this editing process works.

▣ Switch to the Top view and create a polycurve, using the appropriate combination of tools from Rows 2 and 3 (Figure 2.38-a). Then select the Edit Controls tool (M-Tool:4b,2) and apply it to this object. Depending upon which drawing tools were used to generate the polycurve, various *controls* that govern the shape of the object will be displayed (Figure 2.38-b).

▣ Click on any one of the displayed controls to select it. Then move it around and see how the shape of the polycurve changes in response. Manipulate other controls in a similar fashion to completely reshape the object (Figure 2.38-c). Multiple controls can be selected for manipulation at the same time by using the Shift key. How exactly moving a control modifies the shape will depend upon which drawing tool was used to create that part of the polycurve. In the case of an arc, for instance, there are controls for modifying its radius, center point, as well as the start and end points—in short, everything that went into defining the arc when it was created.

▣ The smoothness of the polycurve, which was specified at the time of creation, can also be changed at a later stage. Simply apply the Query tool (M-Tool:11b,1) to it, as you learned in Section 3.6, and click on the Edit button. A dialog will be invoked in which you can specify the new Smooth Interval for the polycurve.

▣ Next, create an analytic primitive using any of the tools in the left column of Row 1. You have seen how the Query tool can be used to edit the parameters of a primitive object numerically through a dialog. For graphical editing of the same parameters, apply the Edit Controls tool to the object. Depending upon the type of primitive, various controls will be displayed for manipulating the size, angles, and closure parameters. Activate and move some of these controls, just as you did for the polycurve, and see how they modify the shape of the object. Remember that multiple controls can be selected for manipulation using the Shift key.

▣ An analytic primitive can also be graphically manipulated using the Edit Surface tool, located immediately after the Edit Controls tool on Row 4. Try it. You will find that this tool allows you to move the *surface* of the object at the selection point, rather than its controls. The little arrow that appears on the surface at the point you click on represents the normal to the surface at that point.

Figure 2.38

Modifying the creation parameters of a polycurve with the Edit Controls tool.

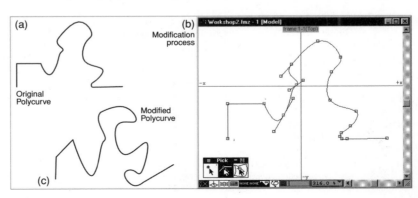

Both the Edit Controls and Edit Surface tools are used to modify a variety of other parametric objects as well, and have a number of options associated with these editing functions. We will study these in detail in Workshop 6.

EXERCISE 5

Insertions: A Convenient Alternative to Booleans

In this exercise, you will work with the four magenta-colored tools located in the right column of Row 2 of the modeling tool palette. These are the *insertion tools*, used for dividing surfaces and adding and subtracting volumes from existing objects. They can often be used as a convenient alternative to the boolean operations, Union and Difference. The four insertion tools represent four different types of insertion modes, and just like the five object generation tools you saw in Workshop 1, they are used in conjunction with the drawing tools on Row 3 to create insertions of various shapes and sizes. Let us see how they work.

■ Open a new project or clear the window of all its contents—both ghosted and unghosted—using the corresponding Clear commands in the Edit menu. Create a few 3D facetted solids. These will be used as the base objects on which the insertions will be performed.

5.1 Inserting Outlines

■ Select M-Tool:2b,1 to set the mode to Insert Outline. This is similar to the Insert Segment tool (M-Tool:10a,8) you used in Section 3.2, except that it can be used to insert not just a single segment, but an entire sequence of lines, a circle, a polygon, or any other desired 2D shape on the face of an object. Also, the face on which the insertion is to be made needs to be prepicked, otherwise an error message is displayed. So go ahead and select a face of any one of your objects by setting the topological level to Face and using the Pick tool.

■ Once the face is selected, use one of the drawing tools on Row 3 to draw a shape on it. For an open shape, both endpoints must lie on the *edges* of the face (Figure 2.39-a), so use the appropriate object snapping option. A closed shape, on the other hand, must lie completely *inside* the face (Figure 2.39-b). Experiment with both types of shapes. Since you are in the Insert Outline mode, these shapes are being inserted on the selected face. It is possible to insert multiple outlines within a single face as shown in Figure 2.39-b, provided they do not overlap with each other.

■ Just like an inserted segment, an inserted outline divides the face on which it is inserted into two parts. Thereafter, one part can be transformed independently of the other to modify the shape of the object. Again, watch out for non-planar faces, as those shown in Figure 2.39-a.

■ The different faces resulting from the insertion of an outline can also be colored in different colors, as shown in Figure 2.39-b. A good application of this would be for façade design in architectural modeling in the early conceptualization phase, when it is too tedious and time-consuming to model the individual openings.

■ Notice that an outline gets selected as soon as it is inserted, so it can be moved, or colored in a different color, or transformed in any other manner right away. If you need to do this at a later stage, remember to select the insertion with the topological level set to Face, not to Outline. When a closed shape is inserted on a face using Insert Outline, a new face is created by cutting a "hole" in the original face. Thus, the edges of the new face will coincide with the edges of the outline (i.e., the hole) of the original face. This might make it difficult to select the new face with the Pick tool in the usual fashion—you will have to resort to the pick parade feature (Section 4.5), or use the Clicking Inside Boundaries option of the Pick tool (Section 3.1).

When the Clicking Inside Boundaries option for the Pick tool is activated, you do not even need to prepick a face for insertion—it is automatically detected when you start drawing the insertion shape. This applies to all the insertion modes, ranging from Insert Outline to Insert Opening, which otherwise require a face to be preselected.

Figure 2.39

Using the Insert Outline mode.

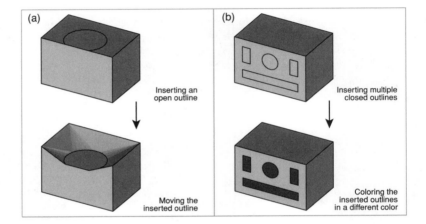

5.2 Inserting Faces

▣ Move on to select the next insertion mode, Insert Face. This works on the same principle as Insert Outline, except that a 3D extrusion is now inserted instead of a 2D shape. The height of the inserted extrusion can be preset in the Heights menu, or input interactively by setting Heights to Graphic/Keyed. Choose the latter option for now.

▣ Select a face of an object and with the appropriate tool from Row 3, draw any shape on it. For an open shape, remember that the start and end points must lie on the edges of the face.

▣ After the base insertion shape is defined, you will be prompted for the height of the inserted volume. Since Heights is set to Graphic/Keyed, you can drag the volume either *into* the object, or *out* of it. The first action will subtract the volume from the object, and is therefore equivalent to the Difference operation (Figure 2.40-b); the second will add the volume to the object, and is thus equivalent to the Union operation (Figure 2.40-c). If you want to specify the height using the keyboard, use a negative height for subtraction and a positive height for addition.

▣ Work with the Insert Face mode some more, using different shapes on different surfaces. Experiment with closed shapes that are *larger* than the faces on which they are being inserted (Figure 2.40-d) and with insertions *within* insertions (Figure 2.40-e), and see how many unique and interesting objects can be generated using these techniques. Notice that when a larger base shape is dragged into the object, it adds to the object instead of subtracting a volume from it.

Figure 2.40

Various configurations created using the Insert Face mode.

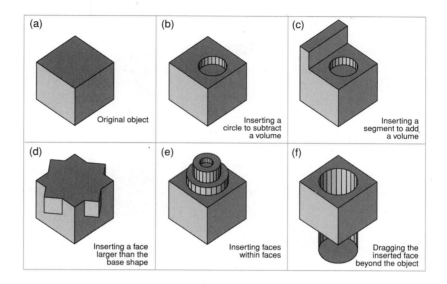

Finally, insert a closed shape on the face of an object and drag it all the way through, beyond the other side. You will see that the insertion creates the expected hole within the solid where it encounters volume, but beyond the solid where it encounters a void, a volume is created and added. It is quite weird! Moreover, the resulting object is not quite right, as you can see in Figure 2.40-f. You should, therefore, avoid using Insert Face in this manner. If you want to drill a hole all the way through an object, use the next insertion mode, Insert Hole.

5.3 Inserting Holes

Select the third insertion mode, Insert Hole. This is almost identical to the Insert Face mode except that it can only subtract volumes from objects and not add them. Depending upon the height of the insertion that is specified, the subtracted volume can be either a cavity or a hole that extends throughout the depth of the object (see Figure 2.41-a). Unlike the Insert Face mode, the inserted shape can be dragged all the way through the object and further beyond—the result will only create a hole without any ill-formed additions at the opposite end like you saw in Figure 2.40-d.

The Insert Hole mode provides a neat and efficient way of drilling identical holes on the opposite sides of a 3D enclosure—an operation you cannot perform with Insert Face. Try it out and see the difference. With Insert Hole, you simply need to select one of the outer faces on one side of the enclosure and then drag the insertion beyond the corresponding face on the opposite side (Figure 2.41-b).

In the same manner, Insert Hole can also be used to drill holes in a curved object like a cylinder, which is made up of many consecutive faces that do not lie on the same plane. Simply select a face where the hole is to be centered and let the insertion shape extend beyond the sides of that face. Then drag the insertion into the volume of the cylinder in the usual fashion. A cavity or hole will be created, depending on the extrusion height specified (see Figure 2.41-c). Again, this is something you could not have achieved using Insert Face.

Figure 2.41

Various uses of the Insert Hole mode.

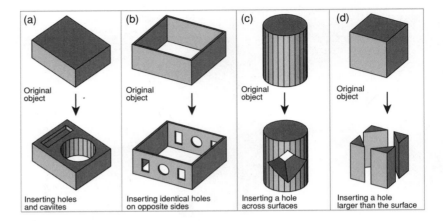

◨ Finally, just as you did with Insert Face, experiment with closed shapes that are *larger* than the faces on which they are being inserted, dragging them all the way beyond the volume of the object. Figure 2.41-d shows a four-sided polygon inserted diagonally on the top face of a cube, extending beyond its sides. You can see that such an insertion results in discontiguous volumes, similar to what you encountered when working with the Intersection and Difference tools in Workshop 1. You already know from that workshop how to deal with such a situation.

5.4 Inserting Openings

◨ Proceed to select the last insertion mode, Insert Opening. This simply punches holes into objects through the selected face. The difference from the Insert Hole mode is that the height of the insertion does not have to be specified—it is simply taken to be the entire depth of the object from the selected face.

◨ Keep in mind that with the Insert Opening mode, the shape of the opening must lie completely *within* the face on which it is being inserted; it cannot spill over the edges of the face, as it can with the Insert Hole mode. The edge of the opening cannot even *overlap* with the edge of the face. This is demonstrated in Figure 2.42, where all the openings in the 3D enclosure were conveniently made using Insert Opening except the corner one, for which Insert Hole had to be used.

Figure 2.42

Insert Opening is the fastest mode for creating openings in objects, since the extrusion height does not have to be specified. However, it cannot be used to create a corner opening as shown.

5.5   Working with Holes and Volumes

Now that you have seen how to add and subtract volumes from objects using Insert Face, Insert Hole, and Insert Opening, let us work with the last topological level in the left column of Row 4, Hole/ Volume, that we did not cover in Exercise 3.

▣   Set the topological level to Hole/Volume (M-Tool:4a,7). Then use the Pick tool to select a volume that you have added to or subtracted from an object. You can select several of these "holes or volumes," as they are called. Because the topological level is set appropriately, you will be able to select just the holes and volumes without selecting the rest of the object.

     In general, volumes that are added to an object are easier to select when the Pick tool option is set to Clicking Inside Boundaries rather than Clicking On Edges.

▣   You can now apply any kind of transformation on the selected holes and volumes, provided they remain on the same face. Try it. You will be able to move, rotate, scale, or mirror them along the surface. You can also perform these transformations in the Copy mode to make additional insertions of the same type on the surface. You can even delete the holes and volumes, which will restore the object back to its original form. All these operations are illustrated in Figure 2.43. Essentially, inserted holes and volumes can be treated just like any other object in form•Z.

Figure 2.43

Working with the Hole/
Volume topological level.

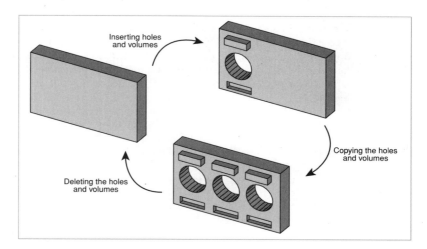

5.6   Triangulation: Getting Rid of Non-Planar Faces

You have seen how objects sometimes acquire non-planar faces when a part of the object such as a point or a segment is moved in a certain way. Examples of such objects were shown in Figures 2.14, 2.15, and 2.39. These objects had been deliberately created, but often, you will inadvertently create an object with non-planar faces without even realizing it. Such objects are problematic because they may not render accurately in some display modes. Even worse, many operations such as the booleans (and others we haven't yet covered) cannot be applied to them. Let us learn how to recognize this problem when it exists, and then, how to fix it.

Figure 2.44

Working with the
Triangulate tool.

- Create an object with non-planar faces, if you do not have one, by simply moving a point, segment, outline, or face appropriately (Figure 2.44-a). Set the topological level to Object, and apply the Query tool (M-Tool:11b,1) to it. In the Query dialog, the number of non-planar faces that the object has is calculated and displayed, as you saw in Figure 2.20-c. This helps you to check an object for planarity. Normally, form•Z allows a certain tolerance while calculating planarity, but you can make the calculation more sensitive by checking the accompanying Strict Planarity box in the Query dialog.

- When the Query dialog reveals that an object does have non-planar faces (which is obvious for the object in Figure 2.44-a, but may not be in many other cases), and you must retain this object in your model, you can apply a tool to it that will convert the non-planar faces to planar faces. This is the Triangulate tool (M-Tool:6a,9). Select it and apply it to the object. You will find that all the non-planar faces get subdivided into triangular pieces (Figure 2.44-b). Recall from basic geometry that a minimum of three points is needed to define a plane, therefore a triangle is the only polygon that is always planar. The process of triangulation thus rids an object of any non-planar faces it might have. Of course, the number of faces the object has will now increase, as you can see.

- Explore the options of the Triangulate tool by invoking its dialog (Figure 2.44-c). You can choose, once again, to activate the Strict Planarity Test while executing the triangulation operation. You can opt to Triangulate All Faces of the object rather than just the non-planar faces, if you would like to give it a uniformly triangulated appearance. And finally, you can select between three different triangulation methods for the use of the tool.

With this, we come to the end of the last exercise for this workshop. It is time to take on the challenge of modeling the basic blocks of a building in our Workshop Assignment.

An Architectural Block Model

ASSIGNMENT 2

- *Locate the drawings of any famous building of acclaimed visual composition. Break it down into volumes and model it directly in 3D using the correct proportions. Keep in mind that this is just a massing model, so you are not aiming for full detail or 100% accuracy. You would, however, like to convey an accurate impression of its form.*

The building selected here is the Guggenheim Museum by Frank Lloyd Wright. The process of modeling it will now be demonstrated step by step, accompanied by the graphic window snapshots at the end of each step. You can also refer to the form•Z files for this assignment in the Assignments > Workshop2 folder of the accompanying CD-ROM, if you get stuck at any stage. A color rendering of the project is in the Assignment2.tif file in the same folder.

Setup

Open a new form•Z project. In the Working Units dialog, select Feet as the Base Unit, set Numeric Accuracy to 1' and Angle Accuracy to 1°. Invoke the Window Setup dialog, and change the Module value for all three axes to 10' with 5 Divisions.

◀ Step 1

We will first model the base, i.e. the site, as a thin slab. Choose an appropriate color from the Surface Styles palette, switch to the Top view, and set Heights to a preset value of 1'. Set the object generation mode to 3D Extruded Solid, and select the Vector Lines tool from the right column of Row 3.

Using direct numeric input, specify the first point as [0,0,0] in the Prompts palette in absolute mode. Then change the mode to relative, and specify the remaining points as follows:

> Pt #2: [220] (Since both the y and z coordinates are 0, they can be omitted from the input.)
>
> Pt #3: [0,150]
>
> Pt #4: [-110]
>
> Pt #5: [0,-15]
>
> Pt #6: [-110]
>
> Pt #7: [c] (Type in a "c" for closing the line sequence)

Step 2

Change the object generation mode to 2D Surface Object. We will use it to draw some construction lines which will be deleted later. We can either draw them in the correct position to begin with, or draw them coinciding with the axes and then move them to where they should be. For example, for the first line, located 35' inside from the lower horizontal site line, input [-10, 35] as the absolute coordinates of the first point and [240] as the relative coordinates of the second point. The second point can also be specified graphically.

Step 3

Set the self-copy mode on Row 11 to One Copy. Select the line you just drew with the Move tool, and specify [0,50] as the relative coordinates of the move. Repeat the process with the same line, this time with relative coordinates of [0,95].

Step 4

Similarly, draw vertical construction lines 15' inside from the left end, and 25' inside from the right end. Notice how easy this is because you started with [0,0,0] as the first point. You can do all this graphically, by setting Grid Snap to 5'.

Step 5

Make copies of the left and right construction lines, 50' and 95' inside respectively.

WORKSHOP **2**

Step 6

Select the Circle tool which lets you draw a circle by diameter (M-Tool:3a,5). Use the construction lines to inscribe two circles with diameters of 50' and 95'. These circles should actually be a little smaller—the construction lines you have created are for drawing the second level later. The easiest way of changing the diameters is to set the Scale tool (M-Tool:12a,3) option to Scale By Absolute Value, and apply it to the circles. Change the X and Y values of the first one to 40', and of the second one to 93'. The circles will be resized but their centers will remain in the same position.

After the resizing is done, switch to a 3D view and set Heights to Graphic/Keyed. Then use the Extrusion tool to extrude the smaller circle to a height of 52' and the larger circle to a height of 28'. These will be referred to as Block1 and Block2 respectively.

Step 7

We will now start modeling the four landmark cylindrical forms that sit on top of the shorter cylinder, Block2. Preselect a height of 10' in the Heights menu. Select the Circle tool which lets you specify the center and radius (M-Tool:3a,4), and set the object generation mode to 3D Extruded Solid. Activate the Center Of Face snapping option, and select the center of the top face of Block2 as the center point for the circle. Specify the radius as 49'. The height is preset, so you will end up with a 10' high cylinder, sitting on top of Block2.

Apply the Move tool to translate the newly created cylinder by a distance of 2' in the +Z direction, either graphically using the Perpendicular Lock, or by typing in relative coordinates in the Prompts palette. This will create the required gap between Block2 and the cylinder.

Step 8

Next, we will give the required inclination to the sides of the new cylinder. Turn off the Perpendicular Lock if it is on. Use the Pick tool with the topological level set to Face and select the top face of the cylinder. This should be scaled so that it is larger than the bottom face, giving the sides of the cylinder approximately the right inclination. Select the Uniform Scale operator (M-Tool:12a,4), invoke its dialog, and set the option back to the default of Scale By Percentage. Use Center Of Face snap to pick the center of the selected face as the base of scale, and specify the scaling factor numerically as 1.05. The sides of the cylinder now have the required inclination.

Note that we could have created this cylinder as a truncated parametric cone, but then we would not be able to scale copies of it non-uniformly, as we need to do next. This is why we have created it as a facetted object.

Step 9

The second cylinder sitting on top of the first one is similar to it in all respects, except that it is larger along the X and Y directions. You could, of course, model it by following the same steps as the first cylinder. However, it would be easier to simply make a copy of the first cylinder and then scale it. Set the topological level to Object, the self-copy modifier to One Copy, and use the Move tool to make a copy of the cylinder exactly 12' above it. Then set the self-copy modifier back to Self and use the Scale tool (M-Tool:12a,3) to scale the copied cylinder by scaling factors of [1.05,1.05,1]. The base of scale should be the top face of the cylinder as usual. Switch to the Front, Right, or any other elevation view to make sure you have the correct results.

Step 10

Repeat Step 9 twice to create two more inclined cylindrical forms, sitting on top of the first two.

Step 11

The last cylinder is actually a little taller than the first three, and the inclination of its sides is also not as much. Both these results can be achieved by simply moving its top face vertically upwards by a distance of 6'. By now, you should know exactly how to go about achieving this.

WORKSHOP **2**

Step 12

To quickly fill in the gaps between all the cylinders, select the top face of the original base cylinder, Block2, and move it vertically upwards by a distance of 58'. It will now project beyond the top face of the last cylinder. This is a quick fix rather than an accurate solution for what are actually strips of glazing sitting between the stacked cylinders. However, it is acceptable since our aim at this stage is to create a massing model that can approximate the appearance of the building, rather than a fully accurate, detailed model.

Step 13

Next, you will create a conical skylight sitting on top of the face you just moved. Select it with the Pick tool if it is not already selected, and choose a color from the Surface Styles palette that is appropriate to glass. Activate the Convergence tool (M-Tool:5a,4), access its Status Of Objects option, and set the Status Of Operand Objects to Keep. Set Heights to a preset value of 16' and apply the Convergence tool to the selected face. The cylindrical block will be crowned with a conical roof as required.

Use the Group tool to bring Block2 and all the objects sitting on top of it into one group.

Step 14

Now turn your attention to Block1, the smaller cylindrical extrusion you created in Step 6. It should have a square block positioned about 8' below its top face. We will tackle this next. Switch to the Top view and preset Heights to 8', which is also the height of the block. Set object snapping to Intersection. Use the construction lines to create a square extrusion around Block1, sitting on the XY plane as shown.

Step 15

The length of the side of the square block is currently 50'. This has to be changed to 45'. As in Step 6, change the **Scale** tool option to **Scale By Absolute Value**, and then apply it to the square block. Change the X and Y values to 45' and the block will be resized appropriately.

Step 16

Two additional operations need to be performed on the square block before it is correct. Move it vertically upwards by a distance of 36'. Then select the top face of the block and apply the **Scale** tool to it. Since the **Scale By Absolute Value** option is still on, you can simply change both the X and the Y values from 45' to 47'. The sides of the square block will now be correctly inclined as shown.

Step 17

Next, complete **Block1** by adding a 2' high cylindrical roof slab of diameter 45'. The top face of this block again needs to be scaled outwards to incline the sides. Modeling this should be really easy by now.

Just as you did for **Block2**, group **Block1** and its related objects together using the **Group** tool.

Step 18

Next, we will add the 100' tall rectangular block at the back of the building. Preset a height of 100' in the **Heights** menu using the **Custom** option. Set object snapping to **Endpoint**, the object generation mode to **3D Extruded Solid** and activate the **Rectangle** tool. For the first point, snap on to the upper left corner of the site, as indicated. For the second point, specify [45,-30,0] as the relative coordinates. A 100' tall block of the required dimensions will be created in the correct position.

◁ Step 19

Complete the back corner of the building by adding a 27' high square block of side 65', starting from the upper right corner of the site as shown. Use **Endpoint** snap and relative coordinates of [-65,-65,0]. As you can see, the relative directions of the second point from the first along both the X and Y axes also have to be taken into account—they will not always be positive.

Step 20

Finally, we will model the second level of the building that projects beyond the first level, using the construction lines we drew in the beginning. The height of this level is 16', so preset that value in the **Heights** menu. Open the **Object Snaps** dialog by double-clicking on any one of the object snapping tools and select the option, **Project Onto Reference Plane**, in the **Projection Views** section. Also, open the **Objects** palette and ghost all the objects in the two groups you had created earlier. From the **Edit** menu, activate the **Hide Ghosted** option, so that the ghosted blocks are totally invisible.

Using the **Vector Lines** and **Arc** tools, and with the help of the construction lines and appropriate object snapping, model the extruded shape as shown. This will be created on the XY plane because of the **Project Onto Reference Plane** option you had activated in the **Object Snaps** dialog.

◁ Step 21

Move the block you just created vertically upwards by a distance of 12'. Unghost the grouped cylindrical blocks you had ghosted in the Objects palette.

Step 22

Finish the model by deleting all the 2D construction lines you had created in the beginning. You can also use the Union tool to combine any objects that touch or overlap, although this is not strictly necessary.

You now have the massing model of the world-famous Guggenheim Museum, which you were able to model quite accurately in form•Z with the knowledge gained from just two workshops. The process was long but relatively straightforward, as you have seen. It would have helped to make use of multiple layers and reference planes, as well as to be able to view the model from different angles. All these aspects of form•Z and more will be covered in Workshop 3, coming up next.

Personalizing Your Environment

You have covered a lot of the "form•Z basics" in the last two workshops and should be well equipped, by now, to model projects of some complexity. However, you have so far been confined to the default settings of form•Z. For instance, you have been working only with the predefined colors in the Surface Styles palette, the predefined views in the Views menu, the three predefined reference planes, and so on. Eventually, you will need to go beyond these defaults and define your own settings, depending upon your style of working and the needs of the project at hand.

In Workshop 3, you will accomplish precisely this—customizing your modeling environment to suit your requirements. You will learn how to modify the default project colors and create new surface styles, as well as change the way the various display options work. You will go on to see how you can enhance your efficiency using multiple layers, and create and save your own reference planes and views of the modeling world. Finally, you will learn how to save the modified settings as "preference files," which you can then recall for use in other projects when needed.

Your Own Colors and Styles

This exercise will briefly lead you through the process of defining your own surface styles, to add to the predefined ones you find in the Surface Styles palette. If you have the non-RenderZone version of form•Z, you will have the Colors palette instead of the Surface Styles palette. However, the basic procedure for creating and managing your colors remains the same, so go through the complete exercise and make the appropriate inferences to work with the Colors palette.

Let us first look at how to change the default color settings of the form•Z interface.

1.1   Customizing Project Colors

form•Z makes use of certain colors for different components of its user interface by default. Thus, the background color of the graphics window that you see when you launch the program is white, the reference plane grid is in teal, the axes are in red, the highlight color to indicate selection is again red, ghosted objects are colored in gray, and so on. These are referred to as *project colors* because they can be different for different projects. (Note that in versions prior to 2.9, project colors were referred to as system colors, so substitute the word "system" for "project" as you work through this section.)

🔳 Launch form•Z and save the default modeling window that appears as a new project using File > Save As. Close all palettes except Prompts and Surface Styles.

🔳 To see the list of default color settings for the current project, select Project Colors from the second group of the Options menu. This will invoke the Project Colors dialog which lists all the display colors used in the project (Figure 3.1).

🔳 To change any of these colors to suit your individual requirements, simply click on the associated box. Thus, for instance, to change the Highlight color to something other than red, click on the red-colored box beside it. You will be presented with the standard color selection dialog for your operating system (Mac or PC), from which you can choose a different color (see Figure 3.4-b). If you now return to the graphics window, create an object, and select it with the Pick tool, you will find that the selection color is the new one you specified rather than the original red color.

🔳 Similarly, you can change any of the other colors as well. The most commonly changed project color is Background—usually set to black or dark gray instead of the default of white. It may be a little hard on the eyes but can make for very attractive presentations (Figure 3.2).

Figure 3.1

The Project Colors dialog, showing the display colors used for various components of the form•Z interface.

Figure 3.2

A different look to the graphics window, created by selecting a dark background color. form•Z automatically adjusts the object color in displays such as Hidden Line so that it contrasts with the background.

WORKSHOP 3

▣ The Project Colors dialog also gives you three options for dealing with the colors of objects created in other files that are pasted into the current project. The default is to transfer the original color of the object. If that color does not exist in the Surface Styles palette, it will be added to it as a new color. If you do not wish the color to be transferred for some reason, you can opt for using either the active color or the best matching color in the current palette.

1.2 Creating a New Surface Style

We have, so far, often been using the word "color" for what is actually a "surface style." This is because, until now, we have worked only with the plain colors present in the Surface Styles palette; therefore, using the term "surface style" would have only led to confusion. It is time to understand, however, that a surface can have various attributes *in addition to color* such as texture, transparency, bumps, and so on, which is why the more fancy term "surface style" is used instead of simply "color." In this exercise, we will only take a brief look at how to define and use surface styles with various attributes in addition to color. More complicated aspects such as sizing textures and mapping them accurately on an object will be left for Workshop 5.

▣ Turn your attention to the Surface Styles palette. Unless you have already modified it in some manner, you should see eight styles immediately visible in the palette. There are sixteen in all by default—scroll down the palette to see the rest. Alternately, you can increase the size of the palette window until all the styles are visible (Figure 3.3-a). As you can see, all of these are plain color styles without any other surface attributes.

Figure 3.3

Working with the Surface Styles palette. (a) Resizing it so that all the default styles are visible. (b) Scrolling down to the bottom to define a new style.

- ▣ Let us now add a new surface style to the default ones that exist in the Surface Styles palette. Scroll down to the bottom of the palette until you come to the blank white row (Figure 3.3-b). Click anywhere in this blank space. You will be presented with the Surface Style Parameters dialog that lets you define a new style (Figure 3.4-a). Here, you can change its default name and specify various attributes for the style. As you can see, Color is only one of them. You can also manipulate the Reflection, Transparency, and Bumps attributes in diverse ways to create, literally, an infinite number of unique surface styles.

- ▣ By default, a surface style is of Plain Color, as you can see from the dialog in Figure 3.4-a. If you want to create a plain style but of a different color, click on the Options button associated with the Color attribute. The standard color selection dialog for your operating system will be invoked (Figure 3.4-b shows the PC dialog), from which you can select the color you want for the new style. Exit the dialog after making your selection.

Figure 3.4

The Surface Style Parameters dialog for defining a new surface style. A specific color is being selected for the Color attribute of the style.

- ▣ On the other hand, you can create a *textured* surface style by choosing one of the other options for the Color attribute instead of Plain Color. Open up the Color attribute popup list in the Surface Style Parameters dialog and select, for instance, the Brick, Textured option. Click on the associated Options button, and you will be presented with a completely different dialog (Figure 3.5). Here, you can modify various parameters of the brick texture such as the color and proportions of the brick and the mortar. Experiment with changes in these parameters and see how they affect the resulting texture.

- ▣ Explore also the various options for Reflection, Transparency, and Bumps in the same manner. You can use the Copy From option in the dialog to copy the parameters of any existing surface style and apply them to the current one. Keep in mind that for a new surface style to be actually created with the selected or copied parameters, you *have* to exit the Surface Style Parameters dialog by clicking on the OK button. To create additional styles, invoke the dialog again by clicking on the blank space in the Surface Styles palette, as you did before.

Figure 3.5

The parameters associated with the Textured Brick option for the Color attribute of a surface style.

■ form•Z also has some predefined textures for different types of objects. Click on the Predefined button in the Surface Style Parameters dialog to access these textures. You can choose from among nine different categories of materials available here (Figure 3.6). After you have finished making a selection, click on Apply Selected Material to return to the main dialog. You will find that all four attributes in the Surface Style Parameters dialog will now have acquired values appropriate to the material selected. Additional modifications to these attributes can be made by clicking on the accompanying Options buttons, enabling you to create your own customized materials. For instance, you can select Glass as a predefined material and then simply change its Color attribute to obtain glass of a different color.

Figure 3.6

Selecting a predefined material for a surface style.

■ Create at least three or four new textured surface styles with different attributes. Then get back to the graphics window and create some objects using these styles. Switch to the RenderZone display mode to see the fully rendered display. The proportion of a texture with respect to the size of the object might not be satisfactory, but don't worry about that for now. You will learn how to map these textured styles precisely on the surfaces of objects in Workshop 5.

■ Switch to the other display modes in turn, and you will find that even the textured objects are displayed in plain color only. Basically, RenderZone is the only display mode that is capable of showing *all* the attributes of a surface style that you just manipulated (which is why it is also the slowest).

■ Double-click on any one of the textured surface styles you created in the Surface Styles palette and its Surface Style Parameters dialog will be invoked. Notice that the Color, Reflection, Transparency, and Bumps attributes are grouped together under the RenderZone section (Figure 3.4-a), indicating that these are applicable only to the RenderZone display. There is an additional option here called Shader Antialiasing, which will be discussed in Workshop 5.

▪ Turn your attention to the options under the Simple section in the dialog. These are used to specify the color and transparency of a surface style as it appears in all the non-RenderZone displays. The default color is a RenderZone Average, but you can deselect this option, click on the box next to Color, and choose a new color. As far as simple transparency is concerned, different display modes deal with it in different ways, as we shall see in Exercise 2.

This is just the tip of the iceberg as far as creating and applying surface styles is concerned. As mentioned, we will revisit this aspect of form•Z in more detail in Workshop 5. You will then be able to carry out more precise and sophisticated texture mapping. For now, it is sufficient to have a basic understanding of how various surface styles can be created and applied to objects.

1.3   Editing and Managing Existing Surface Styles

▪ You have seen that to modify an existing surface style, you need to simply double-click on it in the Surface Styles palette. The same Surface Style Parameters dialog that you saw in Figure 3.4-a is invoked, allowing you to make the required modifications to the attributes of the style.

▪ All the surface styles in a project are managed through the Surface Styles dialog, which can be invoked in two ways: click anywhere inside the Surface Styles palette while holding down the option key (Mac) or Ctrl+Shift keys (PC), or go to Options > Surface Styles. The Surface Styles dialog is similar to the Objects dialog you saw in Section 3.5 of the last workshop, with identical options. You can highlight any style and move it to the top or the bottom of the palette, delete it, edit it (which will again invoke the Surface Style Parameters dialog), or make a copy of it. You can use New to create new styles to add to the palette, Sort to sort all the styles by name, and Purge to delete all the styles that have not been used in the project. The last option, Load Surface Styles, can be conveniently used to import the styles you created in another project into the current one.

Now that we have our choice of project colors and surface styles up and running, we can proceed to learn how to modify the various displays through which these colors are seen.

EXERCISE 2

Controlling the Displays

You were briefly introduced to the various display modes under the Display menu in Section 1.11 of Workshop 1. Since then, you must have switched frequently between these different kinds of displays in the course of your work and must be well acquainted with each of them. However, you probably did not realize that there is a lot more to each display than what meets the eye. Each comes with its own extensive set of options that can be adjusted to suit your requirements, thereby giving you greater control over how your modeling world appears in the graphics window. In this exercise, we will explore the options for all display modes except RenderZone, which will be covered along with texture mapping and imaging in Workshop 5.

- Continue working with the project you have from the last exercise, or open up any other project such as the Assignment from Workshop 2. In the course of the exercise, you will see this project using different displays, modifying the options of each. To access these options, go to Display > Display Options. This will open up the Modeling Display Options dialog (shown in Figure 5.11 of Workshop 5), which has buttons leading to the options for each individual display mode. It also contains some additional options related to lighting and memory management, which will be covered in Workshop 5.

- You can bypass this dialog and go directly to the dialog of a particular display mode by selecting it from the Display menu while holding down the option key (Mac) or Ctrl+Shift keys (PC). You should have guessed so from the * symbol listed next to each mode in the menu.

2.1   Wire Frame Options

- Invoke the dialog for the Wire Frame display mode using one of these two methods and look at the options that are available (Figure 3.7-a). Try out each one of them and see how it affects the display. Most of the options are quite self-explanatory. Show Backfaces, for instance, does precisely this—shows the back faces of objects in addition to their front faces. Deselecting this option will hide the back faces, useful for partially simulating a Hidden Line display in much less time. This is far from accurate, however, so don't rely on it too often.

- Most often, you will find that the default options set for a display are usually the ones that you will use the most. Sometimes, however, you might need a change. For instance, if the colors of some of your objects are so similar to the background color that they can hardly be seen, you can deselect the Show Object Color option; this will display all the objects in a single color which contrasts with the background.

- Recall from Section 3.5 of Workshop 2 that the Objects dialog gives you various options for locating the object axes and centroid of an object. These can be actually displayed in the graphics window by selecting the Show Object Axes and Show Centroid options in the Wire Frame Options dialog. Once displayed (see Figure 3.7-b), you can snap on to them using the Point snap and use them as a reference for any further operation.

Figure 3.7

The Wire Frame Options dialog with the Show Object Axes and Show Centroid options activated, and the resulting display.

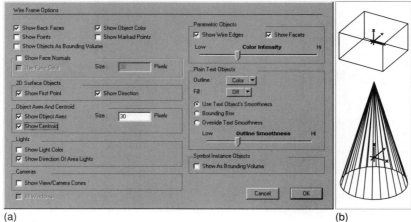

(a)   (b)

WORKSHOP 3

◾ You are already acquainted with the Show Direction option under the 2D Surface Objects section, which you activated while working with the line-editing tools in Section 4.6 of Workshop 2. You can select the Show First Point option as well. Both options are useful in a variety of operations you will work with in due course.

◾ Many options such as those dealing with lights, cameras, text objects, symbols, and others will become comprehensible as and when you cover these topics in later exercises and workshops. You can ignore them for now, but do come back and explore them once the corresponding topics are learned. As far as the All Windows option at the base of the dialog is concerned, recall from Section 2.1 of Workshop 2 that this will be activated if multiple windows are open for the project, allowing you to apply the modified display settings to all the windows. The same option exists for all the other display modes as well.

2.2 Quick Paint and Surface Render Options

◾ Next, open the dialogs of the Quick Paint and Surface Render display modes in turn and look at the options. These are similar and, again, quite self-explanatory. One option that you can expect to activate quite frequently is the Render With Shadows option, particularly for Surface Render, and you will begin doing so when you deal with lights and shadows in Workshop 5.

◾ In the last exercise, you learned how to set the simple Color and Transparency attributes of a surface style for display in the non-RenderZone modes. Both the Quick Paint and Surface Render displays give you the option of showing transparent objects in wireframe to distinguish them from other objects which are shown with shaded surfaces. An object is considered transparent when the Transparency value of its surface style is set to above 0%.

◾ For final renderings in Surface Render, it is a good idea to choose Accurate rather than Quick for the Show Edges option. Of course, you could also choose to not show the edges at all by deselecting this option, resulting in the effect shown in Figure 3.8. Try it.

Figure 3.8

A Surface Render display of the building model project from Workshop 2, with the Show Edges option de-selected.

2.3 Hidden Line Options

◾ Invoke the dialog for the Hidden Line display. Check both the Show Object Color and the Include Open Shapes options and see the resultant display. Contrary to the defaults, it is often useful to have both these options selected: the first, if you have used colors to differentiate between different groupings of objects; the second, if open shapes are an integral part of the scene and must be visible.

▣ The Hide Edges With Angle Greater Than option is useful for hiding the display of edges whose adjoining surfaces meet at an angle greater than the specified value—140° by default. Activate this option, and test it with different values for the angle. For instance, specifying an angle value greater than 90° suppresses the display of all the vertical lines along the cylindrical forms of the sample building model, as shown in Figure 3.9. Compare this with the default Hidden Line display of the same model shown in Figure 3.2.

Figure 3.9

A Hidden Line display of the building model project, with the Hide Edges option activated and set to 100°.

2.4 Shaded Render Options

▣ Move on to the Shaded Render display mode, which has a larger number of options in its dialog (Figure 3.10). Select the first option, Set Image Size. You now have to select a *portion* of the graphics window to render; the rendering is no longer done for the entire window. This same option also exists for the RenderZone display where it is generally more useful, so we will revisit it again when we study the RenderZone options in Workshop 5.

▣ Figure 3.11 shows you a comparison of the renderings that resulted from combinations of various options for Shaded Render. Generate the same renderings for the project you have, so that you can follow the subsequent explanation. Figure 3.11-a shows the rendering with the default options— no smooth shading and no antialiasing. The result, as you can see, is far from perfect.

Figure 3.10

The Shaded Render options, set to default values, and the associated Smoothing Options dialog.

WORKSHOP 3

◼   Now activate the Smooth Shading option and see the difference. The quality of the rendering will be considerably enhanced, particularly for facetted curved surfaces, since the individual facets that these surfaces are made up of get "smoothened out"—the surfaces no longer seem faceted. Needless to say, the rendering will also take more time.

◼   Smooth shading has some additional options in a dialog that is invoked by clicking on the associated Options button. Briefly explore all the options. For instance, you can select the first option to specify that only objects for which the Smooth Shading attribute has been applied using M-Tool:13a,2 (which you will learn about in Workshop 5) should be rendered smooth. The other options will apply smooth shading to all the objects, with or without overriding the individual object smoothing attributes that have been specified using the same tool.

◼   In the Smooth Shade section of the same dialog, you can set the global smooth shading attributes that will be used for the rendering. Choose between smoothing all faces of an object, resulting in inaccurate but nevertheless interesting results (Figure 3.11-b), or smoothing only specific faces. For the second option, you can specify the smoothing criteria in two ways: edges with an angle greater than the accompanying value (Figure 3.11-c), or faces with a specified range of sides. The default smooth shading type is Gouraud, but you can also go in for the more accurate (and correspondingly more time-consuming) type, Phong.

◼   Exit the Smooth Shading Options dialog to return to the Shaded Rendering Options dialog. Just below the Smooth Shading option is the Parametrics popup menu, which gives you three options for rendering parametric objects such as the analytic primitives you created in Workshop 1, as well as nurbz objects, patch objects, and c-meshes, which will be covered in Workshop 6. By default, these are always rendered smoothly. However, you can choose to apply the same smooth shading options to parametric objects that you just set for facetted objects, or use their individual smoothing attributes as set by the Smooth Shade tool (M-Tool:13a,2), which we will study in Workshop 5.

◼   The next option, Antialiasing, is an important one since it removes the jagged edges in your rendering. The difference may not be that obvious in Figure 3.11-d—which has antialiasing in addition to smooth-shading—since this was generated as a high-resolution image for printing, but will be readily apparent at the low resolution you are working in by default. Moreover, the Antialiasing option must be selected in order to activate the Transparencies option, which is used to render transparent all those objects created in surface styles with simple transparency values. Shaded Render is the only non-RenderZone display mode capable of showing the *degree* of transparency specified for the surface style.

◼   The Shadows option will be familiar to you from the earlier displays. It has two sub-options, Opaque and Transparent, which are activated only when the Transparencies option is checked. These sub-options are the same as in the RenderZone display, and we will discuss them when we look at the RenderZone options in Workshop 5. For now, also ignore the two options at the base of the dialog, Unsupported Lights and Wireframe Width. They deal with aspects that will be covered in Workshop 5 as well.

◼   Move on to the Decompose Non Planar Faces option, which is used to control how objects with non-planar faces will be rendered. When this option is checked, non-planar faces are first triangulated and then rendered. Note, however, that the triangulation is temporary, done for the purpose of rendering only, and not permanent as applied by the Triangulate tool you covered in Section 5.6 of the last workshop.

Figure 3.11

Comparison of renderings generated by various Shaded Render options.

(a) No smooth shading or antialiasing

(b) Smooth shading all faces

(c) Smooth shading edges with angle greater than 140°

(d) Antialiasing in addition to smooth shading

WORKSHOP 3

- By default, the display of grid and axes is turned off in a Shaded Render display, as you can see from the illustrations in Figure 3.11. Sometimes, however, you might want to display these to enhance a presentation or add a dramatic touch. In that case, select the Show Grid, Axes And Underlay option. (We will cover underlays in Exercise 5.) For an added 3D effect to the grid and axes display, also check the Render Grid And Axes As 3D Lines sub-option.

2.5 QuickDraw 3D and OpenGL Options

- Since the options for RenderZone will be covered in Workshop 5, that leaves us with only two more display modes to explore at this stage. Recall that QuickDraw 3D is available only on the Mac, whereas OpenGL is now supported on both platforms. The dialogs of these displays are shown in Figure 3.12. Since both modes are similar in that they enable you to carry out interactive modeling of objects using shaded surfaces rather than lines, we will discuss only the OpenGL options. Some options such as those related to smooth shading and transparencies will already be familiar to you from the Shaded Render options you just explored.

- Try out both options for Rendering Type. You will naturally want to settle for the Shaded option (the equivalent in QuickDraw 3D is Interactive Renderer), since the alternate Wire Frame option is not that different from a regular Wire Frame or Hidden Line display.

- In Workshop 5, you will learn how to map images as textures to the faces of objects. Such textures are usually visible only in the RenderZone display mode. By activating the Textures option, such image-based textures can also be seen in OpenGL. However, it will slow down your modeling activity considerably, so it is recommended that you leave this option turned off.

- The Fog option allows you to give a fog-like effect to the scene, as shown in Figure 3.13-a. In the associated Options dialog, you can modify the color of the fog and various other settings. However, keep in mind that this feature does not help in the main purpose of this display mode which is to enable shaded interactive modeling, so don't spend too much time on it.

Figure 3.12

The dialogs for the OpenGL display on the PC and the QuickDraw 3D display on the Mac.

(a)

(b)

◾ The Lights options will not be comprehensible until we deal with lights in Workshop 5. So once again, stick with the default options for now, but come back to explore the alternatives once lights are covered.

◾ The last option, Highlight Edge Size, lets you specify a pixel width for object parts such as points, segments, faces, etc. when they are selected in this display mode. Figure 3.13-b shows an exaggerated width of 10 pixels for a face which has been selected. Complete objects and groups, when selected, get fully shaded in the highlight color.

Figure 3.13

Renderings produced by two different OpenGL options.

(a)

(b)

Render With Fog activated

Highlight Edge Size set to 10 pixels

EXERCISE 3

Working with Layers

A layer in a CAD program is like a transparent screen on which graphical entities are created. There can be many layers superimposed one on top of the other and because they are transparent, all the entities drawn on them are visible. However, just as when writing or drawing takes place, it can only be on one of these transparent screens at a time, similarly, only one layer can be *active* at any given time. All the graphical entities being modeled at that time will be created on this active layer. form•Z allows you to define an unlimited number of layers in a project. When required, some of these layers can be made invisible, making it easier to work with the required entities on the visible layers only. The analogy with the transparent screens is to simply take away some of them from the pile and keep them aside.

Layers are indispensable as a means of segregating the various objects in your modeling world into different categories, so that they can be isolated when required. For instance, if you are modeling a chair, you can create the legs on one layer, the seat on a second, the back on a third, the arm-rests on a fourth, and so on. This makes the overall modeling process much easier, because you can make only the necessary layers visible at a time instead of having each and every object visible in the window. That can very quickly get messy and chaotic, even for a project of moderate complexity only. Moreover, the time required for regenerating the display each time you zoom, scroll, or choose a different display mode increases proportionally with the number of objects visible in the window. In general, you should try and minimize the number of objects on a single layer, so that you can have a minimum number of objects visible in the window at a time.

Another important advantage of using layers is that it enables you to print different combinations or aspects of your model very easily. Let's say, for instance, that in a building model you judiciously use separate layers for different categories of related elements—slabs, beams, columns, exterior and interior walls along with their openings, furniture, lights, and so on. You can then easily isolate and print out various useful layer combinations: the structural components only; walls, slabs, and furniture only; walls, slabs, and lights only; and so on.

In short, *use layers as much as you can*! This cannot be emphasized enough. The payoffs are worth the effort of organizing all your objects into layers, many times over.

3.1 Creating New Layers

▣ Open a new project and create an object. It does not matter what shape or size it is. Look for the Layers palette, through which layers are manipulated in form•Z. If it is closed, open it from the Palettes menu.

▣ Turn your attention to the Layers palette. It is almost identical to the Objects palette we saw in Section 3.5 of Workshop 2, so learning to work with it will be easy. Notice that the palette has a default layer called "layer 1" with a √ mark beside it (Figure 3.14-a). This indicates that layer 1 is the currently active layer. The single object you modeled was created on this layer. Change the default name of the layer by writing over it, just as you did for the entries in the Objects palette. Call it "yin."

▣ You will now create a new layer. Click on the blank space under the yin layer name in the Layers palette; a new layer gets created with the default name "layer 2." The name is highlighted, so you can give the layer a new name right away by typing over it. Call it "yang" to go with "yin."

▣ So you now have two layers, yin and yang. Notice that although you created a new layer yang, the active layer is still yin, as denoted by the √ mark. If you would like to create new objects on the yang layer, you need to simply click in the first column of the Layers palette beside its name. The √ mark shifts to this position, indicating that yang is the active layer (Figure 3.14-b). Now create a new object, and it will be placed on the yang layer.

Figure 3.14

Working with the Layers palette. (a) The single default layer. (b) Creating and activating a new layer, and changing both the layer names.

 (a)

 (b)

3.2   Attributes of a Layer

◼ To check that the second object has actually been created on the yang layer rather than on the yin layer, make the yin layer invisible. Just as with the Objects palette, the visibility of a layer can be turned off in the Layers palette by clicking on the shaded diamond icon in the first column to the right of the layer name. Try it. The icon will become unshaded, indicating that the layer is now ghosted. Correspondingly, the object that was created on the yin layer will appear ghosted, leaving the object created on the yang layer still visible. Thus, there are no doubts that the new object was indeed created on the layer that was active.

◼ So far, the behavior of the Layers palette seems to be identical to that of the Objects palette. However, there is an important difference between ghosting an object using the Objects palette and ghosting a layer of objects using the Layers palette. The first is equivalent to using the Ghost tool; the second is not. To verify this, try going to Edit > Select All Ghosted. You will find that this command is deactivated as no ghosted objects have been detected in the project. For the same reason, even the Hide Ghosted command will not affect the display of the ghosted object in your window. Keep this distinction between the two palettes in mind.

Ghosting a layer is thus a property of the layer rather than of the objects on that layer. The basic notion of ghosting, however, remains the same—the objects on a ghosted layer are displayed in a light gray color and cannot be selected. Ghosting a layer is useful if you do not need to work with the objects it contains but would still like to use them for reference. This feature can also be used as an effective presentation technique, as illustrated in Figure 3.15, where a structural plan of columns is shown in visible mode while the floor that it supports above is shown in ghosted mode. The same image would have been hard to comprehend if the floor was fully visible or if it was not shown at all.

◼ Click on the diamond icon next to the yin layer once more. It will disappear, indicating that this layer is now totally invisible; the object on it will no longer be seen. What you just did was turn the layer "off." Click once more in the same spot, and the diamond icon will reappear in its original state—fully shaded—restoring the visibility of the layer. Thus, the diamond icon in the Layers palette toggles between the three attributes of visibility, ghostedness, and invisibility, just like the corresponding icon in the Objects palette.

Figure 3.15

A structural plan of columns, demonstrating the usefulness of ghosting a layer.

- Now try changing the visibility attribute of the yang layer. You will find that you cannot do so—it must remain in visible mode. This is because it is the active layer, which naturally, must always be visible. To make this layer invisible, you must first designate another layer as the active layer.

- Just like the Objects palette, the Layers palette has two more columns for the attributes of pickability and snapability, indicated by the lock icon and the shaded circle respectively (see Figure 3.16). These toggle-switch icons work identically to the corresponding icons in the Objects palette which you explored in the last workshop. Try them out. Lock one of the layers and you will find that you can no longer select and modify the object on this layer. Click on the circular icon in the last column of the same layer, and none of the Object Snap tools will work any more on the object it contains.

Figure 3.16

Manipulating the pickability and snapability attributes of a layer.

 (a)

 (b)

Locking the layer

Turning off layer snapability

The rationale for turning off the visibility, pickability, or snapability attributes of an entire layer is the same as that for a single object. In a large and complex project in which you have judiciously used many layers for segregating related groups of objects, the layers not being used at any particular time can be made totally invisible. If they need to be used as a reference, they can be made ghosted, so that you can still snap to the objects in them. If a layer needs to be visible but without the possibility of the objects in it being accidentally modified in any way, it can be locked and therefore effectively "frozen." Additionally, if the objects in such a layer do not need to be used for snapping, it is better to turn off the snapability attribute of the layer—this will make it easier to snap only to the desired objects.

You have seen that you can also lock the active layer or turn off its snapability. This is in contrast to the visibility attribute which cannot be turned off for the active layer. The ability to lock even the active layer can be useful, for instance, in a situation where you want to select all the objects in some specific layers for an operation such as Move, Color, Delete, etc. In that case, you would simply lock all the other layers *including* the active one, and then go to Edit > Select All Unghosted to make the desired selection. Very convenient and elegant, as you can see.

In general, manipulating the attributes of an entire layer is much more useful and convenient than manipulating the attributes of individual objects, which is why you will find yourself using the Layers palette far more frequently than the Objects palette. The object listing in the Objects palette is unfortunately not sorted by layer, which makes it very difficult to keep track of which object is in which layer through it. Especially for large projects, this task is almost impossible. Therefore, until such a feature is introduced (hopefully!) in a future version of form•Z, focus on the Layers palette rather than on the Objects palette, and as mentioned earlier, aim for the minimum number of objects on a single layer.

3.3 Moving Objects Between Layers

You created the first object on the yin layer and the second on the yang layer. What if you realize later that the second object should really have been categorized with the first object and should therefore be on the yin layer? Basically, what we need to know is how to move objects from one layer to another *after* they have been created.

- The currently active layer is yang. Since you want to move the object to the yin layer, make the yin layer active.

- Now select the object on the yang layer which is to be transferred. If you've forgotten which of the two objects was in the yang layer, simply lock the yin layer. This will guarantee that the object you select is in the yang layer, which is the one you want.

- After selecting the object, go to the Set Layer command (M-Tool:13b,3). Following the instructions in the Prompts palette, click anywhere in the window. The object gets moved to the active layer which is yin. There is no visible change, but you can verify the move by making the yang layer invisible or ghosted. Both your objects will remain visible, since they are now in the yin layer.

- The method just described can be used to transfer many objects at a time to a different layer by prepicking them with the Pick tool. To change the layer of just a single object, you can also use the Attributes tool (M-Tool:11b,2). Simply apply this tool to an object and in the dialog that is invoked, use the On Layer popup list to specify a different layer for it. We will explore this tool in more detail in Workshop 5.

3.4 Global Manipulation of Layers

By default, layers are visible, unlocked and snapable when they are created (see Figure 3.17-a). Each of these attributes can then be modified for individual layers, as we have seen. You can also conveniently modify the attributes of *all* the layers in one step, when necessary.

- Create about three to four additional layers in the Layers palette. Don't bother changing their names. Having many layers will help you understand better how global manipulation of layers works. Make sure the visibility attribute of all the layers is turned on to start with.

- Click on the diamond icon that appears at the head of the visibility column, as indicated in Figure 3.17-a. You will find that all the layers except the active layer are ghosted (Figure 3.17-b). A second click at the same spot will turn all the ghosted layers off (Figure 3.17-c). So basically, this works as a toggle switch for all the layers in one step, setting them to on, ghosted, or off repeatedly. Of course, the initial setting of a layer will determine how it is toggled. Thus, if some layers are ghosted, they will be made invisible, while invisible layers are toggled back to visibility (see Figures 3.17-d to 3.17-f).

Figure 3.17

Manipulating the visibility settings of all the layers at a time (except the active layer) by using the header visibility icon.

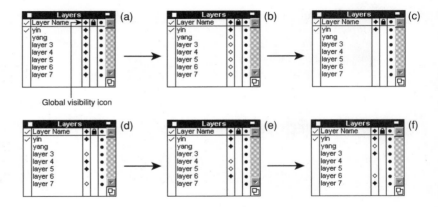

- Try out the same technique with the other two header icons for pickability and snapability. They work in an identical fashion.

- As you can see, this is a very convenient method for changing the attributes of all the layers at a time. However, what if, for instance, you want to change the attributes of only 5 or 6 layers in a project with a total of 12 layers? You cannot use the method just described. If you manipulate the layers individually, you will find it tiresomely slow for a complex project (even in Wire Frame display), since the graphics window is regenerated each time the visibility attribute of a layer is changed. The solution to this problem is to hold down the Shift key as you change the visibility attribute of an individual layer. This will postpone the regeneration of the display until the Shift key is released, which you can do after manipulating all the required layers.

 The Objects palette affords the same ability for global manipulation of attributes as the Layers palette, but it is not so useful there.

3.5 Working with Layer Groups

Starting with version 3.0, form•Z provides the ability to collect together individual layers into layer groups, in a manner similar to how individual objects are collected together into object groups. Thus, you can create layer hierarchies in much the same way as you can create object hierarchies. The rationale for doing so is the same as that discussed in Section 3.4 of Workshop 2, where we worked with object groups. In fact, with the ability to group layers, you might find that you don't need to bother with grouping objects at all.

- Go to the Layers palette, and click on the blank space under the last layer name while pressing the control key (Mac) or Ctrl+Alt keys (PC). This will create a new layer group with a default name, which you can type over. Existing layers can now be moved into this layer group by the drag-and-drop method, identical to how you rearranged objects and groups in the Objects palette. You can create as many layer groups as you want, and move some of them within other layer groups, building up any desired hierarchy (Figure 3.18-a). Try it. Keep in mind that multiple consecutive entries can be selected by clicking and dragging across their names in the palette.

- You can manipulate the attributes of all the layers within a layer group simultaneously by using the corresponding visibility, pickability, and snapability icons next to the name of the group (Figure 3.18-b). Recall that you tried this out for object groups in the Objects palette as well.

- Just as with the Objects palette, the arrows in front of a layer group name work as toggle switches, allowing you to show or hide the list of layers contained within the group.

Figure 3.18

Working with layer groups. (a) Creating groups within groups. (b) Manipulating the visibility attribute of all the layers within a group simultaneously.

3.6 The Layers Dialog

▪ The Layers dialog provides you with some more options for working with layers. It is like the Objects dialog you explored in Workshop 2 and is similarly invoked by one of three methods. The easiest way is to click in the header row of the Layers palette, where the column title Name appears. Alternately, click anywhere inside the Layers palette while holding down the option key (Mac) or Ctrl+Shift keys (PC), or go to Options > Layers.

▪ As you can see in Figure 3.19-a, the information about layers and layer groups displayed on the left side of the Layers dialog is in the same format as the Layers palette. The attributes of visibility, pickability, and snapability for the layers and groups can be manipulated through the same icons and in the same way as you did for the palette. You can create new layers and groups directly in the dialog by using the Layer and Group commands respectively. You can highlight a layer or group, and apply the usual operations to it such as Delete, Copy, Top, Bottom, and Sort. The Active option will make the selected layer active, while the Purge option will remove all the empty layers and groups—which contain no objects—from the project. Be careful about deleting layers or groups that are not empty using Delete, as this action cannot be undone. At the base of the Layers dialog are the options for changing the default layer and group names, if required.

▪ Select a layer and click on the Edit button. This will invoke the Layer Attributes dialog where you can specify various attributes for the selected layer. You can see that this dialog is very similar to the Object Attributes dialog you used in Section 3.3 to change the layer of an object. Thus, you can assign to a layer the same attributes that you can assign to individual objects. Keep in mind that the former override the latter. Thus, if you select a surface style for the layer by activating the Surface Style box, as shown in Figure 3.19-b, *all* the objects on that layer will be rendered with the chosen surface style, regardless of the surface style assigned to them individually. We will learn about all the other attributes shown in the dialog by the end of Workshop 5.

▪ The next option, Load Project Layers, lets you import layers from another project into the current one and is thus similar to the Load Surface Styles option you saw in the Surface Styles dialog. For layers, this option comes in especially useful when you are working on similar projects, or working on parts of the same project in two or more separate files.

Figure 3.19

The Layers dialog, and the Layer Attributes dialog for the selected layer.

■ Move on to the next three options. Draw In Order Shown and Draw Active Last are used to determine the order in which objects are drawn in the window. These are not of great importance, so ignore them for now. Note, however, the Paste On Active Layer option—it is unchecked by default. This means that if you use Cut or Copy after making a selection in form•Z and then use Paste in the same project, the selected elements will be pasted on the layers they were originally in. However, if you want them to be pasted on a different layer, make that layer active and check the Paste On Active Layer option in the Layers dialog. Now the cut or copied objects will be pasted on the active layer, irrespective of which layer they came from. Apart from its obvious use of *duplicating* objects across layers (using Copy and Paste), this method can also be used to *transfer* objects between layers (using Cut and Paste) instead of the Set Layer or Attribute tools. Thus, in form•Z, there invariably is more than one way of doing something. In time, you will find out which works best for you.

■ The remaining two options in the Layers dialog give layers some interesting abilities. If you activate the Show Color option, a layer will be displayed in the Layers palette in the color which has been assigned to it using the Layer Attributes dialog you just saw. And if you activate the Highlight Picked option, selecting an object in the graphics window will highlight the name of the layer it is on in the Layers palette. Activate both these options and test them out. The Highlight Picked one is especially handy.

Now that you know how to properly organize all your objects in multiple layers, let us proceed to learn to use multiple reference planes, which will further improve your modeling efficiency.

EXERCISE

Using Your Own Reference Planes

4

In Workshop 1, you learned how to use the three predefined planes—XY, YZ, and ZX—that are available in form•Z. In this exercise, you will learn how to define and work with your own reference planes that better suit the requirements of the objects you are modeling. For instance, a reference plane passing through a surface can be very convenient for positioning openings accurately on it. Just as you created your own surface styles and layers, defining your own planes is one more step in the direction of customizing your working environment.

4.1   Arbitrary Reference Planes

The three predefined planes may not be sufficient even for a relatively simple modeling situation such as that shown in Figure 3.20, where a 3D triangular enclosure needs to be created on an inclined face of a pyramid. You could, of course, use the Face object snap to create the enclosure on the desired face, as you learned in Section 2.4 of Workshop 2. The only problem is the lack of preciseness. What if the enclosure needs to be sized such that it is, for instance, exactly 3' inside from all the edges of the face? How can this be done without getting into complex numeric calculations in 3D coordinate space?

What would be really useful to have here is the ability to treat the face itself on which the extrusion has to be created as the reference plane for the modeling. Then creating an extrusion on it in a precise location would be as simple as creating the same extrusion on the predefined XY plane, for instance, dimensionally accurate as you learned in Workshop 2.

Figure 3.20

A simple example of a configuration to be modeled.

Well, you *can* do exactly this—create a reference plane passing *through* the face on which you want to locate the extrusion. Such a plane is referred to as an "arbitrary" plane, since it can be located anywhere in 3D space. Let us go through the process of modeling the required configuration using an arbitrary plane.

■ Create and activate a new layer, now that you know how to do so, and make all the other layers invisible. Create a pyramid using the Rectangle tool in 3D Converged Solid mode. Then select a face of the pyramid on which you will situate the enclosure by setting the topological level to Face and using the Pick tool.

■ Turn to the third column of window tools located at the base of the graphics window and select the first tool, Define Arbitrary (W-Tool:3,1). The Prompts palette will ask you to click to define an arbitrary plane, since a face has already been selected. Do so, and a new reference plane will be created passing through the selected face. It has its own axes—called *reference plane axes*—which are colored in teal to distinguish them from the original red-colored axes—known as *world axes*.

■ The orientation of the reference plane axes will depend upon the sequence in which the segments were picked to select the face. Try out different pick sequences, reapplying the Define Arbitrary tool each time. You will get the same plane but with different axes orientations. Figure 3.21 shows all possible variations of the pick sequences for the same face, and the resulting axes. As you can see, the X axis is always aligned with the segment that is selected first. For the purpose of modeling our target configuration, the axes orientation shown in Figure 3.21-a seems suitable, so let us settle for that.

Figure 3.21

Different axes orientations depending upon the picking sequence of the face. The display of the world axes was temporarily turned off.

(a)   (b)

(c)

◻ Try creating any object now, not necessarily the triangular extrusion. You will find that all 2D and 3D objects are created with respect to this "arbitrary" reference plane. Notice that the dimensions of the new grid are the same as those for the predefined planes, and that if the Grid Snap switch is on, it is also active for the new plane. Essentially, arbitrary planes reflect the same grid settings as the regular planes.

Let us get back to the original problem of creating the extrusion so that it is exactly 3' inside the face from all sides. How would you do this? You can, of course, use the grid as a reference and draw the base triangle approximately 3' inside from the edges of the face. But what if you had to be absolutely precise? This is where the arbitrary reference plane you just defined will come in most useful. Execute the following sequence of steps exactly as described.

◻ Invoke the dialog of the Pick tool and select the option, Auto Select New Objects. (So there *is* some use for it after all!) Select the Vector Lines tool in 2D Surface Object mode; with this, draw a triangle that coincides with the face on which the extrusion is to be located, by snapping to its segment endpoints. You now have a base triangle which is of the same size as the face, lying exactly on top of it. It gets highlighted as soon as it is created because of the Auto Select feature, saving you from the bother of having to use pick parade (as covered in Section 4.5 of Workshop 2) to select it. The same base triangle could also have been obtained using the Derivative 2D Surface tool (M-Tool:5a,1), which you will learn about in Section 6.1 of Workshop 4.

◻ You will now scale the 2D triangle with respect to the arbitrary plane, so that it lies exactly 3' inside the face from all sides. Moreover, you will do this graphically using the grid, rather than by typing in a scaling factor. Select the Uniform Scale operator (M-Tool:12a,4). The triangle is already selected, so the scaling will be applied to this object. For the base of scale, specify the center of the triangle by selecting it using the Center of Face snap (W-Tool:6,11).

◻ Next, you need to specify the scaling factor. Activate Grid Snap and set the snapping module to 1'-0". Also, turn off object snapping by setting it to None. Click on any point at the bottom edge of the face which coincides with the plane's X axis; this will be the first point for the scaling factor. Since Grid Snap is on, you should easily be able to click at a point 3' inside from the first point along the same face. This will be the second point for determining the scaling factor. The 2D triangle gets resized according to this factor, and it should now be 3' inside from all edges of the face (Figure 3.22).

◻ Now simply use the 3D Enclosure tool (M-Tool:5a,5) to generate a 3D enclosure from this 2D triangle. By default, the enclosure is centered about the original 2D line, so you will lose some of the 3' margin on all sides. To retain the exact margin, set the Justification option to Left in the dialog of the 3D Enclosure tool, and then apply it to generate the triangular enclosure.

Voila! You have finished creating the target configuration (shown in Figure 3.20) by defining and using your own reference plane.

Figure 3.22

Creating the appropriately sized base triangle with the help of the new reference plane.

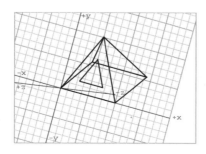

4.2   Switching Between Predefined and Arbitrary Planes

What if you want to switch to the XY plane for creating other objects, but would like to retain the option of returning to the newly created arbitrary plane whenever needed? Let us see how to do this.

◼ Turn your attention to the first window tool palette that contains the reference planes. You will notice that the Arbitrary icon is highlighted, indicating that the currently active plane is a user-defined one. To switch to one of the predefined planes, simply select the corresponding icon from the palette. Create some object on the plane you switched to.

◼ Now select the Arbitrary icon again. The arbitrary plane you had created becomes active once more and can be used for further modeling activity.

◼ Keep switching between the four different kinds of planes in the palette and create various objects. It will give you a feel for the flexibility and convenience afforded by multiple planes, both predefined and arbitrary.

4.3   Using Arbitrary Plane Coordinates

You already know that only one plane can be active, and therefore visible, at any given time. You are always modeling with respect to the currently active plane—predefined or arbitrary—that you see in your window at that time.

◼ Switch back to the Arbitrary plane if it is not active. Your next task is to move the triangular extrusion you created earlier by a specific distance, up and away from the face it is located on in a perpendicular direction, as shown in Figure 3.23-a. Assume that the distance is a fractional number—such as 16'-1/2", for instance—so that it is preferable to execute the Move operation using direct numeric input rather than graphically with the mouse.

◼ You already know from Workshop 2 that you can use relative coordinates to carry out the move. Deselect the box marked A in the Prompts palette to set its mode to relative. Then activate the Move tool, select the enclosure as the object to be moved, and key in 0,0,16'-1/2" as the relative coordinates of the move. What you will get (Figure 3.23-b) is obviously not what you had aimed for.

So what went wrong? Obviously, the coordinates you keyed in were not correct. If you look carefully, you will find that the triangular enclosure *has* been moved by the distance [0',0',16'-1/2"] away from its original position, but with respect to the red-colored world axes rather than the teal-colored axes of the current reference plane. The solution to this problem is really very simple.

Figure 3.23

The next modeling goal, and the erroneous move that occurred at the first attempt.

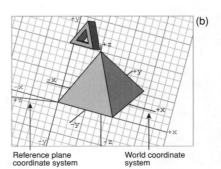

Reference plane coordinate system   World coordinate system

▣ Undo the Move operation you just performed. Then deselect the box marked W in the Prompts palette. Execute the Move again by keying in the same relative coordinates as before, and you will find that it is now executed correctly, giving you the result you want. By deselecting the W box, you specified that all input should be with respect to the coordinate system of the current reference plane rather than that of the predefined planes. That is why your numeric input works correctly this time.

Each arbitrary reference plane that you create comes with its coordinate system, relative to its axes. Such coordinates are known as "reference plane coordinates." In contrast, the coordinates of the predefined planes, relative to the original X, Y, and Z axes, are known as "world coordinates." Just as the A checkbox in the Prompts palette switches between relative and absolute coordinates, similarly, the W checkbox switches between world and reference plane coordinates.

▣ Let us carry out another operation using reference plane coordinates. Delete the triangular enclosure you just moved. We will insert an opening on the same face of the pyramid where the enclosure was initially located. The opening must be of specified dimensions, say 12' by 6' with a depth of 1', and located at a precise distance, say 10' by 8', from the lower left corner of the face (see Figure 3.24). Make sure the arbitrary plane is still active, and that the W box in the Prompts palette is deselected. Go ahead and check the A box, however, so that you can locate the first point of the opening correctly with respect to the plane origin using absolute coordinates.

▣ Prepick the face of the pyramid with the Pick tool. Activate the Insert Hole mode on Row 2, and select the Rectangle tool on Row 3. Specify [10',8',0'] as the first corner point. Then deselect the A box to set the mode to relative, and specify [12',6',0'] as the second corner point. Finally, specify the height as [-1'], and the hole will be inserted, correctly located and sized. Practice with this procedure some more until you are comfortable with it.

Figure 3.24

Inserting a hole on an inclined face precisely, using reference plane coordinates.

4.4 Using Multiple Arbitrary Planes

▣ Suppose that you now want to create a new object with reference to one of the *other* faces of the pyramid. Naturally, you will have to create a new arbitrary plane passing though that face. Select the face and use Define Arbitrary (W-Tool:3,1) as you did before to define a reference plane passing through it. Create any object on this new plane.

◼ Switch to one of the three predefined planes—XY, YZ, or ZX—using the first window tool palette. Then select the **Arbitrary** icon in the same palette. You will find yourself going back to the arbitrary plane you *last* created.

Thus, you can only return to the most recent user-defined plane using the **Arbitrary** window tool. What if you need to use the arbitrary plane you *first* created? Do you have to recreate it every time you need to use it? What if your model is complicated and you are using many such planes?

Fortunately, form•Z has the ability to store multiple user-defined planes, so that you can recall them whenever needed, without having to recreate them each time. This is done through the **Planes** palette, which is closed by default—that is why you never noticed it all this time.

◼ Go to **Palettes > Planes** to open this palette. You can see that it is similar to the **Objects** and **Layers** palettes which you've already worked with. In fact, it is simpler with three columns only: the first designates the active plane; the second lists the name of the plane; and the third indicates what kind of plane it is (see Figure 3.25). The palette is empty in the beginning as no planes have been saved in it. We will proceed to do this right away.

◼ Click on the palette in the space under **Plane Name**. A default name will appear which you can type over; click in the space below or press **Return** or **enter** to complete the definition of the new plane. It will be checked in the first column, indicating that it is the active plane. Also, a tag of **ARB** appears in the column to the right of the name, indicating that it is an arbitrary plane (Figure 3.25-a). What you have effectively done is store the current user-defined plane in the **Planes** palette.

◼ Now create another arbitrary plane, passing through one of the other faces of the pyramid. Save it in the **Planes** palette in the same manner. See how easily you can now switch between these two arbitrary planes, simply by clicking in the first column next to their names in the palette. You can similarly create, store, and recall as many planes as needed. The active plane is indicated by a √ mark, just as for active layers.

◼ The **Planes** palette is so convenient for switching between planes that you might also want to store the three predefined planes in it. Activate the XY, YZ, and ZX planes in turn using the first window tool palette, and create a new entry for each of them in the **Planes** palette. As you can see in Figure 3.25-b, the tag in the third column changes to reflect the type of plane. You can now forget about the first window tool palette altogether, and use only the **Planes** palette for switching between planes—both predefined as well as arbitrary.

◼ Finally, click on the label **Plane Name** in the title row of the **Planes** palette, just as you did for the **Layers** palette. This will invoke the **Reference Planes** dialog which is similar to the dialogs for **Layers**, **Objects**, and **Surface Styles**, containing the same options for managing your planes such as **Delete**, **Rename**, **Sort**, and so on.

Figure 3.25

Working with the Planes palette. (a) Storing an arbitrary plane. (b) Storing and using the predefined planes in addition to arbitrary ones.

4.5 The Reference Plane Manipulation Tools

The third column of the window tool palette contains some other tools, in addition to **Define Arbitrary**, that are used for manipulating the active reference plane, whether predefined or arbitrary. Let us briefly look at each one of them in turn.

▣ The second tool in the palette, **Define Perpendicular**, lets you define a plane which is perpendicular to an existing plane. Try it for one of the arbitrary planes you have created; of course, you need to activate the plane first. Since there can be two planes perpendicular to a given plane (for instance, both the YZ and ZX planes are perpendicular to the XY plane) you will be asked to specify the axis about which the new plane is to be created.

▣ **Move Plane** lets you move an existing plane to a different location. Try it for both an arbitrary plane as well as a predefined one. The distance of the move can be specified graphically or by direct numeric input, similar to how the **Move** tool is used for moving objects. The relocated plane can be saved as a new plane in the **Planes** palette, if required. The **Move Plane** tool has many applications—for instance, in architectural modeling, subsequent floors of a building can be constructed on XY planes that are "moved" up to the required floor heights.

▣ The next tool, **Move Origin**, can be used to change the origin of a reference plane from its default location to any other point on the same plane. The plane itself will not be moved, just its origin. This tool is useful because very often, it is difficult to create a plane with its origin at the exact point that is needed. You can use **Move Origin**, for example, to change the origin of your first arbitrary plane from a vertex of the pyramid to the center of one of its faces (Figure 3.26). The **Endpoint** and **Center Of Face** snapping options can be used to accomplish this precisely.

Figure 3.26

Moving the origin of an arbitrary plane from the vertex to the center of a face.

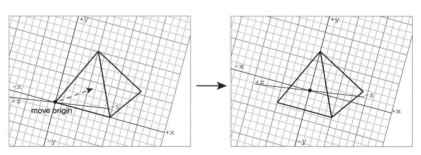

▣ Use the next tool, **Rotate Plane**, to rotate the active plane about its origin by a specified angle, which can be either typed in or indicated graphically. It is thus similar to the **Rotate** tool used for rotating objects, except that this tool works on planes. It is much more convenient than using the **Angle** direction snap (W-Tool:5,4) for working on parts of a project that are rotated at an angle with respect to the rest of the project. This is illustrated in the building model shown in Figure 3.27, where the XY plane is rotated by an angle of 45° to conveniently model the diagonal floor plan.

▣ For those of you who have been yearning to change the size of the reference grid from Day 1, the **Extend Plane** tool can be used to do this in no time at all! Simply grab each one of the four edges of the plane in turn and drag it outwards—the grid will be increased automatically by the designated distance. You can also shrink the plane using the same technique, if needed.

Workshop 3

Figure 3.27

Rotating the XY plane to assist in the modeling of a floor, most of which is diagonally oriented with respect to the rest of the building.

▣ Keep in mind that any plane you modify using these plane manipulation tools can be saved in the Planes palette as a new plane. What's more, the original plane itself can be retrieved by using the last tool in the palette, Reset Plane. This tool discards any changes made to the active plane and restores it to its original configuration. Thus, you can modify a plane and save both the original *and* the modified versions in the Planes palette.

Now that you know how to create and manipulate your own reference planes, you can proceed to do the same with views.

EXERCISE *5*

Having Different Views

So far, you have used the View menu in a very limited fashion, switching between the various predefined views it contains. In this exercise, you will expand your visualization capabilities enormously by creating views from desired positions and angles. You will also work with the Views palette, which lets you save and manage your views in a manner similar to the Objects, Surface Styles, Layers, and Planes palettes you have been working with.

5.1 Predefined Axonometric Views

form•Z has a large number of predefined views that you can use to visualize your modeling world in various ways. All of these are accessible from the View pulldown menu (Figure 3.28), which you were briefly introduced to in Section 1.8 of Workshop 1. We will now study this menu in more detail.

▣ Recreate the configuration shown in Figure 3.20 of the last exercise—the pyramid with the 3D triangular enclosure located on one of its inclined faces. You will be seeing these objects in a 30-60 axonometric view by default. Correspondingly, there is a √ mark against the z=30° x=60° item in the first group of the View menu, which specifies the viewing angle from each one of the three axes; the y angle is not given, indicating that it is 0°. There is also a √ mark against the Axonometric item in the third group of the menu, which denotes the kind of view.

Figure 3.28

The View menu, expanded to show the Plane Projection submenu.

■ Switch to each one of the other four viewing angle options in the first group of the View menu, and see how they give you different axonometric views of your world. The last option in this group, Custom View Angles, lets you define your own viewing angles. Try keying in different values for X, Y, and Z, and see the resultant view. Notice that for the Z axis to be positioned vertically in the window, the Y angle *must* be 0°.

Figure 3.29

The six planar views of the 3D world shown in Figure 3.20, with respect to any of the three predefined planes.

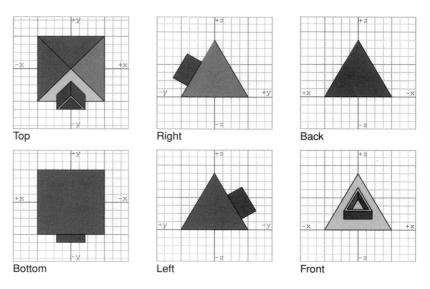

Top Right Back

Bottom Left Front

■ Move to the second group of the View menu. The first six options in this group give you all the six planar (or "projection") views possible—Top, Bottom, Right, Left, Back, and Front—with respect to the world axes. (Think of your modeling world as being inside a box; then you can look at it head-on from only the six sides of the box.) Switch to one of the predefined reference planes, XY, YZ, or ZX; then try out the six planar views to see orthogonal views of your modeling world from all sides (Figure 3.29). For each view, go to the Custom View Angles option and note the angle values for X, Y, and Z. This will give you a better sense of how to define your own viewing angles when the need arises.

You will find that planar views are particularly convenient for more precise and accurate work, as working directly in 3D can sometime be misleading. Even if you prefer to work directly in 3D all the time, you should make it a habit to periodically switch to the planar views to check if the objects are indeed being created or modified as you intend them to be.

The planar views you have just used are with reference to the red-colored world axes. But you may not always be using the world coordinate system, as in the last exercise where you learned to create your own reference planes and use their respective coordinate systems. form•Z conveniently gives you the same six planar views for your customized reference planes as well. This feature is incredibly useful—literally a boon!—which you will not find in other 3D CAD programs.

◻ Activate any one of the non-planar views in the View menu. Then switch to an arbitrary plane coinciding with one of the inclined faces of the pyramid that you had created in the last exercise— it should be saved in the Planes palette. Re-create it if you do not have it any more. Now switch to the Top view. You will find that this still gives you a planar view of the *original* XY plane (shown in Figure 3.29), not of the arbitrary one you just activated.

◻ Go to the last command in the second group of the View menu, called Plane Projection. It has a submenu with six options, as shown in Figure 3.28. If you are still in the Top view (or in any other planar view), all these options will be grayed out. Switch back to a non-planar view, and make sure the active plane is still the arbitrary one.

Figure 3.30

The six planar views of the same 3D world as in Figure 3.29, but with respect to the arbitrary plane shown in Figure 3.21-a rather than the predefined planes.

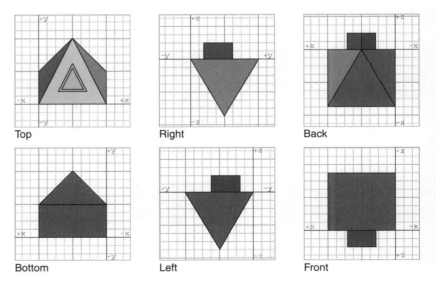

Top   Right   Back

Bottom   Left   Front

◻ The Plane Projection sub-options now get activated. Select Top—the first of these sub-options. This will show you the top planar view of your 3D world, but with respect to the *arbitrary reference plane* rather than the predefined XY plane. Try out the other five planar views in the

Plane Projection submenu as well, all of which work with respect to the arbitrary plane (Figure 3.30). As you can see, these views will be extremely useful when you need to work accurately with the coordinate system of an arbitrary plane.

5.2   Other Types of 3D Views

For the rest of this exercise, use a completed project such as the building model you created in the Assignment for Workshop 2—it should be fun viewing it in various ways. Turn your attention to the third group of the View menu which has four more types of views in addition to the default of Axonometric, which we have been using predominantly so far. All these views have dialogs associated with them, as indicated by the * sign, which can be invoked in the usual fashion—selecting them while holding down the option key (Mac) or Ctrl+Shift keys (PC). You can also invoke the dialog of the *current* view by going to View > View Parameters. Most of the options in this dialog can be graphically (and thus more conveniently) specified using the Edit Cone Of Vision command, which will be covered a little later in Section 5.4; therefore, we will skip the dialog for now. However, let us browse through the remaining four types of views and see how they differ from each other.

■   Switch from Axonometric to Isometric. This mode allows only non-planar views, so all the planar views in the second group of the View menu will not work as expected. Look closely and you will find that in this mode, the actual dimensions of objects, measured in directions parallel to the three orthogonal axes, are retained (see Figure 3.31-a). This is in contrast to the "natural" Axonometric views, in which non-planar views do not convey the real size of objects. When you switch to the Isometric mode, the first group of the View menu changes to give you six different viewing angle combinations. Try out each one of these. There is no Custom option, but more isometric views can be generated interactively through the Edit Cone Of Vision command, which you will soon work with.

Figure 3.31

An Isometric view (x=30° y=60°) and an Oblique view (Inclination = 45°) of the building model created in Workshop 2.

(a) Isometric view

(b) Oblique view

◼ Next, switch to Oblique, which is similar to the Isometric mode in preserving dimensions measured parallel to the axes and in not allowing planar views (see Figure 3.31-b). The first group of the View menu again changes to give you six possible viewing options, which you should browse through. All these options are in terms of the inclination of the Y axis relative to the horizontal direction of the window. Again, you can generate various other oblique views using Edit Cone Of Vision.

Both the Isometric and Oblique modes are not commonly used, since they do not allow for planar views. They can be used in specific cases when a presentation expressly calls for the use of such a mode. But for practical application during actual modeling, these modes can be safely ignored.

◼ Select the next viewing mode, Perspective. You will find that this is identical to Axonometric—it lists the same viewing angles in the first group and the same planar views in the second group, including the Plane Projection submenu. The only difference is that it adds a perspective effect to the view. Try it out for different viewing angles, and see how you can quickly generate one-point perspectives by switching to the planar views with the Perspective mode activated (Figure 3.32). We will look more closely at the Perspective mode and its options when we work with the Edit Cone Of Vision command.

Figure 3.32

A one-point perspective of the building model, obtained by switching to the Front view in Perspective mode.

◼ The fifth and final viewing mode, Panoramic, was introduced in version 2.9. As soon as you select this option, a panoramic view of the project is displayed and all the modeling and windows tools are grayed out. A panoramic view is basically a 360° view of the world, and as you can see, it would be impossible to perform any modeling operations in this mode. It is meant for display only, and can be saved for presentations as an image file or used to generate QuickTime VR movies. We will look at this feature in detail in Workshop 7, along with the viewing parameters for panoramic views.

5.3 Using the Views Palette

As you become increasingly familiar with the various tools in form•Z, you will find yourself working progressively faster. Speed then becomes an important consideration, and you will be constantly searching for the fastest possible way to do something. One such operation you would prefer to spend minimal time on is changing views, particularly since it is done so frequently. You will often need to change views to see what you are doing from various angles, sometimes even in the middle of an operation. (Keep in mind that you *can* do that in form•Z.) Even if you are working only in a single view for an extended period of time, you will still need to constantly zoom in and out of that view to see different parts of the project

Having to constantly navigate through the View menu to select the view you want can get very tiresome and time-consuming. A convenient shortcut is to store all the views you need in the Views palette, so that you can recall them with just a single mouse click when needed. form•Z lets you save as many views as you like in the Views palette. The views can be predefined, such as the ones you have seen so far, or customized, such as the ones you will learn to create in later sections.

■ Go to the Palettes menu and open the Views palette if it is closed. It operates in a manner similar to the Objects and Layers palettes, so working with it should not present any problems. There are some differences, however, which we will explore.

■ The Views palette is currently empty since you have not yet saved any views in it. Let us do that right away. First, switch to the view that you want to save. Then click on the Views palette in the blank space under View Name. Just as with layers and planes, the current view gets saved by a default name which you can change right away. An "eye" mark appears in the column to the left of the newly created view, indicating that it is the active view. The type of view—Perspective, Axonometric, Top, Right, and so on—is also indicated in the column to the right of the view name (see Figure 3.33).

■ Switch to a different view using the View menu. We will save this view using another method. Go to the Save View option, located in the fourth group of the View menu. A dialog will pop up, asking you for the name of the view. Write over the default name and click OK. This view will now appear in the Views palette by the specified name. To switch back to the first view, simply click in the eye-mark column to the left of its name.

■ Any view that is saved in the Views palette can be actually displayed in the graphics window in Wire Frame mode by clicking in the column to the right of its type. A diamond icon will appear there, indicating that the view is visible. To see this graphical view display better, you should switch to another view. Figure 3.33 shows the representation of both an axonometric and a perspective view, seen from an altogether different viewpoint. As you will notice, the representation is made up of various components which you will learn about in the next section (see Figure 3.35). Once a view is made visible, it can also be selected by clicking in the left-most column of the palette. A selected view is indicated by a √ mark. While only one view can be *active* at a time, many can be *selected* at the same time. A selected view can be graphically manipulated using tools such as Move, Rotate, etc., unless it has been locked by clicking in the last column beside its name.

Figure 3.33

The Views palette, and the graphical representation of two views. One of the views has been selected.

▣ Just like the dialogs of other palettes, the dialog of the Views palette can be easily invoked by clicking on the header, View Name, in the title row of the palette. This dialog provides you with similar options for deleting, sorting, loading views from another project, and so on, that you encountered in the dialogs of other palettes. The Edit option here will invoke the same dialog for the selected view as the View Parameters command in the View menu. You will be studying this dialog in detail in Section 5.6.

Not only can you save different viewing types and viewing angles as separate views, you can also save zoomed in or zoomed out versions of the same view under separate names in the Views palette. In a Top view, for instance, you can fit the entire model in the window and save that as a view. You can then zoom in to various parts of the model and save each of them as a separate view. You will quickly learn to appreciate both the convenience of switching between views by simply activating them in the Views palette and the substantial time savings that will accrue.

 Make it a habit to save your most frequently used views in the Views palette, even if they are simple planar views such as Top, Front, and so on.

5.4 Creating Customized Views: The Cone of Vision

In Section 5.2, we saw what seemed to be a vast assortment of predefined viewing angles in different modes such as Axonometric, Isometric, and Oblique. However, even these might often seem to be insufficient or too limiting. You would like to create your own views in which you have full control over where you are and what you are looking at in your modeling world. In a detailed building model, for instance, you will almost certainly want to generate interior views of the building, which would be practically impossible to arrive at using predefined views. Generating such customized views, which let you see your modeling world from any desired angle, is done in form•Z using the Cone Of Vision feature. Mentioned so often since the beginning of this exercise, we are going to be working with it at last!

Figure 3.34

The Edit Cone Of Vision environment.

■ Switch to an Axonometric view. From the View menu, select the very last option, Edit Cone Of Vision. You will be transported to a completely new environment in which the graphics window gets divided into four smaller windows (see Figure 3.34). Three of these windows show the top, front, and right side planar views of the model and are used to manipulate the parameters of the view. They are referred to as the *modification windows*, and only one of them can be active at a time to modify the viewing parameters. The fourth window in the top right-hand corner redraws the actual view after each change of parameter, enabling the desired view to be generated interactively. This window is called the *preview area*.

■ Notice the set of window tools in the lower left corner of the Cone Of Vision environment. These are the same window tools that you find in the modeling environment; here, they are used to control the graphic environment of the active modification window. You can zoom in or out, scroll, use the various kinds of snapping options, and so on.

The Cone Of Vision environment provides control over all the view parameters and lets them be graphically manipulated to obtain desired views. These parameters, which appear in all the three modification windows, are illustrated in Figure 3.35 in the top view window.

The parameters you will most frequently manipulate are the *eye point* and the *center of interest*. The segment connecting the two is the *line of sight*. There is also a *light beam* connecting the *light source* to a *light target*. There can be many such light sources, as you will see in the Lights exercise in Workshop 5. For now, just ignore the light beam and make sure that you do not mistake it for the line of sight. The *view angle* and the *view spin* parameters respectively determine how much you see and in what angle from the vertical. Finally, the front and back clipping planes—referred to as the *hither* and *yon* planes respectively—can be adjusted to prevent objects in front of or beyond a certain plane from appearing in the view. They are especially useful in generating sections or sectional perspectives, as shown in Figure 3.38.

■ To obtain a customized view, you need to make simultaneous adjustments to these parameters in all the three modification windows. An example is shown in Figure 3.36. You will find that certain adjustments can be more conveniently made in specific windows. Horizontal positions, for instance, are best adjusted in the top window, which is active by default. Simply move the eye point and the center of interest individually, by clicking and dragging, to the desired locations along the XY plane. Alternately, you can click and drag on the line of sight, which will move both the eye point and the center of interest.

Figure 3.35

The Cone Of Vision parameters, illustrated in the top modification window.

Figure 3.36

A customized view, gene-
rated by manipulating the
appropriate parameters in
all the three modification
windows.

▣ On the other hand, the heights of the eye point and the center of interest can be adjusted only in
the two lower elevation windows. Activate either one of these by clicking on it. Then adjust the z
coordinates of both points until you see the view you are aiming for in the preview area.

▣ Experiment with changes in the other parameters too—view angle, spin, and clipping planes—
and observe the changes in the resulting view. The clipping planes can be pulled in or out by
dragging them from their sides. Dragging their corners, on the other hand, changes the view spin
but not the position of the plane. The view angle can be changed by dragging the lines connecting
the front and back clipping planes, towards or away from the line of sight.

5.5   The Cone Of Vision Menu

▣ The preview image in Figure 3.36 is in the Surface Render display mode, whereas what you are
seeing in your window is probably a Wire Frame display. You can switch to any other kind of
display mode by selecting it from the Cone Of Vision menu, the only menu that is accessible from
within this environment. You can get to it by clicking anywhere in the title bar of the Cone Of
Vision window (see Figure 3.37). If you try and click on any of the other menus above the title bar,
you will hear a beeping sound indicating an error.

▣ Let us proceed to explore the extensive set of options in the Cone Of Vision menu. Undo and Redo
in the first group work in the usual manner, letting you undo and redo any changes you made to
your viewing parameters. The second group contains six display modes for the image in the preview
area, which are identical to those in the regular modeling environment.

▣ The third group consists of two options that can be turned on (indicated by a √ sign) or off. Turn
the Perspective option on to see your view in perspective mode. Do the same to the Clip Hither/
Yon option, which will activate the clipping action of the hither and yon planes. Now move the
clipping planes in various ways, and you will see how you can literally "chop off" parts of your
model, preventing them from appearing in the view. For a building model in which the interior
has been modeled, this is a great technique for generating sectional perspectives almost
instantaneously, as shown in Figure 3.38.

Figure 3.37

Accessing the Cone Of Vision menu in the Cone Of Vision environment.

■ The first three options in the fourth group of the Cone Of Vision menu allow you to reset the view angle, view spin, and clipping plane parameters to the original values—the ones they had when you entered the Cone Of Vision environment. This is useful if modifications made to these parameters ultimately prove to be unsatisfactory.

Figure 3.38

Generating a sectional perspective of a building model by appropriately positioning the clipping planes and activating the Clip Hither/Yon option.

▣ Align & Scale Views is another very useful option. It will zoom in or out all the three modification windows, such that the axes in all of them are aligned with one another, and all the objects fit in the windows and are displayed in the same scale. This is useful to do from time to time because the windows get de-synchronized quite rapidly as you zoom in, out, and scroll through them independently.

▣ The last option in the fourth group, Window Setup, invokes the same dialog that you used for setting up the graphics window in Section 2.1 of Workshop 2. It is a good idea to use it at least for turning off the grid display in the modification windows, particularly if it is too dense, since it interferes with how well you can see and adjust the viewing parameters. This was done for all the Cone Of Vision figures illustrated so far, starting with Figure 3.35.

▣ Move on to look at the fifth group of the Cone Of Vision menu. Save View in this group is identical to the same command you encountered earlier in the modeling environment. Once you have generated a desired view, you can save it using Save View; you can then proceed to generate and save additional views, all *without* leaving the Cone Of Vision environment. All the views saved in this manner will appear in your Views palette once you exit this mode and return to the graphics window. The next command in the fifth group, Views, invokes the same Views dialog that is accessible through the Views palette. You can use it to delete or sort views, or to switch to another view while remaining in the Cone Of Vision environment.

▣ The sixth group of the Cone Of Vision menu has three commands. The first one, Display Detail, opens up a dialog that lets you choose the level of detail in which objects will be displayed, both in the modification windows as well as in the preview area. If your modeling world is large and complex, it is advisable to choose a lower level of detail; this will save the time involved in regenerating windows each time a parameter is changed. The next command in the sixth group, View Parameters, is a crucial one and is discussed in detail in the next section. And as for the Sun Position command, don't worry about it for now—we will be working with it in Workshop 5.

▣ Before proceeding to the next section, go over all the Cone Of Vision menu options once again, familiarizing yourself well with how they work. Manipulate the various view parameters and generate some interesting views of your modeling world, saving them as you go along. When you are ready to exit the Cone Of Vision environment, select the last option in its menu, Close Cone Of Vision, or simply click on the close button of the Cone Of Vision window. This will return you to the graphics window, and you will see all the views you had saved within the Cone Of Vision environment listed in the Views palette. You can now switch to any of them by activating them in the usual manner.

5.6 The View Parameters Dialog

▣ There are various means of invoking the View Parameters dialog. You can select the View Parameters command from the Cone Of Vision menu, or from the View menu in the regular modeling environment. You can also double-click on a view in the Views palette, click on the Edit button in the Views dialog for a selected view, or select any of the view types from the View menu with the option key (Mac) or Ctrl+Shift keys (PC) pressed. The View Parameters dialog lets you fine-tune your viewing parameters by numerical input, and is thus a good supplement to the graphical input you used in the Cone Of Vision mode. If this dialog is invoked for a saved view, the View Name will be displayed and all options will be active. For an unsaved view, the View Name, Camera View, and Animation options are deactivated. Figure 3.39 shows the View Parameters dialog for a saved view.

Figure 3.39

The View Parameters dialog, showing the parameters of the view depicted in Figure 3.40-a.

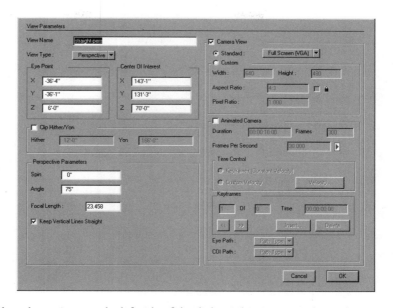

■ Let us first explore the options on the left side of the dialog. The View Type shows the type of view, and also allows you to select a different view type from the popup list. The Eye Point, Center Of Interest, and Clip Hither/Yon options are common to all view types and their exact values can be numerically specified. In the lower left part of the dialog, the parameters specific to the selected view type are displayed. Thus, for an axonometric view, the Spin and Angle values are listed here, while a perspective view has an additional Focal Length value, along with an option to Keep Vertical Lines Straight. The focal length and viewing angle parameters are correlated, so a change in one will automatically update the other. Together, they represent the viewable area of a camera's lens. If the Keep Vertical Lines Straight option is selected, the perspective view will keep all the vertical lines parallel to the Z axis instead of converging them. The difference is illustrated in Figure 3.40.

Figure 3.40

The same perspective view, shown with and without activating the Keep Vertical Lines Straight option.

■ In the right half of the dialog are the Camera View and Animated Camera sections, which are activated only for a saved view. We will study the Animation parameters in detail when we work with animations in Workshop 7, so ignore them for now. Go ahead and select the Camera View option. When you do this, the current view becomes a camera view instead of a regular view. The difference between the two is only seen in a Shaded Render or RenderZone display. In a camera view, the resolution is determined by various parameters which simulate those in a real-life camera. In contrast, the resolution in a regular view is dependent upon the size of the graphics window and is set in the Image Options dialog, which we will explore in Section 1.3 of Workshop 5. To specify the camera settings for a camera view, use one of the standards available in the Standard popup list, or set the parameters individually using the Custom option.

■ Make some modifications to various parameters in the View Parameters dialog for the current view, and see the resulting changes in the graphics window or in the Cone Of Vision environment, wherever you happen to be. One simple instance of where it can be useful to specify an exact numeric value for a parameter is in setting the Z value of the Eye Point to 6'-0" (as in the dialog in Figure 3.39), so as to position it at "human eye level" in a building model (as in the views in Figure 3.40). It is also usually easier to specify exact numeric values for Spin, Angle, Focal Length, etc., rather than set them graphically.

5.7 Setting, Navigating, and Walking Through Views

There are four more view-related tools located in the last window tool palette at the bottom of the graphics window. In this section, we will work with three of these—Set View, Navigate View, and Walkthrough. The fourth tool—Match View—works best with a form•Z feature called Underlay, both of which will be covered together in the next section.

■ Let us start with Set View, which is conceptually the simplest. Activate any of the views saved in your Views palette, then select the Set View tool (W-Tool:8,1). Click on any point in the graphics window. Now move the cursor and you will find that the view gets rotated about its center, with the direction of rotation following that of the mouse movement. Clicking the mouse a second time stops the rotation of the view.

■ Notice that the Set View tool uses the same Continuous Window Tool Control feature as some of the Zoom tools you have seen—all other tools are grayed out when this tool is active, allowing you to apply it repeatedly for manipulating the current view. Thus, you can execute more view rotations with additional mouse clicks in the same fashion. To stop using the tool, simply click on it again or on any one of the deactivated tools, or press the Esc key, and the tool palette display will be restored to normal.

■ The Set View tool can also be used with some modifier keys to move closer or further away from the center of the scene. The effect can be properly seen only in a perspective view, so switch to such a view if your current view is not a perspective one. Then reapply the Set View tool, only this time keep the option key (Mac) or Ctrl+Shift keys (PC) pressed. You will now find that as you move the cursor up, you are moving closer to the scene, and as you move the cursor down, you are moving further away from the scene. As soon as you release these modifier keys, the regular view rotations you saw earlier are performed.

■ Perform some more view manipulations with the Set View tool until you get a sense of how it works. As you can see, it is very useful for quickly manipulating views without having to get into the Cone Of Vision mode. Keep in mind that you can save the new view as a separate entry in the Views palette—you will then have instant access to both the original and the modified views.

Figure 3.41

The navigation marquee invoked by the Navigate View tool, and its various controls.

For more complex manipulation of views outside the Cone Of Vision environment, you can use the next tool on the same tool palette, **Navigate View**. This lets you change many of the viewing parameters interactively, and not just rotate the view. The operation of this tool is again best seen in perspective mode, so switch to a perspective view before experimenting with it. Keep in mind, however, that it works for all types of views.

■ As soon as you select the Navigate View tool, a navigation marquee appears in the center of the graphics window, as shown in Figure 3.41. The marquee is made up of four circles and a number of icons, the functionalities of which are also illustrated in the figure. Move the cursor near each one of the controls indicated, and see how it changes depending upon the control. Each of these controls represents a different view manipulation parameter.

■ To activate a control, position the cursor on it and click. As you now drag the mouse, the view will change depending upon the type of control selected and the associated viewing parameter. Another click of the mouse will terminate the action of that control. The navigation marquee, however, is still displayed, allowing you to continue manipulating the view in different ways by selecting the appropriate controls. Thus the Navigate View tool also uses the Continuous Window Tool Control feature, just like the Set View tool, and its operation can be terminated in a similar fashion.

■ Let us briefly review the five basic types of controls of the navigation marquee. The first is Depth Pan, active when the cursor is inside the innermost circle of the marquee. After the initial click, moving the cursor vertically upwards has the effect of moving you closer into the scene, while moving the cursor vertically downwards moves you away from the scene. Essentially, the eye point and the center of interest are being moved here *along* the line of sight.

■ In contrast, the second control, Pan, moves the eye point and the center of interest *perpendicular* to the line of sight. This control is active when the cursor is positioned between the innermost and second circles. The panning is restricted to the horizontal direction if the cursor is close to the horizontal axis and to the vertical direction if it is close to the vertical axis; it is unrestricted if away from both the axes. The cursor icon changes, based on its position, to reflect these three kinds of panning.

■ The third control, Rotate, is active when the cursor is positioned between the second and outermost circles. It has the effect of rotating the eye point, or the center of interest, or both, about the line of sight, depending upon if the cursor is close to the outermost circle, the second circle, or between the outermost and second circles respectively. In the third situation, the relative rotation of the eye point and the center of interest depends upon the distance of the cursor from the bounding circles—clicking on the middle (third) circle between them will rotate both the eye point and the center of interest equally about the line of sight. The Rotate control of the Navigate View tool is thus a little more involved than the Set View tool, which is only capable of rotating the eye point about the center of interest. The rotation produced by the Rotate control can also be restricted to only the horizontal or vertical directions, if desired, by positioning the cursor close to the horizontal or vertical axes, just like the Pan control. The cursor icon changes to reflect the three kinds of directional rotations in a similar fashion.

◼ The fourth control, Spin, is activated by clicking on either one of the two Spin icons located outside the outermost circle along the horizontal axis of the marquee. Moving the mouse in a circular direction then causes the view to spin around the line of sight.

◼ The last control, Zoom, is similarly activated by clicking on either one of the two Zoom icons located outside the outermost circle along the vertical axis. Moving the cursor to the left then decreases the viewing angle, zooming the view in; in contrast, a rightward movement increases the viewing angle, zooming the view out.

You can see that Navigate View is quite a sophisticated view manipulation tool. Using it can be somewhat confusing at first, but persevere until you have a better understanding of how it works. It is, of course, no match for the simplicity and intuitiveness of the Cone Of Vision feature, but just like Set View, it does have the advantage of not requiring you to exit the modeling environment to obtain a view.

The next view-related tool in the eighth window tool palette, after Navigate View, is the Walkthrough tool. As obvious from its name, this tool is used for obtaining an interactive walkthrough of the scene displayed in the modeling window. Such a walkthrough is often useful for getting a more realistic feel of the modeling project. Since perspective views are the only ones which can simulate the feeling of depth as perceived by the human eye, the Walkthrough tool is most effective when used with such views.

◼ Switch to a perspective view and activate the Walkthrough tool. This will invoke a small marquee made up of a central circle and horizontal and vertical arrows, as shown in Figure 3.42-a. You can see that it is far simpler than the marquee you encountered for the Navigate View tool. It also works a little differently. The movement of the cursor does not directly manipulate the view; instead, the position of the cursor with respect to the horizontal and vertical axes triggers a certain operation, the *speed* of which is determined by the distance of the cursor from the center of the marquee. The greater the distance, the faster the speed. Try it out. First click at the center or close to it, then move away. The view changes rapidly as you move further away from the center, and doesn't stop changing even if you stop moving the cursor. Move the cursor back to the center of the marquee, and the view stops changing. You can continue to change the view by moving the cursor out of the center again, or click to terminate the operation.

◼ Notice that bringing the cursor back to the center of the marquee does not restore the original view; it simply halts further modification of the view. Hopefully, you have the view saved in the Views palette from where you can restore it easily, if needed.

◼ So how does this tool enable you to walk through a scene? The answer to this lies in the various operations which can be triggered by moving the cursor, in combination with some modifier keys, horizontally or vertically away from the center of the marquee. These operations are illustrated in Figure 3.42-b. Experiment with each one of them until you get a sense of how the tool works.

Figure 3.42

The marquee invoked by the Walkthrough tool, and the various operations that can be performed in combination with modifier keys on both the Mac and the PC.

(a)

(b)

5.8   Underlays and the Match View Tool

The last tool in the eighth window tool palette, Match View, is used in conjunction with a background image, letting you match a perspective view of the model with the perspective lines of the image. It is extremely useful when you want to situate your model in an appropriate background and then render it—you would obviously want a realistic fit between the model and the background.

form•Z lets you place a background image in the graphics window in the form of an *underlay*. In this section, we will first see how to place an underlay, and then how to use Match View to align a perspective view of the model with the underlay image.

▣   Open an existing project file for which you have a suitable background image. Otherwise, continue to use the building model project and locate any image to use as the background, even if it is unrelated to the building. Scan a photograph if you don't have access to any collection of image files. You must ensure that the file is in a format recognizable to form•Z: PICT, TIFF, JPEG, Targa, and so on.

▣   Go to Windows > Underlay. The Underlay dialog shown in Figure 3.43 will be invoked. Check the Show Underlay box to activate all the options in the dialog. Then click on the Select Underlay File button—this will invoke the standard File Open dialog for your operating system. Use it to locate and select the image file you want to use for the background. Leave the other options in the Underlay dialog as they are for now, and click on OK to exit the dialog.

▣   Back in the window, you will find that the selected image now appears in the background instead of the usual background color (Figure 3.44). Perform various operations such as zooming in and out, scrolling, changing the window size, switching to a different view, and so on, and you will find that the underlay always fills up the entire window.

▣   If the proportions of your window happen to be different from those of the image, the image will look distorted. To avoid this problem, invoke the Underlay dialog again and select the option, Match Image Size To Underlay Size. Your graphics window will now be resized to match the size and proportions of the underlay image; thereafter, you will only be able to reduce its size but not change its proportions. This is generally a useful option to leave turned on.

Figure 3.43

The Underlay dialog, with the Show Underlay option activated.

◼ Now switch to one of the planar views in the second group of the View menu and select the Axonometric mode. You will find that the underlay is no longer seen. If you have an image that you want to use as a reference in planar views—for instance, the site plan for a building—you would naturally prefer to see the underlay in a planar view rather than in a 3D view. To do so, invoke the Underlay dialog again and switch from the default selection of In 3D Views to In Projection Views. Choose a different image file, if necessary. You can also specify the Scale at which the image should appear in the window, its Origin along both directions, and whether the specified origin should be placed in the center of the window or at the lower left corner. If you now return to the graphics window, the underlay will be visible in all the planar views following your scale and origin specifications, but not in any of the non-planar views.

◼ The only remaining option in the Underlay dialog, which applies to both 3D and planar views, determines whether the underlay should be displayed above or below the grid and axis. The default is below, which is fine as long as you continue to use the grid and axis for reference while you are modeling. However, when you want to generate renderings in which the underlay should be seen but not the grid and axis, you should activate the Display On Top Of Grid And Axis option.

Now that we have looked at underlays, let us see how the Match View tool comes in handy when a model needs to be aligned with an underlay image.

◼ Set the Underlay option back to In 3D Views and select its sub-option, Match Image Size To Underlay Size. Switch to a perspective view of your model, and select Edit Cone Of Vision from the View menu. You will find that the underlay now appears below the model in the preview area of the Cone Of Vision environment. You can try and align the model with the underlay by adjusting the various view parameters, as you learned to do in Section 5.4. While not impossible, this can be quite a tedious process. Fortunately, form•Z provides you with a convenient shortcut—the Match View tool.

◼ Exit the Cone Of Vision environment, and make sure you are still in Perspective mode. Select the Match View tool (W-Tool:8,4). This will take you into the Match View *edit mode* in which all other tools in the modeling and window palettes are grayed out. At the same time, a *match rectangle* appears at the edges of the reference plane grid, with its vertices highlighted by little black boxes indicating that they can be edited (see Figure 3.44).

Figure 3.44

The Match View edit mode, with the selected underlay image in the background.

◼ Click on one of the vertices of the match rectangle and drag it to another position. This will change the shape of the rectangle, which in turns reshapes the reference grid and causes the perspective view to be changed. You can also click and drag the sides of the rectangle to reshape it—the perspective view is redrawn to match it. Keep moving the points and sides of the rectangle in this manner until the perspective view of your model seems aligned with that of the underlay image. When you are satisfied with the view, double-click to exit the Match View mode and save your new view in the Views palette.

◼ The Match View tool takes some time getting used to, but it eventually gets easier and is more convenient than the Cone Of Vision method for generating a properly aligned view of the model with respect to an underlay image. It works best if the image has a rectangular shape somewhere which you can use as a reference for aligning the match rectangle. If you have such a shape in your image, create a new reference plane in the model which, in the final rendering, has to be positioned close to or on top of that shape. Make sure to activate *this* reference plane before selecting the Match View tool; you will now find it much easier to properly align the model with the underlay image.

◼ You can modify the default behavior of the Match View tool by using it with the following keys: Shift to temporarily suspend the regeneration of the view that usually happens after each change, very useful for a complex model; control (Mac) or Ctrl+Alt (PC) for completely moving the match rectangle; option (Mac) or Ctrl+Shift (PC) for moving the view along the reference plane; and finally, control+shift (Mac) or Ctrl+Alt+Shift (PC) along with a mouse click to reset the match rectangle to coincide with the grid, if it has gotten displaced (which it does from time to time).

◼ By default, most of the display modes show the project background made up of the grid, axis, and underlay. For Shaded Render and RenderZone, however, the background is not displayed by default— you need to actually go and activate this option in the dialogs of these displays. You already learned to do this for the Shaded Render display in Section 2.4; you will study the RenderZone display options in Workshop 5. If just the underlay is to be displayed in these modes, you can turn off the grid and axes displays from the Windows menu, or invoke the Underlay dialog and check the Display On Top Of Grid And Axis option.

◼ You have seen how underlays can be useful for rendering and to provide reference points in modeling. When not in use, you should turn off the underlay display so that it does not distract you from the task at hand. To do this, simply deselect the Show Underlay option in the Underlay dialog, and your window background will be restored to its normal color.

5.9   Associated Windows, Tile Windows, and Window Frames

Now that you have learned how to create and use multiple views in many different ways, let us conclude this exercise by looking at three related utilities that can enhance your modeling speed and efficiency.

▣   Go to Windows > New Model Window. A second window of the same project will open up, a status that is reflected by the name of the window in its title bar. You can change the view in this window to a different view of the project. Such a window is called an *associated window*, since it is a different window of the same project. You can open up several such associated windows and set them to different view angles or zoom levels, giving you the ability to quickly observe your model from different points of view or at different scales and levels of detail. You can also use different underlay files for different windows.

▣   Only one of such multiple associated windows can be the active window at a time, but the changes made to the model in the active window will be concurrently reflected in all the windows. All the associated windows of a project are listed in the last group of the Windows menu. The active window is indicated by a √ mark. To switch from one window to another, simply select it from this menu or click on it if it is visible on the screen.

▣   There are a special type of associated windows called *tile windows*, which lie side by side instead of overlapping with each another. Go to Windows > Tile Windows and select Open from its submenu. Four smaller windows automatically open up and position themselves next to one another, each occupying one quarter of the default form•Z window size. The setup is similar to the Cone Of Vision environment. By default, three of the tile windows display planar views—Top, Right, and Back—while the fourth displays a 3D view. You can choose a different view for any window, either from the View menu or the Views palette. Each tile window comes with its own set of window tools for manipulating its graphic environment, and can be resized, closed, etc., just like any regular window.

▣   The Tile Windows submenu has some additional options that can be useful. Arrange goes about rearranging the windows if you have been moving them around. Align & Scale Views synchronizes the views in all the tile windows, in the same way as it was done for the three modification windows in the Cone Of Vision environment. And finally, the Close option closes all the open tile windows in one step.

Tile windows can be a great mode to work in if you have a large monitor. You can create or modify an object by seeing it simultaneously from many different angles, which is always a great help in visualizing a 3D world on an essentially 2D screen. Tile windows, however, do not allow you to continue a modeling operation started in one window in another window. form•Z, however, does have such a feature in the form of *window frames*. You were briefly introduced to the concept of frames in Section 3 of the Introduction. Let us now see how to work with them.

▣   Go to Windows > Window Frames. This will divide the currently active graphics window into four parts or "frames," each one of which is set to a different view by default, just like tile windows (see Figure 3.45). The number of a frame and the view it is set to is indicated at the top of each frame. The active frame is indicated by a red border; any other frame can be similarly activated by clicking on it. Once a frame is active, you can change its view or perform any part of a modeling operation in it. Go ahead and activate each frame in turn, setting them to views that you have saved in your Views palette.

Figure 3.45

Working with window frames.

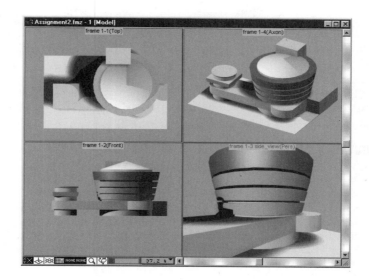

■ We will now see how to continue a modeling operation from one frame to another. Activate a frame which is set to the Top view or to a 3D view, and use the Cube tool to draw the base of a cube in this frame. Do not specify the height of the cube just yet. Instead, take the mouse over to some of the other frames and see how a frame gets activated simply by positioning the mouse over it— you don't even have to click. Go to a frame with an elevation view—Front, Right, etc.—where you can now conveniently specify the height of the cube. Perform some more modeling operations using multiple frames in this manner, until you are comfortable with the technique.

■ You do not have to stick with the default sizes and layout of the frames. To resize a frame, first make it active; then click on and drag any of its edges in the desired direction. To close a frame, drag one of its edges so that it touches the opposite edge. If you carry out this click-and-drag operation while pressing the option key (Mac) or Ctrl+Shift keys (PC), the frame will be split into two frames. You can continue to subdivide frames in this manner up to a maximum of 10, giving you plenty of views of your modeling world to work in simultaneously!

■ When you no longer need to work with frames, go to Windows > Window Frames once again. This option will be deselected and all the frames will disappear, returning you to your original graphics window.

EXERCISE 6

Specifying Your Preferences

Each one of you will end up working in form•Z with "settings" that *you* individually feel most comfortable with and which are best suited to the projects you are working on. Settings here refers to aspects such as working units, window setup, project colors for various interface components, choice of styles in the Surface Styles palette, dialog options for various modeling and window tools and menu commands, open palettes and their positions on the screen, and so on.

You have already learned how to modify all these settings to suit your modeling requirements. However, you must have noticed that each time you open a new project, most of these settings revert back to the default form•Z values. It can be quite tedious having to reset these for every new project to the values that you prefer. form•Z, therefore, lets you store your preferred settings in a *preference file*, which will then be applied to every new project you subsequently create in that session. You can also specify *your* preference file as the default, so that your saved settings are loaded and used each time form•Z is launched. Let us see how to do this.

6.1 Creating and Using Preference Files

◾ Open the project you created for Exercise 1 in which you changed the default project colors and created additional surface styles. If you did not save that project, open a new project and make similar changes. Also, go through dialogs such as Working Units, Window Setup, and so on, and make some changes to the default settings they contain. The aim is to create a project in which the settings are visibly different from the default form•Z settings. Save the file after you have completed this task but do not close it. Close any other open projects that you may have.

◾ Open a new modeling project by going to File > New[Model]. As you would expect, the second project has the default form•Z settings rather than the settings you defined for the first project. Leave it as it is for now.

◾ You will now save the settings of the first project in a preference file. Make sure that it is the active project by clicking on its window or selecting it from the Windows menu. Then go to Edit > Preferences. The Preferences dialog will be invoked (Figure 3.46 shows a modified version). It contains a large number of options, which we will look at in due course. For now, simply click on the Save Preferences button, and specify a file name and location. An extension of ".zpf" is automatically given to the file, indicating that it is a form•Z preference file. Let's say you gave the name My_Pref1—your preference file will be called My_Pref1.zpf.

◾ Open another modeling project by going to File > New[Model]. You will find that the settings of this project are indeed the same as the ones you just saved in My_Pref1.zpf—the project colors, the styles in the Surface Styles palette, and all the dialog options will be identical to those in the first project. This holds true for any new project you now create within the current session of form•Z.

You are not restricted to a single preference file only—any number of preference files can be created from different projects in the same manner. This is useful because different categories of projects often require different settings; for instance, the Working Units settings for urban design projects will be quite different from those for furniture and product design projects. You can create separate preference files for each category of project you work with. A preference file is just like any other regular file, form•Z or otherwise, which you can copy across disks, move, delete, and so on.

◾ Let us see what happens in a new session of form•Z. Quit the program and restart it. You will find that new modeling projects are created with the default settings rather than with the ones you saved. This happens even if you open up the original project file whose settings you had saved in My_Pref1.zpf.

◾ To make form•Z *always* use the settings in My_Pref1.zpf, even after you have quit and restarted the program, open the Preferences dialog and choose the Preference File option for the System Options From parameter. Choose the same option for the Project Options From parameter. This tells form•Z to always load the settings from a preference file rather than its own defaults. You also need to specify what this preference file is. To do this, click on the Load Preferences button and select the file, My_Pref1.zpf (as shown in Figure 3.46). All subsequent sessions of form•Z will now use your stored settings when new projects are created.

■ Not only can you create different preference files for different purposes, form•Z also comes with its *own* set of multiple preference files which you can use whenever appropriate. To access these files, invoke the Preferences dialog again and click on the Load Preferences button. In the File Open dialog, locate the form•Z main application folder, and within it, the form•Z Preferences folder. This contains six preference files, differentiated by the type and scale of the working units as well as by the window setup. Load each one of these preference files in turn, and open a new project to see what the corresponding settings are. For instance, the preference file Lrg_Engl.zpf has the Unit Type set to English, the Base Unit to Feet, and a large grid module of 192'. Thus, it can be conveniently used for large urban design projects.

Figure 3.46

Instructing form•Z to use the settings in the saved preference file, My_Pref1.zpf, instead of the defaults.

WORKSHOP 3

6.2   Other Preferences

The Preferences dialog shown in Figure 3.46 contains a number of other options that determine how form•Z operates. Some of these appear directly in the dialog, while others have to be accessed using buttons. Let us start with the first category.

■ The options for At Start Up Open and Project File Options are self-explanatory and you should go through them to determine if you would like to change them, based on your mode of working and the disk space available to you. As you can see, a backup file is created by default for every project; it can be identified by the ".bak" extension. It is useful to retain the Keep Backup option, so that if you inadvertently lose or delete the original project file, you can use the backup file instead.

On the PC, you must change the extension of the backup file from ".bak" to ".fmz" on your desktop before you can open it in form•Z. On the Mac, you are not required to do this.

Figure 3.47

The Auto Save Options dialog.

◾ Turn your attention to the next four checkbox options. You will recall the Continuous Window Tool Control mode from your encounters with the Zoom and View window tools; you can deselect this option if you are not comfortable with it. The Save Prompts In TEXT File option, if checked, will save all the ongoing content of the Prompts palette to a text file called form•Z Prompts in the form•Z application folder; this can be useful for future reference. The Store New Image Elements In Project option applies only to drafting projects which will be covered in the Appendix. As for the Always Open File Format Options Dialogs option, it is better to leave it turned on, unless you are repeatedly saving form•Z files into a different file format using the same settings.

◾ The remaining two options in the left side of the dialog refer to the zoom percentage and memory availability values that are displayed at the end of the window tool palette by default. You can choose to turn these off if not required. The memory can also be displayed in the form of a "meter" by choosing that option from the accompanying popup menu.

◾ Next, click on the Auto Save button to invoke the Auto Save Options dialog (Figure 3.47). Here you can activate the Auto Save feature and specify how it should operate—how often the saving should happen, and whether it should be saved over the open project file or saved as a separate copy. The second option will take more disk space, but it is useful because it allows you to go back and undo any operations in the original file; this would not be possible if the project was saved automatically, unless you had activated the Save Undos In Project option in the Undo Options dialog, as you learned in Section 3.3 of Workshop 1. You can even go one step further and select the Incremental File Names option in the Auto Save Options dialog, which will create a separate project file for *each* automatic save. Do this only if you have plenty of disk space to spare!

◾ Get back to the Preferences dialog and click on the Dialogs button. This invokes a dialog where you can set the size of the Preview Dialogs, which are dialogs giving you a preview of how a particular operation will be performed. You will be encountering the first of such dialogs in the next workshop. The next option, Use Dialog Buffer, applies only to the Mac and is deactivated in the PC version. Dialog buffering refers to the process of allocating some memory for storing screen information that is hidden from view whenever a dialog is opened. This makes regeneration of the screen faster than it would be if dialog buffering was turned off. It is on by default. You can also specify the amount of memory you wish to allocate for dialog buffering. It is a good policy to activate dialog buffering whenever you have the memory for it, but turn it off for memory-intensive tasks like shadow calculations and rendering. Finally in Dialog Preferences, you can choose between an automatic and custom option for Dialog Centering.

■ The next Preferences option, Fonts, lets you specify the default fonts that will be used in form•Z. This will be relevant when you work with 2D and 3D text in Workshop 7 and the drafting module in the Appendix, so you can skip it for now. Likewise, the Textures and Radiosity preferences will become relevant when you deal with these topics in Workshop 5.

■ The Scratch Disk button invokes the Scratch Disk Preferences dialog, where you can specify the location of the various temporary files that are automatically created by form•Z. These include files containing the Undo and Redo records, rendering information, and other calculations for an open project, as well as the scratch file that is created if the program crashes unexpectedly. It is a good idea to set a Custom location for these files, particularly if you are working in a networked environment, so that in the event of a crash, you know exactly where to locate the scratch file. When you find it, give it a ".fmz" extension if that is missing, and you should be able to open it like any other form•Z file.

■ The Warnings button in the Preferences dialog leads you to several Warning Preferences, some of which you might like to turn off once you become proficient with the program and know what you are doing.

■ form•Z has an Open Recent option in the File menu that lists the last ten files opened by the program. It is a convenient shortcut for opening a file you have recently been working with. The Recent Files button in the Preferences dialog is related to this option. It invokes a dialog where you can change the maximum number of files from the default value of 10. There are also a couple of other options related to how the file names are displayed and sorted. Check them out.

■ And finally in the Preferences dialog, you can change the way your Cursor looks while an operation is being executed. Be sure to choose the one you like best, since you will sometimes find yourself staring at it for an extended period of time while form•Z goes about its business! (Keep in mind that modeling, rendering, and animating complex objects can't help but be a time-consuming affair.)

On that philosophical note, let us end the exercises and move on to the assignment for this workshop.

ASSIGNMENT 3

An Item of Furniture

■ *Model any piece of furniture such as a table, chair, desk, cabinet, etc., in detail and to proper scale. Do not choose something which is too simple!*

The actual exercise of modeling the chair shown here will now be demonstrated step by step. It is a variation of the famous "red and blue chair" by Gerrit Rietveld. You can refer to the form•Z files for this assignment in the Assignments > Workshop3 folder of the accompanying CD-ROM. A color rendering of the project is in the Assignment3.tif file in the same folder.

WORKSHOP 3

Setup

Open a new form•Z project. We first need to set its **Working Units** appropriate to the scale and type of the project, which is an item of furniture. Set the **Base Unit** to **Inches** rather than **Feet** under the **English** measurement system, the **Numeric Accuracy** to 1/16", and the **Angle Accuracy** to 0.5°.

Change also the **Window Setup**. Have a grid module of 1' in all directions with 4 subdivisions.

◀ Step 1

We will start by constructing the front legs of the chair. Create a block with dimensions of 7/8" along X, 3 1/2" along Y, and 23" along Z, starting from the origin [0,0,0] as shown. Create this as a facetted object (with the **Rectangle** tool in **3D Extruded Solid** mode) rather than as a primitive (with the **Cube** tool), since we have to cut out a notch in it later.

Step 2

With coordinate mode set to relative and self-copy modifier set to **One Copy**, apply the **Move** tool to the block and specify the **Move** coordinates as [20 7/8]. This will duplicate the block at a distance of 20" from the original block along the X axis.

Both the blocks have been created in the default layer. Change the name of this layer in the **Layers** palette to **front legs**.

◀ Step 3

The next step is to model the front support. Create a new layer called **front support** and make it active. Create a block of 22 1/2" by 7/8" and a height of 3 5/8" anywhere on the XY plane. This has to be positioned appropriately with respect to the legs.

Draw a temporary line connecting the facing points of the legs as shown.

Step 4

Move the line vertically upwards by a distance of 3 1/4".

Step 5

Use Move again with Midpoint snap to position the front support on this line, centered between the two legs. Its front face should lie on the same plane as the front faces of the legs.

Use pick parade to select the temporary line coinciding with the front support and delete it.

Step 6

You now have to create two notches in the front legs for the support you just modeled. Activate the front legs layer. Use the Difference tool with the Status Of Objects set to Keep so that the front support is retained. Difference the support from each of the legs in turn. Then delete the original, un-notched legs which are retained after the operation. These will overlap with the notched legs, so select them carefully.

WORKSHOP 3

Step 7

The back legs are slightly more complicated and we will model them using reference planes. Turn off the front support layer, and create and activate a new layer called back legs. Create an arbitrary reference plane on one of the inside faces of the front legs, oriented as shown. Using the reference plane coordinates (by turning off the W switch in the Prompts palette), create a 7/8" polygonal slab on this plane, with the base points as follows (all in absolute mode):

> Pt #1: [0]
> Pt #2: [26 3/8]
> Pt #3: [26 3/8,2 7/8]
> Pt #4: [0,13 3/8]
> Pt #5: [c] (for close) or triple-click

Step 8

Define a second arbitrary plane passing through the top, inclined face of the polygonal slab you just modeled. Create a 2D surface on this plane whose dimensions are larger than the inclined face on all sides. Then move this 2D surface in the Z direction so that it lies 4 1/2" below the face as shown.

Step 9

Extrude the 2D surface in the opposite direction from the top face of the polygonal slab, such that it extends beyond the lower face of the slab. Let us call this new block a "temporary block."

Step 10

Set the Status Of Objects option of the Difference tool back to Ghost. Use this tool to subtract the temporary block from the polygonal slab. This will yield one of the back legs in its final form.

Use the Mirror tool in One Copy mode to create another back leg touching the inside face of the second front leg. The reference plane can now be set back to XY.

◁ Step 11

Next, we will add the triangular side supports to the front legs. Turn off the back legs layer as well, so that you can see only the front legs now. Create and activate a new layer called side supports. Since the triangular support is parallel to the ZX plane, we will use it instead of creating an arbitrary plane. With the Prompts palette set to absolute world coordinate mode, create a 3/4" thick slab with the following base point specification.

Pt #1: [0]

Pt #2: [0,0,-13 1/2]

Pt #3: [-6 5/8]

Pt #4: [c] (for close) or triple-click

Step 12

Use the Move tool in Self mode with Endpoint snap to move the newly created triangular block, such that it touches the top corner of the back face of the front leg as shown. Then use the Mirror tool in One Copy mode to make a mirror image copy of it for the other leg.

In the course of all these processes, keep saving your most frequently used views in the Views palette.

WORKSHOP 3

◁ **Step 13**

Next, we will move on to the seat. This is simply a 7/8" slab sitting on top of the inclined faces of the back legs. Turn off all layers except the back legs layer, and create and activate a new layer called seat. Create an arbitrary plane passing through the top face of one of the back legs as shown. Using reference plane coordinates, create a rectangular extrusion of base dimensions 20" by 18 1/8" and height 7/8", which fits exactly on top of the back legs as shown.

Step 14

The back of the chair relates to the seat, so we will model that next. Turn off all layers except seat. Create and activate a new layer called back. In the dialog of the 2D Enclosure tool, set the Justification option to Right and the Wall Width to 3/4". Switch to the Right view. Use the Single Line tool to create a line, the first point of which must snap to the lower, right endpoint of the seat. The second point should be numerically specified as [32 3/4",60°,0] by setting the Prompts palette to relative, polar coordinate mode (deselect the A and C boxes).

◁ **Step 15**

Switch to a non-planar view and extrude the double-line 2D object in a direction perpendicular to its surface, by a height equal to the width of the seat which is 20".

Step 16

Create a reference plane coinciding with the front face of the chair back as shown. Use it to move the back by a distance of 2" towards the front of the chair, i.e., in a direction perpendicular to the plane. In the Right view, it will now be seen cutting across the seat of the chair. Move the reference plane so that it passes through the new position of the front face of the chair back, or create a new one.

Step 17

The back is actually made up of three separate pieces: a central piece of width 10 1/2" and two side pieces of width 2 7/8", with a 3/4" gap between them. The side pieces are also 1 1/2" shorter than the central piece. With the help of the active arbitrary plane, create such a 2D pattern on the front face of the chair back, using a different color. You can switch to View > Plane Projection > Top to make this task easier.

Step 18

Use the 2D pattern to recreate the 3D blocks for the back, with the Rectangle tool in 3D Extruded Solid mode. The thickness of the blocks should be 3/4", oriented in the same direction as the original block. Delete the original block and 2D lines after you have finished creating the new blocks for the back. You can use Select By to easily select all the 2D lines that were created in a different color.

Finally, activate the seat layer, and subtract the blocks making up the back from the seat, in order to create the notches in it for the blocks. You will have to set Status Of Objects to Keep to retain the blocks, and keep deleting the original seat using pick parade each time the Difference operation is executed.

◁ **Step 19**

Now that the back is complete, we can add the back support. This is a simple block measuring 25 1/2" by 4" by 1", attached to the back of the chair. Turn off all layers except back, and create and activate a new layer called back support. Use the same arbitrary plane you had created for the back, and create a block of the required dimensions, starting at the origin.

Step 20

Use Midpoint snap to move the support so that it is now centrally located with respect to the back. Its front face must touch the back faces of the blocks making up the back of the chair.

◁ **Step 21**

Once this is done, simply move the back support by a relative distance of 14" upwards along the back surface of the chair. This would be along the +Y direction, if you have the same arbitrary reference plane shown in the illustration. Check the Right view to see if it is correctly positioned. The back support is now complete.

Step 22

Finally, we come to the most difficult part of the model—the arms. Turn off all the layers except side supports, and create and activate a new layer called arms. Define an arbitrary reference plane passing through the top face of the left side support as shown.

◁ **Step 23**

Move the origin of the arbitrary reference plane by a distance of 1" along the –X direction and 8" along the –Y direction. Make sure the W box in the Prompts palette is deselected when you make this move. Save the new plane in the Planes palette. Switch to View > Plane Projection > Top, and draw a 2D rectangle of size 8 3/4" by 30 7/8" positioned at the origin of the plane.

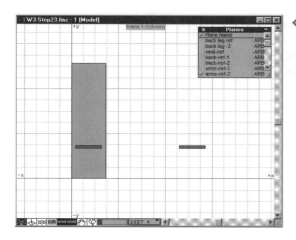

Step 24

Next, draw construction lines 3" inside from all the four sides of the rectangle. In addition, draw one construction line 12" inside from the side facing the front of the chair. Use these construction lines to create a single 2D shape for the arm of the chair, combining lines and arcs. A certain amount of approximation can be used for the gradual curve at the back. You will find the use of Intersection snap indispensable in creating the arcs for the rounded corners.

◁ **Step 25**

Delete the original rectangle and construction lines. Still in Top view, rotate the 2D arm surface by an angle of −11.5°, with the lower left corner of the side support selected as the center of rotation.

Step 26

Switch to a non-planar view and set the reference plane back to XY. Extrude the arm surface in the +Z direction by a distance of 7/8" to yield the 3D slab for the left arm.

◁ **Step 27**

Activate the back layer and use the Difference tool to create a notch in the arm where one of the back panels cuts into it. This completes one arm. Use the Mirror tool in One Copy mode to make a mirror image copy of it for the other arm. Switch to a different view to check if the result is accurate.

Finally, activate the back support layer and use the Difference tool to create a notch in the back support for each of the two arms where they cut into it.

Step 28

With that, the chair is complete. Turn on all the layers to see it in its entirety. Many colors were used to make the modeling of different parts easier, but you can now change the colors to suit a desired color scheme.

The only additional embellishment needed for your chair is for some of the edges to be rounded off. You can leave this for Workshop 4, when you will learn to use the Round tool.

Workshop 3

4

Enhancing Your Modeling Capabilities

In this workshop, you will be introduced to several new modeling tools. Most of these are located in the left and right columns of Row 5; the remaining are scattered across Rows 6, 8, and 12. The number of exercises in this workshop is thus somewhat larger, but the length of each exercise is also shorter, adding up to the same overall content as the other workshops.

You will start by learning how to create complex objects from simple 2D shapes, first by revolving them about an axis, and then by "sweeping" and "skinning" them along various paths. The remaining derivative tools on Row 5 will also be covered. You will then work with the powerful sectioning tools in form•Z, as well as model undulating landforms and terrains. Next, you will look at the processes of rounding object edges and corners, and transforming objects using draft angles. Finally, you will learn how to build up sophisticated configurations by attaching objects to each other in various ways, align and distribute objects, extend and trim them with respect to other objects, and position them along a path to generate interesting forms.

Going Round and Up and Down

In this exercise, we will look at four different tools based on the same principle: deriving objects by the operation of revolution about an axis. These objects fall into four categories—generic objects of revolution, helixes, bolts and screws, and spiral staircases—and we will explore the tools devoted to each one of them. Since we will be working with spiral staircases, it is also a good time to look at the Straight Stair tool, which is used for creating regular staircases in building models.

1.1   Generic Objects of Revolution

▣   Begin a new project and close all palettes except Prompts and Surface Styles. Turn Grid Snap on (W-Tool:4,1) so that your modeling is more precise. Then draw a 2D circle on the XY plane, not too far from the Y axis, but not intersecting or touching it either (see Figure 4.1-a).

▣   Select the Revolve tool (M-Tool:5b,1). You will be asked to first specify the *source shape*. This can be any 2D surface object, 2D enclosure, or a segment, outline, or face of an existing 2D or 3D object. Select the 2D circle in response. Next, you will be asked to specify the *axis of revolution*. Select the Y axis. As soon as you do this, a dialog is invoked, giving you a preview of the revolved object that will be created by the operation, along with the options to make various modifications to it, if necessary (see Figure 4.1-b). We will briefly go through each one of these options and see how they affect the resultant object.

▣   The preview window on the left shows how the circle gets revolved about the selected axis to generate a doughnut-like shape. At the base of the preview window are the same set of tool icons you first encountered when working with the Query tool in Section 3.6 of Workshop 2. They let you see the object from different viewpoints, as well as zoom and scroll. Try them all out to familiarize yourself with them again. You will encounter these icons in all the preview dialogs of various tools in form•Z.

▣   Let us move on to explore the options located on the right side of the dialog. The first parameter you can modify is the Revolution Angle, set to a full 360° by default. You can reduce this angle to create partial revolutions (see Figure 4.2-a). You can also specify whether the Direction should be Clockwise or Counter Clockwise, a particularly important option for a partial revolution.

Figure 4.1

Generating an object of revolution using the Revolve tool.

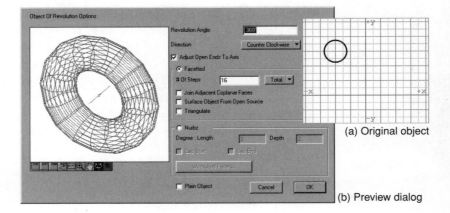

(a) Original object

(b) Preview dialog

Figure 4.2

Various options of the Revolve tool. (a) Partial revolutions, with and without joining adjacent coplanar faces. (b) Adjusting open ends to the axis of revolution.

■ The next option, **Adjust Open Ends To Axis**, is relevant to a situation where the ends of an open source shape intersect the axis of revolution. When this option is checked, the object of revolution is generated by simply clipping off the parts of the shape that project beyond the axis. If the option is turned off, the parts projecting beyond the axis are also revolved (see Figure 4.2-b). The latter might sometimes lead to self-intersecting shapes, so be careful.

 As far as a closed source shape is concerned, it is not allowed to cross the axis of revolution at all. In fact, it cannot even have a segment coinciding with the axis. It can, however, have a point that lies on the axis.

■ By default, an object of revolution is created as a **Facetted** object. Within this section, you can specify its resolution in terms of the **# Of Steps** of the revolution, either for a full 360° angle, or for the specified angle of revolution. Thus, if the **Revolution Angle** is set to 180°, 16 steps specified using the **Total** sub-option will actually create only 8 steps; in contrast, if the **Per Angle** sub-option is used, the partial revolution will be made up of 16 facets.

■ There are three more options in the form of checkboxes which apply to a **Facetted** object of revolution. The first one, **Join Adjacent Coplanar Faces**, is relevant when the **Revolve** operation produces an object with separate end faces that touch each other and lie on the same plane. When this option is activated, such faces will be merged into a single larger face. An example of this is shown in Figure 4.2-a, where a 2D open shape is revolved about the Z axis with a revolution angle of 180°. Two different results of the operation are obtained, one by leaving the **Join Adjacent Coplanar Faces** option unchecked as it is by default, and the other by selecting this option. The second result would naturally be the desired one in this case. See how the source shape in the example is open rather than closed, so that there is no segment coinciding with the axis of revolution, the Z axis. Such a revolution, as we have noted, would not be allowed by form•Z.

■ The other two **Facetted** options are simple. **Surface Object From Open Source**, when checked, will create a one-sided surface object instead of a two-sided surface solid when an open shape located away from the axis is revolved. And the **Triangulate** option works exactly like the **Triangulate** tool you saw in Section 5.6 of Workshop 2. When checked, it automatically triangulates any non-planar faces that might be created in the revolved object. This would happen if the source shape used for the Revolve operation did not lie on the same plane as the axis about which it was revolved.

■ The second type of object that can be generated with the Revolve tool is a parametric Nurbz object, referred to as *derivative nurbz*. You were briefly introduced to the nurbz personality type in Section 2.3 of Workshop 1, and you will be learning a lot more about these objects in Workshop 6. We will also look at the options that govern the creation of nurbz objects in that workshop—these are the same options that appear under the Nurbz section in the revolution preview dialog. You can ignore this entire section for now, but if you are really eager to get a head start on nurbz objects, turn to Section 5.1 of Workshop 6, where you can get all the information you need.

■ By default, an object of revolution is a parametric object—it is stored along with the parameters that created it. So if you exit the revolution preview dialog, and reapply the Revolve tool to the object you just created, the same preview dialog will be invoked again, allowing you to modify various options to edit the object. Try it. If you are sure you will not need to change the creation parameters of a revolved object, select the Plain Object option at the base of the preview dialog. This will delete the creation parameters saved with it, reducing the size of the project file. You will no longer be able to edit that object with the Revolve tool.

■ An object of revolution that has *not* been converted to a plain object can also be graphically edited with the Edit Controls tool (M-Tool:4b,2), which you have already used for editing polycurves and analytic primitives in Section 4.7 of Workshop 2. Simply apply this tool to the revolved object, and a small control arrow will be invoked, positioned near the object. Click and drag this arrow, and you will find that the revolution angle changes, based on the direction of movement. Thus, you can interactively modify the angle of a revolved object to suit your requirements using the Edit Controls tool.

■ Next, invoke the dialog of the Revolve tool and look at its options. All of these are identical to the ones you just explored in the revolution preview dialog, except for the Edit and Adjust To New Parameters options located at the base of the dialog. The Edit option is active by default, which accounts for the preview dialog being invoked when the Revolve tool is applied to an object. The Edit option is deactivated, and cannot be turned off unless the Adjust To New Parameters option is selected. The effect of selecting this option is that if the Revolve tool is now applied to a previously created revolved object, the parameters *currently* set in the Revolve tool dialog will be applied to it, overriding its previous creation parameters. Try it.

Now that we have finished exploring all the options of the Revolve tool, let us look at a few more aspects of the revolution operation.

■ The form of an object of revolution is as much dependent upon the location of the source object in relation to the axis, as its shape. Thus, if you apply the Revolve tool to a semicircular arc whose open ends touch the axis of revolution, a solid sphere will be created, but if the same arc is moved away from the axis and then revolved, the resultant object will be a surface rather than a solid.

■ The axis of revolution when using the Revolve tool can be any line segment—it is not restricted to the three coordinate axes. To see how this works, create a pyramid and draw a 2D shape on one of its faces using the Face object snap, as shown in Figure 4.3-a. You can now revolve this shape about any of the edges of the pyramid by simply selecting it as the axis of revolution—you don't even need to change the topological level to Segment before selecting the edge. You can see from Figure 4.3-b how greatly your modeling capabilities are enhanced by using the tool in this manner.

Figure 4.3

Using the segment of an existing object as the axis of revolution.

(a) Original 2D object   (b) Revolved 3D object

■ Experiment further with the Revolve tool, using various kinds of source shapes and different axes of revolution. Keep in mind that you can also use *parts* of existing objects as source shapes— simply set the topological level to Face, Outline, or Segment in order to make the selection. When you revolve a part of an object, the original object will be ghosted, unless you specify otherwise in the Status Of Objects option associated with the Revolve tool.

We will now proceed to look at the next four tools after Revolve in the right column of Row 5. All these tools work in a manner similar to the Revolve tool: a preview dialog is invoked when the tool is applied, and there are the Plain Object, Edit, and Adjust To New Parameters options in these tool dialogs, carrying out the same functions that you saw for the Revolve tool in this section.

1.2   Helixes

The Revolve tool you just used generates relatively simple objects of revolution, in which a source shape is revolved in a circular path about an axis. In contrast, the next tool, Helix, lets you create more complicated objects in which the source shape is revolved in a helical (i.e., spiral) path about an axis.

Figure 4.4

The preview dialog that is invoked when the Helix tool is applied to a source shape.

(a) Original object

(b) Preview dialog

■ Select the Helix tool (M-Tool:5b,2) and invoke its dialog. It contains a large number of options, most of which will appear in the preview dialog when the tool is applied. Concentrate only on the first three options, which let you choose the type of helix you want to create. We will go with the

WORKSHOP 4

default option, Solid/Surface Helix, to start with. Exit the dialog and apply the Helix tool to a 2D shape, selecting an appropriate axis of revolution (Figure 4.4-a), just as you did for the Revolve tool. Instead of a simple object of revolution, you will be rewarded with a solid or a surface helix, depending upon whether the source shape was closed or open. Examples of both helixes are shown in Figures 4.4 and 4.5 respectively.

▣ There are several parameters which determine the shape and size of the resulting helix. They can be adjusted in the preview dialog that opens up when the Helix tool is applied (Figure 4.4-b). The actual revolution of the helix is determined by specifying the # Of Cycles or the total revolution Angle, while the Length can be given in terms of the total length or the length of a cycle. The Direction of revolution can be Clockwise or Counter Clockwise. The Facetted and Nurbz options remain the same as those you saw for the Revolve tool. Experiment with different values and combinations of these various parameters to get an idea of how they affect the configuration of the resultant object.

▣ Additional parameters for creating helical objects, as seen in the preview dialog in Figure 4.4, include the ability to carry out various kinds of transformations. The path can be scaled along the width and length of the helix, and the source shape can be scaled as well as rotated in the course of its revolution about the path. Again, experiment with different values and combinations of transformations, some of which are demonstrated in Figure 4.5. (a) shows an open 2D shape which is revolved helically about the Z axis to generate the subsequent objects. The total Length of the helix was set at 40', with the # Of Cycles specified as 6. (b) shows the helix generated without applying any transformations. For (c), the Scale Path option was checked, and the Width value was set to 0.5. (d) resulted from scaling the Length of the path to 0.5 as well. For the tree-like object in (e), the Length of the path was reset to 1.0, and the Width was set to 0.05. Additionally, the Scale Source option was activated, and both the X and Y values were set to 0.5. Finally, (f) shows what happens if the Rotate Source option was also turned on with a value of 30°.

Figure 4.5

Different transformations yielding various types of helical objects with the Solid/Surface Helix option.

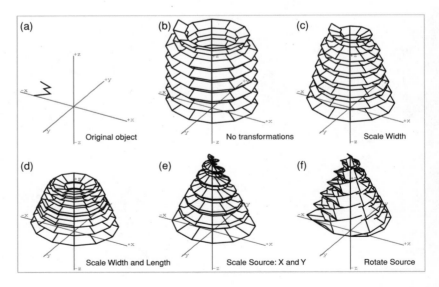

▣ Move on to select the next option in the dialog of the Helix tool, Wire Helix About Axis. Then simply click on one of the coordinate axes or on any line segment. The preview dialog will be invoked, showing a simple wire helix generated about that axis or segment, starting from the point you clicked on and running in the positive direction. The parameters that affect the shape and size of this wire helix are similar to the ones you just explored for the Solid/Surface Helix option. There is, however, an additional Radius value which determines the width of the helix, necessary because there is no source shape here which is revolved. Experiment with changes in these parameters. Two examples of wire helixes are shown in Figure 4.6. (a) was created by clicking on the Z axis, with the Width and Length of the path being scaled by the values of 0.25 and 0.75 respectively. Contrast this with (b), in which the Scale Path option was deselected, one of the vertical segments of the block was selected as the axis of revolution, and the Length was set to the exact height of that segment.

Figure 4.6

Generating simple wire helixes about an axis.

(a) Wire helix about Z axis   (b) Wire helix about line segment

■ Proceed to select the third Helix tool option, Wire Helix Along Path. This is quite similar to the previous one, the only difference being that you can generate a helix along *any* path, not just about a straight axis. Figure 4.7 shows two variations of this type of helix, using the 2D curved path illustrated in (a). The # Of Cycles was set to 40. The version shown in (b) had no path scaling option, while in (c), the Scale Path option was checked and the Width value was set to 0.1. Notice that both the Length value as well as the Length option for path scaling were deactivated, since the helix has to extend through the entire length of the selected path. Also see how the direction of scaling follows the direction of the path object. If you need to have the helix running in the opposite direction, simply reverse the direction of the path first. This can be done by using the Reverse Direction tool (M-Tool:10b,2). Try it.

■ Keep in mind that a helix object to which the Plain Object option has *not* been applied is a parametric object, just like the revolved object you saw in the last section. It is stored with its creation parameters, which can be edited by reapplying the Helix tool to it.

You must be wondering what can be done with the wire helixes you have created using the last two options of the Helix tool—after all, aren't most models made up of solid objects rather than lines and wires? Well, you will soon learn about the Sweep tool in Exercise 2, with which you can generate fascinating coiled objects by simply sweeping a source shape along a wire helix. One such object is depicted on the front cover of this book.

Figure 4.7

Generating wire helixes about a path rather than about an axis.

(a) Path object   (b) Wire helix without scaling   (c) Wire helix with scaling

1.3   Screws and Bolts

◼ If you belong to a field which deals with nuts and bolts in any manner, you will find the next tool on Row 5, Screw/Bolt, really useful. As the name suggests, you can automatically generate screws and bolts by simply selecting an axis of revolution and then specifying a few key parameters in the preview dialog that is invoked. These are quite self-explanatory and you should explore them in detail at leisure. Figure 4.8 shows an example where a screw is required to be depicted connecting two blocks. A line segment is first created in the desired position, passing through the center of one of the two blocks. The screw is then generated by using this segment as the axis of revolution. The direction of the screw is again determined by the direction of the segment, as you can see, so that has to be drawn carefully.

Notice the lucid illustration of the resultant screw shown in Figure 4.8-b, in the Shaded Render display mode. It was generated by applying a surface style with a simple transparency attribute to the blocks, and then activating the Transparencies option in the Shaded Render Options dialog, as you learned in Section 2.4 of Workshop 3. You can see how transparency can be used as an effective presentation technique, even for those objects that are not actually supposed to be transparent in real life.

Figure 4.8

Creating a screw about a line segment selected as the axis of revolution.

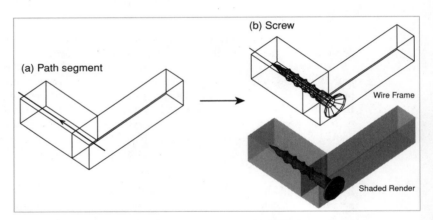

1.4   Spiral Staircases

If you are an architect, you will fall in love with form•Z (if you haven't done so already!) the minute you see how it can generate, in one step, an object that is so tiresome and tedious to draft and model otherwise—a spiral staircase.

◼ Draw a single vertical line segment, with direction from bottom to top, which you can use as the axis of revolution for your spiral staircase. Set object snapping to Endpoint, and select the Spiral Stair tool from Row 5. You will be prompted for the axis of revolution. Select the segment you just drew by snapping to its lower endpoint. Viola! A spiral staircase is generated instantly around the segment, starting from the lower endpoint, as shown in the preview dialog in Figure 4.9.

◼ You will naturally want to manipulate the parameters in the preview dialog which determine the size and configuration of the staircase. The basic parameters include: the inside and outside radius, the difference of which is equal to the Width of the staircase; the total Height as well as related information such as the riser height or the number of steps, each of which will determine the value of the other since they have a reciprocal relationship; the total Length of the stair, given in terms of either the total angle, the angle of one step, or the width of one step; the # Of Segments Per Step, the default value for which is 3, as evident in the staircase shown in Figure 4.9; and finally, the Direction of the staircase. Experiment with changes in these parameters to create staircases of different configurations.

Figure 4.9

The preview dialog invoked by the Spiral Stair tool, showing the default options.

In addition to the basic staircase, you can choose to incorporate various other features such as Tiles, Side Beams, and Railings, by activating the corresponding options in the spiral staircase preview dialog. Tiles are separate slabs that sit on top of each step of the staircase, extending beyond its sides if required. You can specify the height, as well as the front and side extensions of the tiles. Side beams are protective beams running along the two sides of the staircase. Their width, as well as their extensions above the top and under the bottom of the staircase need to be specified. As far as railings are concerned, you can create a customized one by accessing the accompanying Options dialog. A staircase incorporating all these features is shown in Figure 4.10, along with the options used to generate the railing shown with it.

Figure 4.10

A spiral staircase modeled with tiles, side beams, and a railing, the options for which are also shown.

■ There is only one more option that is new to the spiral staircase preview dialog, Warn When Exceeding Limits. You can activate this if you would like to be warned when certain limits related to the tread and riser dimensions of the staircase are exceeded. You can set these limits yourself in the dialog that is invoked by clicking on the accompanying Set Limits button.

■ Finally, keep in mind that just like all the objects you have seen in this exercise so far, a spiral staircase to which the Plain Object option has not been applied is a parametric object. Thus, it can be edited by reapplying the Spiral Stair tool to it.

1.5   Straight Staircases

In versions of form•Z prior to 3.0, "regular" staircases, i.e., staircases that were not spiral, had to be modeled just like any other object, using the modeling tools on Rows 2 and 3 of the modeling tool palette. A single stair could be modeled and the staircase then generated using the Move tool in Multi Copy mode. Landings, of course, had to be modeled separately. The Terrain Model tool (M-Tool:5a,9) could also be used to create certain types of staircases quickly with minimal effort, as illustrated in Section 5.2.

form•Z now has a dedicated tool for modeling regular staircases, similar to the tool for generating spiral staircases which you covered in the last section. This is the Straight Stair tool, located immediately after the Spiral Stair tool in the right column of the fifth row. With this tool, regular (or "straight") staircases of a wide variety of shapes and configurations, complete with landings and railings, can be conveniently generated in one step. In architectural modeling, where straight staircases are so common, this tool saves a lot of time and effort and is therefore a real boon to have! Let us see how it works.

■ To generate a staircase with the Straight Stair tool, the path of the staircase has to be defined first. This can be either an open or closed 2D shape. Go ahead and create such a shape. Keep in mind that the staircase will be generated with respect to the plane of the path shape if it is made up of multiple segments, or with respect to the current reference plane if the path shape is made up of a single segment. Also note that if you want to create a staircase with multiple flights superimposed over the same 2D shape, the shape *has* to be closed. Examples of staircases created using both an open and a closed shape are shown in Figure 4.11.

Figure 4.11

Staircases modeled with the Straight Stair tool. (a) A Solid Stair type single-flight staircase, created using an open shape. (b) A Beam Stair type multiple-flight staircase, created using a closed shape.

(a) Solid Stair   (b) Beam Stair

Figure 4.12

The Straight Stair preview dialog for the single-flight staircase shown in Figure 4.11-a.

Workshop 4

■ Activate the **Straight Stair** tool and apply it to the 2D path shape you have created. A preview dialog similar to the ones you have seen so far is invoked (Figure 4.12), containing an extensive set of options. All the options in the lower half of the dialog, including the ones related to Tiles, Side Beams, and Railings, are already familiar to you from the Spiral Stair tool. Let us look at what is different.

■ The **Type** popup menu lists six different types of straight staircases, the default selection for which is **Solid Stair**. Switch to each one of the other five types in turn, and watch the staircase display in the preview window change in response to your selection. After observing the differences between all the types, settle for one of your choice. Then move on to look at the **Align** option, which has three sub-options for positioning the staircase. They determine whether the left, center, or right of the staircase should be aligned with the line of the path shape.

■ **Layout**, on the other hand, is used to specify how the treads of the staircase are adjusted when the path shape is made up of multiple segments (see Figure 4.13). The default **Continuous** option places the total number of treads along the total length of the shape, without caring about breaks between consecutive segments. In contrast, the **Per Section** option adjusts the treads in such a manner that a complete number of treads is placed in every section of the staircase. The third option, **With Landings**, circumvents this problem altogether by placing a landing at every section break. When this sub-option is selected, you can also specify front and back **Landing Extensions** for your staircase, a little further down in the dialog.

Figure 4.13

The three Layout sub-options of the Straight Stair tool. Landing Extensions for the With Landings sub-option are also shown.

Continuous   Per Section   With Landings

◾ The next three options, Width, Height, and Step Calculation, are those which determine the actual dimensions of the staircase (see Figure 4.11-a). The width is a single straightforward value. The height can be specified for the whole staircase or for a single flight. For a multiple-flight staircase generated from a closed path shape, the number of flights is also specified. And finally, the dimensions of each step are calculated by specifying either the height of the riser, the depth of the tread, or the total number of steps.

 When a single-flight staircase is generated from a closed path shape, the starting point of the staircase is located at the "first point" of the shape. Turn on the Show First Point option in the Wire Frame Options dialog if you are not sure where the first point for your path is located. To change the first point of an existing path, use the First Point tool (M-Tool:10b,1).

◾ There are only a few more options that are new to the straight staircase preview dialog. The Reverse Direction option conveniently reverses the direction of the path shape, and thus of the staircase. The Triangulate option is not new, but note that it is especially relevant to the two Ramp types of stairs, as it will triangulate any non-planar faces that the staircase might have. Then there are the Beam Height and Ramp Height parameters, which appear at the base of the dialog for the Beam Stair and Beam Ramp stair types respectively—they determine the vertical height of the associated beam or ramp. And finally, the S&R Thickness parameter, which appears at the same spot when the Steps & Risers type is activated, is used to specify the thickness of the slabs from which this type of stair is constructed.

◾ Again, keep in mind that a straight staircase is a parametric object by default, which means it can be edited by reapplying the Straight Stair tool to it.

EXERCISE *2*

Sweeping Your Way Through

In the next two exercises, you will learn about two simple yet extremely powerful and unusual tools in form•Z: the Sweep tool and the Skin tool, located at the end of the right column of Row 5. Both of them work on the same principle but in somewhat different ways. The concept is that of generating complex 3D objects—which cannot be created using the regular object generation modes and drawing tools—by tracing the profile of a 2D shape as it moves along a path. Unlike the Revolve or Helix tools, the path need not be circular or spiral but can be of any arbitrary shape that *you* define. Sounds intriguing, doesn't it? Let us see how it works, starting with the Sweep tool.

2.1   Axial Sweep

◾ Clear your window of all its contents or move to a different layer. Using the 2D Surface Object mode (M-Tool:2a,1), draw a small square or circle. This will be used as the *source shape* for the Sweep operation. You now need to define a *path shape* along which the source will be "swept." Using the same object generation mode, draw a larger shape. You can choose to use another reference plane, predefined or arbitrary, for the path—you are not restricted to the same plane used for the source (see Figure 4.14-a).

Figure 4.14

Using the Sweep tool.
(a) The source and path
shapes. (b) The preview
dialog. (c) The resultant
object in Surface Render
mode.

■ Make sure the topological level on Row 4 is set to Object. Now select the Sweep tool (M-Tool:5b,6) and follow the instructions in the Prompts palette. For the source, click on the smaller object; for the path, select the larger shape. This brings up the preview dialog for the Sweep operation (Figure 4.14-b), similar to what you encountered for the tools in Exercise 1. It shows you the resultant object, generated by sweeping the source shape along the path shape. Exit the dialog by clicking OK, and you can see the swept object more clearly in one of the paint display modes (Figure 4.14-c).

■ By default, the object created by the Sweep tool is a parametric object, just like the first five tools on the same row. So you can reapply the Sweep tool to the object to get back to the preview dialog. Do this, then turn your attention to the options in the Source Shape section. Here, the source shape is shown in a smaller window, with a number of tool icons located under it. From left to right, these let you move, rotate, or scale the source shape, flip it horizontally or vertically, or reverse its direction. Each one of these transformations will modify the resultant object in various ways. Try them out. You will see how the transformation is always carried out with respect to the point which marks the crossing of the path shape through the source, graphically indicated in the source preview window by a red cross. It is placed by default at the centroid of the object.

■ The Sweep tool comes with another powerful feature that can greatly enhance your modeling capabilities. This is the ability to scale as well as rotate the source shape from one end to the other end of the path. By default, both options are off. Check the Scale option in the preview dialog and specify a scaling factor, which can be different along the X and Y directions. See how the resultant object changes in shape. Then check the Rotate option as well and explore the changes for different angle values. To flip the direction along which the scaling and rotation occurs, click on the Reverse icon that is located *below* the Source Shape section, next to the Path Shape option. This will flip the direction of the path, and consequently, the direction in which the transformation will occur.

Figure 4.15 shows the variations in the resultant object, generated by sweeping the same source along the same path shown in Figure 4.14-a, but with different transformations. In (a), Scale was turned on

WORKSHOP 4

with a factor of 3.0 for X and 1.0 for Y. In (b), Y was also set to 3.0. In (c), the Rotate option was selected with a total angle of 180°, in addition to the Scale option. Finally, (d) had the same transformations as (c), except that the path was reversed, so the transformations were applied in the opposite direction.

Figure 4.15

Different configurations generated by applying various transformations to the source in the Sweep preview dialog.

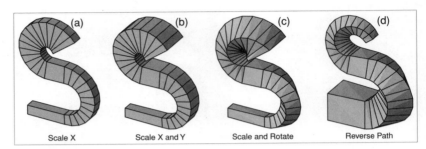

Scale X   Scale X and Y   Scale and Rotate   Reverse Path

▣   Next, turn to the Perpendicular To Plane option located in the Source Shape section, the use of which is illustrated in Figure 4.16. (a) shows the 30-60, top and front views of the source and path shapes created for the Sweep operation. The circular path shape, as you can see, is not parallel to any of the predefined planes—it was created using an arbitrary plane. The XY plane, however, was activated when the Sweep tool was applied. (b) and (c) show the results of the operation with the Perpendicular To Plane option turned off and on respectively. You can see that when the option is off, as it is by default, the source shape keeps adjusting its orientation to be perpendicular to the path as it is swept along it. In contrast, when the option is on, the source always remains perpendicular to the active reference plane. You can make the choice depending upon what you want to accomplish.

Figure 4.16

The effect of the Perpendicular To Plane option available in the Sweep preview dialog.

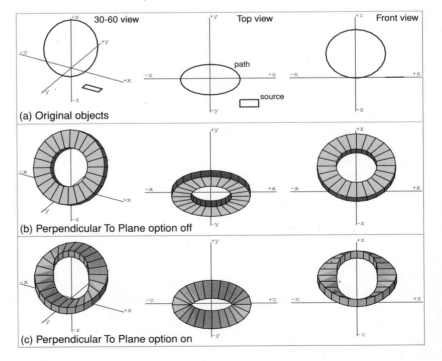

▣ The remaining options in the Sweep preview dialog should be familiar to you from the preview dialogs of the tools you covered in Exercise 1. The swept object can be created with either the Facetted or the Nurbz personality, and you can check the Plain Object option if you are confident that you will not need to modify its creation parameters at a later stage.

▣ Keep in mind that the source and the path shapes for the Sweep operation you have been executing can be open or closed—there is no restriction. Explore various combinations of both types of shapes. As you would expect, a closed source produces a solid, as in the examples in Figures 4.15 and 4.16, whereas an open source results in a surface. 2D enclosures can also be used as source shapes to produce 3D enclosures of various configurations.

The kind of Sweep operation you have performed so far—sweeping a source object along a single axis determined by a path object—is known as *axial sweep*, and it is the default mode for the Sweep tool. There are three additional kinds of Sweep operations: *two source sweep*, *two path sweep*, and *boundary sweep*. The choice of the operation is made in the dialog of the Sweep tool.

▣ Double-click on the Sweep tool to invoke its dialog. You will find the four types of sweep operations listed at the top, of which Axial Sweep is selected by default. We will look at the remaining three types in subsequent sections. All the other options in this dialog are identical to those in the preview dialog, except for the Alignment option in the Source Shape section. This is used to determine the cross section alignment of the path shape with respect to the source shape. Centroid is selected by default, which is why the axis of the path shape has been passing through the center of the source shape all this time. Alternately, you can choose the Origin of the current reference plane, or the First Point of the source for the alignment. Besides, you can always change the axis alignment by moving the source in the source shape window of the preview dialog, if required.

2.2 Two Source Sweep

▣ Select the Two Source Sweep option in the dialog of the Sweep tool. This kind of sweep, as the name suggests, expects two source shapes and one path shape. Back in the graphics window, create any two 2D objects to function as source shapes. Both can be either open shapes or closed shapes, but you cannot have one open and one closed. Also create a path object, which can be open or closed (Figure 4.17-a). Then select the Sweep tool and follow the instructions in the Prompts palette to select, in turn, the first source, the second source, and the path. The preview dialog will be invoked (Figure 4.17-b), showing how the resultant object has a form which changes from the source shape selected first to the source shape selected second, as it is swept along the specified path (Figure 4.17-c).

▣ You will already be familiar with most of the options in the preview dialog which are similar to those for Axial Sweep. There are just a couple of additional options to note. In the Source Shape section, you will now see two source objects instead of one. You can make either one active by selecting the 1st or 2nd options. The active source is shown in color while the other is shown in gray. Only the active source can be graphically manipulated using the accompanying transformation icons.

▣ In a Two Source Sweep operation, what is especially important is the location of the first point and the direction of one source with respect to the other. Preferably, the first points should be aligned and the directions should be the same, otherwise the swept object will be twisted. You can synchronize the sources in the preview dialog itself, using the Rotate tool to adjust the first point and the Reverse tool to adjust the direction of the active source.

Figure 4.17

A Two Source Sweep operation. (a) The two source shapes and one path shape. (b) The Sweep preview dialog. (c) The resultant object in Surface Render mode.

□ Notice, also, that the location of the first point of the path object is where the first source is placed. Thus, if your path object is closed, you have to take care to create it correctly in order to achieve the effect you want. You cannot modify the location of the first point of the path object in the preview dialog, but you can reverse its direction, if necessary, using the Reverse tool in the Path Shape section.

□ Just as with Axial Sweep, the Rotate transformation can be applied in the preview dialog for Two Source Sweep, as in the example illustrated in Figure 4.17, to achieve interesting twisted effects in the resultant object. The Scale option, however, is not available since there are two shapes which determine the two extremities of this type of Sweep.

2.3 Two Path Sweep

□ Move on to select the next mode in the dialog of the Sweep tool, Two Path Sweep. As you can guess from its name, this Sweep type generates an object by sweeping one source along two paths. Go ahead and create these shapes. The only thing to keep in mind is that both the path shapes must either be closed or open—you cannot have one closed and one open path. And at least for now, ensure that the starting points and directions of these paths are aligned, as in the examples demonstrated in Figure 4.18. Later, once you learn how the operation actually works, you can deviate from these guidelines to create unusual objects with desired shapes.

□ Perform the Sweep operation by selecting sequentially, as prompted, the source shape and the two path shapes. You should be able to deal with the preview dialog that opens up like an old hand now! The only new option that you will see in this dialog is Preserve Height. Select it and then deselect it to see how it affects the resultant object. You will find that when this option is not selected—which is the default—the aspect ratio of the source is maintained as it is swept between the two paths. In other words, the source is uniformly scaled, resulting in an object with a constantly varying height. On the other hand, with the Preserve Height option selected, the resultant object has a constant height which is equal to the height of the source. The source is thus scaled only in one direction as it is swept between the two paths. Both scenarios are illustrated in Figure 4.18.

Figure 4.18

Two examples of the Two Path Sweep operation. The First Point and Direction displays were turned on for the original 2D shapes.

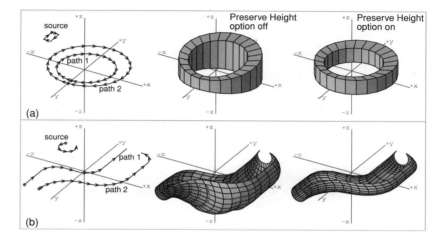

2.4 Boundary Sweep

■ Proceed to activate the last Sweep tool mode, Boundary Sweep. This is similar to Axial Sweep in the sense that it requires only one source shape and one path shape. However, it works a little differently. Not only does it sweep the source shape along the specified path, it also goes on to add faces at the ends to *close* the form. Thus, it will always produce a solid object and requires the source shape to be open, as illustrated in Figure 4.19.

■ Draw an open shape to function as the source, making sure it does not self-intersect. Stick to a fairly simple one for now. Then create a larger closed shape for the path (Figure 4.19-a). Select the Sweep tool and pick the two objects in the correct sequence. You will see that what would have been a surface object in Axial Sweep is a solid object in Boundary Sweep because the open ends are closed up. Also, note that the Scale and Rotate transformations are not available, as they could interfere with the ability to create well-formed closures.

Figure 4.19

Two examples of Boundary Sweep, using a closed and an open path. The contrast with Axial Sweep is also shown.

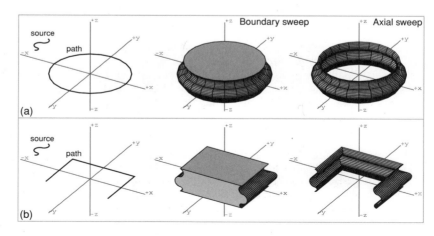

WORKSHOP 4

◼ Now repeat the same Sweep operation, but with a path shape that is open instead of closed (Figure 4.19-b). For the Boundary Sweep to generate a well-formed object using an open path, the path has to meet two requirements: it must have at least two segments, and the "virtual" segment connecting the two open ends of the path must not intersect any of its other segments. If your path shape does not meet these conditions, you will be issued a warning message. Once again, note the contrast between the results obtained by using Boundary Sweep and Axial Sweep for this source and path.

Skinning Your Forms

The Skin tool is located immediately after the Sweep tool on Row 5 of the modeling tool palette. While similar in concept, the two tools operate quite differently, producing different results. The Sweep operation is relatively simple—all it requires is one or two source shapes and one or two path shapes. You do not have to worry about the relative locations of the source and path shapes, as you just saw. The Skin tool also produces 3D objects by sweeping 2D sources along 2D paths, but the difference is that the sources and the paths have to be properly positioned such that they *describe the profile* of the 3D object that is to be created. In addition, there are some other conditions that need to be satisfied. Let us see how to use the Skin tool and explore the conditions involved.

3.1 Skinning Along a Path

◼ Clear everything in your window or move to a different layer. Invoke the Wire Frame Options dialog (as you learned in Section 2.1 of Workshop 3), and select the Show Points option located at the top of the dialog (*not* the Show First Point option located in the 2D Surface Objects section). It is important to always activate this option before using the Skin tool, since the operation works better when the points of source and path shapes are properly matched.

◼ Turn Grid Snap on and create four path objects as shown in Figure 4.20-a. Two of these are on the ZX plane; the other two are on the YZ plane. They can be created with precision by going to the Front/Back and Right/Left views respectively. Ensure that you create them in the same general direction. If you like, turn on also the Show Direction option in the Wire Frame Options dialog, so that there is no confusion about direction.

◼ Next, create a source shape on the XY plane such that it has points touching one end of each of the four path shapes, as shown in Figure 4.20-b. You will execute your first Skin operation with this single source shape. Zoom in closer to ensure that points on the source actually touch points on the paths. You can see how important it is to turn on the point display in the Wire Frame mode, without which you would not be able to tell if the points coincided or how far away they were from each other.

◼ You now have to tell the Skin tool (M-Tool:5b,7) exactly how many source and path shapes you will be using for the operation, and change other settings if necessary. Select it and invoke its dialog (Figure 4.21). It has a large number of options, all of which we will be exploring in due course. The Facetted and Nurbz options will be familiar to you from the tools you covered in the first two exercises. Stick with the default personality of Facetted until you study nurbz objects in Workshop 6.

Figure 4.20

Executing a Skinning Along Paths operation. The original source and path shapes are shown with the display of points turned on.

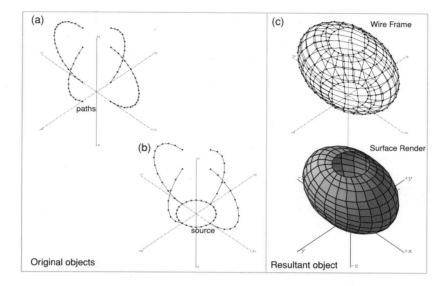

- There are two basic skinning modes. The one selected by default is Skinning Along Paths, which is what you will be executing first. Change the # Sources value to 1, since you have a single source. Skinning Along Paths requires at least 3 paths, so you will not be able to set # Paths to a value less than 3. Try it, and remember this restriction for future use. Then change # Paths back to the default value of 4, since you have four path shapes.

- Look further down in the Skin Options dialog and notice that the Placement Type is set to Current Position, which is fine for now. There is an associated Tolerance value, useful in case there are points on the source shapes which do not coincide exactly with points on the path shapes. You can change this value as necessary, so that the tool is able to relate the sources to the paths.

- Having set all the appropriate options, exit the Skin Options dialog and apply the tool. Following the instructions in the Prompts palette, select the source object first. Then select each of the four path shapes, taking care to pick them in the right sequence. You will find that the source shape is "swept" between the four path shapes, resulting in a 3D surface object as shown in Figure 4.20-c.

Figure 4.21

The dialog of the Skin tool, with the options set to perform the Skin operation illustrated in Figure 4.20.

◼ If you get any error messages at this stage and the operation is not performed, check to see if the directions of the path shapes are synchronized. If they are not, apply the Reverse Direction tool (M-Tool:10b,2) to the path shapes whose directions need to be corrected. If the Skin operation still does not work, increase the Tolerance value in the dialog. That should take care of the problem.

◼ Notice from Figure 4.20-c that the resultant object is a surface with open ends. Go back to the Skin Options dialog and check the option, Close At Ends Of Open Paths. Undo and reapply the Skin operation. If the source shape is closed, such as the one used in Figure 4.20, the resultant object will now be a solid with closed ends.

◼ Let us do another example of Skinning Along Paths in which there are two source shapes. Recreate the configuration of sources and paths shown in Figure 4.22-a. Invoke the Skin Options dialog and set the # Sources value to 2. Also check the Close At Ends Of Open Paths option. The other options should be the same as in the previous example. Apply the Skin tool to this configuration and you should get the result shown in Figure 4.22-b. You can see the ability to sculpt shapes precisely that is afforded by the Skin tool.

◼ We will perform a final example of Skinning Along Paths, this time using closed rather than open paths. Create the paths as shown in Figure 4.23-a in Top view, and move them along the Z axis to space them out vertically. Then create a closed source as shown in Figure 4.23-b, making sure that it has points coinciding with points on all the three paths. As you can see, doing this is much easier when the configuration is centered about the origin; so it is a good idea to always do it this way, even if it means creating the configuration on a separate layer. Make the appropriate changes to the values for # Sources and # Paths in the dialog of the Skin tool and then apply it to the configuration. You should have the result shown in Figure 4.23-c. Notice that the result is a solid object, since both the source and the paths were closed.

◼ Get back to the Skin Options dialog (Figure 4.21), and notice that there are two sub-options for Skinning Along Paths—Centroid Based and Boundary Based—that we did not touch upon at all. The reason is that in most cases they will produce identical results, so it is not necessary to get into the mathematical explanation of how they differ. Simply keep in mind that the default selection, Centroid Based, is better for curved shapes, whereas the alternative, Boundary Based, is better for angular shapes. Therefore, select the sub-option appropriate to the modeling task at hand.

Figure 4.22

Applying the Skinning Along Paths operation to a configuration of two sources and four paths.

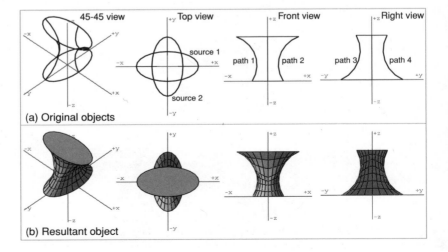

Figure 4.23

Applying the Skinning Along Paths operation to a closed source, using three closed paths.

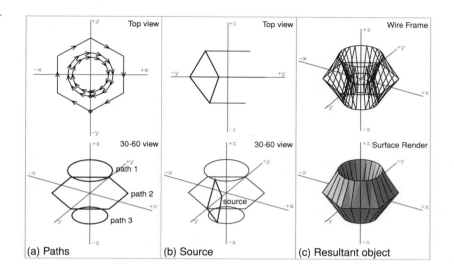

(a) Paths   (b) Source   (c) Resultant object

3.2 Skinning Using Anchor Points

At times, it might be difficult to create a source of the precise shape that is required, in the correct position, touching all the path shapes at the desired points. In such a situation, form•Z gives you the option of creating the source shape in a different, more convenient location, and then telling the Skin tool exactly how it is to be placed. This is done by positioning *anchor points* along both the source and path shapes—these are essentially points on an object that are marked in a special way. Let us now do an example of this type of skinning.

■ Create three path shapes having the same direction, correctly positioned with respect to each other. Then create a properly dimensioned source shape, *not* in the position it should be for skinning, but somewhere else on the plane, as shown in Figure 4.24-a. "Properly dimensioned" means ensuring that *if* the source was drawn in the correct location, it would have points that correctly matched with points on each of the paths. This is very important, so do it carefully.

■ We now have to indicate to the Skin tool which points on the source need to be matched with which points on the paths. As mentioned, you will use anchor points to do this. But first, invoke the Wire Frame Options dialog once more and select the option, Show Marked Points. This will show the anchor points when you mark them. Since you have not yet marked any points, there is no change in the display in the graphics window at this stage.

■ Next, go to the Point Marker tool (M-Tool:10b,4), and apply it to both the source and path shapes, selecting the matching points on each. There should be a point on the source corresponding to a point on every path. The selected points will be displayed with an additional mark in the Wire Frame display mode, as shown in Figure 4.24-b.

■ What remains is to specify the appropriate options for the Skin tool. Invoke its dialog and set the values for # Sources and # Paths as 1 and 3 respectively. In the Placement Type section, activate the By Anchor Points option. That is all you need to do. Exit the dialog and apply the Skin tool in the usual manner. You should achieve a result similar to that shown in Figure 4.24-c.

Figure 4.24

Performing a Skin opera-
tion using anchor points.

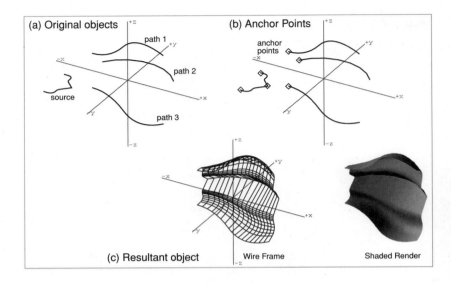

If you were not able to execute the operation successfully, reverse the direction of the source. If it still does not work, do the following: In the Skin Options dialog, check the Place Only sub-option that appears next to the By Anchor Points option; then reapply the Skin tool. This time, the source shape will only be placed in the correct position based on the anchor points, rather than swept along the paths. If you marked the points correctly, this should get done without any error messages. Now set the Placement Type option back to By Current Position in the dialog, specify an appropriate tolerance value, and reapply the Skin tool. This time, the operation should be executed without any problems, giving you the desired result.

3.3 Cross Skinning

So far, all the skinning operations we have executed were of the type, *skinning along paths*. The Skin tool provides us with a second type of skinning operation referred to as *cross skinning*. While the former was similar to the Sweep tool, the latter is similar to the Revolve tool in the sense that one or more sources are revolved about a single path. The path has to be a closed shape, but need not necessarily be circular as with the Revolve tool. We will carry out a few examples of cross skinning in this section.

▣ On a new layer, create a closed path of any shape and a single source as shown in Figure 4.25-a. If the source shape is open, you have to ensure that one of its points coincides with a point on the path shape. For a closed source, two points on the source must match with two points on the path (see Figure 4.25-b).

▣ Invoke the dialog of the Skin tool and select the Cross Skinning option. Change the # Sources value to 1. Notice that you cannot change the # Paths value, which is always 1 for this kind of skinning. Make sure that the Placement Type is set to By Current Position with a suitable tolerance. You are now ready to execute the cross skinning operation. Exit the dialog, and as prompted, select first the source object and then the path object. You will be rewarded with a beautifully skinned form, as shown in Figure 4.25-a.

Figure 4.25

Performing Cross Skinning operations using various sources. (a) An open source. (b) A closed source. (c) Multiple sources.

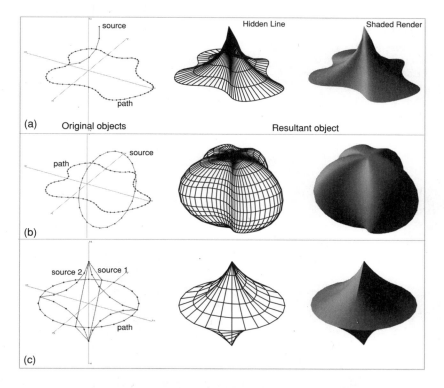

Original objects   Resultant object

■ Repeat the operation with a different source shape, again ensuring the correct matching of points. Figure 4.25-b shows the cross skinning of a closed source about the same path used in Figure 4.25-a.

■ Let us now try a cross skinning operation with more than one source. You can continue using the same path; simply create a second source shape which is open or closed, depending upon the first source. The sources must all be either open or closed—a "mix and match" will not work. There is an additional condition you must satisfy when there are multiple source objects: in addition to touching the paths, all the sources must touch each other at two additional points, referred to as *apex points*, one on either side of the path. Figure 4.25-c shows an example with these points indicated for two source shapes, and the resultant cross skinning operation. Don't forget to change # Sources to the right value in the Skin Options dialog before applying the tool.

■ It might seem tricky to create multiple source shapes for cross skinning, all of which meet each other at the same two points, as well as touch the path object at distinct points. Figure 4.26 illustrates how this task can be accomplished more easily, using the source and path shapes from the last example. After creating the path shape, create single segments going across it at the positions where the sources are to be located, as shown in (a). Use Endpoint snap for accuracy. All these segments should pass through the same point located inside the path shape.

■ Extrude these segments by the same distance on one side of the path, as shown in (b), using the Extrusion tool (M-Tool:5a,3). Then apply the Move tool, with the topological level set to Segment and the Perpendicular Lock turned on, to move the lower segment of each extrusion by the same distance on the opposite side of the path. As shown in (c), this will give you a rectangular surface for each source, correctly positioned, and intersecting the surface of every other source at two apex points, one above and one below the path.

WORKSHOP 4

Figure 4.26

The process of creating source objects for cross skinning that touch the path object as well as other sources at apex points.

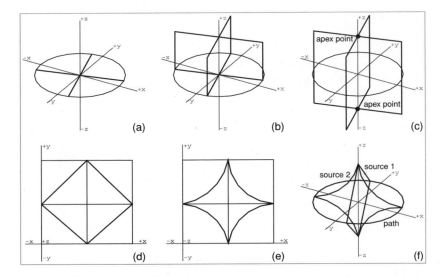

◼ Next, create an arbitrary plane for each of these rectangular surfaces using Define Arbitrary (W-Tool:3,1). Thereafter, for each plane, go to View > Plane Projection > Top and create the source shape for that plane, ensuring that it touches a point on the path (using Endpoint snap) as well as the two apex points (using Intersection snap). This is shown in (d) and (e). Delete the temporary rectangular surfaces after creating the sources. You should finally have your source and path shapes correctly positioned as shown in (f).

◼ You can also use the By Anchor Points method for cross skinning when the source objects are closed, or if they are open but touch the path at both ends. Note that you have to "mark" the apex points in the sources as well, in addition to the points where they touch the path. Do an example of this, following the same procedure you used in the last section.

The Skin tool is a complex one and it is beyond the scope of this book to cover all its ramifications. The best way to master it is to experiment with different sources and paths and observe the results. Therefore, take some time to execute more skinning operations before moving on to the next exercise of this workshop.

EXERCISE 4

Cutting Your Sections

In this exercise, you will work with the Section tool, located in the left column of Row 8, that can be used to "slice" up one or more objects with a cutting plane—almost like a knife passing through butter! Alternately, it can be used to derive the 2D intersection of the cutting plane with the objects. You will also look at the Contour tool, located immediately after the Section tool, that is used to create a sequence of 2D cuts throughout an object.

The Section tool is especially useful from a design presentation standpoint, as it lets you automatically derive plans and sections of your 3D models without having to redraw them. All that is needed is a *cutting plane* created in the position through which the model is to be sectioned. Moreover, this cutting plane does not have to actually cut through (i.e., intersect) any of the objects that are to be sectioned. It can exist anywhere in the model provided that, in an infinitely extended position, it would intersect the objects along the plane of the desired section. In fact, you can even use a *cutting line* from which the cutting plane is automatically derived by extruding the line perpendicular to the active reference plane. Let us see how it works.

4.1   2D Sections

▣ Move to a new layer and create a few 3D objects of various shapes and sizes. Then use the Rectangle tool (M-Tool:3a,1) in 2D Surface Object mode to create a few rectangles in different positions such that, when extended infinitely, they would intersect your 3D objects in different ways. Some rectangles can be created on arbitrary planes or one of their segments can be moved, so as to incline them with respect to the objects. This will generate more interesting sections.

▣ Use the Pick tool to select all the 3D objects—everything except the rectangles created as cutting planes. If you have too many objects which can make individual selection tedious, select everything by going to Edit > Select All UnGhosted, and then click on the cutting planes using the Pick tool to deselect them. Ensure that the topological level continues to be set to Object.

▣ Choose the Section tool (M-Tool:8a,8) from the modeling tool palette. Invoke its dialog and ensure that both the 2D and Plane options are active, which are the defaults. Back in the graphics window, you will be prompted to select a cutting plane—this can be an outline, face, or 2D object. Select one of the rectangles you had created (Figure 4.27-a), and watch your objects disappear, leaving behind 2D sections of the solids where the plane of the rectangle cut into them (Figure 4.27-b). Simple, isn't it? You can change the Status Of Objects from the default of Ghosted to Keep or Delete, if you want the original objects and cutting plane to be retained or deleted.

▣ Undo and repeat with any of the other cutting planes you had created. You can also apply the Section tool without prepicking the objects. In that case, you would first select the object to be sectioned, and then the cutting plane. Obviously, you can section only a single object in this manner. Use the prepick method when you want to section many objects at a time with the same cutting plane.

Figure 4.27

Using the Section tool to generate 2D sections using a cutting plane.

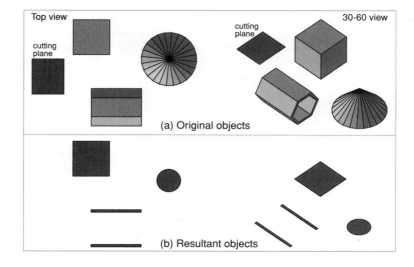

Top view

cutting plane

cutting plane

30-60 view

cutting plane

(a) Original objects

(b) Resultant objects

■ Create a fresh set of 3D objects. This time, draw a single line segment running across them, such that if extruded perpendicular to the current reference plane, it would cut through the objects. In the dialog of the Section tool, set the Cut Objects With option to Line instead of Plane. Then apply the Section tool as you did earlier, this time selecting the cutting line after prepicking the objects. You will have 2D sections of your solids as before. The Line option is thus useful when simple cuts perpendicular to a plane are required.

Only a single line segment can be used as the cutting line with the Section tool. To cut an object with a polyline, polycurve, arc, or any other shape, you have to use the With Line option of the Trim/Split tool, which will be covered in Exercise 5 of Workshop 6.

The new objects created by the Section tool are regular objects and can be used for any other operation. You can also copy them across to the drafting module, where you can then proceed to label and dimension them if you need to create plans and sections of your model. This process is described in the Appendix, which takes a brief look at drafting in form•Z.

4.2 3D Sections

Normally, when you draw plans and sections of your designs, you show not just the cut portion but also what's left beyond the cut, in order to give a clearer picture of what the various objects are. For instance, the 2D section of the circular cone shown in Figure 4.27 is a circle, but it could just as well have been the section of a cylinder. What would have been useful in this situation is to leave the lower half of the cut intact, in which case there would have been no doubts about what the sectioned object was. This is where 3D sections come in useful as far as the generation of plans and sections is concerned.

■ Invoke the dialog of the Section tool, and set the options to 3D and Plane. Create a new set of objects and cutting plane. Perform the Section operation as before. You will find that all the selected objects now get sliced into separate parts along the cutting plane. The cut is indicated by a line appearing on the surface of the objects (Figure 4.28-a). The sliced parts can be selected, moved, deleted, etc., independent of each other (Figure 4.28-b).

■ For generating a plan or section, simply delete those sectioned parts that should not be there, and then switch to the appropriate view. You now have your plan or section, not only cut in the right place but with all the portions beyond the cut also visible, making it easier to read (Figure 4.28-c). You can copy this view across to the drafting module, or save it in the appropriate file format for another labeling or dimensioning program. Remember to Undo the Section operation if you had performed it for the purpose of generating plans and sections only, because you would, of course, want your original model back.

Figure 4.28

Applying the Section tool in 3D mode to the same set of objects shown in Figure 4.27-a, with the same cutting plane. The cut portions can be moved (b), or deleted (c), independently of each other.

⬛ The Section tool in 3D mode, as you can see, is useful not just for generating plans and sections of the model, but also for conveniently trimming away unwanted parts of objects. Remember that you can also use a cutting line instead of a cutting plane by setting the Cut Objects With option to Line, just as you did for 2D sections.

4.3   Contour Cuts

⬛ Select the Contour tool, located immediately after the Section tool in the left column of Row 8, and apply it to any 3D object. You will find that a number of 2D sections of the object are created at regular intervals, parallel to the currently active reference plane (see Figure 4.29-a). Each one of these sections is called a "contour," and the distance between them is referred to as the "contour increment." The Contour tool is thus similar to the Section tool in the sense that it makes 2D sections of the selected object; however, no cutting plane or line is needed here.

⬛ Create an inclined arbitrary reference plane, then reapply the Contour tool to another object. Notice how the contours of the object are now created differently since they are parallel to the new plane. Needless to say, this method of deriving several parallel 2D surfaces from a single 3D object can come in very handy at times.

⬛ Invoke the dialog of the Contour tool and look at its options (Figure 4.29-b). You can see that you have two basic choices: Use Contour Increment, where you specify the distance between two contours; or Use # Of Increments, where you specify the total number of cuts that should be made to the object. You have already worked with the first option, which is active by default. Switch to the second one and see how it works.

Figure 4.29

Applying the Contour tool to the same set of objects shown in Figure 4.27-a, using two different planes. The tool dialog is also shown.

(a)

(b)

⬛ For each of the two main options of the Contour tool, you also have a few choices that determine where the *first* contour will be located. Try them all out. For the Use Contour Increment mode, you can specify the actual starting position relative to the reference plane (Start At), or a value that will be added to the lowest point of the object (Start At Min Plus), or simply opt for the lowest position that is a multiple of the contour increment (Start At Increment Multiple). For the # Of

Increments mode, you can choose between Start At Min Plus, which has the same meaning as before, or End At Max Minus, where the specified value will be subtracted from the highest point of the object to fix the position of the final contour.

▣ There are two additional options that apply to both modes of the Contour tool, and these appear towards the base of the dialog. By default, two discontiguous contours of an object created at the same level are treated as one object. This situation occurs with the 3D enclosure shown sectioned in Figure 4.29-a. By checking the One Object Per Contour option, such discontiguous same-level contours get created as separate objects. Needless to say, you can always use the Separate tool (M-Tool:8b,2) to separate them later, if you forget to select this option.

▣ The last option for the Contour tool is Set All Elevations To Zero. When this is checked, all the contours will be projected on to the current reference plane and will lie on top of each other. You could use this to quickly create, for instance, a set of concentric circles as shown in Figure 4.30.

Figure 4.30

Selecting the Set All Elevations To Zero option for the Contour tool.

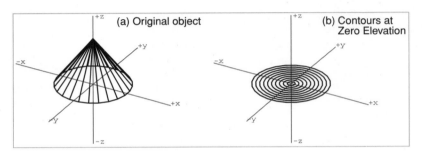

EXERCISE **5**

Moving Over Rugged Terrains

In this exercise, you will learn how to create undulating landforms, i.e., sites for architecture and urban planning that are not flat. form•Z provides you with a dedicated tool for creating such undulating terrains: the Terrain Model tool, located at the end of the left column on Row 5. This lets you create sloping sites in the manner in which such sites are normally represented and illustrated outside CAD— using contour lines and contour intervals. This makes the Terrain Model tool very easy and intuitive to use, as you will see in the course of this exercise.

5.1 Meshed Terrain Model

▣ On a new project or fresh layer, use the drawing tools in 2D mode to draw a site outline and some contour lines, all on the same reference plane. You can switch to the Top view in order to do this more accurately. The site *must* be a closed surface. Take care to ensure that the contour lines which do not form a closed loop within the site cross the boundary of the site. And, of course, you should not create contour lines that cross each other—a basic requirement of the contour concept, in CAD or outside of it.

Figure 4.31

The Terrain Model Options dialog.

WORKSHOP 4

▣ Select the Terrain Model tool (M-Tool:5a,9) and invoke its dialog (Figure 4.31). Notice that there are three types of terrain models, of which Mesh Model is selected by default. This is the terrain type we will be working with first. Leave all the options selected the way they are, except for those in the Contour Heights section. Use Contour Heights is selected by default, but we will explore this later. Switch instead to the alternative, Adjust Heights At Intervals Of. There is an associated contour interval value, which you can also change if required. What this option lets you do is draw contour lines on the same level as the site (which is what you have done), and then use the specified contour interval to automatically space them out perpendicular to the site plane. Exit the Terrain Model Options dialog after making this change.

▣ Back in the graphics window, use the Pick tool to select each one of the contour lines in the correct height sequence, starting with the lowermost contour. The sequence of selection is very important for the Contour Heights mode you just activated, since it will determine the height of each contour line.

 If some contours need to be at the same height, group them first using the Group tool. Then pick all the contours with the topological level set to Group rather than Object.

▣ When all the contour lines have been prepicked, select the Terrain Model tool and watch the Prompts palette. You will be asked to select a 2D object or the face of a 3D object to serve as the site for the landform. Click on the shape you created for the site. A meshed terrain model of your site will be instantaneously created, following the shape, heights, and sequence of your contour lines (Figure 4.32).

Figure 4.32

Creating a meshed terrain model with the option set to Adjust Heights At Intervals Of. The picking sequence of the contour lines is indicated.

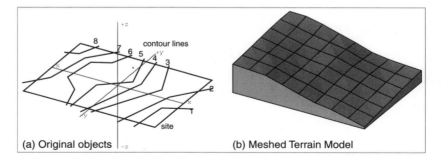

▣ Return to the Terrain Model Options dialog and set the Contour Heights option back to the default of Use Contour Heights. Undo the Terrain Model operation you just performed; you will redo it using the new option. Since you will now be using the actual heights of the contour lines, apply the Move tool with the Perpendicular Lock turned on to move each contour line to the desired height (Figure 4.33-a). As you can see, the advantage of this method is that you can have variable heights between contours rather than a uniform contour interval. After you have finished rearranging the contour lines, prepick them—the sequence of selection will not matter now—and apply the Terrain Model tool as before. You should see a different landform based on the new heights of your contour lines (Figure 4.33-b).

◼ You might wish to have a smoother terrain, which requires having a denser mesh with smaller subdivisions. This can be done by invoking the Terrain Model Options dialog and clicking on the Mesh Options button. This will bring up a dialog in which you can change the dimensions of the mesh. This is the same dialog associated with the Mesh tool (M-Tool:6a,1) which will be covered in Workshop 6, and we will explore all the options in this dialog at that time. For now, simply change the X, Y, and Z values of the mesh, deselecting the XYZ Lock option if you require them to be different from each other. Then get back to the graphics window, Undo the Terrain Model operation, and reapply it with the new settings. The meshed terrain should now be denser, and therefore smoother, than before (Figure 4.33-c).

Figure 4.33

Using the Terrain Model tool with the option set to Use Contour Heights. Two versions of the resultant model are shown, each with different mesh settings.

◼ Go back and look at the Terrain Model Options dialog and you will see that there are four Interpolation options for the Mesh Model type. These options determine how the elevations of each point of the mesh are related to the heights of the contour lines you create. The four different options lead to very minor changes, so we will not get into the technical details of how the interpolation is actually done. All that you really need to know is that the Fall Lines method is considered to be more accurate (and therefore more time-consuming), but the default of X&Y works reasonably well and you can leave it as such.

◼ The Terrain Model Options dialog contains a number of other options that apply to all the three types of models. The value of the Site (Starting) Height determines the elevation of the base of the site when it is a 2D object, as in the examples used so far. It has no effect when the face of a solid object is selected as the site. Test it with a height that is different from the default value.

◼ The Smooth Contour Lines At Distance option is more relevant to the Stepped Model, so we will look at it later. Turn to the last option, Precheck For Intersecting Contours—this will warn you if it finds intersecting contours before attempting to carry out the Terrain Model operation. As already mentioned, contours should not intersect, but if you have a large site and many closely spaced contours (which you may have entered through a digitizing tablet), you might inadvertently have some of them intersecting each other. Therefore, for modeling large sites and complicated terrains, it is advisable to turn this option on, otherwise it is not necessary.

> *A very common error when working with terrain models is to leave contour lines drawn on the same plane as the site, and then neglect to change the Contour Heights option from the default of Use Contour Heights to Adjust Heights At Intervals Of. This will result in a flat landform since the actual contour heights will be used, which are the same height as the site. Watch out for this error, and rectify it by selecting the appropriate height option.*

5.2 Stepped Terrain Model

▣ It is time to move on to the other types of terrain models. Get back to the Terrain Model Options dialog and select the second type, Stepped Model. Undo the Terrain Model operation you last performed and redo it using the new mode. You will see that instead of a smooth mesh, the landform now has actual steps between the contour lines (Figure 4.34-a).

▣ Since the individual contours are now actually visible, these might need to be curvilinear to give a better appearance to the stepped site. You could, of course, created them as curved to begin with. An easy alternative is to activate the Smooth Contour Lines At Distance option in the Terrain Model Options dialog, and specify the desired smoothing distance in the associated box. If you now Undo and reapply the Terrain Model tool, the steps of the terrain will be smoothly curved, unlike before (Figure 4.34-b).

Figure 4.34

Creating a stepped terrain model, using the same site and contours as in Figure 4.32. The result of activating the Smooth Contour Lines At Distance option is also shown.

(a) Stepped Model   (b) Smooth Contour Lines option on

▣ The Stepped Model terrain type can be used to create a simple staircase very quickly with minimal effort. And unlike the Straight Stair tool, the steps can be of any shape. Draw the outline of the staircase, and the individual steps as contours projecting beyond the outline, as shown in Figure 4.35-a. You could simply draw one contour and then transform it in Multi Copy mode to generate the rest. Activate the Adjust Heights To Intervals Of option and specify the required riser height as the contour interval. Apply the Terrain Model tool to this configuration in the usual manner, and you have your staircase ready in a jiffy! The result is shown in Figure 4.35-b.

Figure 4.35

Creating a staircase quickly using the Stepped Terrain Model.

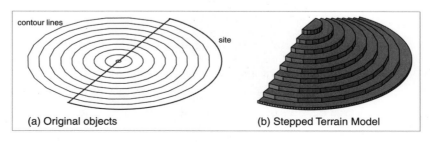

(a) Original objects   (b) Stepped Terrain Model

WORKSHOP 4

5.3   Triangulated Terrain Model

■ Move on to select the third type of terrain, Triangulated Contour Model, in the dialog of the Terrain Model tool. Apply it to a new set of contour lines and site. This time, use a 3D slab rather than a 2D surface as your site (Figure 4.36-a). This means that after you finish prepicking your contour lines, you will have to set the topological level to Face and apply the Terrain Model tool to the top face of the slab. Note that the contour lines themselves can be created at the level of the lower face, which coincides with the reference plane and is therefore more convenient.

■ You will find that the resultant terrain model is derived by preserving the shape and height of the contours and triangulating the resulting faces (Figure 4.36-b). Since the shape of the contour lines is preserved, it might again be advisable to check the Smooth Contour Lines At Distance option to smoothen them out.

Figure 4.36

Creating a Triangulated Terrain Model, using the top face of a 3D slab as the site. The sequence of contour selection is also indicated. The same height contours were first grouped.

(a) Original objects   (b) Triangulated Terrain Model

■ You can increase the level of triangulation by selecting the Triangulate Non Sloping Triangles sub-option for the Triangulated Contour Model in the tool dialog. This will give you a more accurate terrain. Try it.

5.4   Combining Terrain Model Types

It is possible to combine different terrain model types on the same site. Let us end this exercise by executing one such combination example.

■ Create a horizontal slab with a thickness and then draw a single contour line such that it coincides with the top face of the slab, as shown in Figure 4.37-a. This contour will serve as the divider between the two different types of terrains that you will create on the top face.

■ Invoke the Terrain Model Options dialog, and select the Stepped Model type with the Use Contour Heights option. Select the single contour and apply the Terrain Model tool to the top face of the site, as you did in the previous section. Since the contour is at the same level as the top face, the result of the Terrain Model operation will simply be to divide the top face into two separate faces, as shown in Figure 4.37-b. (Thus, you could also use the Terrain Model tool simply to divide the face of an object into two or more parts.)

■ Now create two separate sets of contour lines for each of the two faces, as shown in Figure 4.37-c. You can move these contour lines to the appropriate heights, or set the Contour Heights option in the Terrain Model Options dialog to Adjust Heights At Intervals Of, with a suitable interval value.

■ Preselect one set of contours and apply the Terrain Model tool to the corresponding face by setting the topological level to Face. That part of the site will become a stepped terrain (Figure 4.37-d).

■ Choose another terrain type in the Terrain Model Options dialog, say the Mesh Model. Change the value of the contour interval if necessary. Then apply the Terrain Model tool to the other set of contour lines and face. The final result will be a landform with both types of terrains (Figure 4.37-e). Thus, you can see how versatile the Terrain Model tool is.

Figure 4.37

Creating a Terrain Model with two types of terrains on the same site.

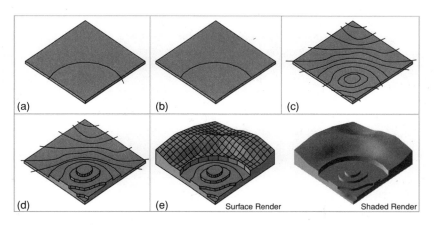

EXERCISE 6

The Remaining Derivatives

The left column of Row 5 of the modeling tool palette contains all the *derivative object tools* that are used to derive new objects from existing ones in various ways. In Workshop 1, you worked with three of these tools, Extrusion, Convergence, and 3D Enclosure, while in the last exercise, you worked with one more, the Terrain Model tool. In this exercise, we will explore the remaining derivative object tools and see what they can do for us.

6.1   Deriving 2D Objects and Enclosures

■ The first two tools in the left column of Row 5 are the Derivative 2D Surface and Derivative 2D Enclosure tools respectively. Let us look at Derivative 2D Surface first. Select this tool and apply it to any 3D object, ensuring that the topological level is set to Object. There is no visible change. However, apply the Move tool to the object and you will find that you can select each one of its faces separately and move them away, leaving behind the original object in ghosted mode (Figure 4.38-a). What this tool has done is derived 2D shapes from a 3D object by literally splitting it up into independent faces. The original object can, of course, be retained by setting the Status Of Objects option to Keep.

Figure 4.38

Applying the Derivative 2D Surface tool with the topological level set to Object. (a) To a 3D object. (b) To a 2D enclosure with the option set to Boundary Of Surface Object.

(a)   (b)

⬛ The Derivative 2D Surface tool comes in especially useful when you want to use the face of an object for performing some operation—extrusion, for example—but need to retain the original object as it is. This tool can also be used to derive segments and faces from other 3D and 2D objects by setting the topological level appropriately. The dialog of this tool has some additional options that you should explore—for instance, the Boundary Of Surface Object option transforms a 2D enclosure into a 2D surface object by extracting only its outermost boundary (Figure 4.38-b).

⬛ The next tool, Derivative 2D Enclosure, functions identically to the Derivative 2D Surface tool, except that it generates enclosures instead of single lines or faces. The wall width and justification options for the enclosure can be set in the tool dialog in the usual manner. Use it for various 2D and 3D objects and observe the results.

6.2 Creating Parallel Objects

⬛ Create a few 2D and 3D objects on a fresh layer. Select the Parallel tool (M-Tool:5a,6) and apply it to each one of these objects. What this tool essentially does is create offsets of existing objects at a specified distance. For surface objects, you will find that the object is moved parallel to itself in a positive direction with respect to the coordinate axes. For solid objects, all the faces are moved out parallel to the original faces, resulting in the entire object being enlarged by a certain factor. Thus, the Parallel tool always creates parallel surfaces, an operation which can often come in handy. As you can see from the examples illustrated in Figure 4.39-a, you can also apply the Parallel tool repeatedly to the same object to progressively increase the offset distance.

⬛ Invoke the dialog of the Parallel tool and experiment with the options available. Here, you can change the direction as well as the distance of the offsets, both for surface and solid objects. While the In and Out options are obvious for a solid object, for a surface object they relate to the direction in which the parallel surface gets created. The default is Out, which means that the surface object will be moved in the positive direction of the axes. Change this to In for moving in the opposite direction.

⬛ You can also see that the default option is Single Parallel (Surface), which is why the Parallel tool has so far been creating a single surface parallel to the original face. Switch to the alternate option, Double Parallel (Solid), and you will find that the Parallel tool now converts every single surface to a pair of surfaces with solid between them. Thus, 2D surfaces get transformed to 3D extrusions, while 3D objects themselves get transformed to hollow enclosures (Figure 4.39-b). The offset distances apply in the usual manner, and there is an additional option, Center, which will offset the pair of surfaces equally about the center of the original surface.

Figure 4.39

Applying the Parallel tool to a set of objects. The original objects are in ghosted mode.

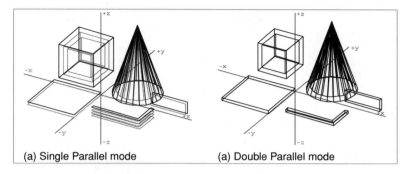

(a) Single Parallel mode (a) Double Parallel mode

- For surface objects, parallel surfaces are created in a direction perpendicular to the plane of the surface by default, as you can see in Figure 4.39. To create parallel surfaces on the *same* plane as the object, simply activate the Parallel On Same Plane option in the dialog of the Parallel tool. The surface will now be reduced or enlarged (depending on whether the In or Out option is activated), instead of simply being moved parallel to itself. Try it.

- You can also apply the Parallel tool with the topological level set to Face or Segment. This comes in useful if you are trying to create faces or segments parallel to existing objects, an operation which is frequently necessary. You can set Status Of Objects to Keep, so that the original object is not lost but you can still use it as a reference for deriving a parallel face or segment.

6.3 Making Projections

- Move on to the Projection tool (M-Tool:5a,7) which is used to derive 2D projections of 3D objects. There are two different kinds of projections that can be obtained. The default type is Projection Of View, as you can verify in the dialog of the Projection tool.

- Create a 3D block and make multiple copies of it. Make sure you are in a non-planar view; then apply the Projection tool to one of the copies. Switch to a different non-planar view and apply the tool to another copy. Repeat this for a few other views. Finally, use the Top view for the last copy. Still in the Top view, look at the results of all the projections (Figure 4.40-a). Then see them in a non-planar view (Figure 4.40-b). You will find that in each case, the current view of the object was projected on to the current reference plane, transforming the 3D object to a flat 2D object. To put it in simpler terms, the way you see the object on the screen is mapped and then placed on the active reference plane. Because the views kept changing, the projections kept changing as well. The projections would also be different for the same view but a different reference plane.

Figure 4.40

Using the Projection Of View mode to derive projections of the same object on the XY plane using four different views: 30-60, 45-45, 60-30, and Top. The original objects are seen in ghosted mode.

Top view   30-60 view

Figure 4.41

Using the Orthographic
Projection mode to derive a
rudimentary plan and
elevation of a model.

▣ Switch to the alternate option, Orthographic Projection, in the dialog of the Projection tool and apply it to some objects. You will find that this kind of projection is derived by simply projecting the object straight on to the current reference plane, thus making it independent of the current view. Not only is this less confusing, it has greater utility in modeling as well. It can be used to derive plans and elevations, of sorts, from a model, which can then be reworked into more accurate drawings. This is illustrated in Figure 4.41, using the example of the chair modeled in Workshop 3. Its orthographic projection was derived on both the XY and YZ planes to give a plan and side elevation respectively. The Status Of Objects was set to Keep the first time, and both planes were moved some distance away from the chair prior to projection.

6.4 Unfolding Objects

▣ Select the next derivative object tool, Unfold (M-Tool:5a,8), and try it on some objects. You will find that, true to its name, this tool unfolds the object completely and lays out all its surfaces on the current reference plane, retaining some, but not all, of the surface adjacencies. (Needless to say, some connections have to be broken in order to "unfold" the object.) You can easily see the analogy of this in real life to dismantling a box by cutting along a few of its edges until all the faces are laid out flat on the ground. In the case of the Unfold tool, where the cut is made is determined by where you click on the object to apply the operation to it. Also, the unfolded object is always located at the origin of the current reference plane relative to how the object was selected, and oriented in the positive axes direction. A couple of examples of the Unfold operation are shown in Figure 4.42.

The Unfold tool can be used to create the 2D layout of a 3D object that is to be constructed manually, for instance, the physical "block models" of cardboard or wood that so many design professionals build for design conceptualization. Needless to say, this tool is most useful when applied to a preliminary massing model of an object or a design rather than a detailed model.

▣ The Unfold tool has a number of options which you should explore in detail at leisure. The Reposition Overlapping Parts option, which is selected by default, moves any overlapping parts the original object might have to a new position in the unfolded object, where they do not overlap. Triangulate Non-Planar Faces has the usual meaning. When the Unfold tool is used for constructing a physical model of a design, it is helpful to activate the Generate Connectors option. This will create a connector on each edge of the unfolded object, which can be used to attach adjacent faces to each other in the physical model. You can also set the width and other specifications for the connectors in the included sub-options.

Figure 4.42

Two examples of the Unfold operation. The original objects are seen in ghosted mode.

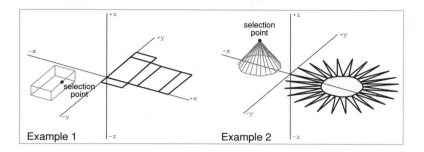

6.5   Deriving Objects from Other Objects

There are no more derivative tools left on Row 5 to work with. But there is still one more option that we haven't yet explored, which is *deriving objects from complete objects*. Let us do one example of this.

■ Create any extruded or converged solid (Figure 4.43-a). Let us suppose that you want to derive other solids from all the faces of this object simultaneously. Instead of tediously carrying out the operation for each face separately, use this simple shortcut. First, set the topological level to Object. Then, select any of the derivative object tools from Row 5, say the 3D Enclosure tool. Invoke its dialog and set the extrusion direction as Perpendicular To Surface. Also, preselect a height from the Heights menu.

■ Now apply the 3D Enclosure tool to the object. You will find that all its faces are simultaneously converted to 3D enclosures of the same height and thickness, completely transforming the original object (Figure 4.43-b). Experiment to see what other interesting forms can be generated using this method.

Figure 4.43

Deriving 3D enclosures of a predefined height simultaneously from all the faces of an object.

(a) Original object   (b) Resultant object

EXERCISE 7

Rounding Objects and Drafting Angles

In this exercise, we will work with the two tools located in the right column of Row 6 of the modeling tool palette: Round and Draft Angle. The Round tool is useful for rounding or beveling the points and edges of an object, while the Draft Angle tool is used to provide a desired inclination to the surfaces of an object with respect to a plane. Let us start with the Round tool.

7.1   Plain Rounding

▣ Create a simple solid object whose points and edges you can round. Then select the Round tool (M-Tool:6b,1) and invoke its dialog. The default option is set to Controlled Rounding. However, go ahead and activate the Plain Rounding option—we will work with it first, since it is simpler. Under this option, set the Rounding Type to Corner Point and leave the Rounding Method to the default selection of Use Radius (Figure 4.44). Change the default value of the rounding radius if it is not proportionate to the size of your object. Leave the # Of Rounding Points to the default value of 4. Click OK to exit the dialog after you have finished making all these specifications.

Figure 4.44

Activating the Plain Rounding option in the dialog of the Round tool.

▣ Back in the graphics window, set the topological level to Object and apply the Round tool to the object you have created (Figure 4.45-a). You will find that all the points of the object get rounded (Figure 4.45-b). Undo and set the topological level to Point. You can now round only selected points with the Round tool (Figure 4.45-c).

▣ Zoom in closer to one of the rounded points and you will find that the rounding actually takes place in 4 segments or facets. To increase the resolution of the rounding, get back to the Rounding Options dialog and increase the value of # Of Rounding Points. Apply the Round tool to a new object, or undo the previous operation and reapply the Round tool to the same object. You will find that the rounding is now smoother (Figure 4.45-d).

▣ You can also increase the resolution by checking the High Density option, which generates additional faces for the rounding operation (Figure 4.45-e). Note that this applies to the currently selected Corner Point option only.

▣ Measure the rounding offset of the object, i.e., the distance from the original point to where the rounding begins (Figure 4.45-f), and you will find that it is equal to the value accompanying the two Rounding Method options in the dialog. You can change this value depending upon the extent of rounding you want.

▣ The two options for Rounding Method differ only slightly. Use Radius draws an imaginary sphere of the specified value around a point and uses the intersection of this sphere with the object to determine the area that will be rounded. Use Distance, on the other hand, simply uses the specified value to mark the distance on each edge from the point, within which the rounding will then take place. If the angle subtended by the edges of the object at a point is 90º (as in the cube example in Figure 4.45), the two methods will produce identical results. However, if it is less than or greater than 90º, the rounding radius will be less than or greater than the specified value respectively. The difference is so small that you should not worry about which Rounding Method to use, unless you are working with a very high level of precision.

WORKSHOP 4

Figure 4.45

Applying the Round tool with the option set to Plain Rounding and Corner Point. (a) The original object. (b) Rounding all points. (c) Rounding only selected points. (d) Increasing the number of rounding points. (e) Checking the High Density option. (f) The rounding offset, indicated in a planar view.

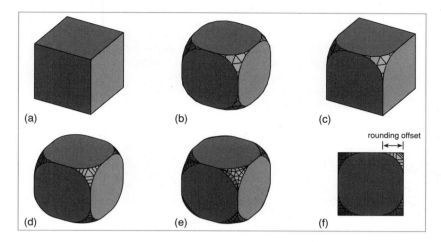

■ Let us move on to look at the other two types of Plain Rounding. Select the Edge option in the Rounding Options dialog and apply the Round tool to a fresh object (Figure 4.46-a), first with the topological level set to Object, then with it set to Segment. Now the edges of the object will be rounded rather than the points (Figure 4.46-b). All the other related options such as Rounding Method, # of Rounding Points, and so on, work in the same manner for edges as for points.

■ Repeat the process for the third Plain Rounding option, Edges & Points. As you would expect, both points as well as edges now get rounded simultaneously (Figure 4.46-c). You should use this option whenever a point is to be rounded along with its associated edges; rounding the point and edges separately will not yield accurate results.

Figure 4.46

Applying the other two types of Plain Rounding.

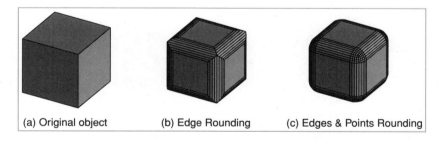

(a) Original object   (b) Edge Rounding   (c) Edges & Points Rounding

■ Proceed to explore the remaining three options located at the end of the Plain Rounding section in the Rounding Options dialog. These apply to all three types of plain rounding. When the Bevel option is selected, the edges and points will be beveled rather than rounded. The Triangulate option, as usual, triangulates any non-planar faces that are produced by a rounding operation. The last option, Adjust Radius To Fit Angle, is useful when the rounding value specified is too large for rounding an edge or a point. When this option is checked, the rounding value gets adjusted automatically (up to a maximum of 25%) and the rounding operation is reapplied. If the rounding still cannot take place after the adjustment, only then is the error message issued. For precise rounding, however, you should turn this option off and adjust the values yourself.

■ Try reapplying the Round tool to any of the objects you just rounded. You will be greeted with a message telling you that the object has non-planar faces and cannot be properly rounded, or that some points and segments cannot be rounded at all. You will have to reduce the rounding value substantially to round the new points and edges that were created as a result of the first rounding. Basically, you can no longer modify the rounding operation applied to the original object. Thus, the new object that gets created is a *plain* rather than a parametric object, which is why the rounding operation that yielded it is called plain rounding.

7.2   Controlled Rounding

The Round tool can also be used to create a parametric object, in which the creation parameters are stored along with the object and can be edited later by applying the same tool. Such an object is also referred to as a *controlled* object, and the rounding operation that produces such an object is referred to as controlled rounding.

◼ Invoke the dialog of the Round tool and select the first option, Controlled Rounding. Apply the Round tool to any object which you have not rounded so far. A Rounding Preview dialog will be invoked, as shown in Figure 4.47-a. It is very similar to all the preview dialogs you have seen so far. The object is shown in a preview window on the left, with the familiar tool icons at the base of the window. There is only one additional tool, Pointer, which we will soon explore. On the right side of the dialog are a variety of options for controlling the rounding, most of which are similar to what you encountered for Plain Rounding in the last section.

◼ Notice that in the preview window, all the edges and points of the object are in the ghosted color, which is gray by default. This indicates that none of them are selected for rounding. Use the Pointer tool to select some edges and points, and click on the Preview button. You should now see the selected entities rounded according to the values specified in the dialog (Figure 4.47-b).

Figure 4.47

Using the Round tool with the option set to Controlled Rounding. (a) The Rounding Preview dialog, invoked when Controlled Rounding is first applied to an object. (b) Rounding three edges and a point by selecting them in the preview window. (c) Changing the rounding parameters of a previously rounded entity to new values using the Edit option.

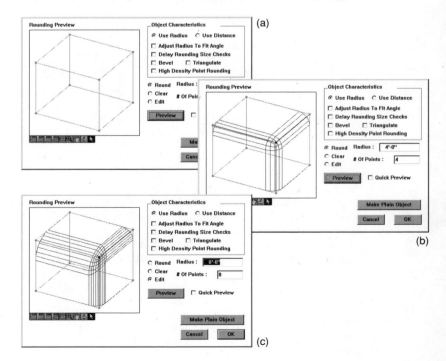

▪ You could, of course, also have achieved the same result by applying Plain Rounding with the Edges & Points option. The difference, however, is that you have now created a controlled object rather than a plain one, and you can come back and modify it at any time. Try it. First, exit the Rounding Preview dialog by clicking OK. Your object should be rounded according to the parameters you had specified. Reapply the Round tool to the same object, and the Rounding Preview dialog will be invoked, showing the original shape of the object, along with the rounded shape (as in Figure 4.47-b). You can now modify the size and resolution of the rounding, round other edges and points, or remove the rounding from any edge or point. All this would not have been possible with Plain Rounding.

▪ Let us see exactly how these modifications can be made. Change the Radius and # Of Points values and select a new edge or point with the Pointer tool. Hit the Preview button and you will see the newly selected entities rounded according to the new specifications. To modify any previously rounded entity, activate the Edit option and select the rounded edge or point with the Pointer tool. The Radius and # Of Points boxes will show the current values for that entity. Modify these and click on the Preview button. The rounding will now be changed according to the new specifications (Figure 4.47-c).

▪ Next, activate the Clear option and select some rounded edges and points in the preview window. Click on the Preview button and you will see these entities restored to their original unrounded condition. Thus, you can, if required, clear the object of all its rounding and restore it back to its original state.

▪ There are only three options in the Rounding Preview dialog that are new to Controlled Rounding. Delay Rounding Size Checks is a useful option to activate when many adjacent entities are to be rounded, because rounding values can sometimes conflict when the rounding is done sequentially but not when done collectively. Having this option selected will postpone the rounding calculation until you complete the selection of entities, and click on the Preview button or the OK button to exit the dialog.

▪ The Quick Preview option, when checked, will display the rounding in the preview window at a low resolution of 2 points, irrespective of the actual # Of Points value. This is useful when complex objects are being rounded. The actual resolution will be applied once you exit the Rounding Preview dialog.

▪ Finally, the Make Plain Object button, when clicked, will convert the rounded controlled object to a plain one. You should do this only when you are sure that you will no longer need to modify the rounding parameters of the original object. Conversion to a plain object has two advantages. First, it saves memory since you are deleting information that is no longer useful. Second, it is essential when you want to do *recursive rounding*, i.e., round a point or segment that was not originally present in the object but gets created as the result of a rounding operation. It is illustrated in Figure 4.48. This could not have been done on a controlled object.

Figure 4.48

Recursive rounding applied to a plain object. (a) Original object. (b) Rounding an edge with a large radius value. (c) Rounding the points of the resulting edges with a much smaller radius value.

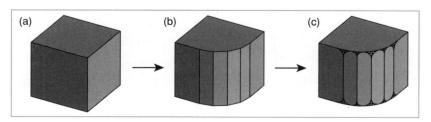

7.3 Stitch Rounding

The third type of rounding available in the Rounding Options dialog is Stitch Rounding. A "stitch" is a continuous, closed sequence of segments in a solid object, with the angles between adjacent segments equal to or greater than 100°. The Stitch Rounding option enables you to conveniently round stitches without having to select each segment of the stitch. Let us see how it works.

◼ Create a circular or elliptical extrusion, as shown in Figure 4.49-a. Invoke the dialog of the Round tool and activate the Stitch Rounding option. It has the same rounding parameters—Distance and # Of Rounding Points—as the other two rounding methods. You can modify these values from the defaults if necessary.

◼ With the Round tool selected, click on one of the segments of any face of the object that meets the condition of a stitch. All the edges of the face get rounded simultaneously according to the specified parameters (see Figure 4.49-a). Note that you could have achieved the same effect by using the Plain Rounding option with the rounding type set to Edge, activating the Face topological level, and applying the Round tool to that face. The Stitch Rounding option saves you from the bother of changing the topological level—it can remain as Object.

◼ Another example of Stitch Rounding is illustrated in Figure 4.49-b on an object with insertions created using the Insert Face mode. Note again, that you could have achieved the same result by using Plain Rounding in Edge mode with the topological level set to Outline.

Figure 4.49

Two examples of applying the Round tool with the mode set to Stitch Rounding.

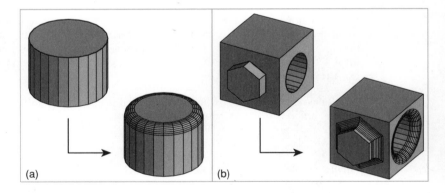

(a)   (b)

The examples shown in Figure 4.49 are very simple examples of stitches, which is why Plain Rounding could have been used just as well by setting the appropriate topological level. There can be, however, more complicated stitches in non-planar meshed and patch objects, which cannot be selected by setting the topological level to Face or Outline. Stitch Rounding is really indispensable for such objects. You will learn to create such objects in Workshop 6, so keep the Stitch Rounding option in mind for later use.

7.4 Applying Draft Angles

The Draft Angle tool, located immediately after the Round operator, is a nifty little tool that can be used to quickly incline a surface object, or one or more faces of a solid object, to the desired extent. The inclination takes place with respect to a specified reference plane. Let us see how it is done.

Figure 4.50

Applying the Draft Angle tool to the same object, but with respect to two different planes.

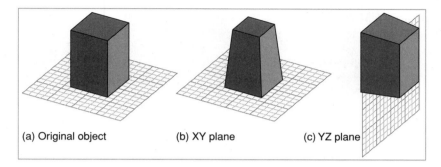

(a) Original object   (b) XY plane   (c) YZ plane

▣ Create a solid extrusion on the XY plane, as shown in Figure 4.50-a. Set the topological level to **Object**. With the XY plane still active, select the **Draft Angle** tool (M-Tool:6b,2) and apply it to the solid. You will find that all the faces of the solid perpendicular to the XY plane are splayed inwards, changing the shape of the solid (Figure 4.50-b). **Undo** the operation, switch to a different plane, and reapply the **Draft Angle** tool to the solid. The same transformation happens, but now with respect to the new plane (Figure 4.50-c).

▣ The **Draft Angle** tool comes with a number of options in its dialog (Figure 4.51), which we will explore next. The first option is **Base Reference Plane** which is set to **Active Plane** by default. This is why all inclinations have been taking place with respect to the current plane. You can also choose to specify one of the three predefined planes as the base plane for executing the operation, irrespective of the currently active plane.

▣ The **Position Of Base Plane** option determines where the inclination calculation will begin. Consider the example illustrated in Figure 4.52-a of three identical objects whose lowest and highest points are 20' and 50' above the reference plane respectively. The draft angle calculation can be applied in three different ways depending upon where the base plane is located, leading to different results as shown in Figure 4.52-b. Try out all three. **At Current Position** uses the current location of the base plane, which is 0' in the example. For the **At Minimum Of Object/Faces** method, the base plane is moved to the lowest point of the object and then the inclination is calculated, leading to a larger object size. For the third method, **At Maximum Of Object/Faces**, the base plane is moved to the highest point for calculating the inclination, leading to the largest object size, even bigger than the original object.

▣ The next option in the **Draft Angle Options** dialog is **Inclination**, which lets you specify the required inclination value. The default is 5°. Try higher values and watch your object, at some point, end up with surfaces crossing each other. Such objects are mathematically not very sound, so be careful if you apply this technique.

Figure 4.51

The dialog of the Draft Angle tool.

WORKSHOP 4

Figure 4.52

The effect of different Position Of Base Plane options for the same set of objects, while applying the Draft Angle operation.

(a) Original objects

(b) Resultant objects

■ The last two options in the dialog let you decide which faces of an object will be affected by the Draft Angle operation. The Use Faces Within option, which is selected by default, lets you specify an angle—only faces which are at an inclination of less than this angle with respect to the base plane will be affected by the operation. Going by the default value of 2°, a pyramid, for instance, will not be affected at all, unless its height is so large compared to its base that its sides are almost vertical. On the other hand, choosing the Use All Faces option will apply the Draft Angle operation to all the faces, irrespective of what their inclinations are.

EXERCISE 8

Cultivating Attachments

The remaining two exercises of this workshop will cover the Attach, Align, Extend, and Place tools, located in the right column of Row 12 of the modeling tool palette. The operations executed by these tools are, in fact, special types of geometric transformations in which the positions of selected entities can be transformed *relative* to other entities.

We will begin by exploring the Attach tool in this exercise, which gives us the ability to move and position an object (referred to as the *source*) relative to another object (referred to as the *destination*), by attaching one of its parts to a part of the other object. The attachment can even be applied to another part of the same object. There are two basic types of attachments, Object Part and Entire Object, the choice of which is made in the dialog of the Attach tool (see Figure 4.53). In the first, only the selected part of the source object gets displaced, distorting its shape; in the second, the entire object itself gets repositioned. The default mode is Entire Object. Additionally, attachments can be carried out at various topological levels: points, segments, faces, and entire objects. The Attach tool can also be used to reposition an object with respect to a reference plane. We will explore each of these options in turn, after making some basic preparations.

■ Clear your window of all its contents or move to a different layer. On the XY plane, create two 3D objects of substantially different sizes, not touching each other, as shown in Figure 4.54-a. The Attach tool, as pointed out, works in many different ways, so you can create multiple copies of these two objects—this will let you explore all the various permutations of the tool in relation to the same set of objects.

Figure 4.53

The dialog of the Attach tool.

8.1   Point-to-Point Attachments

■ In a point-to-point attachment, the selected point of one object is moved to coincide with the selected point of another object (or of itself). Set the topological level to Point and the self-copy mode to Self. Then select the Attach tool (M-Tool:12b,1), and verify that the Entire Object option is the one that is active in its dialog (as in Figure 4.53). Also, the Attach Kind option must be set to Per Topological Level. Don't worry about the other options in this dialog for now—they are not relevant to this kind of attachment.

■ Turn your attention to the Prompts palette and follow the instructions. For the *source point* (the point that will be displaced), select a point of the smaller object. For the *destination point* (the point to which the source point will be attached), select a point of the larger object. As soon as you do this, the smaller object is moved to reposition itself so that the selected source point coincides with the selected destination point (Figure 4.54-b). Undo the operation and repeat it with different combinations of source and destination points; this will give you a better understanding of how the tool operates.

Figure 4.54

A point-to-point attachment, executed using both the Entire Object and Object Part options.

(a) Original objects   (b) Entire Object option   (c) Object Part option

■ Now repeat the operation with the option set to Object Part in the dialog of the Attach tool. Switch to the Surface Render mode for a more accurate display of the result. You will see that the source object gets completely deformed in the process of being "attached" to the destination object through the selected points (Figure 4.54-c). Such an object will often have non-planar faces, so watch out for these. In general, you will find yourself using the Entire Object option for the most part.

▣ Another variation you should try is to set the self-copy mode on Row 11 to one of the Copy modes rather than Self. The Attach operation will now produce a copy of the source object in the attached position, retaining the original object.

▣ The versatility of the Attach tool is greatly enhanced by its ability to attach a part of an object to another part of the *same* object. This can be done with the Object Part attachment type and the self-copy mode set to Self, which will result in transforming the shape of the object itself, as shown in Figure 4.55-a. Alternately, use the Entire Object attachment type with the self-copy mode set to One Copy to attach additional copies of the object to itself, as shown in Figures 4.55-b and 4.55-c. This involves selecting two different points of the same object as the source and destination points. You can see how easy it is to build any kind of repetitive 3D configuration or 2D pattern using this option of the Attach tool.

Figure 4.55

Examples of a point-to-point attachment of an object with itself.

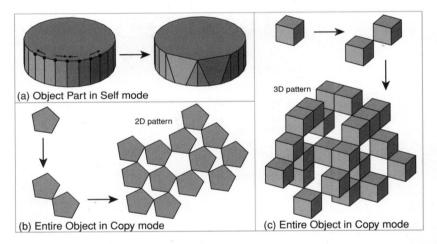

(a) Object Part in Self mode

2D pattern

(b) Entire Object in Copy mode

3D pattern

(c) Entire Object in Copy mode

Only actual points can be selected for attachments. You cannot, for instance, choose to attach the midpoint of a segment of an object to another object. This is because the midpoint is calculated interactively, it is not actually stored as part of the object description; so it cannot be selected. If there is any confusion, invoke the Wire Frame Options dialog and turn on the Show Points option so that all the points of an object are highlighted and clearly visible.

8.2   Segment-to-Segment Attachments

▣ Let us move on to segment-to-segment attachments. Use a fresh set of solids, as shown in Figure 4.56. Set the topological level to Segment, and repeat the entire sequence of operations you performed in the last section. The only difference is that you are now attaching objects through segments rather than through points. Try out a few variations of source and destination segments, using both types of attachments, Entire Object and Object Part. You might find it necessary to change to the Wire Frame display mode to be able to choose your segments correctly.

Figure 4.56

Illustration of how point mapping affects a segment-to-segment attachment. Two different results are obtained, depending upon how the source and destination segments are selected.

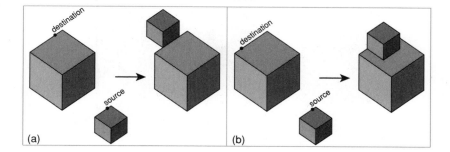

- You will soon find yourself getting very unpredictable results with this type of attachment. This is because the operation is affected by *where* you click on the source and destination segments to select them—the ends must correspond according to the result you wish to achieve. Thus, if you are clicking near the endpoint of a source segment, you must click on the destination segment closer to the end to which the source segment is to be mapped. Figure 4.56 illustrates two different results of attaching the same source segment to the same destination segment, but selected in different ways. The attachment type was Entire Object.

- Notice also that the attached objects are being aligned according to the midpoints of the selected segments, which might not always be what is required. To specify a different segment alignment, invoke the dialog of the Attach tool and choose a different option for Adjust To under the Segment column. The default, as you can see, is Midpoint Of Segment, which is why objects were being attached through segment midpoints. Select each one of the other options in turn, and repeat the Attach operation to see how the results differ. Figure 4.57 illustrates all the four adjustment options. Notice how the All Points option scales only the selected source segment so that it matches the size of the destination segment, while the Scale option scales the entire object so that it matches the destination segment.

- As with point-to-point attachments, the source and destination segments in a segment-to-segment attachment can belong to the same object, transforming it (Self mode) or attaching identical copies to it (one of the Copy modes). The results would be similar to those illustrated in Figure 4.55. Carry out a few such attachment operations before moving on to the next section.

Figure 4.57

Segment-to-segment attachments with various Adjust To options. The attachment type was Entire Object throughout.

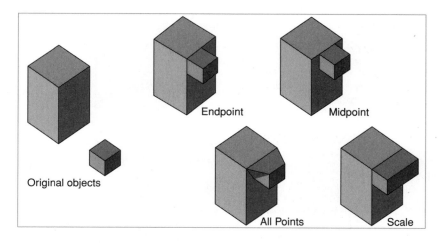

Figure 4.58

Face-to-face attachments in various modes with various adjustment options.

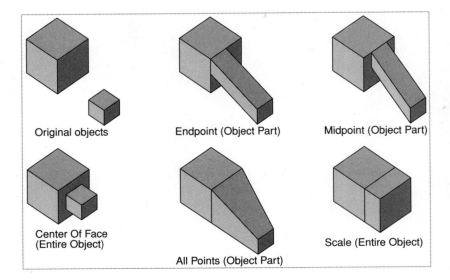

Original objects   Endpoint (Object Part)   Midpoint (Object Part)

Center Of Face (Entire Object)   All Points (Object Part)   Scale (Entire Object)

8.3   Face-to-Face Attachments

▣ The next type of attachment is through the faces of objects. Use a fresh set of objects and with the topological level set to Face, explore the Attach tool in both modes, Object Part and Entire Object. Notice that here again, the order in which you select the segments that delineate a face affects the resultant operation—the segment picked first on the source face is mapped to the segment picked first on the destination face. Therefore, make the selection carefully.

▣ Experiment also with all the Adjust To modes for Face that are available in the Attach dialog. These are illustrated in Figure 4.58. You will find that for face-to-face attachments, the Object Part option becomes a very convenient way to extend or trim an object with respect to the face of another object. Notice also that the first two Adjust To options for Face, in Entire Object mode, work identically to the corresponding options for Segment, and are, in fact, easier to carry out using segment-to-segment attachments rather than face-to-face attachments.

Figure 4.59

A good application of face-to-face attachments: stacking objects on top of each other about the same central axis.

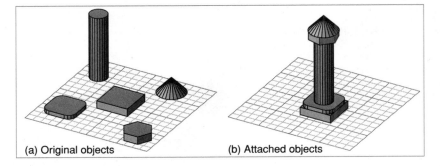

(a) Original objects   (b) Attached objects

▣ The face-to-face attachment is a great technique for stacking solids on top of each other to create interesting configurations. Consider the generation of a column, for instance. You can create all the various elements—the base, pedestal, shaft, cornice, etc., separately (and thus more conveniently) on one plane, as in Figure 4.59-a. Then you can simply use the Attach tool to stack them up to create the final column, as shown in Figure 4.59-b. Try it out. Make sure that your attachment type is set to Entire Object and the adjustment option to Center Of Face.

8.4   Object-to-Object Attachments

▣ You can also use the Attach tool for attaching one object *simultaneously to all faces* of another object. Create two solid objects, one relatively smaller than the other. You will attach the smaller object to all the faces of the larger object. Set the topological level to Object, and the attachment type to Entire Object. (The self-copy modifier setting has no effect here, as it is always executed in Copy mode.) If you now perform the Attach operation, copies of the source object will be attached to every face of the destination object in one step, as shown in Figure 4.60. The attachment happens through the first face of the source object, which in turn is determined by how the object was created.

▣ To perform an object-to-object attachment through *any* desired face of the source object, without being restricted to the first face, activate the second Attach Kind option in the dialog of the Attach tool, Selected Face To All Faces. You can now use the Attach tool to select first a face and then an object; copies of the first object will be attached to all faces of the second object through the *selected* face. Try it out.

▣ Object-to-object attachments are affected by the same Adjust To option that is active for Face in the Attach Options dialog. Different results will be obtained depending upon the option selected—check them all out. Two of these are illustrated in Figure 4.60.

▣ Carry out some more examples of object-to-object attachments. You will soon discover how some of the freakiest objects can be created with this mode! But also, be careful—it is very easy to make a mistake by picking the wrong objects or the wrong faces.

8.5   Repositioning Objects Using Attach

▣ We have worked with all the options of the Attach tool, except the third Attach Kind option, Selected Face To Reference Plane. Go ahead and activate this option. Then select any face of an object and click somewhere on the active reference plane. You will find that the selected face gets placed exactly on the plane, repositioning the object to which it belongs. Try this out for different face selections. Also, keep in mind that this repositioning operation is governed by the same Adjust To option that is active for Face in the Attach Options dialog.

Figure 4.60

Object-to-object attachments using two different Adjust To options.

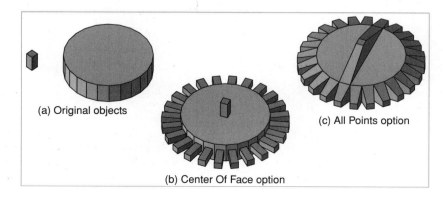

(a) Original objects

(b) Center Of Face option

(c) All Points option

Alignments, Extensions, and Placements

This final exercise will cover the Align, Extend, and Place tools, located immediately after the Attach tool in the right column of Row 12 of the modeling tool palette.

9.1 Aligning and Distributing Objects

The Align tool can be used to align objects located anywhere in 3D space along the X, Y, or Z directions, relative to each other. It can also be used to distribute selected objects at equal distances. Let us see how it works.

▪ Create a number of objects scattered randomly in 3D space, and prepick them with the Pick tool. Then select the Align tool (M-Tool:12b,2) and click anywhere in the window. As soon as you do this, the Alignment/Distribution Options dialog is invoked, showing the selected objects in the preview window and providing you with options for aligning and distributing them in various ways (see Figure 4.61-a).

▪ First, explore the Align and Distribute options located at the top of the dialog in the form of icons, spread out in a row and column format. There are three rows for each of the three axes, X, Y, and Z, and eight columns, three for Align, four for Distribute, and one for indicating no alignment or distribution. To begin with, the Off option is activated for all three axes, as you can see in Figure 4.61-a. Choose one of the three alignment options—Min, Center, or Max—for one or more axes and see how the objects in the preview window line up accordingly, along the minimum, center, or maximum of the chosen directions respectively (Figure 4.61-b). Switch to the Top view to see the results more clearly.

▪ Explore also the four Distribute options in the same manner. The icons do a good job of explaining how the respective operations work. Thus, the Min option will distribute the selected objects equally between the minimum point of the first object and the minimum point of the last object, along the chosen axis. In contrast, the last option, Between, will distribute the objects between the maximum point of the first object and the minimum point of the last object. Note that for a given axis, you can activate either one of the Align or one of the Distribute options, but not both (see Figure 4.61-b).

Figure 4.61

Aligning and distributing objects with the Align tool. (a) The Alignment/Distribution Options dialog, when first invoked. (b) Applying Align and Distribute operations along the X and Y axes.

(a)   (b)

- Now proceed to explore the remaining options located in the lower half of the Alignment/ Distribution Options dialog. By default, the Between Ends option is activated for all three axes, X, Y, and Z, which makes the distribution operation work as explained earlier—the first and last objects along the axes are determined, and the remaining objects are distributed between them at equal distances. In contrast, when the At Distance option is activated, the first, central, or last object along the axes is determined (depending upon whether the Min, Center, or Max distribution option is selected), and the remaining objects are placed sequentially at the distance specified in the accompanying box. The objects are placed in the order in which they were selected. If the fourth distribution option, Between, is selected, objects are distributed at the specified distance about the point which is the average of the maximum point of the first object and the minimum point of the last object. It might sound confusing, but will be clear once you try it out.

9.2 Extending Segments and Faces

Let us move on to look at the next tool, Extend. It is used for extending a segment, or the face on which a number of segments end, in various ways. The extension happens in such a manner that the "directionality" of the segment is maintained. Thus, the Move tool, for instance, cannot be used instead of the Extend tool, as it is not always possible to confine the direction of movement. Since objects are basically comprised of segments and faces, the Extend tool is indispensable for extending and trimming objects accurately with respect to each other.

- Create any two 3D objects, located close to each other, but not touching or overlapping. Activate the Extend tool (M-Tool:12b,3) and watch the Prompts palette for instructions. For the *segment to extend*, select any segment of one of the objects. You will then be prompted for the *face to extend to*. Select any face of the other object that is not parallel to the segment. As a result of the operation, the selected segment is stretched out to meet the selected face, distorting the object it belongs to in the process (Figure 4.62-a).

Figure 4.62

The default operation of the Extend tool, along with the tool dialog.

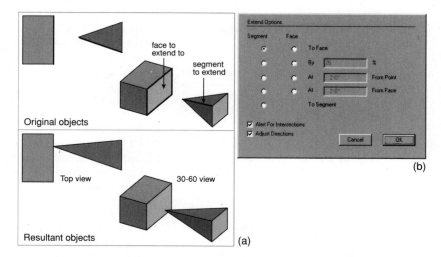

- Invoke the dialog of the Extend tool and examine the options it contains (Figure 4.62-b). There are five methods for extending a Segment and four for extending a Face. By default, the Segment option is active using the To Face method, which is why you were asked to select a face for extending the segment to, in the last step. Explore all the other methods for extending segments as well. You can extend the segment by a percentage of its original length, or by a specified distance from its endpoint or the face at which it ends. These three methods only require the segment to be selected. For the remaining method, To Segment, you have to select a second segment for extending the first segment to.

■ It will often be more convenient to extend the face on which a number of segments end, rather than each individual segment, as in the example illustrated in Figure 4.63 where the corners of two walls in a building model need to be "flushed." Activate the To Face method for the Face entity in the Extend Options dialog. Then select the end face of one wall and extend it to the appropriate face of the other wall, as shown. Repeat the process for the second wall to trim it up to the first wall. Choose the further surface of the wall this time, so that the walls are properly flushed against each other.

Figure 4.63

Extending a face to another face with the Extend tool to flush two walls with each other.

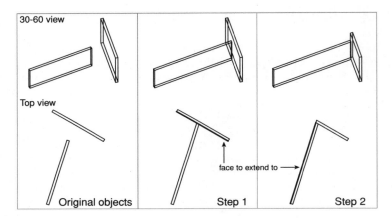

30-60 view

Top view

face to extend to →

Original objects   Step 1   Step 2

■ Explore the other three methods for extending a face, which work in the same manner as for a segment. Also, note the remaining two options at the base of the Extend Options dialog, which are selected by default. When using the To Face extension method, occasionally a self-intersecting object may be produced, or the directions of a solid may get reversed. It helps to be alerted when either of these two situations occur, so it is advisable to leave both options turned on.

9.3   Placing Objects

Place, the last tool in the right column of Row 12, is used to place an object, called the *source*, on an edge or a corner point of another object, called the *destination*. Both the source and destination objects can be 2D or 3D. Multiple copies can be placed, if desired, in one step. The Place tool can also generate a 3D mesh out of multiple 2D placements, as well as apply a macro transformation while placement. We will explore all these capabilities in the remaining sections of this workshop.

■ Clear the window or move to a different layer. Create one large 2D shape and a smaller 3D object. Set the topological level to Object, and the self-copy modifier to Self. Then activate the Place tool (M-Tool:12b,4), and following the instructions in the Prompts palette, select the smaller object as the source and the larger shape as the destination (Figure 4.64-a). The source now gets placed on the destination at the point where you clicked on it to select it (Figure 4.64-b). This is the basic operation of the Place tool.

Figure 4.64

The basic operation of the Place tool, using different Orientation options.

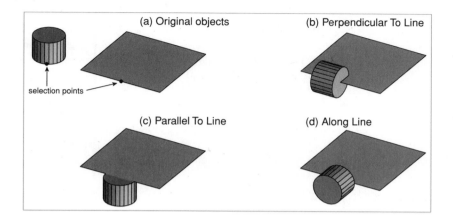

- Invoke the dialog of the Place tool, shown in the next section in Figure 4.66. It has an extensive set of options, all of which we will now study. Let us start with Orientation, which determines how the source object will be oriented when it is placed on the destination object. The default option is Perpendicular To Line, which accounts for the result you obtained in the last step. Explore all the other options, some of which are illustrated in Figure 4.64. Some of these give the same result, depending upon the location and orientation of the destination object.

- Next, turn to the Alignment options. You can see from Figure 4.64 that the source is placed by aligning it through its Centroid. This is the default alignment, but there are four other options. Explore each one in turn. You can mark any point of the source with the Point Marker tool (M-Tool:10b,4), and then use the Reference Point option to place the source through that point. Using the First Point of the source is another option. The Middle Of Open Ends option is applicable only to an open 2D source object—the placement happens through the midpoint of the imaginary segment joining the first and last points of the shape. And finally, the World Origin option places the source through the origin [0,0,0] of the world coordinate system. To use this option effectively, you must create the source in such a way that the origin passes through the point you want for the alignment.

Figure 4.65

The effect of the Snap To Points Within Distance Of option, when placing objects on endpoints.

■ Next, try placing a few objects on the endpoints of various segments of the destination object, using Endpoint snap, rather than on the edges (Figure 4.65-a). You will find that in all cases, the source is oriented perpendicular to the line of the segment ending at the selected point (Figure 4.65-b). Go back to the Place tool dialog and check the Snap To Points Within Distance Of option. Change the accompanying value to 4'-0". Undo all the Place operations you just did, and reapply the tool to place a source on an endpoint of the destination object. You will find that the source is now oriented, not perpendicular to the segment as before, but on the *bisector* of the angle between the two consecutive segments of the destination object at the selected point (Figure 4.65-c). The distance of 4'-0" that you specified will make the Place tool always snap to an endpoint rather than to a segment if you click within 4'-0" of the point; it will then place the source along the angle bisector at the snapped point.

9.4   Multiple Placements

■ The real power of the Place tool is evident when it is used in one of the Copy modes. Set the self-copy modifier on Row 11 to Continuous Copy; then apply the Place tool to a different set of source and destination objects. You will find that you can now place many copies of the source along the destination object by clicking on it at various points. In fact, you can even place multiple copies of the same source on *other* objects, without having to reselect the source and destination object combination each time.

■ For placements at a uniform distance, set the mode to Repeat Copy. You can now place many copies of the source at regular intervals—determined by the first interval you specify—on the destination object, by simply clicking anywhere in the window after the first two placements. The source object will automatically wrap around all the individual segments of the destination object. For a 3D destination object, the face you click on is used for the placement. If the Snap To Points Within Distance Of option in the Place dialog is checked and a segment endpoint happens to become a placement location, the placement will automatically happen along the angle bisector, as you saw in Figure 4.65-c.

■ Now switch to the Multi Copy mode. This lets you place the required number of copies of the source in one step. However, it works a little differently from the usual manner in which you use Multi Copy. Here, the number of copies made is determined not by the value set in the dialog of the Multi Copy tool, but by the value set in the dialog of the Place tool.

Figure 4.66

The dialog of the Place tool.

■ Invoke the Place tool dialog and look at the Multi-Placement options in the lower half of the dialog (Figure 4.66). You can choose between two modes: Between Selected Points or End-To-End. The default is the first mode. Here, you specify the # Of Placements; also, you can choose between indicating by the first two placements, either the placement increment, or the entire placement distance which will then be divided into the specified number of placements. Experiment with both options. The Divide Distance method is more convenient when you want to precisely locate the ending placement in addition to the starting placement. Figure 4.67-b shows a Multi-Placement using this method, with the # of Placements set to 14.

■ Now activate the End-to-End method. This will automatically place the source along the entire length of the destination object, and it can do this in four ways. Explore each one of them in turn—they are quite self-explanatory. The only thing to note is that for all except the first option, only a single click on the destination object is needed to execute the placements. But for the Use Increment option, two clicks on the destination object are needed to specify the increment distance. Figure 4.67-c shows a Multi-Placement using the End-to-End method with the Use Increment option. A small increment distance was indicated.

■ If your source object is a 2D shape, there is an additional option you can apply when you perform multiple placements. Go to the Place Options dialog and check the Generate C-Mesh option. If you now apply the Place tool using a 2D source in the Multi Copy mode, a solid mesh will be generated instead of mere 2D placements (see Figure 4.67-d).

Figure 4.67

Executing multiple placements in one step, using different options.

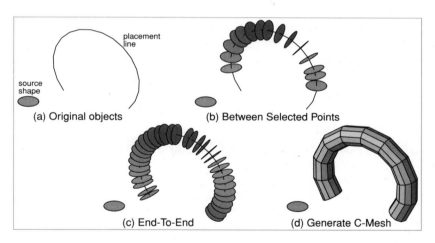

(a) Original objects   (b) Between Selected Points

(c) End-To-End   (d) Generate C-Mesh

The actual parameters of this mesh—curvature, density, etc.,—are determined by the options specified in the dialog of the C-Mesh tool (M-Tool:7a.2), which we will study in Workshop 6. Don't worry about it for now. Note, however, that this object is a "controlled mesh"—or c-mesh—and can be edited at any time using the C-Mesh tool. This is what makes the meshed object generated by the Place tool in the Copy modes different from that generated by the Sweep tool, which also creates objects by sweeping 2D shapes along paths. The Place tool is, in fact, really useful for creating meshed objects of desired configurations.

■ The final word on the Place tool—you can also combine it with the use of macro transformations, which you learned about in Section 4.4 of Workshop 2, to create some very interesting objects. Use Define Macro (M-Tool:11a,6) to create a simple macro transformation, for instance, Move and Scale, or Rotate a Scale. Then go to the Place dialog and check the option, Apply Macro

Transformation. This option was deactivated earlier when no macro transformation had yet been created and stored in the project. If you have defined more than one macro, you can select a specific one from the accompanying popup list, which shows all the macros in the project.

◾ Now apply the Place tool in Multi Copy mode to a different combination of source and destination objects. The source, in addition to being placed multiple times on the destination, also gets transformed according to the applied macro as it is placed, resulting in a potentially interesting configuration. A simple example is illustrated in Figure 4.68. As you can see, the versatility of the Place tool is greatly enhanced by combining it with macro transformations.

Figure 4.68

Combining macro transformations with the Place tool operation.

With that, we come to the end of the exercises for this workshop. Let us proceed to take up the challenge of the Workshop Assignment next.

WORKSHOP 4

Site Planning for Urban Design
ASSIGNMENT 4

◾ *Take any urban design project, preferably on a contoured site. Model the buildings that are to be placed within the site as blocks only. Model the site first, and then concentrate on the placement of the building blocks within the site.*

The actual exercise of modeling the site plan shown on the following page will now be demonstrated step by step. You can refer to the form•Z files for each step of the assignment in the accompanying CD-ROM, under the folder Assignments > Workshop 4. A rendered image of the model is in the Assignment4.tif file in the same location.

Working on this assignment will require the use of only a few of the new tools that have been covered in this workshop. The rest of the tools will be used in the assignment for the next workshop. So you can rest assured that you *will* get the opportunity to put into practice all the enhanced modeling capabilities you have recently acquired!

With all the experience gained from the previous workshop exercises and assignments, you should be very comfortable with the basic modeling operations of form•Z. Therefore, the instructions for this and subsequent assignments will be more concise and less detailed than the instructions for previous assignments.

Setup

Open a new form•Z project. Let us first set up the Working Units appropriate to the scale of the project. Set the Base Unit to Feet under the English measurement system, the Numeric Accuracy to 1', and the Angle Accuracy to 1°. Change also the Window Setup to a grid module of 10' in all directions with 2 subdivisions.

Change the Display Scale to 1/16"=1'. Turn off the display of the default light in the Lights palette.

◁ Step 1

Switch to the Top view, set the Heights menu to 16', turn Grid Snap on, and create a base block of 30' by 30'. We are making the height of the base deliberately this large so that we can adjust it at various positions within the contoured site.

Set the Heights menu to 10', and still in Top view, create two blocks within the base as shown. Then move these blocks upwards by a distance of 16' so that they sit on top of the base.

Step 2

Give the top face of the blocks the required slope for the roofs, as shown, by moving the corresponding segments vertically upwards by a distance of 4'. Also select these top faces and Color them in a different color.

Use the Mirror tool to create a mirror image of the blocks on the base as shown.

Finally, select all these blocks and use the Join tool to combine them into one object. Change the layer name to unit1.

WORKSHOP 4

◁ Step 3

Move to a new layer, unit2, and turn the unit1 layer off. Create the same base block of 30' by 30' with a height of 16'.

Create three 10' high blocks as shown, resting on top of the base.

Step 4

Give the roofs the required slope by moving the corresponding segments vertically upwards by 4'. Again, color the top faces of the blocks in a different color.

Once again, use the Join tool to combine all the parts of this unit into one object.

◁ Step 5

Using these two unit types, create ten different clusters as shown. Each cluster should be created on a separate layer. To copy the units from their individual layers into the cluster layers, activate the Paste On Active Layer option in the Layers dialog. Now you can simply use the Copy and Paste commands to make copies of the units in the cluster layers.

After creating a cluster, select all its individual units and combine them into one object using the Join tool.

Step 6

We will now model the contoured site. Activate a new layer, site, and turn off all the other layers. Switch to the Top view, and draw a 2D rectangle of dimensions 520' by 335'.

Then use the Vector Lines tool to draw the contour lines as shown.

Step 7

Prepick the contour lines in the correct sequence using the Pick tool.

Select the Terrain Model tool and make the following specifications in its dialog: Select the Stepped Model type; let the Site Starting Height remain 1'; for Contour Heights, choose the Adjust Heights option with a contour interval value of 2'; and, check the Smooth Contour Lines At Distance Of option with a value of 5'.

Then apply the Terrain Model tool to your site rectangle. It will be converted to a stepped terrain model.

Step 8

Switch back to the Top view and draw the road lines passing through the site. Connect their ends on either side using the Connect tool (M-Tool:10a,4), so that they form a closed shape.

◀ Step 9

In a non-planar view, move the closed shape for the road vertically downwards below the base of the site. Then extrude it so that its top face is higher than the highest point of the site.

Step 10

Use the road block to perform a One Way Split of the site, so that it is broken up into three separate pieces: one each for the two portions of the site, and the third for the road.

Move the separated road piece vertically upwards by 1' so that it is clearly distinguishable from the rest of the site. You can then move its base vertically downwards by 1' as well, so that it is aligned with the base of the site.

Apply appropriate colors to both the road and the site blocks. You will have to set the option for the Color tool to Clear All Face Surface Styles in order to do this.

◀ Step 11

Switch to the Top view. Turn on all the cluster layers and rearrange them on the site as shown, using the Move, Rotate, and Mirror tools. The location can be approximate rather than exact at this stage. You can use the Align tool to align the sides of the clusters wherever required.

Step 12

Switch to a paint display mode and you will find that parts of the clusters are buried into the site. Obviously, the height of each cluster now has to be adjusted according to the slope of the terrain. A simple way to do this is to apply the Query tool at the Point topological level to a point of the highest contour passing through each cluster, and take note of its Z coordinate. Add 2'—the contour interval—to it for the next contour. So, for instance, for the cluster in the lower left corner of the site, this value is 21'+2'=23'. To make the units in this cluster accessible from the highest point of the site, the base should be at a height of at least 24'. We modeled the base of each unit as 16' high. So we need to move this cluster upwards by a distance of 24'–16'=8' (assuming that all the units in a cluster are built at the same level). Do this and then check the paint display. You will find that the cluster is now fully visible above the surface of the site.

Step 13

Repeat this process for all the other nine clusters as well. Some of the clusters located at lower contours will have to be moved downwards rather than upwards. Check the results for each cluster in a non-planar view.

Step 14

Finally, model the "community building" blocks located in the open space between the clusters in the upper left corner of the site.

You now have your basic site plan design which you can build upon by adding pathways, community spaces, steps to the individual units, surrounding areas, and so on.

Illuminating and Texturing Your World

This workshop is devoted to imaging, lights, and textures. You will start by exploring the extensive set of options available to you for rendering your models in the RenderZone display mode. You will learn how to save these rendered images in files which can then be used in various other applications, as well as work with the Imager Set that enables you to render a set of images efficiently in a batch mode.

You will then move on to work with multiple lights, including the sun, and render your images realistically with shadows. Exercise 3 is devoted to exploring the radiosity-based rendering feature, which enhances lighting effects considerably. In Exercise 4, you will see how to map textures to objects more precisely, and apply multiple textures to the same surface using decals. Finally, you will study the remaining object properties you have not yet covered, which can be modified to achieve various rendering effects.

Note that color versions of all the rendered images illustrated in this workshop are included in the CD-ROM accompanying this book.

Imaging

A crucial component of any modeling activity is the generation of rendered images. The RenderZone display mode has an extensive set of options which let you create realistic images of your modeling world. Naturally, you would like to be able to save some of these renderings, either for reference, or for printing, or for importing into an image-editing program, where you can make additional modifications. form•Z gives you the ability to save these renderings in various image file formats such as TIFF, Targa, JPEG, PICT (on Macs only), and BMP and Metafile (on PCs only). There are also many associated utilities such as viewing image files from within form•Z, specifying the size and resolution of these files, efficient management of rendering memory, and generating and saving renderings in a batch mode rather than individually. This exercise is devoted to exploring all these imaging capabilities.

1.1   RenderZone Options

■   Open one of your completed projects for which you would like to explore various rendering techniques. You will use the same project throughout this exercise.

■   In Exercise 2 of Workshop 3, you explored the options accompanying all the display modes except RenderZone. Now go ahead and invoke the dialog for the RenderZone display mode in the same fashion: select it from the Display menu while holding down the option key (Mac) or Ctrl+Shift keys (PC), or access it through the Display Options command available under the same menu. There are a large number of options associated with the RenderZone display, as you can see from its dialog (Figure 5.1). A detailed discussion of each and every one of these options is beyond the scope of this book. We will, however, work through all the crucial options in this section.

■   There are seven possible options for Rendering Type in the accompanying popup list, ranging from Flat to Full Raytrace, each one progressively more accurate and therefore more time-consuming. Test this out by trying each one in succession. The difference will be very obvious if you have used complex surface styles with textures, reflections, transparencies, and so on. You can use the low-end rendering modes for drafts, and the high-end ones for final renderings. Most often, the default type of Full Z-Buffer should be sufficient. Use Full Raytrace only when the highest quality of rendering, with the maximum degree of realism, is required for an image.

Figure 5.1

The RenderZone Options dialog, showing the default settings for this display mode.

Figure 5.2

Some of the RenderZone display Background options, illustrated together in a single image.

▣ The Z-Buffer and Raytrace rendering types have some additional options which can be accessed by clicking on the associated Options button. These advanced options involve an in-depth understanding of the mathematics and technicalities of computer graphics and rendering, and we will not deal with them here. For all practical purposes, you should also not need to worry about them.

▣ The next two options are relatively simple. Estimate Memory Usage is useful before executing a complex rendering to ensure that enough memory is available to finish the rendering with the specified options. Decompose Non Planar Faces should already be familiar to you from the Shaded Render display options you explored in Section 2.4 of Workshop 3.

▣ Set Image Size, again an option you already encountered for Shaded Render, is especially useful in RenderZone as it lets you render only selected parts of the image to check if textures, lighting, shadows, etc., are appropriate before doing a full rendering. You can also employ it, as shown in Figure 5.2, to make a collage of various RenderZone display options in a single image—an interesting presentation technique in itself!

▣ Let us now look at the Background options located on the right side of the dialog, some of which are illustrated in Figure 5.2. The rendering type throughout was Full Z-Buffer, which you can also stick with. To obtain a full initial rendering, deselect Set Image Size and set the Background to any option other than the default of Project Color. The one used in Figure 5.2 is Sky. This provides a background with a base plane and sky, complete with clouds and the sun. Naturally, you have to adjust the view to suit the background, which you have already learned to do in Workshop 3.

▣ Click on the Options button associated with Background. This will bring up a dialog containing various parameters that define the selected background. For Sky, these include parameters such as the colors of all the individual components, the scale, coverage, and density of the clouds, the size and location of the sun, and the location of the horizon line. Experiment with different parameters to create different variations of the same background. The Sky options used to generate the image shown in Figure 5.2 are illustrated in Figure 5.3.

▣ Notice the Match Horizon With Perspective View option in the Sky Options dialog that is checked by default. This automatically adjusts the horizon line for a perspective view, and lets you specify the exact distances of the clouds and the ground, above and below the selected reference plane respectively. For a non-perspective view, or if the Match Horizon With Perspective View option is deselected, the Horizon slider bar can be used to specify the location of the horizon line from the lower margin of the image.

Figure 5.3

The Sky Options dialog, showing the settings used for generating the background in Figure 5.2.

- Now that you have generated a full background rendering, activate the Set Image Size option in the RenderZone Options dialog, and explore some of the other types of backgrounds by rendering only parts of the image. Those illustrated in Figure 5.2 are Project Background, with the grid and axes rendered as 3D lines, and Image, which lets you load any image file to use as the background. Explore the associated Options dialog for each type of background.

- In the Background Image Options dialog, for instance, you can not only load another file to replace the default image (which is the logo of auto•des•sys Inc., the company that makes form•Z), but also specify how it should be scaled with respect to the scene (see Figure 5.4). If you choose to Keep Image Size rather than Fit Image To Window and the image size is smaller than the window size, the image will be "tiled" across the width and height of the window, creating an interesting effect. Figure 5.2 illustrates this technique, using a plan view of the same building project for the image file. You can also specify only a part of the image to be used for the background rather than the entire image, with the help of the View option. Note that none of these variations would have been possible if you had used the image as an Underlay. This shows that the two utilities are not interchangeable—each is important in its own right.

Figure 5.4

Specifying an image as the background for part of the RenderZone display shown in Figure 5.2.

█ There are plenty of other options for Background which are self-explanatory and can be explored at leisure. The one called Environment is deactivated by default; we will study it later and find out why it is so. The last option, Alpha Channel, calls for some explanation. When this is selected, the background is rendered in black, but each pixel of the image stores an additional channel of information called the *alpha channel*, in addition to the three regular channels of color information—red, green, and blue. The alpha channel stores information on the level of transparency of each pixel relative to the background, and is used in image-composition programs to smoothly blend images into one another for photo-realistic rendering effects. The Alpha Channel background in form•Z will capture the transparency information for those pixels in the image that belong to objects having a transparent surface style, or that lie on the antialiased edges of objects, or those that represent the glow of a light (coming up in the next exercise). For more information on how to work with alpha channels, you should refer to the manuals accompanying your image-editing program.

In form•Z, it is possible to surround your model with an "environment" to accurately simulate how it would be in real life. Objects in the modeling scene that have reflective surfaces will then reflect this environment in addition to reflecting other objects in the scene. This effect cannot be achieved by using a "background" only.

█ To add an environment to your scene, activate the Environment section located just below the Background section. You can choose between three options: Cubic, Spherical, and Rendered. The Cubic option positions an imaginary cube around the scene, while the Spherical option positions an imaginary sphere around the scene. We will look at the Rendered option a little later. To explore these three options, apply reflective surface styles to some of the objects in the currently open project.

█ Just as you had a choice of different types of backgrounds, you can also choose from among a variety of environments with which to surround the scene and produce reflections. Explore some of these environments and see what kind of reflections are produced. One of these—the Sky option—is illustrated in Figure 5.5-a for both cubical and spherical environments. You can see that for the cubical environment, the sky is reflected many times, as it is mapped to each side of the imaginary cube surrounding the scene. The spherical environment, on the other hand, gives more accurate results since the sky is mapped only once around the image. The Sky settings were the same as those illustrated in Figure 5.3.

WORKSHOP 5

Figure 5.5

Rendering with the Cubic and Spherical environment options. (a) Environment set to Sky. (b) Environment set to Image. The six image files used for the Cubic environment are also shown.

▣ The Environment can also be set to Image, letting you specify image files with which to surround the scene. For a Spherical environment, only one image file is needed, but for a Cubic environment, six different image files can be specified for each of the six faces of the imaginary cube. Thus, it is possible to simulate the environment very precisely. A simple example of Image environment mapping is illustrated in Figure 5.5-b, again for both cubical and spherical environments. The six image files used for the Cubic environment are also shown, all of which were previously generated from the same project. The Spherical environment example uses the single image file shown in Figure 5.4. For realistic effects, you would, of course, use actual photographs of the surroundings of your project for these environment maps.

▣ Now go back and open up the popup menu for Background, and you will find that the Environment option, which had previously been grayed out, is now activated. If this option is selected, the pattern of the current environment cube or sphere will be rendered as the background, in addition to being visible on reflective surfaces. This will most realistically simulate a real-life situation. It is especially useful when generating an animation, as you will learn to do in Workshop 7—a different portion of the environment will be rendered as the background for each separate perspective view that makes up the animation. Thus, the impression of moving through the scene will be more vivid than it would be if the background remained the same for every view.

▣ Let us now look at the third Environment option, Rendered. This is relevant only when the scene contains objects whose surface styles have their Reflection attribute set to Environment in the Surface Style Parameters dialog. This setting is similar to the Mirror setting for Reflection, but is faster and less sharp. There is also a more crucial difference between the two. An object with a Mirror reflection attribute reflects only the surrounding objects, not the project background, as you can see in Figure 5.6-a where the background is set to Sky. (It can, of course, reflect a Cubic or Spherical environment map, as you saw in Figure 5.5.) An object with the Environment reflection attribute, on the other hand, will also reflect the project background, as shown in Figure 5.6-b, when Environment is set to Rendered.

WORKSHOP 5

Figure 5.6

Setting the Environment option to Rendered. (a) Surface style of objects has the Reflection attribute set to Mirror. (b) Surface style of objects has the Reflection attribute set to Environment.

(a) (b)

▣ Additionally, when the Rendered option for Environment is selected, it activates the accompanying Render At field. Here, you can specify the resolution of the environment in pixels, which in turn will determine the degree of sharpness of the reflections that will be produced. For sharper reflections, increase the resolution value.

▣ Proceed to explore the options in the Depth Effects section, which let you apply additional effects to your rendering (see Figure 5.7). Activate the first option, and you will find that it has three sub-options: Depth Cue, Fog, and Snow. Depth Cue lets you merge the colors of your model with the color of a specified background to the desired extent. Fog, as is obvious from its name, creates a fog-like effect, while Snow is used to create simple snow flakes in the rendered image. Each one of these sub-options has several settings, which you can access and explore by clicking on the associated Options button.

■ The second option in the Depth Effects section is Blur. It can be activated to achieve an "out of focus" effect in a rendering, similar to what you would find in a photograph. You can specify the beginning and the end of the focussed area; the remaining area of the scene will be blurred. You can also alter the degree to which the blurring will take place. Click on the associated Options button to access all these parameters.

Figure 5.7

Rendering with various options in the Depth Effects section.

Depth Cue   Fog   Blur

■ Next, turn to the options in the Shading section on the left side of the RenderZone Options dialog. You are already familiar with two of these—Shadows and Smooth Shading—from the other displays such as Shaded Render. Shadows in RenderZone has two sub-options which will be discussed in Section 2.1, so skip it for now. If you have applied image-based textures to any of your objects (as you will learn to do in Section 4.5) and want them to be displayed in the rendering, the Texture Maps option should remain selected. Likewise, the Reflections, Transparencies, and Bump Mapping options should be selected if you have any textures with these attributes, so that they are rendered accurately.

■ The two remaining options in the Shading section are Shader Antialiasing and Super Sampling. The first is relevant only to the Full Z-Buffer rendering type. When it is activated, the level of antialiasing in such a rendering is significantly improved, resulting in a greater clarity of the image, particularly when textured surface styles are used. (Recall from Workshop 3 that the Surface Style Parameters dialog for an individual surface style also has a Shader Antialiasing option, which can be turned on or off for that style.) A still higher degree of antialiasing in the image can be obtained by activating the Super Sampling option. This is especially useful for reducing flickering while generating an animation. Keep in mind, however, that activating these options for a rendering will also consume more time and memory.

The Parametrics section, located below the Shading section, should be familiar to you from the Shaded Render display options covered in Workshop 3. That leaves only two more options for the RenderZone display, Illumination and Wireframe Width. The first relates to lighting while the second relates to the Rendering Attributes tool, both of which will be covered in later exercises of this workshop. So you can skip these options for now, and move on to explore the various imaging options of form•Z in the rest of this exercise.

1.2 Saving and Viewing Image Files

Recall from Workshop 1 that the QuickDraw 3D and OpenGL displays are meant for interactive modeling only and cannot be saved. Apart from these, all the other six display modes can be used to generate image files. RenderZone and Shaded Render images can only be saved in bitmapped file formats such as Targa, TIFF, JPEG, and BMP. In contrast, the other four displays—Wire Frame, Quick Paint, Hidden Line, and Surface Render—can also be saved as vector-based images in file formats such as PICT, Metafile, and EPS. Vector-based images are resolution independent, and will therefore print faster and without the "jagged edges" of low-resolution bitmapped images.

🔲 Generate a rendering of your project that you would like to save. Then use File > Save As, as you learned in the Introduction, to save the file in any of the 2D image file formats that are available. The file will automatically be given an extension, depending upon the file format selected.

🔲 Once you have saved an image file in this manner, you can open it in any program which recognizes that format to view, modify, or print it. You also have the option of viewing the same file within form•Z itself by going to File > View File. From the file selection dialog that is invoked, select the image file you just saved. A new window will open up, displaying the image (Figure 5.8). In fact, you can use this option to view even those image files that were not created in form•Z, but are in formats recognizable to it.

Figure 5.8

Viewing an image file within form•Z.

🔲 You can change the size of the window in which the image is displayed, as well as use the Zoom tool to zoom in or out of the image. To zoom out, select the Zoom tool while holding down the option key (Mac) or Ctrl+Shift keys (PC). If the entire image is not visible in the window, the scroll bars and the Hand tool will be activated, allowing you to view different parts of the image. The image size is displayed in pixels at the top of the window. You have to close this window to get back to the regular form•Z environment.

1.3   Image Options

The image file you just saved was stored using the default form•Z settings for image size and resolution, set respectively to the current window size and the screen resolution of 72 pixels/inch. This resolution is adequate for screen displays of your bitmapped image files, such as the one you just saved. Try printing the file, and you will find that the image is not very sharp. A much higher resolution is needed for acceptable printed images, depending upon the printer you will use. You might also want to specify an image size that is different from the default value. form•Z gives you the option of customizing the image size and resolution for the images that you generate.

▣ Select the last item in the Display menu, Image Options. In the dialog that pops up, you can choose from among various options for Image Size. The default size is set to the current size of the window. Choose the alternate option, Use Custom Size. You can now specify the image size in two ways: By Number Of Pixels, or By Size And Resolution. The second method is more intuitive, allowing you to specify the exact size and resolution of the image (Figure 5.9). Since the Maintain Proportions option is checked by default, you need to specify either the width or the height—the other dimension will adjust itself appropriately. Change also the Resolution to a higher value.

▣ You will now see the values for Width and Height in the By Number Of Pixels option change to reflect the actual number of pixels that will be contained in the specified image size at the specified resolution. A larger resolution increases the number of pixels—as seen in the Image Options dialog in Figure 5.9—which in turn means longer rendering times for the Shaded Render and RenderZone displays, since these are bitmapped rather than vector displays.

Figure 5.9

Specifying the Image Options for a rendering. An image size of 8 by 6 inches at a resolution of 300 pixels/inch is equivalent to 2400 by 1800 pixels.

▣ Select the Use Custom Size option and exit the dialog. You will find that the graphics window gets resized and you are no longer able to change its size—it has been locked. Also notice that the window size is determined by the total number of pixels. Thus, for the specifications shown in Figure 5.9, you will see a window of 2400 by 1800 pixels rather than a window measuring 8 by 6 inches. If the window size is too large to fit on the screen, the Maximize Window In Screen option, which is checked by default, resizes the window so that it fits on the screen. The resizing is for display purposes only; the actual number of pixels that will be rendered remain the same as those specified in the Image Options dialog.

▣ After you have generated your renderings at the specified size and resolution and want to resume regular modeling activity, you should go back to the Image Options dialog and select the Use Window Size option. Now you will be able to resize your window in the usual manner. At the very least, you should reduce the Resolution value back to 72 pixels/inch, so that your modeling work is not slowed down needlessly.

▣ The Image Options dialog also lets you modify the depth of color of your image. You can choose from among three options: 8 bits, 16 bits, and 32 bits. A larger color depth can capture more shades and hues of colors, but also results in larger files. You could settle for the lower color depth values for prefinal images, which will considerably reduce the time required for generating these images and subsequently working with them. However, be sure to always use the highest color depth for final renderings.

WORKSHOP **5**

Figure 5.10

The effect of the Apply Alpha Channel When Present option, when saving an image file rendered with the Alpha Channel background.

Apply Alpha Channel option off   Apply Alpha Channel option on

▣ When working with the RenderZone display options, you saw how the image Background could be set to Alpha Channel to produce images having an additional alpha channel in addition to the red, blue, and green channels. The option, Apply Alpha Channel When Present, in the Image Options dialog is relevant to such images. If the alpha channel is to be retained when an image file is saved for use with other image-editing programs, leave this option turned off, as it is by default. On screen, however, the image will be displayed without the alpha channel and is therefore not fully accurate. To view the image *with* the alpha channel in form•Z, turn on the Apply Alpha Channel When Present option. However, if the file is now saved, the alpha channel will not be exported. The difference is illustrated in Figure 5.10, which has objects with a transparent surface style.

▣ The final option in the Image Options dialog, Correct Exposure When Present, lets you conveniently adjust the exposure settings of the image within form•Z itself, rather than leave it for an image-editing program. To work with this option, you first need to activate the Generate Exposure Data option in the RenderZone Options dialog under the Illumination section. Then in the Image Options dialog, select the Correct Exposure When Present option and click on the accompanying Options button. This will invoke a dialog showing the image, along with various Intensity and Brightness settings. These can be changed numerically, or graphically by moving the control points of the associated graph. Explore different values for both settings and see how it affects the image.

1.4   Saving Incomplete Renderings

As a project gets larger and more complex and the number of textures and lights increases, a high-end RenderZone image will take an increasingly long time to render. form•Z therefore gives you the ability to interrupt a rendering, save the partial rendering in a file, and continue the rendering at a later time. Needless to say, this is an extremely useful option to have since a lot of time and effort is invariably invested in a high quality rendering, which would be a shame to waste.

▣ Open up your most complex project to date and switch to a perspective view. Invoke the RenderZone Options dialog and set the Rendering Type to Full Raytrace. Also, check the Shadows box, and select the Cubic option and Image type for Environment. In short, do whatever it takes to increase the rendering time for the image. If necessary, you can also increase the complexity of some of the surface styles applied to the objects in the scene.

▣ Activate the RenderZone display to begin the rendering. Wait until about half of the window has been rendered, then press the Shift key along with the command+period (Mac) or Ctrl+period (PC) or Esc (Mac or PC) keys. This will bring up a dialog in which you can choose to continue or cancel the rendering, or save it to a file. (Note that if the Shift key is not pressed while pressing these other keys, the rendering will simply be cancelled.) Click on the Suspend Rendering To File button, which will invoke the usual File Save dialog for your operating system. Specify an appropriate name and location for the file. An extension of ".spd" is automatically given, indicating that it is a suspended rendering file. Once this is done, you are returned to a Wire Frame display of your project.

▣ A suspended rendering can be resumed at any time, even if the original project file is not open. To test this, close the project file that you used for generating the partial rendering. Then go to File > Open and select the suspended rendering file you had saved. The partially rendered image opens up and the rendering is resumed from the point it left off.

▣ Let the rendering be fully completed this time. As soon as it is done, the standard File Save dialog will open up again, allowing you to save the completed rendering in any one of the image file formats you saw earlier. You are also conveniently given the option of deleting the suspended rendering file from disk, which you would usually choose to do in the interest of maximizing your disk space.

1.5   Plotting and Rendering Memory Management

By now, you must have had first-hand experience of the fact that generating a Hidden Line or Surface Render display (i.e., *plotting*) or a Shaded Render or RenderZone display (i.e., *rendering*) for a complex project is a time-consuming and memory-intensive process. This is because a lot of calculations are involved such as hidden faces, the lines of intersections of objects, and so on. All this information is referred to as the *rendering record*, and is, by default, stored in memory. This makes subsequent renderings of different views of the same project faster, but also takes up more memory. It is important to know how to manipulate this rendering memory, particularly when memory is at a premium.

▣ The memory management options for plotting are more extensive than those for rendering. To access them, go to Display > Display Options. This invokes the Modeling Display Options dialog (Figure 5.11), which you first encountered in Workshop 3 as a means of accessing the options of all the display modes in form•Z.

Figure 5.11

The Modeling Display Options dialog.

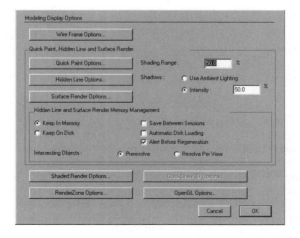

▣ Turn your attention to the section, Hidden Line and Surface Render Memory Management, in the dialog. This gives you two basic options for storing the rendering record during a form•Z session:

Keep In Memory or Keep On Disk. What you choose depends upon what your computer has more of—memory or disk space. Needless to say, keeping calculations in memory makes them more easily accessible and, therefore, faster to retrieve than if they were stored on disk. If the Keep On Disk option is chosen, a temporary file is created to store the calculations.

▣ Rendering calculations, whether stored in memory or on disk, are automatically deleted once a project is closed. They have to be recreated when the project is reopened in subsequent sessions, so the initial renderings will be slow. If you have plenty of disk space, you can afford to check the Save Between Sessions option, which saves the rendering record in a separate file when the project is saved. Even if the project is now closed and reopened, the previous rendering record is immediately available, speeding up any renderings which might be executed. Be careful, however, since these files are quite large, so use this option judiciously.

▣ The next option, Automatic Disk Loading, is relevant only when multiple project files are open and the rendering record is stored in memory rather than on disk. Checking this option will automatically load the rendering record of an inactive project file from the disk (where it is stored by default) into memory when it is made active. Only the rendering record of the active project file can be stored in memory at a given time.

▣ In addition to the rendering record, the Hidden Line and Surface Render displays make use of a *display buffer*, which contains a copy of the pixel map of the image on the screen. The display buffer is used to refresh the screen without any recalculation whenever palettes are moved, dialogs are opened and closed, and axonometric views are zoomed or panned. However, for changes such as zooming and scrolling in perspective views, the display buffer cannot be used and recalculations have to be performed. If the Alert Before Regeneration button is checked, you will be warned when this happens, giving you the option to switch to a Wire Frame display rather than performing the recalculations to refresh the display.

▣ Move on to the Intersecting Objects option, which applies to plotting only. You can decide if intersections will be precalculated for all the objects in the project (Preresolve) or calculated separately per view for only those objects appearing in that view (Resolve Per View). The first option is faster when different views are rendered because all the intersections are precalculated, but it also takes up more memory or disk space to store these calculations.

▣ Additional memory management options which apply to both plotting and rendering are located directly in the Display menu, so go ahead and exit the Modeling Display Options dialog. Look at the last-but-one section of the Display menu. The Clear Rendering Memory command, when selected, will delete the rendering calculations from memory at any time. This is useful when memory is running short. When memory is really tight, you can select the Always Clear Rendering Memory option, which will automatically erase the rendering record after each rendering. Each new rendering will then be recalculated from the beginning, taking more time.

▣ The last option related to memory management in the Display menu is Redraw Buffers. Select this option, and a dialog will be invoked in which you can activate or deactivate the *window redraw buffers*. Unlike a display buffer which stores project plotting information, a window redraw buffer simply stores the window image information, which is used to refresh the screen almost instantaneously when a palette is moved or windows are switched. This buffer occupies memory, so turn it off when memory cannot be spared; you will, however, have to put up with slower screen refresh rates as a consequence.

▣ If you have sufficient memory available for window buffering, leave the Window Redraw Buffer Active option activated, as it is by default (Figure 5.12). There are two additional sub-options you can manipulate, both of which are also active by default. Match Buffer Depth To Screen Depth leads to faster refresh rates but takes more memory if the color depth of your monitor is set to thousands or millions of colors. To conserve memory, you can deselect it and the buffer will work in 256 color mode. Update Screen During Redraw updates the screen at the specified interval even if the buffer is still being regenerated for a complex image, making the image generation process more visible. However, it does slow things down, so turn this option off for fastest performance—provided you can live with the suspense of not seeing the image until it is fully regenerated!

Figure 5.12

Activating the Window
Redraw Buffer option.

1.6 Using an Imager Set

form•Z has an extremely useful built-in utility called the *Imager* which allows you to render as well as print a set of form•Z images in a batch mode. With this utility, you can leave a whole set of renderings to be generated on the computer and come back when they are all done, instead of sitting at the computer throughout and attending to each one individually. This is particularly indispensable for rendering images that require a considerable amount of time, such as when the display of shadows is turned on, when using the RenderZone display mode for scenes that involve a considerable amount of lighting and texture mapping, or even for a Surface Render display of a complex project. We will take a detailed look at the Imager utility in this section.

◻ Start by creating additional views in your project if you don't have at least four or five—you will render these in a batch mode in an *Imager Set*. Save the file immediately so that these views are recorded and available for rendering. Then select New Imager Set from the File menu. (To open an existing Imager Set, you would use File > Open.) This will invoke the Imager Set window shown in Figure 5.13. While this window is open, you cannot access the regular environment of form•Z—you must close the Imager Set to get back to it.

◻ Once an Imager Set is created, it can be saved in the usual fashion using File > Save As. An Imager Set file is saved with a ".fis" extension. Although saving is not mandatory for the rendering to take place, it can be very convenient for reasons we shall soon see. So go ahead and save it.

◻ The next step that you need to perform is selecting the project file or files, along with the views from each file that are to be included in the Imager Set. This can be done by clicking on the Add button in the window. As soon as you select a form•Z file from the File Open dialog that is invoked, all the views saved for that project are loaded in a separate dialog, from which you can select those that you would like to render. Just click on Select All for now. You are not restricted to the views from a single project, but can use the Add button to load more project files and their views in a similar manner. It is advisable not to have more than 10 or 12 views in one Imager Set, so that if an error occurs, processing time is not wasted on too many unusable images. Figure 5.13-a shows the Imager Set window, containing five views from a single project listed in the upper portion of the window.

WORKSHOP **5**

Figure 5.13

Working with the Imager Set. (a) Loading all the views from a single project. (b) Activating one of the views to change its rendering parameters.

▣ Each *view* in the Imager Set is an *image* that will be rendered. Along with the project file and the view that identifies it, an image is listed along with three other attributes—Image Types, Printing (abbreviated to Prt), and Status. Each one of these attributes has a corresponding option in the lower half of the window. These options are global options that apply to all the images in the list. Image Types sets the type of rendering which will be applied while generating an image. Change it from the default of Wire Frame to Surface Render or RenderZone from the accompanying popup menu. Printing determines whether or not to print the images as they are being generated. You should preferably turn this off so that you can check if an image is satisfactory before it is printed. The third option, Image Status, can be used to change the status of all the images to Make All Pending, if you need the images to be regenerated for some reason.

▣ Now click on one of the images in the list. It gets highlighted, activating some of the grayed out buttons in the Imager Set window (Figure 5.13-b). The selected image becomes the *active image* on which these newly activated options can be applied. You can Remove it from the Imager Set, or Preview it to check that it is indeed the image that you want to render. The images will be rendered in the order in which they appear in the list. This can be changed by using the Up and Down arrow buttons to change the order of the active image in the list. Image Specs lets you choose a different rendering type for the selected image—thus, all the renderings do not have to be of the same type—as well as change its default size, resolution, and color depth settings. Display Options brings up the same dialog you saw earlier in Figure 5.11. Through it, you can set the desired rendering parameters for the selected image, depending upon the rendering type you have selected for it. The Print/Plot Setup button is active only if the Printing option has been turned on, letting you modify the default printing parameters of the selected image.

▣ Next, deselect the active image by clicking on the blank space just below the last image in the list. No image is now active, and you will find that all the buttons you just looked at get deactivated.

▪ Click on the Imager Setup button, which is still active. This brings up a dialog which contains certain options that apply to the Imager Set as a whole (see Figure 5.14.) Here is where you can change the default image type, as well as the default file formats of the image files that will be generated for both groups of displays—line (Wire Frame and Hidden Line), and paint (the other four displays). For each file format, the associated Options are accessible and can be modified. For line images, it is also possible to save them as form•Z files that can be read by the drafting module.

▪ The Imager Set Up dialog provides you with two options for clearing the rendering memory. Although the first option, When Switching Between Projects, is on by default, it is better to opt for the second option, After Each Image Is Complete. This will increase the time required for the generation of the Imager Set as a whole, but will make more memory available for the generation of each individual image.

▪ Finally, a very *crucial step in the entire process* involves the last option of the Imager Set Up dialog— Set Destination Folder. Click on this button. You can now select a folder in which the images will be saved as they are generated. If you click on the New Folder button, a new folder is automatically created in the specified location and conveniently named with the current date. It helps tremendously to set such a folder as the destination folder.

If you saved the Imager Set in the beginning, the destination folder gets automatically set to the folder where the Imager Set is located. But if you did not save the Imager Set, the default destination folder for the images is the form•Z program folder. This means that if you move to a different computer, your images will remain on the hard drive of the computer you were working on, and *will no longer be accessible to you*. This happens all too often when students work in computer labs at school, where they are usually not working on one computer all the time. So take care to set up a destination folder on your *own* disk for every Imager Set that you create.

▪ Now that you have finished setting all the necessary options, you are ready to begin the generation process. Return to the main Imager Set window and click on the Generate button. This will set the rendering process in motion. The Status of each image will change from Pending to Generating while it is being generated, Printing while it is being printed, and Complete when it is done. If an error occurs in the rendering, the error number will be displayed. A more detailed explanation of the error can be found by double-clicking in the Status column of the image.

Figure 5.14

The Imager Set Up dialog contains options for the Imager Set as a whole.

WORKSHOP 5

Figure 5.15

The five images generated automatically by the Imager Set shown earlier in Figure 5.13.

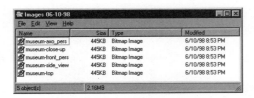

▣ At any stage, the image generation can be interrupted by pressing the Command+period (Mac), Ctrl+period (PC), or Esc (Mac or PC) keys. This gives you the option of proceeding to the next image or of canceling all subsequent image generation. If the generation is canceled, it can be resumed from the point it left off rather than from the beginning the next time the Imager Set is opened and the Generate command is given. This is one compelling reason why it is desirable to save the Imager Set.

▣ Once the generation process is completed (which could take from a few minutes to several hours, depending upon the complexity of the renderings), any of the rendered images can be displayed by highlighting it and clicking on the View button. If the Imager Set is saved and reopened, the rendered images can be viewed in the same manner. Thus, you can also use the Imager Set as a presentation medium, where all your images are rendered and saved and can be displayed in a sequence at the touch of a button. This is another good reason for saving the Imager Set.

▣ As the final step in this exercise, go back to your desktop and locate the folder which you had specified as the destination folder in the Imager Set Up dialog. If you open this folder, you should see all the image files saved in it, with automatic file names assigned to them (see Figure 5.15). These image files can now be used like any other image file—they can be opened and edited using other image-editing programs, as well as viewed within the regular form•Z environment using the View File command under the File menu.

EXERCISE 2

Lights Galore!

form•Z provides you with a vast array of light-related options, including both the type of light as well as how the lighting will be rendered. We will explore all these options in this exercise, starting with a detailed look at how shadows are rendered in form•Z.

2.1   Rendering with Shadows

Shadows make a great difference in our perception of shapes and forms, so they are a crucial component of any rendered image. You have already learned how to activate the Shadows option for the various paint display modes. In this section, we will see how the shadows are actually displayed in these modes. For now, we will only deal with shadows cast by the "sun," which is the single light source existing in a modeling project by default. Shadow casting by additional light sources will be dealt with in later sections. Also, we will not worry at the moment about how the shadows are determined but simply with how they are displayed, given that they exist for a certain position of the sun with respect to the model.

▣ Continue working with the same project you used in the last exercise. If it does not have some kind of base plane, add a large one so that you can capture the shadows of the objects on the "ground." For an existing base plane which is not large enough, extend it by moving each one of its side faces outwards, as in Figure 5.16.

▣ Make sure that you are in a non-planar 3D view. Invoke the Quick Paint Options dialog and check the Render With Shadows option. Now watch how the rendering takes substantially longer than usual, despite which the end result is even more inaccurate. Moral of the story—don't rely on the Quick Paint display when you want shadows! Use one of the other displays instead, even if they take more time.

▣ Move on to Surface Render and enable the Render With Shadows option for this display. The shadows have to be calculated, which takes time, particularly when you do it for the first time. Rendering information, including shadow calculations, is stored by default in memory, as you saw in Section 1.5, therefore subsequent renderings take less time to execute. The result of the rendering will be a nicely shaded image (Figure 5.16-a). Notice how the base plane is essential to capture the shadows of the building on the ground.

▣ You also have the ability to control the quality of the shading. Go to Display > Display Options to invoke the dialog you saw earlier in Figure 5.11. Notice the Shading Range and Shadows specifications in the Quick Paint, Hidden Line, and Surface Render section of the dialog. The Shading Range affects how the objects themselves are shaded rather than the shadows that they cast. Change it from the default value of 50% to, say, 1% and notice how the sides of the objects are no longer differentiated by separate hues, making the model look very "flat" (Figure 5.16-b). Now change the Shading Range to 100% and see the reverse happen (Figure 5.16-c). If you encounter any errors in the display, select Clear Rendering Memory from the Display menu so that the shadows are recalculated when the display is refreshed.

Figure 5.16

Different flavors of shades and shadows in the Surface Render mode.

WORKSHOP **5**

▣ The Shadows option, on the other hand, affects the intensity of the shadows that are cast by objects. The default setting is Intensity with a value of 50%. Change this to 1% and watch the shadows darken so that they are almost black. Changing the Intensity to 100%, as you can guess, will lighten the shadows to such an extent that they become invisible. Now set Shadows to the alternate option, Use Ambient Lighting, and bring the Shading Range back to 50%. You will see shadows similar to Figure 5.16-a but of a lighter shade, as shown in Figure 5.16-d. Later on in this exercise, you will learn how to change the intensity of the *ambient light*—i.e., light that is always there in a scene. For now, explore the shading and shadows options some more to get a better sense of how they affect the resultant image.

▪ Generate shadows for the Shaded Render and RenderZone displays as well in the same manner. Notice that the Shadows option in the RenderZone Options dialog has two sub-options: Opaque and Transparent. The default is Opaque, and with this, even transparent objects will cast opaque, i.e., black shadows. By activating the Transparent option, light passing through a transparent object will take on the color and transparency of that object. This will lead to more realistic renderings, but will also take more time to execute. Try it on an object with a transparent surface style. There is, however, an additional step you need to perform first: Open up the Lights palette from the Palettes menu (if it is closed) and double-click on the single entry, Light1, in the palette. This will invoke the Light Parameters dialog for that light (see Figure 5.20), containing an extensive set of options which we will be exploring later on in this exercise. For now, simply change the Shadows option from Soft (Mapped) to Hard (Raytraced) and exit the dialog. You will now obtain transparent shadows, as shown in Figure 5.17.

Figure 5.17

Opaque versus transparent shadows in the Render-Zone display mode.

Opaque shadows   Transparent shadows

Be careful to turn the Shadows feature off while you are in the early stages of modeling and don't really need it, as it will slow down the display process, and thus your work, considerably.

2.2   Positioning the Sun

The single entry, Light1, in the Lights palette that you encountered in the last section represents the sun by default. Naturally, you would like to be able to specify the exact position of this sun and thereby control how the shadows are cast.

Figure 5.18

The sun in Wire Frame in Top view, and the corresponding shadows in Surface Render.

(a)   (b)

▪ Select the Wire Frame display mode and switch to the Top view. You already know from the Cone of Vision exercise (Section 5.4 of Workshop 3) that the black arrowed line visible in the graphics window in this display mode represents a light beam. Zoom out sufficiently so that the entire line is visible to you (Figure 5.18-a). This light beam, in the absence of any other light source, represents the sun. Verify this by doing a rendered display with shadows in the Top view, and see how the shadows are in accordance with the direction of the light beam seen in the Wire Frame mode (Figure 5.18-b).

▣ You can apply any of the transformation tools on Row 12 to the light beam just like any other object. Thus, you can graphically change the position of the sun by moving the entire light beam, or just the light source (the shaded circle) or the light target (the arrow). The last two will result in the line being stretched or shrunk. You can switch between different planar views to fix the direction of the light more precisely. Do this a few times and see how the shadows change according to the orientation of the light. Make sure that none of the Copy modes are active when you apply the Move tool to the light, otherwise you will be making new copies of the light with every transformation. You can do this, however, once you learn to work with multiple lights in Section 2.4.

The capability to generate shadows for any specified direction of the sun might, in itself, seem more than adequate. But what if you want *real* shadows? In other words, what if you want to know *exactly* how various parts of your model (if it is a building) are going to be shaded at different times of the year, in a specific location in a specific country of the world? You might think this is too much to ask for from a modeling program, but form•Z can do this as well!

▣ Go to View > Sun Position. This will invoke a dialog in which you can specify the location of your site, as well as the date and time for which you are interested in generating shadows (see Figure 5.19-a). By default, the date and time options are deactivated since no site is initially selected. Click on the Choose Site button. You will be presented with an extensive list of cities around the world from which you can make your choice of location. You can also add your own location to this database, if it is not included, by specifying its latitude, longitude, and time zone.

▣ After selecting a location in the Geographic Position dialog (or adding your own), you will be returned to the Sun Position dialog. Here, you can specify the date and time for which the shadows have to be determined. For accurate shadows, you should also specify the angle (measured, by default, as positive in the anticlockwise direction) that the North line of your site makes with the X axis. The default value for this angle is 90°, which means that North is in the +Y direction, following the usual convention in architectural practice. Try different variations of dates, times, and site angles, and watch the black line reorient itself accordingly in the window. Render the image to actually see the corresponding shadows that your model would have on the selected site, at the specified date and time (Figure 5.19-b).

Figure 5.19

The Sun Position dialog, with the site, date, and time specifications, and the resultant rendering with shadows.

(a)

(b)

2.3   The Light Parameters Dialog

◾ A light source is defined by a large number of attributes. In this section, you will explore the attributes associated with the default light source which is the sun. Double-click on its name, Light1, in the Lights palette, as you did a short while ago, to invoke the Light Parameters dialog for this light (Figure 5.20). Here, you can modify various parameters of the light, starting with its name. The Name field is highlighted and can be changed right away. Call it "The Sun" since you have assigned a sun position to it, and are treating it as such.

Figure 5.20

The Light Parameters dialog for the default light source.

◾ The Type of the light is automatically set to Distant. There are various other light types that you can create and position for achieving desired lighting effects in your renderings, and you will be learning about these in the next section. A *distant* type of light is located at an infinite distance away and emits parallel rays in a single direction. It is indicated by a single line with an arrow at the end, as you have seen for the sun. Try selecting another light type for the sun from the Type popup list, and you will find that you are not allowed to do so. The light which is being used as the sun cannot be set to any type other than Distant.

◾ The color of the light is white by default. Click on the box beside Color and you will be able to select a new color from the Color selection dialog of your operating system. Similarly, you can change the Basic Intensity of the light from the default value of 100%. Intensity values normally range from 0% to 100%, but you can go below 0% or above 100% to create effects of underexposure and overexposure respectively (see Figure 5.21). The changes in color and basic intensity are reflected in the little preview window, located in the top, right corner of the Light Parameters dialog. Here, you can verify the effects of the current light, applied to a white cube sitting on a white surface. A different object type can also be chosen from the accompanying popup list. Experiment with different colors and basic intensities and see the corresponding changes in the lighting effect.

◾ There is an Accurate Intensity button located below the Basic Intensity value you just explored. Click on this button, and a dialog will be invoked in which you can specify the intensity of the sun, which is a distant light, as it would be in real life. The Output Power value stands for the effect of such a light on a surface. The default value of 100 Watts Per SqFt is highly misleading—change this to 2 Watts Per SqFt for simulating sunlight on a bright sunny afternoon, with lower values for overcast days or evening light. You can also activate the Apply Atmospheric Light option, which will incorporate in your scene, the indirect light reflected from the atmosphere that illuminates indoor spaces even when there is no direct light shining into them. Choose between three kinds of Cloud Coverage and three kinds of Sky Color, and specify the brightness of the sky in Candelas Per SqFt, all of which will affect the amount of atmospheric illumination calculated. Additionally, you can choose the level of quality of the solution. Applying atmospheric light is useful for generating realistic daytime interior renderings.

Figure 5.21

Different basic Intensity values for the same light source.

100% Intensity   500% Intensity

■ The resultant image, seen using accurate rather than basic light intensity, will be much more realistic, but will also take more time to render. Note that it can be seen only in a RenderZone display, for which you need to have activated the Accurate Intensity option in the Illumination section of the RenderZone Options dialog.

 Modifications in the attributes of a light made in the Light Parameters dialog do not affect the Quick Paint and Surface Render displays. They will, however, be reflected in the Shaded Render, RenderZone, QuickDraw 3D, and OpenGL display modes.

■ In the last section, before you actually fixed the location of the light using Sun Position, you saw how you could change the location and direction of the sun graphically by using any of the transformation tools on Row 12 such as Move. The Light Parameters dialog lets you perform the same operation by modifying the X, Y, and Z values of the Location and the Center Of Interest of the light. In most cases, however, it is far more convenient to manipulate these values graphically rather than by keying in coordinates, so you would usually not worry about these values at all. In particular, if you have already set the light to a certain sun position, you absolutely should not change these values as that would render your sun settings inaccurate.

■ The next facility that is available in the Light Parameters dialog is the ability to manipulate the quality and accuracy of the shadows that will be cast by the light. For shadows to be cast, the Shadows option must be checked. Under Shadows, you can choose between Soft (Mapped) and Hard (Raytraced) shadows. The first option requires a lot of memory but is faster than the second. The Hard option, however, produces shadows with crisper edges (Figure 5.22-a), and you have already seen that transparent shadows in RenderZone can only be produced with this option.

■ Soft shadows have some additional options you can manipulate. Click on the accompanying Options button to access these. The Quality of the shadows can be low, medium, or high, progressively requiring more time and memory. You can vary the degree of Softness of the shadows from 0 (hardest) to 100 (fuzziest). As the softness is increased, self-shadowing of objects also increases (Figure 5.22-b), which can be reduced by a proportionate increase in the Tolerance value (Figure 5.22-c).

WORKSHOP 5

Figure 5.22

Different shadow characteristics for the Shaded Render and RenderZone displays.

(a)
Hard Shadows

(b)
Soft Shadows with Softness = 50%

(c)
Tolerance = 50%

(d)
Resolution = 0.25 Times Image Size

◼ The Resolution option in the Soft Shadow Parameters dialog determines the resolution of the shadow map, relative to the image size, that is generated prior to rendering. For rough drafts, this can be reduced to less than 1 times the image size for faster but less accurate shadows (Figure 5.22-d). Alternately, you can specify an actual pixel value. The last option, Limit Map To, applies to distant lights only and determines for which objects the shadows are calculated. The default choice of All Objects will calculate shadows for all the objects in the project, even if they are outside the current view. If you are rendering only a small portion of your model, choose one of the other two options, All Completely Visible Faces or All Completely Visible Objects. It will result in crisper shadows.

◼ Let us now proceed to explore the options located on the right side of the Light Parameters dialog, below the preview window. By default, a light is visible and can be seen in the graphics window in the Wire Frame display mode. By checking the Ghosted option, the same light will be seen in ghosted mode and cannot be selected. This is useful when you do not want a light to be inadvertently selected and operated upon by a modeling tool, along with your regular modeling objects. If you deselect the Visible option, the light becomes totally invisible. Alternately, you can keep the light visible but check the Locked option which will prevent it from being selected and accidentally operated upon.

◼ Keep in mind that making a light invisible does *not* mean that the light is inactive and does not illuminate the scene and cast shadows. The Visible option merely affects the *display* of the light in the graphics window. To actually deactivate the light, you need to deselect the Shining option. The light then still exists but does not contribute to the illumination of the scene. This feature is extremely useful, allowing you to create a large number of lights in various parts of your model and activate only a desired number of them at a time for different views and lighting effects.

◼ The Use Sun Settings option allows you to set the position of any *distant* light to a specific site, date, and time, using the Sun Position dialog. You have already done this earlier for the current light source. However, if you were to create more distant lights in your project (as you will learn to do in the next section), you can use this option to conveniently set each one of them to a specific sun position, if required.

The only remaining options in the Light Parameters dialog that we have not covered are the Falloff and Glow options, both of which are deactivated for a distant light. We will look at them in the next section, where we will work with the other light types in form•Z.

2.4 Distant, Point, Cone, and Projector Lights

form•Z lets you create and position any number of different light sources in your model in addition to the single light source which exists in every project by default. You are already acquainted with a *distant* type of light such as the sun, located at an infinite distance away and emitting parallel rays in a single direction. There are five other types of lights. A *point* light is located at a specific finite point and emits rays equally in all directions about the source. A *cone* light is also located at a given point, but emits rays in all directions contained within a specified conical shape. A *projector* light projects a rectangular light in a given direction through a specified image, just like a slide projector. We will be exploring all these light types in this section. There are two additional light types—*area* and *custom*—which will be covered in the next two sections.

 Working with multiple lights is only possible in the Shaded Render and RenderZone display modes. Quick Paint and Surface Render use only the single distant light source which is the sun. Moreover, the shades and shadows resulting from point, cone, projector, area, and custom lights can be seen in the RenderZone display mode only. Shaded Render works just with distant lights.

▣ Let us actually get down to working with multiple lights. Continue to use the same model that you have been working with so far. Multiple lights in form•Z are manipulated through the Lights palette which is very similar to all the other palettes—Views, Layers, and Planes—that you have worked with so far. Currently, the palette has only one light, which you renamed as The Sun in the last section.

▣ To add a new light to your model, click on the blank space in the Lights palette below the last light name, The Sun. (The procedure is basically the same as creating a new layer or a new view in their respective palettes.) A new light will be created with a default name. Double-click on it to invoke its Light Parameters dialog where you can define the parameters of the new light. This time, select the Point option for the Type parameter of the light. You can also change its default name of "Light 2" to something more appropriate, such as "Point Source."

▣ Most of the parameters for the Point light type such as Color, Basic Intensity, Shadows, and so on, are the same as those you explored for the distant light in the preceding section. Change these if required. Then move on to explore the other options. The first concern would be to accurately position the light where it should be. A default position is automatically assigned to it, as indicated by the coordinate values in the Location box. (The Center Of Interest option is deactivated since a point light is not restricted to a single direction.) You could change these values in the dialog, but as you saw for the sun in the last section, it is more convenient to do this graphically. Exit the Light Parameters dialog by clicking on the OK button. You will see the new light in your window, represented graphically by a shaded circle for the location and 2D circles along all the three planes—XY, YZ, and ZX—indicating the radius of the light (Figure 5.23-a). Use the Move tool to position the light as desired, switching to some of the planar views for more accuracy. Note that you have to click on the *center* of the light to select it.

▣ To see the effect of the new light, turn off the Shining attribute for the first distant light, The Sun, in its Light Parameters dialog. (You will soon see a shortcut for performing the same operation.)

Then switch to the RenderZone display mode, making sure that its Shadows option is activated. Also set the Background to a dark color. You should see the unmistakable effect of the point source in the rendered image (Figure 5.23-b). If necessary, get back to the dialog of this light and increase or decrease the Radius value, located at the base, for a larger or smaller light spread.

⬛ Switch to the Shaded Render display and you will find that the image is completely blacked out, since the point light is not recognized and the distant light is no longer shining. Get to the Shaded Render Options dialog and set the Unsupported Lights option to Approximate rather than Ignore. Refresh the display and you will find that the point source is approximated by a distant source, resulting in the model being lighted this time.

⬛ To explore the other attributes of the new point light, invoke its Light Parameters dialog once again by double-clicking on its name in the Lights palette. Experiment with the three Falloff options in the Intensity section, which allow you to choose how the light intensity decreases with distance from the light source: Constant results in a constant intensity irrespective of distance and is the default, Linear decreases the intensity linearly with distance, while Square decreases the intensity exponentially with distance. Since the total intensity of the light has to remain the same, a larger falloff (i.e., lesser intensity at a greater distance) results in a higher light intensity in and around the center of the light. This is evident from Figure 5.23-c where the Falloff was set to Square, as opposed to the Constant option active for Figure 5.23-b.

⬛ Next, click on the Accurate Intensity button, and you will find that the dialog which is invoked is different from the one you encountered for a distant light. Both point and cone lights use the same options for specifying the Accurate Intensity, using one of two methods: the Radiometric method, where the input power of a light in watts is given along with its output efficiency; and the Photometric method, where the brightness of the light is specified in lumens or candelas. Generate and compare renderings using both techniques, with different values for power and brightness (Figure 5.24). In the Photometric method, there is an additional option to specify the Color Temperature of the light: lower values give the light an orange color while higher values make it closer to white.

Figure 5.23

Adding a Point light to the model. (a) In Wire Frame display. (b) The resultant lighting in RenderZone display, with default light settings. (c) Falloff set to Square.

(a)

(b)

(c)

Figure 5.24

Specifying the Accurate
Intensity for a point light.
Two different specifications
are shown, leading to two
different lighting qualities
in the rendering.

- The only remaining option in the Light Parameters dialog that is new for the Point light type is the Glow option, which is unchecked by default. This means that only the illumination from the light source is shown in renderings but not the light itself. By checking the Glow option, the light source will also be displayed as a glowing volume in a RenderZone display. Note that the rendering type in the RenderZone Options dialog has to be set to Preview Z-Buffer or above, and the Light Glow option under the Illumination section must be checked for the light glow to be rendered.

Figure 5.25

Activating the Glow option
for a point light. The corresponding Glow Options
dialog is also shown.

- If you do not achieve the glowing effect at the first attempt, click on the accompanying Glow Options button and increase the Intensity, Falloff, and Glow Area values under the Simple section until the glow is visible. If the Falloff option in the Light Parameters dialog is set to Square, the Accurate section in the Glow Options dialog will also be activated, allowing you to select it and experiment with the options it contains. Figure 5.25 illustrates the glowing effect for a point light, along with the corresponding options. The Glow option is very useful in obtaining realistic rendering

▣ effects for a lamp, for instance, which can be created by enclosing a light source in a semi-transparent material. You will work on such a project in the Assignment for this workshop.

▣ Let us move on to look at the other types of lights. Create two new lights following the same procedure you used to create the point light. Set one of them to Cone and the other to Projector. Open up the Light Parameters dialog for each of them and make the necessary adjustments to the attributes, most of which are identical to those for distant and point lights.

▣ The cone light is directional and has both a location and a center of interest, just like a distant light. Again, you will find it easier to position it graphically using the Move tool rather than by specifying coordinate values in the Light Parameters dialog. Additionally, the spread of a cone light is controlled by two angles—the inner and the outer. Experiment with changes in these values, located at the base of the dialog, and see how they affect the resultant lighting. Figure 5.26-a shows a cone light rendering with all the other lights turned off. The Glow option was turned on in order to see the actual light.

▣ The projector light, as mentioned earlier, projects a specified image in a certain direction (Figure 5.26-b). The location and direction are, as usual, best modified graphically. Other attributes such as the angle and the spin of the light, as well as the image to be projected can all be modified in the Light Parameters dialog (Figure 5.26-c). To change the image from the default logo, simply click on it and you will be presented with a dialog through which you can select a new image.

Figure 5.26

Rendering with a cone and a projector light. The Light Parameters dialog for the projector light is also shown.

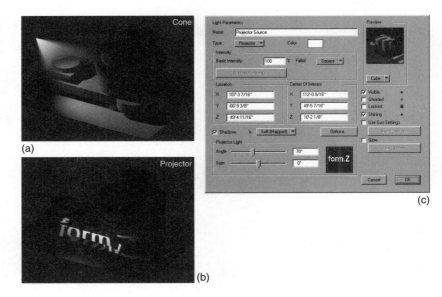

2.5 Area Lights

form•Z lets you convert any modeling object in the project into a primary light source. Such a light is known as an *area light* and is extremely useful in different modeling situations. For instance, when modeling a lampshade, you can convert the lampshade itself into an area light and bypass the step of modeling a cone or point light to place inside the lampshade. You can convert a window pane into an area light to provide subtle nighttime lighting effects inside a space. Any object, of any shape and size, can be made to emit light. This provides enormous flexibility and versatility in creating interesting, unusual, and beautiful lighting effects.

Figure 5.27

Working with an area light.
(a) The Light Parameters
dialog defining the light.
(b) Wire Frame display of
the scene, showing the
area light. (c) RenderZone
display of the scene, with
the Render Light Object
option turned on.

(a)

(b)

(c)

■ Select an object in your scene that you would like to convert to a light source, or create a new object and then select it. With the object still selected, click in the Lights palette to create a new light. Double-click on the new entry to invoke its Light Parameters dialog, and select Area from the Type popup menu (Figure 5.27-a). Click OK to exit the dialog and return to the graphics window. You will notice that the selected object is now replaced by an area light symbol, depicted by surfaces with arrows pointing outwards to indicate the direction of the light (Figure 5.27-b).

■ Generate a RenderZone image with the area light activated; you can turn off all the other lights to get the full impact of this light. Notice that the area light itself is not shown, simply the light from it as it illuminates nearby surfaces. If you want the light itself to also be depicted, invoke the Light Parameters dialog again and check the Render Light Object option located in the Area Light section at the base of the dialog (as in Figure 5.27-a). Refresh the display after making this change, and you will find that the area light itself now appears as a glowing object in the scene (Figure 5.27-c).

■ The Ignore Light Object Color option in the Area Light section enables you to specify that the color of the original object should be ignored in the lighting effect. If this option is checked, only the color specified in the Color box at the top of the Light Parameters dialog is used for the light. If the object color *is* to be considered, as it is by default, you can go one step further and modify the original surface style of the object by clicking on its display in the adjoining preview window. Additionally, you can set the Quality of the illumination and shadows generated by the area light using the accompanying slider bar. A higher value will naturally also take more time to render.

■ The Accurate Intensity of an area light in the Light Parameters dialog is specified using the same options as a point or cone light. But notice that both the Basic Intensity and FallOff options are grayed out for this light, since this light type is not recognized in displays other than RenderZone. You are, however, given the convenient option of specifying an alternative point light that will be used instead of this light. To do this, click on the Alternative Light button, located below the Glow option. In the dialog that opens up, you can specify the radius, intensity, falloff, and shadows options for the alternate light, just as you did for the point light in the last section. To actually ensure that the alternate light is used in a Shaded Render display, choose Approximate rather than

Ignore for the Unsupported Lights option in the Shaded Render Options dialog. The RenderZone Options dialog also has an option for Area Lights under the Illumination section—you can choose to Ignore, Approximate, or Use them.

▫ Once an object has been converted to an area light, modeling operations can no longer be applied to it since it is no longer regarded as an object. If you need to retrieve the object, simply change the light type from Area to something else in its Light Parameters dialog. Don't try and retrieve it by deleting the area light, since this will also delete the object that was converted to the light!

2.6 Custom Lights

The area light you saw in the last section is one step towards customization of lights, enabling you to convert an object of any shape and size into a light, without being restricted to predefined light types such as point, cone, etc. form•Z goes a step further and allows you to create a light with a *customized spread* instead of a uniform spread. In other words, you can define what the light intensities should be in different directions about the light source, rather than settle for a uniform intensity in all directions. Such a light is called a *custom light* and it enables you to simulate real-world lighting situations, which almost invariably have varying light intensities in different directions about a source.

▫ Create a new light in the Lights palette. Open its Lights Parameters dialog and set the Type to Custom. Most of the options for this light are identical to those you have explored for the other light types. Modify some of these familiar options if you like, and exit the dialog.

▫ You should see your new light represented as a sphere in Wire Frame by three perpendicular circles, two of which intersect the *axis* of the light (Figure 5.28-a). The axis is the line which starts at the center of the spherical shape—the *origin*—and ends with the larger arrow—the *center of interest*. The other line starting from the center and ending with a smaller arrow is perpendicular to the axis and represents the *zero angle line*, with respect to which light intensities in different directions are defined. This line coincides with the 0° plane for light distribution, which you will learn about very soon. For now, adjust the position of the light so that it is visible in the scene you want to render.

Figure 5.28

Adding a custom light to the scene. The Intensity Distribution dialog for this light, showing the default intensity spread, is also illustrated.

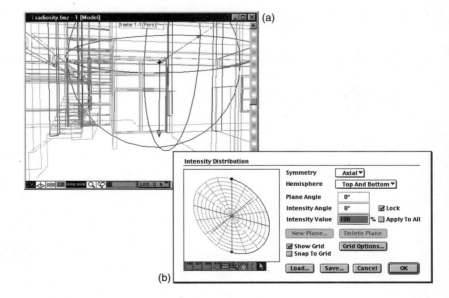

■ Generate a rendering with all other lights turned off except the custom light. With the default intensity settings, you will find that the illumination from the custom light is not very different from that of a point light.

■ We will now proceed to customize the intensity spread of this light. Invoke its Light Parameters dialog once again and click on the Intensity Distribution button, located at the base. The dialog that opens up contains a preview window and a number of options (Figure 5.28-b). The preview window shows the current light distribution curve against a planar grid with radial subdivisions. (It is radial because light, by nature, travels radially outwards from a source.) The distance of each point on the curve from the central axis—which is the axis of the light you saw in the Wire Frame display—represents the intensity of light in that direction, at that position, and on that plane. The custom light will be completely defined by similar intensity curves for different planes, all of which pass through the axis. Only one of these planes is shown in the preview area to begin with.

■ Use the tools icons located at the base of the preview window to switch to the planar view in which you can see the intensity curve head-on. Then select the Pointer tool and use it to move the active endpoint of the curve, which is colored in the highlight color. As you move the point, the shape of the curve changes. Notice that the Intensity Value field, located to the right of the preview window, also changes as you move the point. Try changing this value, which is expressed as a percentage, directly and see the location of the active point change in response to the specified value.

■ Activate the other point and move it as well. You are not limited to moving within the grid that is displayed; you can zoom out as much as you want to manipulate the spread of the light. Thus, you can have intensity values well over 100% if required.

■ By default, there are only two points on the curve that you can move—the endpoints. To insert additional points on the curve so that you can further manipulate its shape, click on any part of the curve while pressing the option key (Mac) or Ctrl+Shift keys (PC). This will insert a new point at the location of the click, which can now be moved just like the earlier points (see Figure 5.29-a). Notice that the movement of this point seems constrained—this is because the angle that the point makes with respect to the origin is locked by default. To unlock it, deselect the Lock option next to the Intensity Angle box; now watch this value change in addition to the Intensity Value when you move the point. The intensity angles of the two endpoints of the curve remain constant and cannot be changed.

■ Repeat the insertion and moving of points until you have a light distribution curve that is very different from what you had earlier (Figure 5.29-a). An inserted point can be deleted, if necessary, by selecting it with the control key (Mac) or Ctrl+Alt keys (PC). When you are satisfied with the curve, generate a rendering with this light to see what it looks like (Figure 5.29-b).

Figure 5.29

Modifying the light distribution curve of the custom
light, and the resultant
rendering.

(a)

(b)

WORKSHOP 5

◼ Invoke the Intensity Distribution dialog for the custom light once again in order to explore the other available options. Start with the four options in the Symmetry popup menu. The default is the Axial option, which requires only one light distribution curve (i.e., a curve on one plane) as you just saw in the last step. The overall spread of the light is derived by revolving this single curve a full 360° about the axis of the light.

◼ Switch to the Quadrant type of symmetry and click OK in response to the query that pops up. Here, the light distribution is symmetrical in each quadrant. Therefore, at least two distribution curves are required to define the light spread within a single quadrant, one at the 0° plane and the other at the 90° plane. Curves at additional intermediate planes can be defined, if required, by specifying the plane orientation in degrees in the Plane Angle field.

◼ As soon as you switch to Quadrant symmetry, you will see a second curve in ghosted mode, perpendicular to the first curve. Click on this curve with the Pointer tool to activate it; the first curve will now become ghosted. Notice also that the Plane Angle value has changed from 0° to 90°. The new curve is initially the same shape as the first curve and is placed on its own planar grid which is now visible. Use the Pointer tool to manipulate the shape of this curve, just as you did for the first curve, adding new points if necessary. You will find that any changes you make to the second curve are also reflected in the first curve—new points are added, and if a point is moved on the active curve, corresponding points on the ghosted curve also get displaced slightly. This happens because the light spread ultimately has to be defined by smoothly blending all the curves, so they must have some correspondence with each other. If you want the changes made to the Intensity Value of the points on the active curve to be exactly duplicated in the ghosted curve, simply select the Apply To All option, located next to the Intensity Value field.

◼ Still in Quadrant symmetry, specify an angle value between 0° and 90° in the Plane Angle field and modify the light distribution curve for this plane as well (Figure 5.30-a). You can modify the curves for any number of quadrant planes in this manner. After you are done, render the image to see what the resulting light spread looks like (Figure 5.30-b).

Figure 5.30

Working with Quadrant symmetry light distribution curves for the custom light, and the resultant rendering.

(a)

(b)

◼ Similarly, explore the remaining two Symmetry types as well. Plane is very similar to Quadrant except that the distribution is symmetrical in each of the two half-planes rather than the four quadrants. You can specify any number of distribution curves between 0° and 180° planes—the two extreme curves have to be specified as a minimum. The remaining option, None, as you can guess from its name, uses no symmetry in calculating the light distribution. It lets you specify the distribution curves for any number of planes. A minimum of three is required: the first at 0°, the second at any angle, and the third at any angle greater than 180°.

◼ Move on to explore the three Hemisphere options. By default, the Top And Bottom is active, which is why your light distribution curves so far could extend both above and below the origin of the light—represented by the center of the radial grid. Physically, this translates to a light source that provides illumination both above and below it, as you can see from the preceding illustrations. Change the Hemisphere option to Bottom for a downward pointing light, or to Top for an upward pointing light. The light distribution curves will be automatically adjusted, with points removed if necessary. Figure 5.31 shows the specifications of a downward pointing custom light and the resultant rendering.

Figure 5.31

Changing the Hemisphere option of the custom light to Bottom, and the resultant rendering.

(a) (b)

▣ There are only a few more options left to explore in the Intensity Distribution dialog for the custom light. New Plane lets you create a new plane at a specified angle for the symmetry types which allow multiple planes—which includes all except Axial symmetry. Delete Plane lets you delete the active plane; if a plane cannot be deleted such as the 0° plane, this option is dimmed. Show Grid and Snap To Grid are toggle switches for grid visibility and grid snapping respectively. You can also make changes to the distance and angle specifications of the grid by clicking on the Grid Options button and specifying the desired values in the dialog that is invoked.

▣ A custom light can be saved in a data file, by clicking on the Save button, in one of three standard light formats: IES (Illumination Engineering Society of North America), CIE (International Commission on Illumination), or the British CIBSE (Chartered Institution of Building Services Engineers). The parameters of a saved light can be recalled for a custom light in any project by clicking on the Load button. In addition to your own saved files, this is particularly useful for loading actual data files, supplied by the manufacturers, for commercially available lights that you plan to use in your project.

▣ We have covered all the options in the Intensity Distribution dialog, so go ahead and exit from it. Back in the Light Parameters dialog, notice that there is an Alternative Light button that allows you to specify an approximation to be used for this custom light, just as you did for Area lights. Additionally, you can change the Spin value at the base of the Light Parameters dialog to rotate the custom light about its axis—this angle is measured with respect to the zero angle line, i.e., the 0° plane orientation.

2.7 The Lights Palette and Dialog

▣ It is time to take a closer look at the Lights palette and see the functionalities it affords. By this time, your palette should have six entries, one for each of the light types you have created in your model so far. The name of each light is preceded by an icon, indicating what its type is (Figure 5.32-a).

▣ Go ahead and create one more light in the usual fashion, and set its type to Distant. Position it graphically in the desired location, or use the Sun Settings option in the Light Parameters dialog to specify a sun position for it. Make sure its direction is sufficiently different from the first distant light you had.

WORKSHOP 5

Figure 5.32

Working with the Lights
palette. (a) Entries for each
of the six light types.
(b) Creating an additional
distant light. (c) Designating
the new distant light as the
sun. (d) Manipulating various attributes of the lights.

◼ Deactivate all the other lights and switch the display to RenderZone. The scene will be rendered, as expected, according to the new light. But switch to Surface Render, and you will find that it ignores the new distant light and goes by the old light, even though the Shining attribute of that light has been turned off. Recall that the Surface Render and Quick Paint displays can only work with a single light source which is the sun. Obviously, these displays are still regarding the first light as the sun for some reason.

◼ Look closely at the icon accompanying your first distant light, and you will find that it is highlighted (Figure 5.32-b). This is why that light is considered to be the sun by the Surface Render and Quick Paint displays. To designate the *new* distant light as the sun, simply click on *its* icon. It will get highlighted, clearing the highlight from the icon of the first light (Figure 5.32-c). A Surface Render display will now give you the correct result, treating the new light as the sun. Thus, you can have many distant lights in your model, but only one of these can be designated as the sun at any given time by highlighting its icon.

The ability to create multiple distant lights but designate only one of them as the sun is very convenient for carrying out daylighting studies of an architectural or urban design model. Many lights can be created, each set to different dates and times for the same site by activating the Sun Settings option in its Light Parameters dialog. To render the model in Surface Render for different sun positions, simply highlight the corresponding icon in the Lights palette. To obtain the same renderings using Shaded Render or RenderZone, activate one light at a time by turning off the Shining attribute for all the others. This is how you can explore the variation in shades and shadows in a model at different times of the day or year, without having to keep changing the sun position every time.

◼ Now turn your attention to the various columns in the Lights palette. To the right of the Light Name are four columns—these provide a convenient way of manipulating some of the light attributes that you previously changed using the Light Parameters dialog. From left to right, these columns correspond with the Visible/Ghosted, Locked, Shining, and Shadows attributes respectively (see Figure 5.32-d). Just like the other palettes you have seen, icons in these columns work as toggle switches, reversing the corresponding attributes of the lights when selected. Try out each one of them.

 It is particularly useful to make lights ghosted or invisible before entering the Cone Of Vision mode, so that you have a less chaotic display and can concentrate on adjustments to the line of sight. Locking a light is always convenient to prevent accidental selections and

transformations. As far as the Shining attribute is concerned, it should always be turned off for those lights that will not be contributing to the illumination of a particular scene. Thus, for daytime external renderings, the interior lights can be switched off, while for nighttime internal views, the external distant lights should be switched off.

▣ The column to the left of the Light Name is the familiar selection column. It can be used to conveniently select a light that is visible and not locked, for instance, when you want to move the light. Try it out. Very often in complex projects, lights get buried under mounds of modeling objects and are difficult to select using the Pick tool, so this is a really useful shortcut.

▣ Just like all the other palettes you have seen so far, the Lights palette has a dialog associated with it which you can access in the usual manner—click in the top bar of the Lights palette where the column title, Light Name, appears, or go to Options > Lights. Here, you have the usual options for creating new lights and editing, deleting, copying and sorting existing lights (Figure 5.33-a). The New and Edit buttons invoke the same Light Parameters dialog that you have already worked with. The Load Project Lights option can be used to load all the lights defined in another form•Z project into the current one—a useful option if you have divided up a complex modeling project into two or more smaller, more manageable projects and would like to synchronize them.

▣ The Ambient Light option in the Lights dialog will be new to you. It is important to remember that the sun, and any other lights that you create in a project, are in addition to the *ambient* light which is always present. The color and intensity of this ambient light is defined in the Lights dialog. The default is white light of 10% intensity. These attributes can be changed in the same way as you change the color and basic intensity of an individual light. Try it. You will find that changes in the intensity of the ambient light affect all the display modes, while changes in the color are visible only in the Shaded Render, RenderZone, QuickDraw 3D, and OpenGL display modes. Figure 5.33-b shows the same lighting scene by the projector light as Figure 5.26-b, but with an ambient light of blue color and 80% intensity.

Figure 5.33

The Lights dialog, and the result of changing the ambient light settings from the defaults, for the scene using a projector light shown in Figure 5.26-b.

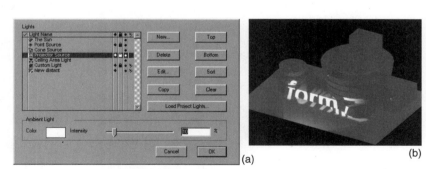

(a) (b)

2.8 Performing an Illumination Analysis

We have, by now, already explored all the options under the Illumination section of the RenderZone Options dialog that we had skipped in Section 1.1, except one—the Analysis option. When this is activated, the current scene will be rendered, not with object colors as is usually done, but with a color coding scheme that shows the *light intensity* on every visible surface. Thus, you can analyze the illumination in any part of your model with this option. It is most useful in architectural modeling for designing the lighting conditions inside a space.

Figure 5.34

Rendering the illumination
analysis of a scene. The
Illumination Analysis Options
dialog is also shown.

Rendered scene

Illumination analysis

(a)

(b)

◻ Open a building project you have modeled to a sufficient extent to be able to generate some internal views. If you don't have such a project, create a simple one: a 3D enclosure sitting on a base plan, its top enclosed by a flat or sloping slab, with a couple of openings in the walls. Generate a few interior views of the space with the openings in sight, using Edit Cone Of Vision. Add lights as appropriate. For a distant light, invoke its Light Parameters dialog, click on the Accurate Intensity button, and set the Output Power to 2 watts per sq. ft.

◻ Bring up the RenderZone Options dialog (shown earlier in Figure 5.1) and turn to the Illumination section. By default, the Analysis option is grayed out, as you can see. You have to check the Accurate Intensity option for the Analysis option to become available. Do so, and then activate the Analysis option as well. Exit the dialog. You will find that the rendered image now shows contour-like patches on all the surfaces in various colors, corresponding with various light intensities (Figure 5.34-a). All areas having the same intensity will be shown in the same color. Thus, you can visually get a quick estimate of the lighting conditions in the current scene.

◻ Go back to the RenderZone Options dialog, and click on the Options button accompanying the Analysis option. In the dialog that is invoked (Figure 5.34-b), you can modify the colors used for different intensity values in the list on the left, by clicking on the color box accompanying each value.

◻ You can also choose whether the rendering will show the Illuminance or the Luminance of a surface. The first option is selected by default. Illuminance is the amount of light intensity *received* by a surface, and can be used to determine if the lighting conditions in a space are proper. Luminance, on the other hand, is the amount of light intensity *reflected* by a surface, and is used to detect areas with a high degree of glare.

◻ The next option in the Illumination Analysis Options dialog is Blend Colors. When this is selected, the edges between adjacent color contours in the illumination rendering are blurred rather than sharp, caused by a smooth blending of colors from one contour to the next. Select or deselect it, based on your rendering requirements.

■ Next, click on the Set Range button. This invokes a dialog where you can specify the Minimum and Maximum illuminance or luminance values that will appear in the Color/Value list. The other values in the list will then be divided into equal increments between the minimum and maximum values. Alternately, you could also specify the Increment value instead of the Maximum value.

■ The remaining buttons in the Illumination Analysis Options dialog perform a variety of functions. Insert is used to insert a new color/value entry above the currently selected one, while Delete will remove the current one from the list. The Revert, Save, Load, and Default buttons have their usual meaning.

Having explored all the basic lighting options, let us move on to learn what radiosity is all about and how it affects the lighting in a rendered image.

EXERCISE 3

Radiosity Based Rendering

Radiosity is a technique that enables the generation of very realistic renderings of the lighting conditions in a scene. The contrast is illustrated in Figure 5.35, which shows a RenderZone display of the interior of a space illuminated by a single distant light, with and without radiosity. You can see how much more real the radiosity rendering appears to be.

We will not get into the technical details here of how radiosity works. It is sufficient to understand that radiosity simulates light very accurately—for instance, it takes into consideration the indirect light reflected off surfaces that are not directly illuminated, which is how light behaves in real life. Ordinary lighting calculations of the kind you have done so far do not account for such light. That is why the radiosity rendering of the scene in Figure 5.35 appears much brighter, and therefore more lifelike, than a non-radiosity rendering of the same scene.

Radiosity is not a rendering technique like the various rendering types—Gourand, Phong, Z-Buffer, Raytrace, and so on—available in RenderZone. Rather, it is a description of the project model incorporating radiosity calculations. This description of the model is referred to as the *radiosity solution*, and its generation can be extremely memory-intensive and time-consuming, depending upon the complexity of the model. Once the radiosity solution has been generated, it can be rendered in the Shaded Render, RenderZone, QuickDraw 3D, and OpenGL display modes.

WORKSHOP 5

Figure 5.35

Radiosity and non-radiosity based renderings of the same scene, using a single distant light.

Radiosity rendering

Non-radiosity rendering

Radiosity based rendering in form•Z is executed by commands grouped in the third group of the Display menu. We will start this exercise by going through one complete cycle of initializing, generating, and rendering a radiosity solution, using the default radiosity settings. Then, we will look at some basic aspects of radiosity. Finally, we will explore all the radiosity options and see how they can be manipulated to enhance the quality of the rendering, or reduce the time it takes to generate a solution.

3.1   Initializing, Generating, and Rendering a Radiosity Solution

As mentioned earlier, radiosity takes into account the indirect light reflected off surfaces, which accounts for the more realistic lighting effects it produces. This is done by meshing each surface of the model and treating each mesh subdivision as a *secondary* light source. *Primary* light sources, as opposed to secondary light sources, are the lights that you create and position in the model, which are listed in the Lights palette. There are three steps involved in the radiosity process: *initialization*, where the subdivisions on each surface are created; *generation*, where the radiosity calculations are performed; and *rendering*, where the radiosity solution is rendered. Let us see how the process works.

🔳   Use the same building project that you used for exploring illumination analysis in the last section. Set the appropriate RenderZone parameters, render the image, and save it as an image file. This will help you compare the non-radiosity solution with the radiosity one.

🔳   Switch to the Wire Frame display mode and go to Display > Initialize Radiosity. This will subdivide the surfaces of all the objects into a dense mesh (see Figure 5.36). At the same time, all the modeling tools and many of the window tools are grayed out, indicating that you are in the *radiosity mode*, within which no changes can be made to the model. The larger the number of initial subdivisions, the greater the number of secondary light sources, and the more physically accurate the lighting simulation becomes. We will see how to increase the density of the initialization mesh in Section 3.3.

🔳   Change the display mode to RenderZone. All the surfaces of the model will be fully blacked out—this is because the radiosity calculations have not yet begun, let alone been completed. Switch back to Wire Frame and go to Display > Generate Radiosity Solution to set the process in motion. For a complex model, the calculations may take quite a bit of time. The slider bar shows the progress of the calculations, and periodically, all the windows get updated to reflect the lighting calculations. These would be visible to you if you were still in the RenderZone display mode, but refreshing the rendered display constantly consumes time and memory, so it is better to remain in the Wire Frame mode.

🔳   Once the calculations are completed, switch the display to RenderZone to see the result. You will find that the overall lighting is brighter and more realistic as compared to the non-radiosity rendering you saved earlier. You might, however, find some deficiencies in the radiosity rendering such as jagged edges, spots, and so on, which we will soon learn to fix.

🔳   Now switch to another view of the model and refresh the RenderZone display. You will find that the new view takes hardly any time to render. This is because the radiosity calculations are, by default, performed for the whole model and are therefore view-independent. Thus, once the solution is generated, any number of views can be rendered very quickly, taking even less time than a new view takes to render outside radiosity.

🔳   To leave the radiosity mode, select Exit Radiosity from the Display menu. A dialog will pop up, warning you that the current solution will be deleted; click OK in response. You will be returned to the regular modeling environment in which all the tools are activated and accessible.

Figure 5.36

Initializing radiosity for the same model and view shown in Figure 5.35.

3.2 Other Radiosity Basics

We have gone through one complete radiosity cycle, comprising initialization, generation, rendering, and exit. Before moving on to look at the radiosity options in detail in the next section, it is important to understand a few other basic aspects of radiosity.

▪ Create and activate a point and a cone light in your model; at the same time, turn off any distant lights that are shining. From the Display menu, select the Generate Radiosity Solution option directly this time. Notice that the initialization process takes place anyway, followed immediately by the generation process. Thus, you can bypass selecting the Initialize Radiosity command if you like.

▪ After the radiosity solution had been generated, switch to the Shaded Render rather than the RenderZone display. You will see that the lighting effects of the point and cone lights can also be seen in Shaded Render, which, outside of radiosity, works only with distant lights (Figure 5.37). This is a clear indication that radiosity effects are achieved by calculations incorporated in the model itself, rather than generated by any rendering technique.

Figure 5.37

A Shaded Render display of a radiosity solution with a point and a cone light, compared with a Render-Zone non-radiosity display of the same scene. Notice that bumps in the surface style cannot be seen in radiosity.

Shaded Render, radiosity   RenderZone, non-radiosity

WORKSHOP 5

◼ Now try generating a radiosity solution with a projector light in the scene and you will find that a cone light is substituted instead of the projector light, and the lighting effects generated accordingly. So if a projector light is essential to your scene, you will have to settle for a non-radiosity solution.

◼ Next, modify some of the surface styles of the objects or faces visible in the current radiosity solution, using the Surface Styles palette. As soon as you make a change, you will be warned that the changes will only be reflected in the radiosity solution from that point on; click OK in response. Now refresh the display and you will find that the surface style changes have been incorporated, *without* requiring the radiosity solution to be regenerated. This is of great advantage, letting you fine-tune your surface styles without going through the time-consuming process of regeneration after every minor change.

◼ With lights, however, it is a different story. Any changes made to the lights that are active for the current solution require the solution to be regenerated. Test this by deactivating a shining light in the Lights palette or changing its color or intensity, and you will be warned that the solution will have to be regenerated. You have no choice but to click OK if you want to see a solution with the required changes. The regeneration will not take place automatically—you have to select the Generate Radiosity Solution command after you have finished making all the desired modifications.

◼ Recall from Workshop 3 that there are some radiosity options located in the Preferences dialog. To access these, go to Edit > Preferences and click on the Radiosity button. You will see a dialog with three radiosity preferences, out of which the first two are selected by default. You can deselect the first option if you do not wish to be warned before entering or exiting radiosity.

◼ Pay special attention to the second option, Save Solution In Project File. This will save the current radiosity solution when you save the file, *provided you are still in radiosity mode*. To test this, exit the Preferences dialog and while you are still in radiosity mode, go to File > Save A Copy As. This will let you save a copy of the current file under a different name. Then exit radiosity, thereby deleting the radiosity solution, and save the original file. Switch to the desktop and compare the file sizes of the original file and the copy you created. You will find that the copy is substantially larger than the original, since it has the radiosity solution stored within it. Open up the copy in form•Z and select the Generate Radiosity Solution command. This will simply load the saved radiosity solution from the file, without needing it to be recalculated. It is convenient to do this once you have finalized both the project model and the radiosity solution, and do not anticipate making any more changes to either of them.

◼ Get back to the Preferences dialog and look at the third radiosity preference, Preserve Solution During Working Session, which is deselected by default. This explains why the radiosity solution gets deleted every time you exit the radiosity mode. If you want the solution to be preserved, simply check this option. However, considering that the radiosity solution has to be regenerated from scratch if any change is made to the model or to the lights, there is not much advantage to preserving the solution during a working session, especially considering the overhead of a larger file size.

3.3   Radiosity Options

Radiosity has a large number of options, both for the processes of initialization as well as generation, which, as you have seen, take place in two distinct stages. These options can be manipulated to reduce the time required to produce a solution in the initial stages, when you are still in the process of experimentation, and later, to increase the quality of the solution when you are ready to produce a final one. Let us get down to exploring these options.

Figure 5.38

The Radiosity Options
dialog.

▪ Go to Display > Radiosity Options. This opens up the substantial Radiosity Options dialog shown in Figure 5.38. You can see that the various parameters are clearly divided into two groups: Initialization and Generation. Rather than plunging right away into an explanation of what each parameter stands for and exploring how it affects the quality of the solution, let us adopt a different, more convenient approach. Look at the Preset Parameters popup menu located in the lower left corner of the dialog. This contains ten numbers, each corresponding with different preset values of the various radiosity parameters that will produce different qualities of the solution. It is set to 6 by default.

▪ Start by setting Preset Parameters to 1, which will produce the lowest quality solution in the least amount of time. Notice the values that each of the Initialization and Generation parameters acquire. Then exit the dialog, generate a radiosity solution, and display it in RenderZone. Compare the quality of the solution, as well as the time taken to generate it, with the results you obtained in the last section. The quality might be so poor that it may never make sense to use this preset parameter, even if the solution is generated instantaneously.

▪ Repeat this process by setting Preset Parameters to increasingly higher values, and notice how all the Initialization and Generation parameters change in response. This will give you a good understanding of how they affect the quality of the solution. Generate and render the radiosity solution for each preset parameter to see the results of the parameters visually. Preset parameters of 9 and 10 might take too long to complete, depending upon the complexity of your model and the capabilities of your computer. In that case, simply observe the maximum values acquired by each parameter and remember to stay below these values when you choose to specify your own combination of parametric values.

In many cases, the preset parametric values will be sufficient in enabling you to produce the kind of radiosity solution that you need, and you do not necessarily have to know what each individual parameter in the Radiosity Options dialog stands for. These will be discussed in the rest of this section, so you can briefly skim through it for now if you are in a hurry to get on with the rest of the workshop. Do come back to study it in detail, though, when you are ready for a better understanding of the radiosity parameters.

▪ Let us start with the Initialization parameters. There are two kinds of mesh density values you can modify. Sources deals with the subdivisions of the area light sources in the model, while Patches refers to the subdivisions of all object surfaces, which, as you have seen, are secondary light sources in radiosity. The level of subdivision for each of these two parameters can be modified by using the accompanying slider bar or numerically specifying a percentage value. The larger the number of subdivisions, the better the quality of the solution, but the greater the processing time.

▣ The subdivisions for both area lights and object surfaces can be further increased by using the next option. The value you enter for Polygons indicates how many more polygons will be generated on top of the initial source and patch subdivisions. To get an estimate of the number of sources, patches, and mesh polygons before the radiosity mesh is initialized, click on the Estimate Mesh Density button.

▣ The Generate Shadows option should be self-explanatory. The radiosity process, unlike the regular rendering methods, usually does not produce very crisp shadows, unless you use a high density initialization mesh. It is more suited to capturing the distribution of reflected light accurately. By selecting the next option, Render Direct Illumination, the computation of the direct illumination in a scene is not done within radiosity, but is postponed until the solution is rendered using the Shaded Render or RenderZone displays. This combines the best of the radiosity and non-radiosity techniques, leading to crisper shadow boundaries in the final solution. The accompanying sub-option, Include Area Lights, can be selected to specify that area lights be treated as direct illumination and rendered outside radiosity. However, since area lights do not usually cause sharp shadow boundaries, it is more efficient to leave this sub-option turned off.

▣ By default, a radiosity solution is calculated for an entire project, that is, it can be seen simultaneously in multiple views. In other words, it is view independent. One way of reducing the time required to produce a high quality solution, particularly when you are only interested in a single view, is to check the View Dependent Solution option. The solution will now be calculated only for the active view, and will take less time than if it were being calculated for the whole project.

▣ The Resolve Intersections option, when activated, improves the quality of the solution by splitting up patches which happen to intersect with other patches. This will lead to less jagged edges, cleaner shadow lines, and no shadow leaks in the solution. It will, however, increase the processing time considerably.

▣ One useful technique for improving the quality of a radiosity solution substantially, without adding exponentially to the time required to generate it, is to apply a highly dense mesh only to those surfaces on which shadows are expected to be cast (using the Rendering Attributes tool, which will be covered in Exercise 5). Low density specifications can be set in the Radiosity Options dialog for the remaining surfaces. The radiosity calculations will then proceed taking into account these different density values, unless you check the Ignore Object/Face Meshing Attribute option, in which case all surfaces will be subdivided according to the same mesh density specified in this dialog.

▣ You are already familiar with the Smooth Shading and Parametrics options from the RenderZone Options dialog. Therefore, all that remains in the Initialization section are the Sampling parameters, which determine how the lighting calculations are performed with respect to each source or patch polygon. For each polygon, a number of randomly selected sample points is chosen for emitting the light that is supposed to leave that polygon. The minimum and maximum number of these sample points has to be specified. In addition to how light leaves a polygon, you can also control how light is recorded when it arrives at a polygon. At Vertices will record the light intensity at each vertex of the polygon, while At Center records it only at the center. As you may have noticed when exploring the preset parameters, vertex sampling is more accurate and used when higher quality solutions are required. Under Sampling, you can also choose between three different levels of lighting quality available in the Quality popup menu: Simple will use the minimum number of sample points specified, while Best will use the maximum.

▣ Now move on to look at the Generation parameters, the first of which is Adaptive Meshing. When this option is turned on, the mesh produced by the initialization process is further subdivided during the generation process, leading to a better quality solution. The extent to which the subdivision occurs depends upon the values of the next three parameters. A higher Density value will create more subdivisions—a value of 80% is adequate for high quality images, and you should be wary of exceeding this limit. The Threshold parameter determines when a mesh polygon will be subdivided based on intensity differences with adjacent polygons—the lower this value, the greater the subdivision. The third parameter, Cutoff, is used to control mesh subdivision in poorly illuminated areas which do not need dense meshing—a higher value reduces the mesh density in such dark areas.

- The next set of four mutually exclusive options determines the sensitivity of the mesh subdivision as the generation process progresses. Continuous Meshing ensures the highest quality solution but may be inefficient and needlessly time-consuming, since it also leads to high mesh density in areas of small contrast where it is not necessary. Decrease Meshing, which reduces the meshing density as the solution progresses, is a better option, being a good compromise between speed and quality. No Meshing After Processing Lights takes even less time since meshing is stopped after all the area sources have emitted their light; the quality of the image might still be acceptable. The last option lets you stop the meshing process after a specified number of Iterations. A single iteration is defined by a single area source or secondary source patch emitting its light to all the other subdivisions of the radiosity mesh.

- The next two Terminate After conditions are very important since they are used to determine when the generation process will stop and the solution will be completed. You can choose to stop when a specified percentage of the total light in the scene has been absorbed—a value of around 85% will yield a high quality solution within a reasonable amount of time. Alternately, you can specify a desired number of iterations that the solution must go through before terminating.

 During the actual process of generating a radiosity solution, the process can be terminated manually at any time by pressing the usual stop-processing keys—command+period (Mac), Ctrl+period (PC), or Esc (Mac or PC).

- The Current Statistics section displays several important aspects of the generation process of the previously executed solution. It is useful when the radiosity solution is being generated in an iterative manner. Based on the values displayed for one attempt, e.g., for # Of Iterations, the termination conditions for the next attempt can be set to stop after a larger number of iterations, if a higher quality solution is desired.

- The last parameter for the Generation process is the Apply Reflected Light As Ambient option. It is turned on by default, causing reflected light which is not yet recorded to be applied as ambient light to all the mesh subdivisions. This causes a scene to appear brighter in the initial stages of the generation process than it would be if the option was turned off. The difference between the two scenarios will reduce as the solution progresses and more and more of the light gets absorbed.

- The final option in the Radiosity Options dialog has to do with the preview that is periodically updated in the graphics window as the radiosity solution progresses. A number of parameters determine the quality of this preview and the frequency with which it is updated. You can access these parameters by clicking on the Preview Options button, located at the base of the dialog. Explore them on your own at leisure—they are quite self-explanatory.

This marks the end of our exercise on radiosity. Keep in mind that a radiosity rendering is not guaranteed to always be better than a non-radiosity rendering. For instance, textures with bumps do not render well in radiosity. Therefore, always generate both radiosity and non-radiosity renderings for a scene, compare the results, and then pick the one that best captures the effect you wish to achieve.

WORKSHOP 5

A Closer Look at Textures

In Section 1.2 of Workshop 3, you briefly went through the process of creating a new surface style (which will here be referred to as a *texture*) using the Surface Styles Parameters dialog. You saw how you can create almost an infinite variety of textures by choosing different attributes for Color, Reflection, Transparency, and Bump, and making further modifications in the Options dialog for each attribute. As you work with textures to produce realistic renderings of your models, you will find that one of the biggest problems is how to scale and position a texture accurately on the surface of an object. Exercise 4 is devoted to understanding and solving this and other texture-related problems, such as mapping an external image to an object as a texture, and applying multiple textures to the same surface.

4.1 Scaling Textures

◼ Open a new form•Z project. You will start by creating a new surface style. Click on the blank space at the lower end of the Surface Styles palette to invoke the Surface Styles Parameters dialog. For the Color parameter of the new style, choose Checker from the selection list. Make sure you do not choose the Checker, Solid option, which is a solid texture rather than a wrapped texture like the first Checker option. (You will see the difference between the two types of textures later.) Leave Reflection, Transparency, and Bump to the default values. Give the new style an appropriate name, say "Checks."

◼ Click on the Options button for the Checker color parameter to open its dialog (Figure 5.39-a). Examine the options and change the two checker colors to different ones if you like. Don't, however, change the Scale value for now. What you see in the preview area is referred to as a single *tile* of the texture.

Figure 5.39

Scaling a texture. The Checker Options dialog for the texture is also shown.

(a)

Scale = 100%
(b)

Scale = 200%
(c)

◼ Exit both the Checker Options dialog and then the Surface Styles Parameters dialog by clicking on their respective OK buttons. With this new surface style, create a few simple objects and switch to the RenderZone display mode (Figure 5.39-b). Notice that an individual tile of the texture is quite small in proportion to the size of the object. (Of course, you could have different results depending upon the size of the objects you create.)

■ Let us see if there is a simple solution to this problem. Double-click on the Checks style you just created in the Surface Styles palette and invoke the Checker Options dialog as you did earlier. Change the Scale value to 200%, return to the graphics window, and regenerate the RenderZone display. You will find that the tile size has doubled from what it was earlier (Figure 5.39-c).

As a quick fix, what we just did was fine. But what if we wanted to specify the exact size of a single tile of the texture? (And where is it coming from anyway?) What if we also wanted to orient the texture differently on different surfaces and on different objects? We can do all this and more by utilizing a special tool in the modeling tool palette devoted to this task, called the Texture Map tool.

4.2   Precise Texture Mapping

■ First, go back and reset the Scale of the Checks style back to 100%. Then select the Texture Map tool (M-Tool:13a,4), and apply it to one of your objects. This will invoke the Texture Map Controls dialog for that object, containing various options for precisely adjusting how the texture is "mapped" on the faces of the object (Figure 5.40).

■ At the top, left corner of the dialog is the preview window, showing the object along with the "shape" based on which the texture is mapped—referred to as the *mapping type*—and its origin. The mapping type will be explored in detail shortly. You are already familiar with all the tool icons located at the base of the preview window except for the last tool. Select this tool and change the preview, first from Wire Frame to Tiled, and then to Rendered. Settle for Tiled, which is convenient for the actual manipulation of the texture, as shown in Figure 5.40. You can occasionally use Rendered to check how the texture mapping actually looks.

■ Let us now see how to adjust the size of the tiles. Turn to the section which says Wrapped Textures. (Recall that you chose the *wrapped* Checker style rather than the *solid* Checker style when you defined the surface style, Checks.) Ignore Mapping Type for now. Instead, look at the Horizontal Tiling and Vertical Tiling options. Here, you can change both the horizontal and vertical sizes of a texture tile from the default values. Do so. To enable different horizontal and vertical values, change the Lock Size To option from Square Tile to None. The changes will be immediately reflected in the preview window since the Auto Preview option is turned on (Figure 5.40-a). Ideally, you should choose tile sizes that are proportionate to the dimensions of your object.

■ You might also like to change the orientation of the texture. As you can see from the axes display in the preview window, a texture map has its own coordinate system which determines how the texture will be mapped. The origin of this system, by default, lies at the center of the object, and its axes are parallel to the world coordinate axes. Thus, for an object not parallel to the axes, like the one shown in Figure 5.40, the tiles will be positioned non-orthogonally on some faces, such as the top and bottom faces of the sample object. This problem can be fixed by aligning the origin and axes of the texture map *with* the object: either numerically by changing the Origin and Rotation values located at the top of the dialog, or graphically by using the Pointer tool to move the origin and rotate the axes in the preview window. Try both methods, and observe the changes in how the texture gets mapped (Figure 5.40-b). You can always reset the Origin and Rotation values back to the defaults, if required, by using the options provided in these sections.

Figure 5.40

Working with the Texture
Map Controls dialog.
(a) Changing the tile sizes
from the defaults.
(b) Aligning the origin and
axes of the texture map
with the object instead of
the world coordinate
system.

(a)

(b)

◾ There are two points you should note when manipulating the origin and axes graphically. The Snap option, which is checked by default, allows you to snap to the points, midpoints, and segments of the object, making the task of moving the origin and rotating the axes easier. Also, you cannot rotate the "current" axis of rotation which is shown in red in the preview window. Thus, if Y is the current axis, you can rotate only the X and Z axes about the Y axis. To change the current axis, go to the Axis/Plane popup menu, which is located just above the surface style preview window in the lower left corner of the dialog. Here, you can change the current axis, depending upon which one you would like to rotate the other two axes about.

◾ Now that you know how to adjust the origin of the texture coordinate system according to your requirements, proceed to explore the Center and Mirror options for both Horizontal Tiling and Vertical Tiling. As obvious from their names, Center will center the tile in one or both directions relative to the origin, while Mirror will mirror the tile in one or both directions. Both are off by default.

◾ Move on to look at the Mapping Type for Wrapped Textures, which determines how the texture will actually be wrapped around the object. As you saw in Figure 5.40, the default mapping type is Cubic. This is reflected by the shape of the mapping area in the preview window. You can deselect the Show Object option momentarily to have a better look at this shape.

■ Switch to the Flat, Cylindrical, and Spherical mapping types in turn by selecting them from the Mapping Type popup menu. For each mapping type, notice the change in the shape of the mapping area in the preview window. While the Cubic, Cylindrical, and Spherical mapping types wrap the texture around the object in the shape of a cube, cylinder, and sphere respectively, the Flat type places the texture along a single plane rather than wrapping it around the object. The default placement plane is XY, but you can reorient the texture map either numerically or graphically, as you learned a short while ago.

■ Each mapping type also has different tiling options. For Flat and Cubic, the tile sizes are specified in terms of distance, for Spherical, they are measured in angles, while Cylindrical uses distance vertically and angles horizontally. The Flat, Cylindrical, and Spherical mapping types also give you the option of specifying the total number of tiles in one or both directions, rather than the tile sizes. Experiment with changes in these and see how they explore the resulting textures.

■ The kind of mapping type you choose will usually depend upon the shape of the object to which the texture is being applied. Thus, cylindrical mapping is the obvious choice for cylindrical objects, spherical for spherical objects, and so on. Of course, you can also deliberately select a mapping type that is different from the shape of the object to get some interesting results. This is illustrated in Figure 5.41. Flat mapping is most useful for mapping textures to individual faces rather than the entire object, a procedure which will be covered in Section 4.4. As far as the Parametric mapping type is concerned, it is active only for parametric objects and can be applied to them to make the texture mapping parametrically calculated as well.

Figure 5.41

A comparison between Cubic and other mapping types for objects of various shapes.

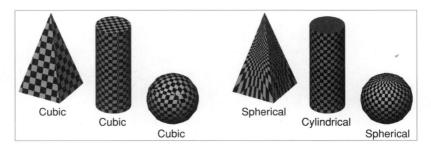

There is only one remaining mapping type, UV Coordinates. This "freezes" the horizontal (U) and vertical (V) values of the current texture mapping on the object and stores them at the vertices. Thereafter, the scale of the texture on the object can be changed by simply expressing the two Size values as a percentage of the original values. This is useful once the texture mapping of an object has been finalized and you want to prevent it from being accidentally changed.

■ Let us now look at solid textures and see how they differ from wrapped textures, whose options we have been exploring all this time. You can apply a solid texture to the current object without exiting the Texture Map Controls dialog—simply click on the Assign button located in the lower left corner. This will invoke the Surface Styles dialog you explored in Section 1.3 of Workshop 3. Click on the New button to create a new surface style, and this time, select the Checker, Solid option for the Color attribute. Return to the Texture Map Controls dialog once your selection of the new style is complete.

■ Your object now has a solid texture rather than a wrapped texture. It is not easy to tell the difference since the Wrapped Textures options are not grayed out. Also, the Tiled display option in the preview window continues to show the tiles according to the wrapped textures specifications. However, make a change to the Solid Textures Size value, located below the Wrapped Textures section, and it will be reflected in the Rendered display. You can see that a solid texture is not wrapped two-dimensionally about an object but exists as a textured block in 3D space. It's almost as if the object is carved out of the material that the texture is made up of. A solid texture, unlike a wrapped texture, has a single tile dimension along all the three axes, which you just changed. However, it does have a coordinate system which you can modify by making changes to the Origin and Rotation values, as you did before for wrapped textures (Figure 5.42).

Figure 5.42

Applying a solid texture to an object.

🔳 There are a few remaining options in the Texture Map Controls dialog which we will explore over the next three sections. For now, experiment further with all the options you have learned. When you are satisfied with the texture mapping of the object you see in the preview window, click OK to apply all the changes you have made and return to the modeling environment. Edit the texture maps of the remaining objects in a similar fashion, choosing different surface styles, mapping types for wrapped textures, coordinate systems of the texture maps, and tile sizes.

🔳 Back in the graphics window, double-click on the Texture Map tool in the modeling tool palette. This will invoke a dialog containing essentially the same options as those you have just explored in the Texture Map Controls dialog. The only difference is that in the Texture Map Options dialog, you can specify the default mapping characteristics that will be applied to *every newly created object*. This is done by using the default option, Edit Default Parameters. You can also specify a different set of texture mapping characteristics for *objects that will be selected with the Texture Map tool* by using the alternate option, Edit Parameters For Next Assignment. Experiment with both options and see the convenience they afford.

4.3 Transformations to Textured Objects

🔳 Textured objects retain their texture mapping for geometric transformations such as Move, Rotate, and Mirror, since these transformations do not change the shape of the object. But other operations such as scaling, moving a point or a face, creating a hole, and so on, which change the shape of the object necessitate a change in the shape of the texture map as well. Apply some of these transformations to the textured objects you just created, and notice how, in most cases, the texture map reshapes itself appropriately without having to be reapplied.

▣ Look at the scaling operation in particular. Observe that if an object is scaled using either of the Scale tools on Row 11, the texture gets scaled with the object by default. If you would like the object to always retain the original size of the texture, reapply the Texture Map tool to it and deselect the Scale With Object option that appears at the base of the Texture Map Controls dialog. Scaling will now change the shape of the object but not the size of the texture. Notice that the Scale With Object option is grayed out for UV Coordinates because this mapping type will always scale the texture with respect to the object.

 There is an aberration with regards to scaling for the Cubic mapping type. Even when the Scale With Object option is activated, scaling the object independently, rather than uniformly along all directions, may not scale the texture as expected.

▣ If you transform the shape of an object by moving a point, segment, or face, the results are not the same as those you would get if you scaled the object. Figure 5.43 shows a comparison. The Scale With Object option was selected for the cylindrical object, therefore when its height is reduced using the Scale tool (M-Tool:12a,3), the texture is scaled down in the Z direction. However, when its height is reduced by simply moving the top face down, the texture is not scaled but retains its proportions, and also "spills" on to the top face. Watch out for results such as these and be aware of what is causing the difference.

Figure 5.43

Different results in texture map scaling, depending upon the method used for transforming the object.

(a) Original object   (b) Scaled object   (c) Move operation applied to top face

4.4 Mapping Textures to Individual Faces

So far, you have been making adjustments to the texture mapping of an object as a whole. But sometimes, different faces of an object have different textures applied to them which need to be adjusted individually. You could also have the same texture applied to all the faces of an object, but which require different mapping for different faces. The Texture Map tool lets you map textures to the individual faces of an object as well.

▣ Create an object for which you need one or more faces to have a different texture map from the rest of the object. If you like, you can use the Color tool, with the topological level set to Face, to change the surface style of these faces *before* you use the Texture Map tool. Alternately, you could wait and see how to make such a change once you get to the Texture Map Controls dialog.

▣ Select the object with the Texture Map tool, and change the display of the preview window to Rendered. If you have already changed some of the individual face colors, you will see the different textures of the object in the display. Notice also the surface style display at the lower left corner of the dialog. If the object has a total of two surface styles, it would say **1 Of 2** below the surface style display and give you the option to view the second one by clicking on the forward arrow button (Figure 5.44). Moreover, any of these surface styles can be edited directly by double-clicking on its display here. Keep in mind, though, that these changes will affect all the objects to which that style has been applied.

▣ You can make the usual changes to the mapping type, tile sizes, and the position and orientation of the coordinate system. These will affect the entire object, including the face or faces to which a different texture has been applied. Try it.

▣ What we would now like to do is manipulate the texture map only on the faces of the object which have a different texture. To do this, we need to create a new "texture group" which is comprised only of those faces. Turn to the section called **Texture Groups** in the lower right portion of the **Texture Map Controls** dialog, and click on the **Current Group** popup menu. It has only a single group called **Object**, which is why all the mapping modifications are being applied to the entire object. To create a new group, click on the **New** button and change its default name if you like.

▣ Change the display of the preview window to **Wire Frame**. You will see that all the faces of the object are now grayed out, indicating that the newly created texture group is currently empty. You now need to add to this group all the faces whose texture is to be mapped separately. There are two ways to do this. Click on the **Pick By** button, located next to the surface style display at the base of the dialog. This lets you pick a surface style from all of those present in the object, and automatically selects the faces which have that style. Alternately, you can use the **Pointer** tool to select the required faces. Use either technique to select the faces with a different texture for the new texture group (Figure 5.45).

▣ Make some changes to the mapping type, tile sizes, and so on, and see the changes in **Tiled** or **Rendered Display**. You will find that these changes affect only the faces that are contained in the new texture group.

Figure 5.44

The Texture Map Controls dialog for an object which has two surface styles— one for the object, and the other for one of its faces.

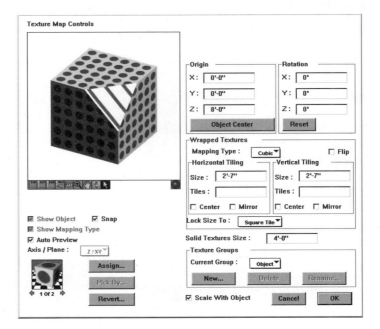

Figure 5.45

Applying the Flat mapping type to a texture group comprising only the face shown in Figure 5.44 that has a different texture. The origin and rotation of the axes were modified so as to be aligned with that face.

▣ Let us now see how to manipulate the texture map on an individual face, using the Flat mapping type. Use the Pointer tool to deselect the selected faces until you have only a single face in the texture group. Change the mapping type to Flat. It would help if the texture coordinate system were to be aligned with the selected face (as in Figure 5.45) instead of the complete object. Try to do this by moving the origin and rotating the axes—you will find that it is not an easy task. Try holding down the option key (Mac) or Ctrl+Shift keys (PC) and watch the Object Center button under Origin change to Texture Group Center. Click on it. The origin is now at the center of the face but the plane is still parallel to the original XY plane rather than the face.

▣ Fortunately, there is a shortcut to get precisely what we want. Deselect the face using the Pointer tool. Now holding down the same keys as before (option or Ctrl+Shift), select the face. This time, you will find that the origin has shifted to the center of the face, the X and Y axes are on the face, and the Z axis is perpendicular to it (Figure 5.45). You may still want to modify the exact orientation of the X and Y axes, but this is much easier now since the Z axis does not have to be changed. (Remember to ensure that the Axis/Plane is set to Z/XY.) You can also simply move the origin to one of the corners of the face if necessary.

▣ Continue to create different texture groups for different faces, or groups of faces, of the same object in this manner, and apply separate mapping techniques to them. Then switch back to the original texture group, Object, and see how all the faces assigned to other groups are no longer part of this group. Keep in mind also that the Rendered display in the preview window will always show the complete object. Individual mapping and tiling of the different texture groups can be seen in the Tiled display. Other options in the Texture Map Controls dialog such as Assign, Scale With Object, and so on, work in the same manner for other texture groups as they did for the default group, Object.

4.5 Image Mapping

In Workshop 3, you saw how the Surface Styles Parameters dialog lets you create an enormous variety of surface styles using various permutations of the Color, Reflection, Transparency, and Bump parameters. For each one of these parameters, it is also possible to use an external image, adding infinitely to the numbers of textures you can create and apply to your objects. In this section, we will explore image mapping for all the four attributes of a surface style.

▣ Let us start with a simple application of using an external image for the Color attribute—the modeling of a picture frame for a room interior. Locate an image that you can use for the picture frame, or scan a photograph to convert it to a digital file. Remember that the file format must be one that form•Z can recognize. Find out the dimensions of your image, either by viewing it in form•Z using File > View File or by using any image-editing program, and calculate the aspect ratio. Thus, for the example shown in Figure 5.46-a, the ratio of the width to the height would be 1200:1770, or 0.68:1.

▣ Model the body of the picture frame in form•Z on a new layer, taking care to maintain the same aspect ratio as the image, so that the final mapping is not distorted. The inset for the picture can be created using the Insert Hole operator (M-Tool:2b,3), as shown in Figure 5.46-b. For this object, use a surface style appropriate to the body of the frame.

▣ You will now create a surface style that uses the image shown in Figure 5.46-a, instead of a plain color or any other texture. Invoke the Surface Styles Parameters dialog for defining a new style and select the option, Image Map, from the Color popup menu. Click on the accompanying Options button and you will see an Image Map Options dialog that is similar to the one you encountered when working with the RenderZone display options in Exercise 1. Click on the Load button to load your image file instead of the default logo image. In the Repetitions section, select 1 Times and the Center option, both Horizontally and Vertically. Then click OK to exit the dialog. In the preview window of the surface style, you will see this image wrapped on all sides of the default cubical shape.

▣ The next step is to apply this style only to that face of the frame object where the image should appear. Use the Color tool at the Face topological level to do this. Check the effect by switching to the RenderZone display mode. As you would expect, the image will not be correctly sized to fit exactly on the selected face, so you will have to resort to the Texture Map tool to make the necessary adjustments.

Figure 5.46

Preparing to model a picture frame. (a) The image that will be used. (b) The body of the frame.

(a)

(b)

Figure 5.47

Using the Texture Map Controls dialog to accurately map an image on the inset face of the frame object.

▣ Select the frame object with the Texture Map tool, and create a new Texture Group consisting only of the face on which the image is being mapped, as you learned to do in the last section. Switch to the Flat mapping type for the new texture group, adjust the origin and orientation of the axes so that image map is correctly positioned on the face, and finally, specify a tile size which matches the face dimensions (see Figure 5.47). At the end of all these steps, you should have the image correctly mapped on the desired face, as shown.

▣ Let us now see how to use an external image for the other attributes of a surface style, which enable you to create extremely interesting rendering effects. Locate a relatively simple image, or create one using a drawing or painting program, ensuring that it is in a recognizable file format.

▣ Create four new surface styles as described next, and illustrated in Figure 5.48. For Style 1, set the Color parameter to Image Map and load the selected image. The procedure is identical to what you just did for the picture frame example. Don't forget to select 1 Times and the Center option both Horizontally and Vertically in the Repetitions section of the Image Options dialog.

▣ For Style 2, set the Color parameter to any Plain Color other than white. For the Reflection parameter, stick to Matte, but click on the accompanying Options button to set some additional parameters. Set Ambient Reflection to Ambient Map and Glow to Glow Map. Click on the Options button for each, and load the same image with the same settings as you did for the Color image map in Style 1.

▣ For Style 3, set the Color parameter to any Plain Color other than white and leave Reflection as Matte with the default settings. Set the Transparency parameter to Transparency Map. Click on the accompanying Options button and load the same image.

▣ For Style 4, set the Color parameter to any Plain Color, the Reflection and Transparency parameters to default values, and the Bump parameter to Bump Map. Click on the Options button for Bump Map and load the same image. In the Repetitions section, select the usual 1 Times and Center options. Additionally, you can adjust the Amplitude to a desired value. A positive value will make the bump project *out* from the surface, while a negative value will project it *into* the surface of the object.

▣ After you have finished defining the four styles, invoke the dialog of the Texture Map tool, and set the mode to Edit Default Parameters, as you learned in Section 4.2. Make only a single modification in this dialog—change the tile size to 8'-0". This will ensure that any new object that is created has a texture map with a tile size of 8'-0".

WORKSHOP 5

Figure 5.48

Four different surface styles
created using the same
image, but for different
parameters.

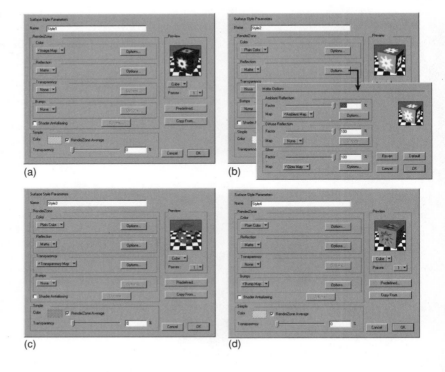

(a)   (b)

(c)   (d)

▪ Back in the graphics window, move to a new layer and create a cube with dimensions of 8' by 8' by 8'. Make three more copies of it. Then apply each one of the four styles you just created to the four boxes, and change the display to RenderZone. You can see the contrast in the four styles, all of which were created using the same image but in different ways (Figure 5.49-a).

Figure 5.49

Applying the four different
styles shown in Figure 5.48
to four identical boxes,
using identical Texture Map
settings. (a) With lights
activated and project
background set to white.
(b) With lights deactivated
and project background
set to black.

(a)

(b)

■ You must be wondering what the difference between Style 2 and Style 1 is—they seem identical, except that Style 2 seems to look brighter. To find the answer to this, move to the Lights palette and turn off all the lights in the model, including the sun. (Remember to click on the circular icon rather than on the diamond icon to turn off the Shining attribute of a light.) Change the project background to a dark color and refresh the RenderZone display. You will find that the box with Style 2 is the most visible one since it is "glowing" in the dark; all the others are blacked out and cannot be distinguished (see Figure 5.49-b). You can use this technique to create various kinds of glowing effects in your models.

■ End this section by exploring various other combinations of predefined textures and external images for the four parameters of Color, Reflection, Transparency, and Bump. You can save all these new styles for use in future projects.

4.6   Decals

So far, you have learned to map predefined textures as well as external images to objects and their surfaces. You have also seen how to apply different textures to different faces of an object by creating texture groups comprising one or more faces. However, you might sometimes need to apply more than one texture to a single face. Rather than create faces within faces to apply different textures to—which can get very tedious—you can use the Decal tool, located immediately after the Texture Map tool, which lets you apply multiple styles to a single face. These styles can even overlap and if some of them are transparent, you will be able to see the styles that lie underneath them as well! *Decals* is the term for additional styles that are applied to a face or to an object. In this section, we will learn to work with decals by using two of the four surface styles that were created in the last section.

■ Create a cube of size 8'-0", just like the one you used in the last section, in a plain surface style. Then apply the Decal tool (M-Tool:13a,5) to it. You will be greeted with a message saying that the object has to have at least one texture map control, and if you would like the default controls of the Texture Map tool to be applied to it. Click OK since you have used a plain surface style for the cube, so the kind of mapping will not matter. If you had used a textured style, you should first have ensured that the texture was mapped correctly to the object, before using the Decal tool.

■ Applying the Decal tool to an object invokes the Decals dialog (Figure 5.50), which is very similar to the Texture Map Controls dialog you have seen. When the dialog first opens up, most of its options are grayed out. This is because no decal has been created as yet for the object. To do so, click on the New button in the lower right portion of the dialog. You will be prompted for the New Decal Name. Stick with the default name if you like. As soon as you have created a new decal, all the options in the Decals dialog get activated. Change the preview display to Tiled, and you will see a default mapping of the decal, using the same surface style as the object.

■ The next step is to select the desired style for this decal, replacing the default style applied to it. Click on the Set Style button in the lower left corner of the dialog and choose Style 4, the style with the bump map you had created earlier (shown in Figure 5.48-d). Set the mapping type to Cubic and the tile size to 8'-0". Also, select the Bumps option and deselect the Color option, both of which are located next to the style preview window. As you can see in Figure 5.50-a, this applies only the bump of the texture but not its color to the rendering of the object.

■ What you have got so far could easily have been achieved using the Texture Map tool. It is what we will do ahead that can be done only with the Decal tool. Create a second decal by clicking again on the New button. For this decal, select Style 2, the style with the transparency map, and change the settings to those shown in Figure 5.50-b. The mapping type should be Cubic and the tile size should be slightly smaller than the size of the top face. In the rendered display, you will see the transparent texture beautifully superimposed on your first "bumped" decal.

▪ But that's not all you can do with transparent decals—there's more! For the same decal, click on the Opacity box to select it, and choose the Transparency option from the popup menu. The entire box except the edges will be rendered transparent as shown in Figure 5.50-c.

▪ Set the second decal back to Opacity, and create a third decal. This time, select a style with a predefined texture, such as the Grid. If necessary, click on the Set Style button and create a new style in the Surface Styles dialog that is invoked. Apply a Spherical mapping for this decal, with the settings and tile sizes as shown. The final result will be an object with three overlapping decals, as shown in Figure 5.50-d.

Figure 5.50

Using the Decal tool to apply multiple overlapping surface styles to an object.

(a)　(b)

(c)　(d)

▪ So far, you have been applying decals to the entire object, but keep in mind that you can also apply decals to selected faces. Each time a new decal is created, all the faces of the object are activated by default. Use the Pointer tool to deselect the faces you don't need, or deselect all the faces first and then select the ones you need. You can use the following shortcut keys: command+A (Mac) or Ctrl+A (PC) for selecting all the faces, and command+tab (Mac) or Ctrl+Tab (PC) for deselecting all the faces.

▪ To go back and modify the settings of any of the decals that are already created, simply highlight its name from the decal list. This makes it the active decal whose parameters are listed in the dialog and can be changed. You can Delete or Rename it, if required. You can choose whether or not to scale the decal with the object using the Scale With Object button, just like you did for a regular texture map. You can also choose to temporarily hide the decal, if necessary, by deselecting the Visible button.

▣ You can have as many as 32 decals for a single object. Overlapping decals of the kind you have created are rendered in the reverse order in which they appear in the list. Thus, for the object shown in Figure 5.50, Decal 3 will be applied first, followed by Decal 2, and finally Decal 1. You can change the order simply by dragging a decal to a new position in the list. Experiment with changes in the order and see what happens.

▣ Another simple application of the use of decals is demonstrated in Figure 5.51—creating mullions on a window pane. A glass surface style was first applied to the pane object. Then a decal was created, using a surface style with both the Color and Transparency attributes set to Grid. It is a simple and fairly effective shortcut, useful when you do not have the time to model the mullions as separate objects.

Figure 5.51

Using decals to simulate the appearance of window mullions on a glass pane.

This marks the end of the exercise on texture mapping. Let us end this workshop by looking at the remaining object properties that we have not yet covered.

EXERCISE 5

Other Object Properties

We have already worked with most of the tools in both columns of Row 13 of the modeling tool palette—Color, Texture Map, Decal, Ghost, Unghost, and Set Layer—that manipulate various attributes of objects. In this exercise, we will work with the remaining four attribute tools on this row, starting with Smooth Shade. We will also look at the related Attributes tool, located after the Query tool on Row 11.

WORKSHOP 5

5.1   Smooth Shading

You already encountered the concept of smooth shading when you worked with the options of the Shaded Render and RenderZone displays. Recall that you could limit the smooth shading effect only to those objects which had the "smooth shading attribute" assigned to them. This attribute can be applied to an object using the Smooth Shade tool.

▣   Select the Smooth Shade tool from the left column of Row 13. Invoke its dialog and select the option, Smooth Shade Object/Face. It has two sub-options, which should be familiar to you from the Smooth Shading options in the Shaded Render Options dialog we studied in Workshop 3. Recall that the Smooth All Faces option is not very realistic but can be used for special effects, whereas the Smooth option will operate only on those edges or faces meeting a specified condition, smoothing curved surfaces in a realistic manner. The difference between the two options was illustrated in Figure 3.11. Activate one of these options for the Smooth Shade tool, and then apply it to an object. The object will acquire a smooth shading attribute, based on the selected options.

▣   Remember that to actually see the results of the Smooth Shade tool on an object in the Shaded Render or RenderZone displays, you must turn on the Smooth Shading option in the dialogs of these displays.

▣   To remove the smooth shading attribute from an object, i.e., to make it "flat shaded", simply deselect the Smooth Shade Object/Face option and then apply the Smooth Shade tool to it.

5.2   Rendering Attributes

The next tool in the left column of Row 13 is the Rendering Attributes tool, which groups together a number of attributes related to how an object will be rendered. Changes are made to these attributes in the dialog of this tool, after which it is applied to the objects whose rendering attributes are to be changed. Let us see what these attributes are.

▣   Select the Rendering Attributes tool (M-Tool:13a,3) and invoke its dialog (Figure 5.52-a). The first modification you can make is to turn on or off the shadow-casting ability of an object. For instance, the base plane in a building model has no other object to cast shadows on, so it would speed up rendering if its shadow-casting ability was turned off and its shadows not calculated unnecessarily. There is an added advantage to doing this—the shadows *received* by an object which does not cast shadows are sharper and crisper.

▣   Similarly, you could turn off the ability of an object to receive shadows if it was not in a position to do so anyway, or if you did not want shadows to be displayed on an object for aesthetic reasons.

▣   The next two options give you the ability to combine wireframe and shaded displays of objects in the same rendered image, generated by the Shaded Render and RenderZone displays. An object can be rendered only in wireframe with the specified pixel width, or only as a shaded surface, or both in wireframe and with shaded surfaces. All three situations are shown in Figure 5.52-b. As you can see, this effect can be used to create very interesting, unusual, and informative renderings.

▣   Notice that if the Object Renders As Wireframe option is not selected, the Object Renders As Shaded Surface option cannot be deselected, and vice versa. In other words, an object must have at least one of these two attributes, if not both.

Figure 5.52

Using the Rendering Attributes tool. (a) The tool dialog. (b) An image rendered with both wireframe and shaded surfaces.

(b)

(a)

▣ Recall that the dialogs for both the Shaded Render and RenderZone displays have a Wireframe Width option that we ignored while working with them earlier. This option relates to the wireframe display activated for an object using the Rendering Attributes tool, for which you can specify different pixel widths, as you have seen. When the image is rendered, you can instruct the display to scale all the wireframes by a certain factor, using the Scale By option. This is useful, for instance, when you are generating the same image at different resolutions, and want to avoid the tedium of reapplying the Rendering Attributes tool each time to change the wireframe widths of the objects in proportion to the resolution. Alternately, you can instruct the display to ignore all the individual wireframe widths set for various objects and use one specified width, by choosing the Set To option for Wireframe Width. Try out both options for an image with some wireframes in the rendering.

▣ The last option in the Rendering Attributes dialog lets you apply Radiosity Meshing to specified objects and faces. The sub-options are similar to what you had encountered in the Radiosity Options dialog in Section 3.3. As you learned in that exercise, you can improve the quality of your radiosity solution and reduce the time required to generate it by applying a dense radiosity mesh only to those surfaces where you expect large variations in light and shadow. A much less dense mesh can be specified in the Radiosity Options dialog for the remaining surfaces.

 Remember that after making the desired changes in the Rendering Attributes dialog, you have to apply this tool to an object to make the specified changes in its attributes.

5.3   Setting and Getting Attributes

There are only two more tools remaining on Row 13 that we have not yet covered—the related tools of Set Attributes and Get Attributes. Let us see what they can do for us.

▣ The Set Attributes tool allows you to modify some or all attributes of an object in a single step. Select this tool and open its dialog. You will find that all the attribute options are off by default. You can turn some of them on by clicking on their checkboxes. To turn them all on, click on the

All button (Figure 5.53). For each attribute that is turned on, you can choose from among various options to set it to. Thus, for Layer, you can choose from among all the existing layers in the project. After making the desired attribute settings in this dialog, simply apply the Set Attribute tool to an object, and all its attributes will be modified as specified in the dialog.

Figure 5.53

The dialog of the Set Attributes tool.

■ The Get Attributes tool works in conjunction with the Set Attributes tool. It can be applied to an object to retrieve some or all of its attributes which are then recorded in the Set Attributes tool, from where they can be easily applied to other objects. Thus, if you need to apply the attributes of one object to another object, all that you need to do is select the first object with the Get Attributes tool, then apply the Set Attributes tool to the second object. You can choose to retrieve only some, rather than all, attributes of the selected object by making the appropriate selections in the dialog of the Get Attributes tool.

5.4 Querying for Attributes

■ Select the Attributes tool, located immediately after the Query tool in the right column of Row 11, and apply it to an object. This invokes a dialog which conveniently lists all the attributes of the object and allows them to be modified (see Figure 5.54). For instance, a different surface style can be applied to the object by simply selecting it from the Surface Style popup menu in the dialog.

■ The Attributes tool can also be applied to faces to get information about their attributes. However, it cannot be applied to entities at other topological levels such as points, segments, and so on, since they do not have attributes as such, merely geometric information associated with them. You have seen in Workshop 2 how you can get such information about these entities using the Query tool.

Figure 5.54

The dialog that is invoked when the Attributes tool is applied to an object.

A Table Lamp

■   *Model a standard table lamp in detail, with proper dimensions. Include the light bulb and actually position a light source inside it to complete the effect.*

The actual exercise of modeling the table lamp shown here will now be demonstrated step by step. You can refer to the form•Z files for each step in the accompanying CD-ROM, under the folder Assignments > Workshop 5. A rendered image of the model is in the Assignment5.tif file in the same location.

Setup

Launch the form•Z program, but do not open a new project. Instead, go to Edit > Preferences and load the preference file, Sml_Engl.zpf, located in the form•Z Preferences folder in the main program folder.

After this is done, open a new form•Z project. Check the settings for Window Setup and Working Units, which should be appropriate to the small scale of the project we are going to model. The Window Setup should show 1" modules with 4 subdivisions. The Working Units should be set to English for the Unit Type, Inches for the Base Unit, 1/64" for Numeric Accuracy, and 0.01° for Angle Accuracy. Change the last two values to 1/16" and 1° respectively, since we do not need such precise levels of accuracy.

Finally, check to see that the display scale in the first group of the Display menu is set to 6" = 1'-0". You can also turn off the display of the default light in the Lights palette for now.

Step 1

Start by modeling the base of the lamp. This is a simple cylindrical extrusion of radius 2 3/4" and height 1". For the sake of convenience, center it at the origin [0,0,0]. For a smoother cylinder, increase the resolution in the Arc/Circle/Ellipse Resolution dialog to 48 segments.

After creating the extrusion, use the Round tool to round the edges of its top face by a small radius value. Also change the name of the layer in which this object has been created to base.

◁ Step 2

Next, we will move on to the striated cylindrical support that connects the head of the lamp to its base. Move to a new layer called support and switch to the Right view. Use the Vector Lines tool in 2D Surface Object mode to draw a line with the following coordinates. (Remember that all dimensions entered are in inches.)

> Pt #1: [0,0,1] Absolute, cartesian mode
>
> Pt #2: [0,0,8 1/2] Relative, cartesian mode
>
> Pt #3: [3 1/2,135,0] Relative, polar mode
>
> Pt #4: [e] or double-click to end

Step 3

Next, the angled point of this line needs to be rounded off. For this, select the Fillet/Bevel tool (M-Tool:10a,6), and set the # Of Edges and Radius values in its dialog to 10 and 1 1/2" respectively. Apply the tool, with the topological level set to Point, to the angled point of the line and it will be nicely rounded off as shown.

◁ Step 4

We will now proceed to model the striated support with the help of the 2D line we just rounded. Turn off the base layer so that only the 2D line is visible. Switch to a non-planar view, reduce the circle resolution to 16 or 20 segments, and create a cylinder of radius 1/2" and height 1/12".

Step 5

Select the Place tool (M-Tool:12b,4) and set the Multi-Placement option in its dialog to End-To-End. Further, select the Use # Of Placements sub-option and set # Of Placements to 70. With the self-copy modifier set to Multi Copy, apply the Place tool by selecting the cylinder as the source object and the 2D line as the placement line. This should give you 70 copies of the cylinder placed along the line.

Select all these cylinders and use the Join tool (M-Tool:8b,1) to join them into one object. The Union tool cannot be used since the cylinders do not touch each other.

Step 6

Create a 2D circle of radius 7/16". Activate a different color in the Surface Styles palette in order to be able to differentiate new objects from existing ones. Then use the Sweep tool (M-Tool:5b,6) to sweep the circle about the 2D line, which should still be there after the Place operation. Zoom in, if necessary, to perform the operation correctly.

Step 7

Now perform a Union operation of the swept object with the cylinders you had placed on the 2D line. This will give you the completed cylindrical support following the shape of the line, and striated as required. The Union operation might take some time, so if you are in a hurry, you can skip it and move on—in a rendered view, the un-unioned objects will look the same as the unioned one.

If you are able to Union the objects, apply the Color tool with the Clear All Face Surface Styles option activated in order to color the unioned object in a single color.

Step 9

Turn off the support layer so that you can see only the square. Zoom in close and use the square as a guideline for drawing the 2D shape made up of lines and arcs on one half of the square as shown. Don't worry about the exact dimensions—just get the proportions right. This shape is going to be revolved about the Y axis of the plane, so make sure you do not cross the axis while drawing the shape. Use grid and object snapping for preciseness. Delete the square after you are done.

◁ **Step 8**

Next, we will proceed to model the little piece—which will be referred to as the "knob"—that connects the support to the bulb holder at the head of the lamp. Activate a new layer in the usual manner and switch to the Right view. The knob is oriented in the same direction as the angled top part of the support. To simplify the process of modeling it, use the Rotate Plane tool (W-Tool:3,5) to rotate the current plane (which will be YZ in the Right view) by an angle of 45°. Also use Move Origin (W-Tool:3,4) to move the origin of the plane to the center of the top face of the support. Save the resulting plane as a new plane in the Planes palette, and turn off the display of the world axes from the Windows menu to avoid confusion.

Use the coordinates of the new reference plane to draw a 2D square of side 1 1/2", attached to the top part of the support. Take care to see that it is centered about the support axis.

◁ **Step 10**

Select the Revolve tool (M-Tool:5b,1) and increase the # Of Steps under the Facetted section in its dialog to 32. Then apply it to revolve the open shape about the Y axis. The object of revolution that is created is the knob which will connect the support to the head of the lamp.

It is time to move on to the head itself. Activate a new layer, head. Create two rectangles of sizes 2 3/4" by 2 1/2", and 2 3/4" by 4"—the first dimension being along the X axis of the plane—and position them as shown.

Step 11

Draw a line parallel to the X axis connecting the midpoints of the opposite sides of the two rectangles. This will function as the axis of revolution for the shape we will create next. This shape has to be created as a double-line since the head is a hollow object rather than a solid object. Therefore, activate the 2D Enclosure mode (M-Tool:2a,2) and set its Enclosure Wall Width to 1/16". Also, choose the Right justification option if you are drawing the shape from top to bottom, and Left if you are drawing from bottom to top.

Now use the rectangles as a guide for creating the double-line "half-shape" of the holder, as shown. It can be done graphically by using a combination of Endpoint and Segment object snapping and Ortho 45 direction snapping, the last two for the angled segment.

Step 12

Turn off the knob layer and delete the rectangles you had created as guidelines. You should be left with just the double-line shape and the single line segment you created as the axis. Before deriving a revolved object from these shapes, use the Fillet/Bevel tool, as you did in Step 3, to round off the six intermediate points of the double-line shape. Set the fillet Radius to 1/16" and # Of Edges to 4 before performing the operation.

Increase the # Of Steps in the dialog of the Revolve tool to 48, and use it to revolve the double-line shape about the line. This will give you the head of the lamp. Notice that its resolution is optimal—not excessive but such that the individual facets are not visible in a rendered display. (We are creating it as a *facetted* rather than a *nurbz* object, which would be rendered more smoothly, because we have to insert holes in this object at a later stage.)

Step 13

The next task is to model the holder for the light bulb, located inside the head we just modeled. Move to a new, appropriately named layer. Ghost the head layer rather than make it invisible, as you will need it for reference. Create a rectangle of 1 3/4" by 1 1/2", centered within the head and touching its top inside surface. Use grid rather than object snapping, since the head object has too many overlapping points in a planar view for object snapping to work accurately. If you *must* use object snapping, make sure you select the Project Onto Reference Plane option for Projection Views in the Object Snaps dialog.

Step 14

Make the head layer completely invisible. You should now see only the rectangle in the window. Draw a line connecting the midpoints of the two smaller sides of the rectangle. Use this line and the rectangle as guidelines for constructing the 2D shape as shown. Use the Fillet/Bevel tool with the appropriate radius for rounding the required points. This 2D shape will be revolved about the line in the usual fashion, so be careful to remain within the bounds of one half of the rectangle.

Step 15

Delete the rectangle. Reduce the # Of Steps in the dialog of the Revolve tool back to 16 and use it to revolve the 2D rounded shape you just created about the line. The revolved object will be the holder we're looking for.

Technically, we should also be modeling the screw plate inside the cavity of the holder where the bulb screws in, but we will ignore that detail in this assignment since it will not be visible in the views of the lamp you are likely to generate. If you are a product designer, you will, of course, incorporate such details in your model.

Step 16

Let us move on to model the actual bulb. This consists of two parts: the head which screws into the holder and is solid; and the body which is hollow and contains the light source. We will not worry about modeling the filament and other internal details of the light bulb. Move to a new layer called bulb and transfer the 2D line left over from the previous Revolve operation to it. Ghost the holder layer so that you can use it for reference.

Select the Screw/Bolt tool (M-Tool:5b,3), and set its dialog options as shown. Note that the Tip, Neck, and Head options are all deselected, and that the Radius and Length values for the Body are different from the defaults. Then apply the Screw/Bolt tool, selecting the line as the axis of revolution. Click on it approximately at the point where it intersects the top of the holder cavity. This will position the screw object correctly inside the cavity. If you are not able to position it correctly the first time, simply move it to the right position afterwards.

WORKSHOP 5

Step 17

Now make the holder layer completely invisible. Draw a 3 1/4" by 2 1/4" rectangle and position it so that the midpoint of its shorter side coincides with the endpoint of the 2D line you used as the axis of revolution in the last step. Then draw another 2D line connecting the opposite midpoints of the shorter side of the rectangle. This will function as the axis of revolution for the 2D half-shape which we will create next for the light bulb.

Step 18

Delete the previous 2D line you had created as the axis of revolution for the screw. Then invoke the Arc/Circle/Ellipse Options dialog and increase the resolution to 48 segments. Also, open the dialog of the 2D Enclosure tool, set the Enclosure Wall Width to 1/16", and the Justification option to Left. Now use the Arc tools to inscribe a double-line curved shape for the bulb in one half of the rectangle as shown.

Step 19

Delete the rectangle you had drawn as a guide. Then select the Revolve tool, increase the resolution to 48 segments, and apply it to the curved shape to revolve it about the line. This will give the curved, hollow object for the body of the light bulb. Of course, we have to change its material characteristics, but we will do that later, once we have finished modeling all the objects.

The body of the bulb is actually supposed to be attached to the head that was created in Step 16. However, it would not be wise to Union or Join them, since we want to be able to apply different surface styles to them. It is sufficient that they are on the same layer. You can group them with the Group tool if you like.

◁ **Step 20**

The configuration of objects making up our lamp is almost complete except for the switch located at the top of the head. Before we model that, however, we need to finish modeling the head object. Turn off the last bulb layer and make the head layer visible. Change to the 120-20 Axonometric view, the third in the View menu. Change the display to Surface Render and create an arbitrary plane passing through the top face of the head as shown. Don't worry about where its origin is located for now.

Step 21

Switch to View > Plane Projection > Top. You should now be seeing the circular head of the lamp straight-on from the top. It has a hole in its center. Draw a 2D line spanning across this hole by connecting two diametrically opposite points. Then move the origin of the arbitrary plane you created in the last step to the midpoint of this line. You should now have the plane positioned exactly at the center of the head.

◁ **Step 22**

Delete the line you had created to position the center. The head needs to have a series of circular holes of diameter 1/4", located at the rim of its top surface. Rather than using Insert Hole, it will be more convenient to create a series of solid cylinders and then subtract them from the head object. With a circle resolution of 12 segments, create a single cylinder with a height of about 1/2", positioned at one of the locations where the holes are supposed to be. Then use the Rotate tool in Repeat Copy or Multi Copy mode to make seven more copies of it, all centered about the origin of the arbitrary plane.

Step 23

Switch to a non-planar view and use the Move tool with the Perpendicular Lock activated to position these cylinders so that they cut through the head object. Then use the Difference tool to subtract each cylinder from the head. At the end of this process, you should have your head object correctly punctured as shown.

Step 24

The head of the lamp is now complete, so let us move on to the switch. Activate a new layer, switch, and make the head layer ghosted. Set the object generation mode to 3D Extruded Solid. Select the Polygon tool and set the # Of Segments in its dialog to 32. Also activate its Polygon Pattern option and select the fifth pattern—the middle one of the nine squares. Use this tool to create a patterned polygon, positioned at the origin of the arbitrary plane, having an outer radius of 1/2", an inner radius of 7/16", and a height of 1/4". It should completely cover the large circular hole located at the center of the head.

Step 25

Reduce the # Of Segments in the Polygon Options dialog to 16, and reapply the tool to create a second polygon, also positioned at the center. The outer and inner radii are 1/8" and 1/16" respectively, and the height is 3/4". Turn off the head layer completely and switch to a non-planar view to check if the two extruded polygons have been created properly. You can Union them if you want to apply the same color to both of them, but don't do so if they are to be colored differently.

◀ Step 26

With this, all the individual component parts of the lamp are complete. Turn on all the layers, and delete any extraneous objects that had been created as guidelines. Then change the colors of all the objects as appropriate. We used a multitude of colors to differentiate the objects while modeling, but in all likelihood, you will have just 3 to 4 colors in the final rendering. To change the color of the head object in which holes were inserted, you will first have to select the **Clear All Face Surface Styles** option in the dialog of the **Color** tool.

Take care to apply a suitably transparent surface style to the body of the bulb. Ideally, it should be reflective as well, but this will add to the rendering time considerably. You can go in for a quicker alternative-make the bulb have a glowing effect in addition to being transparent. For this, set the **Reflection** attribute of its surface style to **Matte** and increase the **Glow Factor** in the **Matte Options** dialog to about 75%.

Step 27

After the colors have been taken care of, create a new light source in the **Lights** palette. Invoke its **Light Parameters** dialog, change its **Type** to **Point**, and specify a suitable value for the **Radius**, say 8". Activate the **Glow** option. Also, change the **Location** value to [0,0,0] in the dialog, so that you can locate the light source easily in the graphics window. Exit the dialog and apply the **Move** tool to position it accurately inside the light bulb.

◀ Step 28

Your lamp is now ready to go. A RenderZone display of just the lamp will not be very effective. But put it on a flat, slightly reflective surface, and you should be able to see the effect of the lamp in lighting up this surface quite clearly. Remember to deactivate the **Shining** option of the default light first.

You can copy this lamp object, along with the point light, to an interior design project for use within a room. The cord for the lamp can be generated by using the Sweep tool so that it runs across the surface on which the lamp is placed. You can even connect it all the way to an "electric outlet" on a wall, for good measure!

Becoming Enmeshed in Your Creations

This exercise is devoted to exploring the various mesh-related tools of form•Z which can greatly enhance your ability to do organic modeling, i.e., modeling of non-rectilinear forms. You will start by creating plain and smooth meshes on the surfaces of objects. You will then proceed to apply movements, disturbances, and various kinds of deformations to meshed objects, all of which can be used to mold the object in various ways. A more sophisticated technique of sculpting an object is to use an image as the basis for displacing a meshed surface, which will be covered in Exercise 3. All these tools are located in the left column of the sixth row of the modeling tool palette.

In Exercise 4, you will move on to work with the tools in the left column of the seventh row, which produce special types of derivative objects. Curves can be derived from straight lines, and various kinds of meshed objects from groups of 2D shapes. You will also look at how to create as well as modify nurbz and patch objects. Finally, you will learn how to carry out boolean operations on meshed objects.

Most of the objects that will be created in this workshop are "controlled" objects—they are internally stored with the control parameters that generated them, making them easier to modify and reshape than regular objects.

Plain and Smooth Meshes

In this exercise, we will learn how to mesh the surface of an object, either plainly or by smoothening it out in addition to meshing it. We will also look at the reverse process—reducing the mesh density of an object that is already meshed. These operations involve the use of the first three tools in the left column of Row 6.

1.1   Plain Meshes

It is possible to transform a 2D closed shape or the face of a 3D object into a flat meshed surface. Such a mesh is not a controlled object and cannot be edited after it has been created. So it is referred to as a *plain mesh*. Let us see how plain meshes are created and what they can be used for.

▣ Open a new form•Z project, and create a rectangular block with a base dimension of 40' by 56' and a height of 80'. Set the topological level to **Face** and use the **Pick** tool to select one of the vertical faces of the block (Figure 6.1-a). Then select the **Mesh** tool (M-Tool:6a,1) and watch the Prompts palette for instructions. Since you have already selected a face, you simply need to click anywhere in the window for the mesh operation to be executed. The selected face will be subdivided into many smaller faces, each measuring 8' by 8' (Figure 6.1-b). This is the default size of the mesh, set in its dialog. Since the original surface is an exact multiple of 8', the mesh will fit exactly within the surface.

▣ Now use the **Pick** tool to try and select the face you just meshed. You will find that you can no longer select it, since it has been split up into many smaller faces. Essentially you have lost the original face. You can, however, retrieve it by using the **Reduce Mesh** tool, which we will cover later on in this exercise.

So what can this meshed surface be used for? In Exercise 2, we will work with sophisticated tools that can deform and displace meshed surfaces in various ways to yield non-rectilinear, "organic" forms. For now, let us apply some simpler transformations to the mesh.

▣ Using the **Pick** tool still at the **Face** level, select some of the mesh subdivisions, which are now basically faces in their own right. Apply a different color to them using the **Color** tool and switch to any of the paint display modes to see the result (Figure 6.1-c). The result is particularly impressive in **Shaded Render** and **RenderZone**, since the individual subdivisions of the mesh are not seen. Imagine how useful this would be, for instance, in quickly designing an architectural facade.

▣ Now select the mesh subdivisions you just colored (you can use **Edit > Select Previous**) and use the **Move** tool to drag them outside the surface of the block. You can create some interesting surface deformations in this manner (Figure 6.1-d).

▣ You could also use the mesh subdivisions for deriving various kinds of extruded objects. Undo the **Move** operation you just performed. The same faces will still be selected. In the dialog of the **Extrusion** tool (M-Tool:5a,3), select the **Perpendicular To Surface** option and set **Status Of Objects** to **Keep**. From the **Heights** menu, preset a height, say 8'-0". Now apply the **Extrusion** tool to the selected faces. You should have the extruded objects hanging off the meshed surface, as shown in Figure 6.1-e.

Figure 6.1

Creating and using plain meshes in various ways.

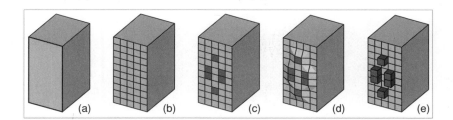

One useful application of the Mesh tool that immediately comes to mind is creating a regular construction grid on a surface. This will facilitate the use of object snapping, enabling further operations on that surface or plane to be carried out more easily and accurately. In architectural modeling and urban design, for instance, you could use the Mesh tool to create a gridded base plane that the building or buildings will be located on. Since the individual mesh subdivisions are not seen in the Shaded Render and RenderZone display modes, they will not affect your rendered images in any way.

1.2 Plain Mesh Options

▣ You will, of course, need to work with different mesh sizes and orientations from the defaults. Invoke the dialog of the Mesh tool to see what its options are (Figure 6.2). First of all, you can change the size of the mesh from the default of 8'-0" along the X, Y, and Z directions. Since the XYZ Lock option is selected, any change you make to one value is automatically made to the other two values as well. Try it and test the new mesh size on another face of the object.

▣ Note that the X, Y, and Z values that you specified do not stand for mesh divisions along the X, Y, and Z directions of the world or reference plane axes. To understand what they denote, create a new block of the same dimensions as before (Figure 6.3-a). Then invoke the Mesh Options dialog, deselect the XYZ Lock option, and key in sufficiently different mesh values for X, Y, and Z—say 4', 8', and 10' respectively. Also, deselect both the Y and the Z boxes to start with. This means that the mesh will be created only in the X direction, giving you the chance to see what it stands for.

▣ Use the Mesh tool to apply the new settings to one of the vertical faces of the block as before. You will find that the mesh now runs only in one direction (Figure 6.3-b), perpendicular to the segment that is first selected (if you are using the Clicking On Edges picking method) or the segment that is closest to the pick point (if you are using the Clicking Inside Boundaries picking method). To test this, undo the operation and reapply the Mesh tool to the same face but by selecting it through a different segment (Figure 6.3-c). Then apply the tool with just the Y direction selected—the mesh now runs parallel to the segment that is picked (Figure 6.3-d). Use both X and Y, and the mesh will run in both directions, as expected (Figure 6.3-e).

Figure 6.2

The dialog of the Mesh tool.

Figure 6.3

Different meshes produced by different direction settings. The segment selected first is indicated in each case.

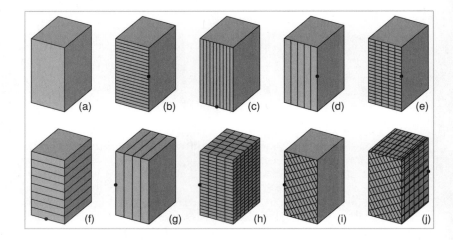

■ Apply the X and Y direction settings to the top face of the block, and you will achieve the same mesh effect shown in Figure 6.3-e. This shows that the X, Y, and Z mesh directions have nothing to do with the X, Y, and Z axes of the active reference plane—they are relative only to the selected face and oriented according to the manner in which the face is picked. To verify this, change the mesh settings so that only the Z direction is activated. You will find that applying the mesh tool now to a face produces no result, since the Z direction is perpendicular to the plane of that face, not lying on it.

■ Why then have a Z direction at all? To find the answer to that, apply the Mesh tool to a new block with the topological level now set to Object. Only the Z option should be activated. You will find that the mesh is applied in a direction perpendicular to the face that is picked, which in turn is determined by the segment used to select the object (Figures 6.3-f and 6.3-g). Thus, applying the Mesh tool at the Object level leads to a 3D rather than a 2D mesh, which is why all three directions are needed.

■ Undo the operation, and check the All Directions option in the Mesh Options dialog. This will activate all the three directions—X, Y, and Z—in one step. Reapply the Mesh tool to the block, and you will see the full three-directional effect of the mesh (Figure 6.3-h).

■ So far, all the meshes you created were parallel to the segments of the rectangular faces to which the Mesh tool was applied. But what if you want meshes that are oriented differently? Go to the Mesh Options dialog and under the Mesh Direction section, pick the From Angle option. This lets you specify a different orientation for the mesh by assigning two angle values for the X-Z and X-Y directions. Experiment with different values of these, both at the Face level (Figure 6.3-i) and at the Object level (Figure 6.3-j). Notice that at the Face level, it does not matter how the face is selected, but at the Object level, the alignment of the mesh does depend upon which segment is picked first. As you can see from Figure 6.3-j, the result of this method at the Object level is not very "clean," and is therefore best avoided.

■ Move on to the four mesh alignment options, located on the right side of the Mesh Options dialog. Notice that the default is Normal Alignment. To see what this means, turn on the XYZ Lock option and specify a value for the mesh size, say 9', that is *not* a factor of the block size. Also, switch to the default From Picked Segment option under Mesh Direction.

Figure 6.4

Different mesh alignment options demonstrated on the top face of a block, seen in Top view.

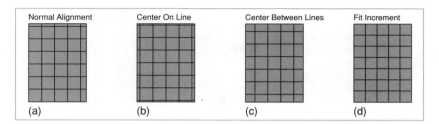

- Undo any previous mesh operations and reapply the Mesh tool with the new settings to the top face of the block. Switch to the Top view to see the results better. You will see that since the mesh dimensions are not synchronized with the face dimensions, there are smaller pieces of mesh "left over" after the mesh is placed relative to the segment first picked (Figure 6.4-a).

- Undo and repeat the operation with each one of the other three mesh alignment options, and observe the difference. The Center On Line option distributes the leftover pieces equally on all sides of the face, ensuring that the mesh lines pass through the center of the face (Figure 6.4-b). The Center Between Lines option also does an equal distribution of leftover pieces, but in such a way that a mesh subdivision lies exactly at the center of the face (Figure 6.4-c). And finally, the Fit Increment option nicely readjusts the mesh size so that it is uniformly distributed across the face (Figure 6.4-d), and is thus a very useful option.

- The only remaining option in the Mesh Options dialog is the Triangulate option which, when checked, creates the mesh and then breaks it down into triangles.

- Since a mesh is actually breaking up a face into many smaller faces, you can also create meshes within meshes. First, create a mesh of a fairly large dimension on a face. Then reduce the mesh dimensions and apply the Mesh tool to one of the smaller meshed faces you just created. You could repeat this ad infinitum, creating fractal-like patterns on the face or other interesting variations (Figure 6.5).

Figure 6.5

Creating meshes within meshes on the top face of a block, seen in Top view.

All in all, it is obvious that even a "plain" mesh is not quite so plain after all!

1.3 Smooth Meshes

The next tool on Row 6, Smooth Mesh, creates a mesh on the surface of an object in the same way as the Mesh tool you just saw. The difference, however, is that instead of uniformly subdividing the face of an object into a flat mesh, the Smooth Mesh tool subdivides a face non-uniformly into a pattern that matches the shape of that face. The mesh patterns would thus be different for rectangles, triangles, pentagons, hexagons, irregular polygons, and so on. Additionally, the Smooth Mesh tool can also smoothen out the edges of the object by giving them a curvature.

Figure 6.6

Using the Smooth Mesh tool with the option set to Keep Flat.

(a) Original objects

(b) Preview dialog

(c) Resultant objects

◾ Clear everything you have in your project or move to a different layer. Create three extruded blocks with different base shapes—a rectangle, a hexagon, and an irregular polygon (Figure 6.6-a). Set the topological level to Object and apply the Smooth Mesh tool (M-Tool:6a,2) to the rectangular block first. A preview dialog will be invoked, containing various options for the Smooth Mesh operation.

◾ Don't worry about getting to know all these options right away. Instead, simply make the following changes to the dialog, as shown in Figure 6.6-b: reduce the Maximum # Of Subdivisions value from 4 to 2; check the Keep Flat option instead of the Smooth option; finally, select the Meshed Object option rather than the Original Object option. This will update the image in the preview window to show you the mesh created on the object. Exit the dialog by clicking on the OK button.

◾ Next, apply the Smooth Mesh tool in exactly the same manner to the other two blocks, with exactly the same options. Notice how the mesh is different for each of the three blocks and is adapted to the shape of the face that is being meshed. (Figure 6.6-c).

1.4 Smooth Mesh Options

◾ Apply the Smooth Mesh tool again to one of the objects you just meshed. Choose the one with the irregular base for more interesting results. The Smooth Meshing Preview dialog will open up in the usual manner, showing the original object in its unmeshed state.

◾ The iconic tools at the base of the preview window for changing views, zooming, scrolling, and selection will be familiar to you from a variety of other tools, the most recent being Texture Map and Decals in Workshop 5. The icon at the end of the row can be used for changing the preview display from wireframe to rendered, whenever necessary.

◾ Go ahead and use the Pointer tool to deselect all the faces of the object in the preview window. Then exit the dialog. You will find that you have just retrieved the original unmeshed object by "removing" the meshes from all of its faces. The Smooth Mesh tool thus produces a *controlled object*, where the control parameters are stored and can be modified at a later stage.

◾ Now set the topological level to Face and apply the Smooth Mesh tool to the same object by selecting only its top face. In the preview dialog, you will see that all the faces are gray except the one you had selected. Activate the Meshed Object option to see the result. Rotate the object in the preview window so that you can see its top face clearly, or better still, switch to the Top view. We will use this meshed face to explore some of the other options in the Smooth Meshing Preview dialog.

■ Change the Maximum # Of Subdivisions value to 1. (A warning: Don't hit the return or Enter key for this value to be registered, or you will unintentionally exit the dialog. Instead, click on the Maximum Segment Length box, located right below the subdivisions box, for the change to be registered.) The Update button, which was grayed out all this time, will now be activated, indicating that the mesh parameters have changed. Click on it to view the results of the change. You will see that the mesh subdivisions have decreased. Do the same for the value of 2, then for 3, and finally for 4. Notice how the mesh subdivisions get finer each time (Figure 6.7-a). You can also clearly see the subdivision methodology at work—the mesh lines run from the midpoints of the boundary segments and end at the center of the face. For an irregular polygon like the one you have, it is first divided into regular polygons and then the subdivision begins.

 You should settle for the lowest value of Maximum # Of Subdivisions that you can do with, as higher values correspondingly increase the complexity of the object.

■ Notice in Figure 6.7 that for the Maximum # Of Subdivisions value of 4, a certain amount of non-uniformity exists in the subdivision. Try changing this value to 5, 6, and larger numbers. After a point, you will find that further subdivisions are no longer being created. Obviously, some other parameter is at work here. This is the Maximum Segment Length option which is currently set at 2'-0". Change it to 1'-0". Also switch to the highest subdivision value which gave you some different results. Compare the result now to the earlier mesh for the same subdivision value, and you will find an increase in the number of subdivisions in certain areas of the mesh (Figure 6.7-b). Step down one subdivision value and you might still see some difference from the earlier result.

Figure 6.7

Exploring the Smooth Mesh subdivision options.

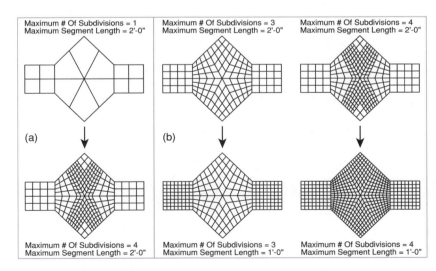

■ The Maximum Segment Length option basically ends the subdivision process as soon as all the individual mesh segments become smaller than the specified segment length. This accounts for the non-uniformity you saw in Figure 6.7-a, where the maximum segment length was specified as

2'-0". It is also due to the same option that an increase in the Maximum # Of Subdivisions value beyond a certain point does not actually increase the mesh subdivisions. The Maximum Segment Length option can be turned off altogether so that no check for segment length is made. However, it is recommended that you keep it selected with a reasonable value (depending upon the scale of the project) to avoid an unwieldy subdivision explosion!

▢ Let us move on to the Smooth mode and see how it differs from the Keep Flat mode that we have used so far. Change the topological level to Object and apply the Smooth Mesh tool to one of the objects you had completely meshed in the last section. Activate the Smooth option in the Smooth Meshing Preview dialog and click on the Meshed Object option to view the result. You will find that the object is now not only meshed but "smoothened out" as well in the process (Figure 6.8).

▢ The Smooth option has three sub-options, as you can see in Figure 6.8. The Maximum Face Angle option determines the level of subdivision of the mesh, superseding both the Maximum # Of Subdivisions and Maximum Segment Length options. The subdivision will stop as soon as all the angles between the meshed faces are less than the value specified for Maximum Face Angle. To understand how it works, keep increasing this value gradually and observe the changes in the configuration of the mesh. As you can see in Figure 6.9-a, a smaller value leads to a denser mesh, particularly in the areas of strong curvature, while a value of more than 90º does not mesh the object at all. The Maximum Face Angle option can also be turned off, which is the same as setting its value to 0º.

▢ The Curvature option comes next. This determines the amount of curvature of the mesh. The slider can go from 0% to 100%. Try out both extremes, as well as some intermediate values. You will see that for a lower value, the object will be curved more around the edges and less at the face centers. It is exactly the opposite for a larger value. For the default value of 50%, the curvature is uniformly distributed between the edges and face centers. Figure 6.9-b shows all three scenarios. The Maximum Face Angle value was left at the default of 10º.

▢ Finally, there is the familiar Triangulate Mesh option which triangulates the resultant mesh. However, it is a little different from the usual triangulation option accompanying other tools which triangulates only non-planar faces. The Triangulate option for Smooth Mesh triangulates *all* faces uniformly, planar or non-planar. Moreover, each triangular face is further subdivided. The overall result is a much smoother mesh. To see how it works, apply the Triangulate tool (M-Tool:6a,9) to one of the objects you used Smooth Mesh on and note the triangulation pattern. Then Undo the operation, and reapply the Smooth Mesh tool to the object with the Triangulate Mesh option checked. The difference between the two operations should be clear (Figure 6.9-c).

Figure 6.8

Choosing the Smooth option as opposed to the Keep Flat option for the hexagonal object shown in Figure 6.6.

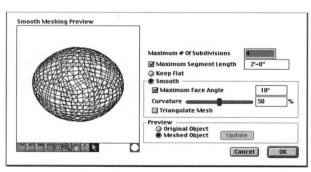

Figure 6.9

Exploring the options for the Smooth mode of the Smooth Mesh tool.

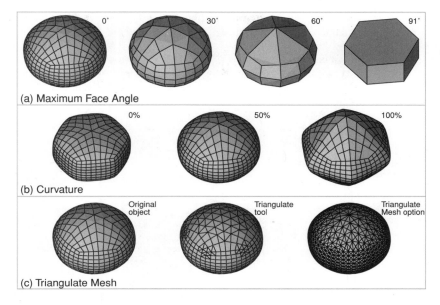

(a) Maximum Face Angle

(b) Curvature

(c) Triangulate Mesh

■ Conclude this section on the Smooth Mesh tool by applying variations of the Smooth tool parameters only on some faces of the object rather than the entire object. You can see from the examples illustrated in Figure 6.10 how it is possible to achieve many interesting effects using the tool at the Face level.

Figure 6.10

Applying the Smooth Mesh tool, with the Smooth option on, only to selected faces of an object.

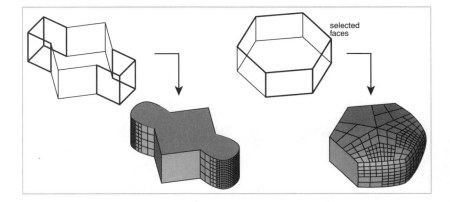

selected faces

1.5 Reducing Mesh Density

■ Select the next tool in the left column of Row 6, Reduce Mesh, and apply it to one of the meshed objects you have. A preview dialog, very similar to the one you just saw for Smooth Mesh is invoked (Figure 6.11-a). Here, you can specify the criteria that will be used to reduce the mesh density of the selected object.

■ The Reduce Mesh tool works by merging the adjacent faces of an object and the adjacent segments of a face. The merging happens only when the angles enclosed by the faces or the segments are less than the values specified for the Face Angle and Edge Angle parameters respectively. Experiment with different values and see how they affect the reduction in mesh density of the object. One example is illustrated in Figure 6.11-b.

▣   The remaining options in the preview dialog are very simple. You can choose to limit the merging only to those faces which have the same Color or Texture Map Control. The options under the Preview section are the same as those for Smooth Mesh. And finally, information is given to you about the number of faces and edges that are merged, which you may find useful.

▣   The Reduce Mesh tool can also be used to reduce the number of segments in a regular 2D object, and the number of faces in a regular 3D object. This is demonstrated in Figure 6.11-c. Try it.

Figure 6.11

Applying the Reduce Mesh tool to meshed as well as regular objects. The preview dialog for the meshed object is also shown.

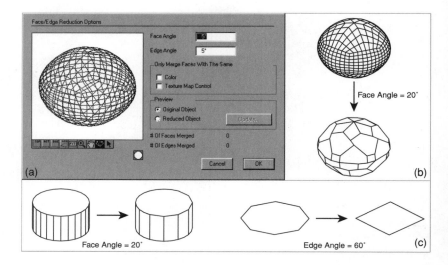

EXERCISE *2*

Moving, Disturbing, and Deforming Meshes

You have, by now, worked with two types of meshed objects. At times, you might not need to go beyond creating such meshes, using the different options that they afford—they might be the final form of the objects you wish to model. However, at other times, these meshed objects might only be the intermediary objects on which further operations have to be performed to generate the forms you need. In this exercise, we will look at three tools that are specifically targeted towards meshed objects, allowing you to further modify and sculpt them into forms you could not achieve with regular unmeshed objects.

2.1   Moving Meshes

▣   Move to a different layer and create an extruded slab—a solid whose base dimensions are much larger than its height. Select the top face of this slab, and apply the Mesh tool to it. The size of the mesh should be relatively small compared to the size of the slab (Figure 6.12-a).

WORKSHOP 6

Figure 6.12

Moving a mesh with the
Move Mesh tool. (a) Original
object. (b) Defining the area
to be moved. (c) Defining
the movement height.
(d) Resultant object.

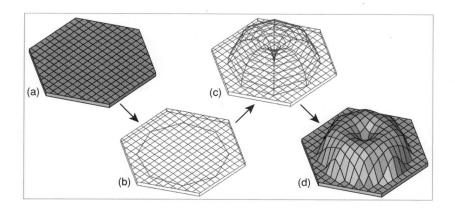

■ Select the Move Mesh tool (M-Tool:6a,5) and watch the instructions in the Prompts palette. The default behavior of this tool is to move parts of meshes in a radial fashion. Since the most logical movement direction for the flat mesh is perpendicular to its surface, turn on the Perpendicular Lock (W-Tool:2,1) to restrict the movement to that direction. Also, make sure that none of the Snap options are active so that the vertical movement is unhampered.

■ The Move Mesh tool is still active, prompting you to select the center of the mesh movement. Click on any point within the top meshed surface, preferably closer to the center. An octagonal shape will be rubber-banded as you move the mouse (Figure 6.12-b). This shape defines the area of the mesh to be moved. Click when you have a sufficiently large octagon, oriented as desired. You now have to indicate with the mouse how much movement you want. Drag the cursor upwards and as you do so, the meshed area you marked gets rubber banded and moves following the shape of a certain *profile* (Figure 6.12-c). Position it at the desired height and click to freeze the mesh movement. You should have your mesh transformed as shown in Figure 6.12-d. You can see why it is important for the mesh to be relatively dense—the denser the mesh, the smoother the transformation.

■ Undo what you just did and repeat the operation up to the point where you have defined the base octagon and are moving it in the vertical direction. While it is being rubber-banded in this manner, try manipulating it in other ways with the following key combinations: option key (Mac) or Ctrl+Shift keys (PC) for changing the radius of the octagonal area in addition to the height of the profile; control key (Mac) or Ctrl+Alt keys (PC) for changing the orientation of the octagon as the mouse is moved; and finally, option+control keys (Mac) or Ctrl+Shift+Alt keys (PC) for scaling the octagon independently in both directions. Thus, you can see that you are not limited to your initial shape definition of the movement area.

■ Try applying repeated mesh movements to the same surface but in different directions—some upwards and some downwards. Interesting effects can also be obtained by partially extending the base octagon *beyond* the meshed surface. Play with it.

2.2 Creating and Using Profiles

The question that emerges based on what we just did is: Where does the shape of the profile that is used to move the mesh come from? The answer is simple: from the Profiles palette.

Figure 6.13

Working with the Profiles palette. (a) Choosing different profiles and the corresponding mesh movements, applied to the same original object shown in Figure 6.12-a. (b) Creating a new profile and applying it to transform the meshed object.

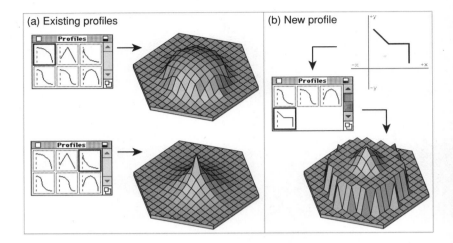

■ Go to the Palettes menu and open the palette called Profiles. It contains a number of 2D profiles, out of which one is highlighted. This is the currently active profile which is applied to the mesh movement. Choose some other profile from the palette. Then undo the previous mesh movement operation, and reapply the Move Mesh tool to the mesh. You will find that it is now transformed differently, following the shape of the newly selected profile. Repeat with some other profiles and see the difference in the results (Figure 6.13-a).

The Profiles palette contains only six profiles by default. What if the profile you need to use for your mesh movement is not there? In that case, you can create your own profiles and store them in the Profiles palette, just as you created your own surface styles and stored them in the Surface Styles palette.

■ Create an open 2D object in the shape of your profile. (It obviously cannot be a closed shape, as you can see from the existing profiles in the palette.) Then select the Define Profiles tool, located just before the Move Mesh tool on Row 6, and apply it to the 2D object. It will immediately appear as a new profile in your Profiles palette (Figure 6.13-b). You can now use it just like any other profile for moving meshes, as shown in the illustration. The ability to create and use your own profiles gives you a lot of control over how to transform your meshed objects.

■ Each profile in the Profiles palette can be further refined, if necessary, by clicking on it while pressing the option key (Mac) or Ctrl+Shift keys (PC). A dialog will open up in which you can change the width and the height of the profile. The proportions of the profile specified here will affect the shape of the mesh when it is moved using that profile. You can also delete the profile if it is no longer needed by clicking on the Delete button in the same dialog.

2.3 **Mesh Movement Options**

■ Double-click on the Move Mesh tool to invoke its dialog. It contains a large number of options that determine how the mesh movement operation is executed (Figure 6.14). The first option, Move Relative To, is set to Reference Plane by default, but you should select the alternative, Perpendicular To Base Point, instead. This will ensure that the mesh is always moved perpendicular to the plane of the meshed surface, even if it is inclined. It will also save you from the hassle of turning on the Perpendicular Lock—which you will find yourself invariably forgetting to do in the beginning—for meshed surfaces parallel to the reference plane, as in the last example. Unless, of course, you have set up a reference plane in such a way that you want to move relative to it rather than perpendicular to the meshed surface, in which case you should stick with the Reference Plane option.

Figure 6.14

The Move Mesh Options dialog.

■ The Movement Shape option lets you choose between different ways of specifying the base shape that defines the area of the mesh to be moved. Try them all out. The default, as you can see, is set to Radial # Of Sides with a value of 8, which is why your base shape was always octagonal so far. This value can be changed to get a base polygon of a different size. The Linear option, on the other hand, lets you define a sequence of lines (i.e., a polyline) about which the mesh will be moved. The last option, From Path, lets you use any existing 2D shape as the base shape for the mesh movement. This is very convenient and flexible, as it lets you precisely define the area of the mesh you want to move. Figure 6.15 illustrates the From Path option using two shapes—an arc and an ellipse. The mesh movement was applied vertically upwards for the arc and vertically downwards for the ellipse.

■ The three options for Move Points come into play when a mesh move is applied on top of a previous mesh move. Undo all mesh movements you have done so far, and create two or more intersecting 2D shapes for moving the mesh using the From Path option (Figure 6.16-a). Apply the Move Mesh tool to the meshed surface using each one of your two path shapes. You will find that the resultant mesh movement is like a *union* of the two individual mesh movements (Figure 6.16-b). This is with the Move Points option set to the default of Points Under Profile Only. Undo and reapply the same operation with the other two options in turn. You will find that with the All Points Within Profile option, all points that fall within the move area are brought back to their original position first and then moved, resulting in the *partial loss* of the earlier movements (Figure 6.16-c). Finally, with the Relative To Original Position option, all points in the move area are still moved, but in relation to their previous height rather than in an absolute manner. In a sense, therefore, this *adds on* to any earlier mesh movements (Figure 6.16-d). The choice of which of these three options you use will depend upon what you wish to accomplish.

Figure 6.15

Using the From Path option for the Movement Shape of the mesh.

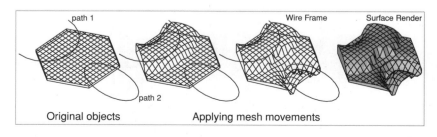

Original objects   Applying mesh movements

Figure 6.16

Using the various Move Points options of the Move Mesh tool.

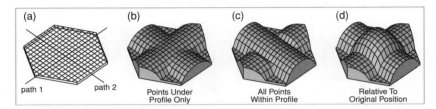

▪ Let us turn to the next two options in the Move Mesh Options dialog. The Movement Interface is set to Edit by default, which lets you define the movement dynamically. However, you can also set it to Generate Directly, in which case the movement will be applied automatically in a single step. For Movement Type, the default Stretch option, as you have seen, scales the mesh movement profile based on the specified height. The alternative Push option will retain the proportions of the profile, stretching the base of the mesh movement area if the specified height is greater than the height of the profile.

▪ There are only a few remaining options. Move Points Of Front Faces Only restricts the mesh movement to only those points on the surface to which the Move Mesh tool is applied, which will almost always be what is required. Deselecting this option will move *all* points of the object that lie within the profile, even if they lie on other surfaces. The Random Point Disturbance option can be selected to "disturb" the surface of the mesh by the specified values, in addition to moving it. You can also choose to apply it to the entire mesh rather than only to those points of the mesh that are moved. The final option, Triangulate, operates in its usual manner.

All the mesh movements you have worked with in this section were applied to plain meshes. However, they can be applied in the same manner to meshes created with the Smooth Mesh tool as well as the C-Mesh tool, which will be covered in Exercise 4. The only difference is that these tools create controlled objects, and modifying them with the Move Mesh tool will cause them to lose their original controls, with the result that they can no longer be edited. You will therefore be warned before you apply the Move Mesh tool to such objects. This also applies to the remaining mesh manipulation tools we will look at in this workshop.

2.4   Disturbing Points

▪ Select the next tool in the left column of Row 6, Disturb Points, and invoke its dialog (Figure 6.17). Here, you can choose between two basic disturb operations, Random Disturbance and Wave Disturbance, each of which comes with its own set of options.

Figure 6.17

The Disturb Point Options dialog.

Figure 6.18

Applying Random
Disturbances with the
Disturb Points tool.
(a) Displacement in all
directions. (b) Displacement
only along the Z direction.

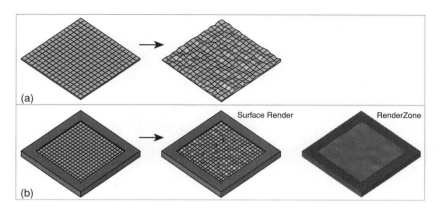

▣ Let us start by exploring the Random Disturbance option which is selected by default. Continue working with the same meshed slab you used in the last section, or create a new one and mesh its top face densely. Apply the Disturb Points tool to it. You will find that each point of the object gets slightly displaced. Switch to the Top view and then to the Front view, and you will see that the displacement has happened along all three directions—X, Y, and Z. The displacement value is quite small but because of the meshed surface, you can see the rippling effect quite clearly (Figure 6.18-a). The same operation applied to an unmeshed block would have been practically indiscernible.

▣ Move on to explore the parameters for Random Disturbance. There are two options, Relative To Reference Plane and Along Point Normals, which have the same meaning as the two Move Relative To options you saw earlier for the Move Mesh tool. To apply disturbances to inclined, curved, or any other non-orthogonal surfaces, use the Along Point Normals option to make sure that the disturbance always takes place perpendicular to the surface. For both options, you can specify the minimum and maximum values of the disturbance.

▣ For the Relative To Reference Plane option, deselecting the Lock box allows you to specify different values for the X, Y, and Z directions. On the other hand, you could choose to apply the disturbance only along a single direction by deactivating the other two options. Figure 6.18-b shows a random displacement only along the Z direction, applied to an object that is supposed to represent a "pool of water" bounded on the sides and bottom. The RenderZone image of the result shows how effective this technique is in realistically modeling a rippling effect such as that in water. (Of course, you have to add the appropriate reflection and transparency attributes to the surface style of the object for full realism.)

▣ Now activate the second Disturb Points option, Wave Disturbance. As it evident from its name, this option disturbs a meshed object in the form of waves. The default wave type is Linear. Apply the Disturb Points tool to a meshed object that has not been moved or disturbed (Figure 6.19-a), and you will get the linear wave-like effect shown in Figure 6.19-b. The undulation of the wave is along the X axis of the current plane. Undo and repeat the operation a few more times, and you will notice that the location of the wave with respect to the object is different each time, depending upon where you click on the object to select it. Go to the dialog and check the accompanying Through Centroid option. Now the wave is always located with respect to the centroid of the object, no matter where you click on it.

▣ Next, select Circular instead of Linear as the Type in the Disturb Point Options dialog—the waves will now be located in a circular fashion about a center. Again, this is affected by the Through

Centroid option. If it is checked, the waves will automatically be centered about the center of the meshed surface. If not, the waves will be centered about the point that you click on to select the surface. The difference is illustrated in Figures 6.19-c and 6.19-d.

Figure 6.19

Different options for Wave Disturbances, applied to a meshed surface.

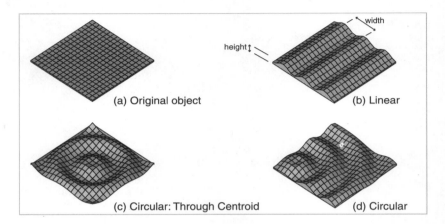

(a) Original object (b) Linear

(c) Circular: Through Centroid (d) Circular

- If you are looking for mathematical precision, you can also choose between the Sine and Cosine wave formulas that are applied to generate the waves. Experiment with both types, keeping all other options the same, to see how they differ. Sine generates a wave that passes through the selection point, whereas Cosine generates a wave that peaks at the same point. You can also check the Inverse option which will flip the *crests* (or peaks) and *troughs* (or valleys) of the wave.

- Next, experiment with different values for the Width and Height of the waves. The width is the distance between two crests or two troughs, whereas the height is the distance between the highest point of a peak and the lowest point of a trough (see Figure 6.19-b).

- Finally, explore what happens if you apply the Wave Disturbance to an object which has all its faces meshed. Figure 6.20 shows an example of such a situation. The wave type was set to Linear and the Width was more than twice the Height. Also, both these values were relatively small compared to the dimensions of the slab. The result of the operation is a "corrugated" form which can be used for modeling roofing sheets and similar objects.

Figure 6.20

Applying a linear Wave Disturbance to an object which has all its faces meshed.

(a) Original object (b) Resultant object

2.5 Deforming Objects

- We will end this exercise by exploring the next mesh manipulation tool, Deform (M-Tool:6a,7). Invoke its dialog and you will find that you have a choice of seven options, each of which can be used to deform a meshed object in different ways. Click on each one of these options—Shear,

Taper, Twist, and so on—and notice the diagram in the little window at the left which changes to illustrate what the selected option does (Figure 6.21). Settle for the Twist option to begin with and exit the dialog.

Figure 6.21

The Deformation Options dialog, with the option set to Twist.

■ On a new layer, create an extruded block such that its height is much larger compared to its base dimensions. Use the One Copy tool to make a copy of it. Mesh all the surfaces of one block using a relatively small mesh value; leave the other one as it is (Figure 6.22-a).

■ Apply the Deform tool to the meshed block first. As soon as you click on the object, it gets highlighted and goes into an edit mode. Move the cursor around the object and you will find that it changes in appearance when it detects a corner point or edge on the upper or lower surfaces of the block. Click on any one of these points and you will find that as you move the mouse, a twisting motion is applied to the block about an axis (Figure 6.22-b). Click when you are satisfied with the amount of twist, and you will be rewarded with a smoothly twisted block.

■ Now apply the same operation to the other unmeshed block. You will find that although it seems to work the same way, the end result is not the same. The meshed block can be smoothly twisted since it is subdivided into many faces, whereas the unmeshed block is forced to retain its straight lines and cannot be properly deformed. The difference between the two is shown in Figure 6.22-c.

■ Most of the other Deform options also work best with meshed objects. Therefore, for the sake of convenience, a Mesh Object option is supplied in the Deformation Options dialog, along with a button to access the same options that accompany the Mesh tool. If you check this option, the Deform tool will mesh the object before applying any of the Deform operations.

■ Work with each of the remaining six Deform options, applying them to the same or to similar objects. Look at the accompanying illustration in the dialog before performing the operation to get an understanding of how it works. Figure 6.23 shows these six options applied to the same meshed block. Note that you can also numerically key in the amount of movement or rotation. The axis about which the deformation takes place is called the *deformation axis*.

Figure 6.22

Applying the Twist operation to a meshed as well as an unmeshed object.

Figure 6.23

The other Deform operations applied to a meshed block.

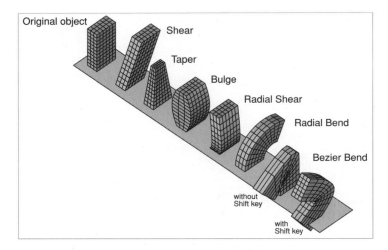

▪ For the Bezier Bend operation, different effects can be achieved by using various combinations of the option, command, control, and shift keys (Mac) or the Ctrl, Shift, and alt keys (PC). The Shift key is particularly useful as it bends both the opposing sides of the object, rather than just the selected side. The contrast is illustrated in Figure 6.23. Be sure to explore this and the other key combinations before moving ahead.

▪ In addition to the seven basic operations, the Deformation Options dialog contains a number of associated sub-options which affect the way in which some or all of the operations work. Let us first look at those located on the right. The All Objects At Once and Base Reference Plane options should be familiar to you. The values for Initial Limits define how much of the object is affected by the applied deformation. Change the Lower Limit to 25% and the Upper Limit to 75% and watch how only the middle half of the object gets deformed (Figure 6.24-a). The Bezier Controls option applies only to the Bezier Bend operation, and is used to locate the control points for the bending along the deformation axis. Bringing the points closer, for instance, by setting the Lower and Upper values to 45% and 55% respectively, will create a sharper bending at the center of the object (Figure 6.24-b).

Figure 6.24

The effects of various other Deform options.

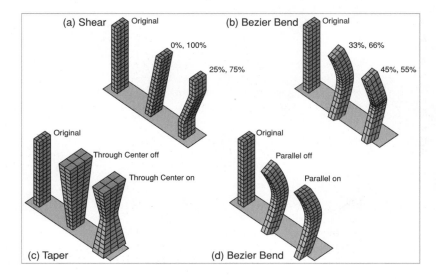

■ There are two remaining options, located just below the operation preview window. The Through Center option affects the first six Deform operations. When checked, these operations are anchored about the midpoint of the deformation axis (Figure 6.24-c). The Parallel option, on the other hand, affects only the Bezier Bend operation, where it ensures that the top surface of the bent object continues to remain parallel to the top surface of the original object (Figure 6.24-d). The change in mode for each operation caused by both the Through Center and Parallel options is reflected in its accompanying illustration diagram. Try them out for all the operations.

EXERCISE 3

Displacing Meshes

The next tool in the left column of Row 6, Displacement, uses a regular 2D image as the basis for the 3D movement of a meshed surface, sculpting it in the form of the image. The image has to be in grayscale rather than in color. Areas on the meshed surface that correspond to white on the image will have the maximum displacement, while areas that correspond to black will have the minimum displacement. Displacement in other areas is proportional to the corresponding shade of gray in the image. Sounds fascinating, doesn't it? Let us see how it works.

3.1   Image-Based Displacement

■ The first step is to find or create an appropriate grayscale image for carrying out the displacement. You can easily create one using any paint program. The important thing to keep in mind about this image, apart from the fact that it must not have color, is to avoid sharp contrasts between black and white. A gradual gradation will produce a smoother displacement. If your paint program does not let you create such a gradation, you can use any photo-editing program for blurring the image. Figure 6.25 shows an image created using a paint program, which was then taken to Adobe Photoshop where the Blur filter was applied to it. This image will be used for illustrating how the Displacement tool works in this exercise.

Figure 6.25

An image created for use with the Displacement tool. (a) The image as created using a paint program. (b) Blurring the image with an image-editing program to remove sharp contrasts.

(a)   (b)

■ Get back to form•Z and create a simple 3D block. Apply a dense mesh to its top surface using the Mesh tool (M-Tool:6a,1) at the Face topological level.

■ Set the topological level back to Object. Then select the Displacement tool (M-Tool:6a,8) and apply it to the block. A dialog will open up containing a large number of options for "mapping" the displacement. It is similar to the Texture Map Controls and Decals dialogs you encountered in the last workshop—it has a preview window and various options to make the required adjustments to the displacement.

◨   Notice the smaller window located at the lower left corner of the dialog. This shows the image that will be used to carry out the displacement. To replace the default logo image with your own image, click on it and a dialog will be invoked, which should be familiar to you from the Image Mapping exercises of the last workshop. Use the Load button to load your image file instead of the logo. The Displacement Mapping dialog will be updated to show the new image (Figure 6.26-a).

◨   Now that the image has been chosen, we can attend to the actual business of displacement. Turn your attention to the preview window, where the object is shown in its original state. Click on the Displaced button in the Show Object section, located just below the window, to see the result of the displacement without modifying any of the settings. You will see the meshed top face of the object take on a slight curvature that corresponds to the selected image. Click on the last iconic tool located below the window and choose the Rendered display mode (Figure 6.26-b). This should help you to visualize the displacement better. Exit the Displacement Mapping dialog, change to Top view, and zoom in for a closer look at the displaced surface (Figure 6.26-c).

Figure 6.26

Using the Displacement tool. (a) The Displacement Mapping dialog, showing the original object and the image that will be used for the displacement.
(b) Rendered display of the displaced object. (c) Top view of the displaced surface in the Surface Render mode.

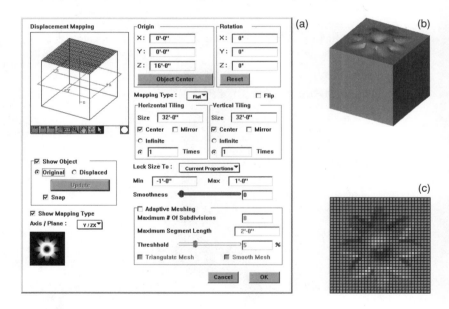

3.2   Basic Displacement Options

You can see that the meshed surface in Figure 6.26 does bear some semblance to the specified image, but the actual displacement seems to be of a rather low resolution. Obviously, further adjustments are necessary. We will now explore how the options in the Displacement Mapping dialog can be used to modify the displacement in various ways.

◨   Apply the Displacement tool to the same object once again, and you will be back in the same Displacement Mapping dialog shown in Figure 6.26-a. Thus, the object created by the Displacement tool is a controlled object—you can continue to reshape it with the Displacement tool, provided that it has not been modified by any other tool.

Figure 6.27

Increasing the resolution of the displacement by using the Adaptive Meshing option.

■ The first task is to increase the resolution of the displaced surface. Choose the Top icon located below the preview window so that the changes in the top meshed surface are easier to view.

■ Next, check the Adaptive Meshing option which is located in the lower right portion of the dialog. This option makes further subdivisions on all the necessary faces, thereby increasing the resolution of the surface for more accurate displacements. The amount of subdivision is controlled by two sub-options which you have already explored for the Smooth Mesh tool in Exercise 1. Leave the Maximum # Of Subdivisions to 8 for now, but keep reducing the Maximum Segment Length until you see a noticeable difference in the displacement resolution. Make sure the Displaced option is selected, and keep clicking on the Update button to see the changes. Figure 6.27 shows the object in the preview window with a noticeably higher resolution than before. Notice how additional subdivisions have been made only in the necessary areas.

 Don't reduce the Maximum Segment Length too much as you might run out of memory for the Displacement operation. As always, you should settle for the largest value you can get away with.

■ The Adaptive Meshing section has a Threshold value that you can change as well. This is used to adjust the sensitivity of the displacement to the gradations in grayscale of the image. A lower value increases the sensitivity and vice versa. Test this by previewing the displacement for the two extreme Threshold values. There is also the usual Triangulate Mesh option which you can use when required, as well as a Smooth Mesh option which is grayed out for now. We will learn how to apply it when the time comes.

■ Next, turn off the Adaptive Meshing option and concentrate on the Smoothness slider bar located just above it. Try out different values for this option and Update to see the results. You will find that larger smoothness values soften out areas of sharp contrast in the image, leading to a smoother displacement (Figure 6.28). At the same time, however, there is a loss of detail. If your original image has no sharp contrasts, the Smoothness can remain at the default value of 0%, since the displacement will already be fairly smooth.

Figure 6.28

Increasing the Smoothness value of the displacement from 0% to 50% to 100%.

■ Set Smoothing back to the default value of 0% and go up further to look at the Min and Max values. As mentioned earlier and as you can verify from the actual displacement, areas corresponding to white in the image have the most displacement, while those corresponding to black have the least. The actual *extents* of these displacements come from the Max and Min values respectively. Keep increasing the value of Max and watch the "white" areas project out of the original surface more considerably (Figure 6.29-a).

■ Similarly, keep decreasing the value of Min to well below 0'-0". You would expect the "black" areas to dig deeper into the surface of the object as a result of this change. That doesn't really happen, but the total projection of the displacement beyond the surface does increase proportionately to the difference between the Max and Min values (Figure 6.29-b). Look carefully at the object in the preview window as you further reduce the value of Min. You will find that the distance between the top face and the XY plane running through the center of the object keeps decreasing, and this is what is causing the total projection to increase (Figure 6.29-c).

Figure 6.29

The effect of increasing Max and decreasing Min values on the displacement. The Displacement preview window as the Min value is reduced is also shown.

(a)   (b)   (c)

This XYZ coordinate system that you see in the preview window in Figure 6.29-c dictates how the displacement is mapped to the object. Not only can the displacement be mapped in a planar fashion, as it is by default, it can also be mapped in a cylindrical or spherical fashion, on the entire object or only on selected faces. We will explore the different mapping types in the remaining sections of this exercise, as well as learn how to adjust the location and orientation of the coordinate system to achieve the desired displacement effect.

3.3   Flat Mapping

■ Start afresh with a new object to explore the various mapping types. It can be just a simple 3D block like the one you had earlier. This time, however, do not mesh it, but apply the Displacement tool to it directly. Load your image as the displacement image in the Displacement Mapping dialog as you did before. Notice that the Mapping Type, located below the Origin and Rotation sections, is currently set to Flat. You will soon see what these options are all about.

Figure 6.30

Applying the Displacement tool to an unmeshed object, with the mapping type set to Flat.

▪ Click on the Displaced option below the object preview window. Since the original object is unmeshed, there will be no displacement. Turn Adaptive Meshing on and adjust its values so that some displacement is obtained. You might also have to increase the level of Smoothing a little for the displacement to occur. Change the Min and Max values too if you like. You will now find that both the top and bottom faces of the object get displaced this time (Figure 6.30).

▪ Since the original object was not meshed, the displacement with adaptive meshing is applied to all its faces. Also, the mapping type is set to Flat which means that the displacement will occur in a planar fashion only along the +Z direction. This is why only the top and bottom faces of the block shown in Figure 6.30 get displaced, and in the +Z direction. Look closely at the axes in the preview window to verify this.

▪ These axes can be rotated in order to make the displacement happen in a different direction, and therefore to different surfaces. Turn to the Rotation section located in the top right corner of the Displacement Mapping dialog, and change the rotation of Y to 90°. You will now find that the displacement coordinate system flips and the displacement now occurs along two of the vertical opposing faces of the object (Figure 6.31-a). A value of -90° for Y will still displace the two same faces but in the reverse direction (Figure 6.31-b). A value of 90° for X will displace the other two sides of the block (Figure 6.31-c). Try out other values in a similar fashion and see the changes in the displacement.

▪ You know from working with the Texture Map and Decal tools in Workshop 5 that you can rotate the axes graphically in the preview window. To do this, you first need to set the Show Object mode back to Original. Now use the Pointer tool to rotate the axes. Keep in mind the current Axis/Plane selection below the preview window, and recall that the current axis shown in red cannot be rotated. You can also switch to one of the planar views in the preview window to adjust the orientation better. After positioning the axes in a desired fashion, switch back to the Displaced mode to see the result. Figure 6.31-d shows the Z axis aligned along the diagonals of the block and the resultant displacement.

Figure 6.31

The effect of rotating the axes on the displacement.

      (a) Y = 90°   (b) Y = −90°   (c) X=90°   (d) Z axis along diagonal

▣ Switch back to the Rotation value of 90° for Y to get the displacement along the two vertical faces of the block (6.32-a). If you want only one of these faces to be displaced without affecting the other, this is what you need to do: Set the Show Object mode back to Original and select that face which is not to be displaced in the preview window using the Pointer tool. It gets grayed out, indicating that it is no longer available for displacement (Figure 6.32-b). Now switch to the Displaced mode and you will find that the displacement is only restricted to the other face (Figure 6.32-c). Note that you could have achieved the same result by applying the Displacement tool at the Face topological level to only the face you wanted to displace. The same technique applies to other faces at different axes orientations.

▣ Switch back to the Original mode and press the command+tab (Mac) or Ctrl+Tab (PC) keys. This has the effect of deselecting all the faces in the preview window, with the result that no face of the object will now be displaced. Thus, you can retrieve your original, "undisplaced" object whenever required. To reselect all the faces of the object for displacement, use the command+a (Mac) or Ctrl+a (PC) keys.

▣ Now turn to the Horizontal Tiling and Vertical Tiling sections in the Displacement Mapping dialog, which should be familiar to you from the Texture Map and Decal tools. These let you fix the size of the displacement map and the frequency with which it is repeated across a surface. By default, the displacement map is first scaled according to the size of the object, so that the Size values for both Horizontal Tiling and Vertical Tiling take on the size of the face they are applied to. Larger or smaller areas can be displaced by increasing or decreasing the Size values. One of the two values can be changed independently of the other by selecting None from the Lock Size To popup menu, in which case it might not be proportionate to the image size. Figure 6.33-a shows an example of such a displacement, applied to all the faces of the object. Notice how the side faces are affected by the displacement "spilling over" the top and bottom faces of the block.

Figure 6.32

Manipulating faces for displacement. (a) Displacement of the entire object. (b) Deselecting one of the faces. (c) The resulting displacement.

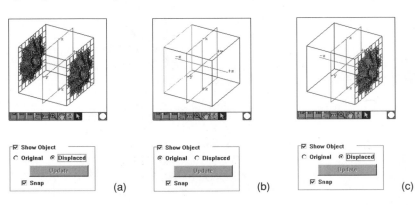

◻ You can also change the position of the displacement with respect to the object by moving the origin, placed by default in the center of the object. The move can be done numerically, by specifying the coordinates in the Origin section, or graphically with the Pointer tool. To use the graphical method, the Original option must be selected in the Show Object section. Since the Snap option in the same section is checked, you can readily snap to the points of the object. By default, the displacement is centered about the specified origin, as you can see from all the preceding illustrations. To position, instead, the lower left corner of the displacement at the origin (so that the displacement happens along the +X and +Y directions only), deselect the Center option in both the Tiling sections. Figure 6.33-b shows an example of such a displacement applied only to the top face of the block. All the faces were first deselected and only the top face was selected, after which the origin was moved to the lower left corner of the top face.

 A shortcut to move the origin from the center of the object to the collective center of only those faces that are selected for displacement—hold down the option key (Mac) or Ctrl+Shift keys (PC) when the preview window is in Original mode. The button in the Origin section will change to Center Of Faces instead of Object Center. Click on it to make the change in the origin position.

◻ If the specified tile size is much smaller than the face which is to be displaced, you can choose to have more than one tile along both directions by specifying the required number in the Times boxes. Or else, you can choose the Infinite option which will repeat the tiles along the entire extent of the face, as shown in Figure 6.33-c.

Figure 6.33

Manipulating the Tiling and Origin values for displacement. (a) Tile size disproportionate to the image size and larger than the object size.
(b) Moving the Origin to a corner of the object and deselecting the Center option. (c) Tiling the displacement infinitely along both directions of a horizontal slab.

3.4   Cylindrical and Spherical Mapping

▣ To make a fresh start with Cylindrical and Spherical mapping, create a new object similar to the one you used for Flat mapping. This will provide you with a good basis for comparison between the three mapping types. Do not mesh the object. Apply the Displacement tool to it directly, and choose your displacement image in the usual manner in the Displacement Mapping dialog.

▣ Change the Mapping Type to Cylindrical and set the preview window to the Displaced mode. Turn Adaptive Meshing on, and adjust the values until you can see some displacement in the object. You might have to increase the Smoothness value. Change the Min and Max values if necessary. What you will see is the use of a cylindrical shape as the displacement mapping boundary, with only a single displacement in the +X direction (Figure 6.34-a).

What you see might be no big deal—after all, you could have easily obtained the same result using Flat mapping with the appropriate axes orientation. So why bother to use Cylindrical? In response to that, make the following changes to the Tiling values and see what happens.

▣ First of all, set the Lock Size To option to None. Then change the horizontal tile Size value, so that it is equal to 360° divided by the number of vertical faces of the object. This is equal to 90° for the sample object shown in Figure 6.34. You can also adjust the vertical tile Size value if it does not match the aspect ratio of your image. Note that Vertical Tiling is specified in distances while Horizontal Tiling is specified in degrees for Cylindrical mapping. Finally, choose the Infinite option for Horizontal Tiling rather than 1 Times. You will now see the displacement along all the vertical sides of the object, facing outwards (Figure 6.34-b). This was something you could not have achieved with Flat mapping.

Figure 6.34

Using Cylindrical Mapping for image-based displacements. (a) Making some minor changes to the default parameters to displace one face.
(b) Selecting the Infinite option and adjusting the Tiling sizes to displace all the vertical faces.
(c) Activating the Smooth Mesh option to smoothen out the object.

Figure 6.35

Displacing a cubical block using Spherical Mapping with the Infinite Tiling and Smooth Mesh options activated.

■ Take the additional step of selecting the Smooth Mesh option which is now activated in the Adaptive Meshing section. Your object will now acquire a nice cylindrical curvature in addition to the displacement (Figure 6.34-c).

■ Needless to say, there's a lot more that you can do. You can change the horizontal tile Size to 360° to wrap a single displacement around the entire object. You could change the orientation of the axes to change the direction of the cylinder and thereby displace different areas of the object. Explore these and more options until you are comfortable with the Cylindrical mapping type.

■ Next, simply change the Mapping Type from Cylindrical to Spherical in the Displacement Mapping dialog for the same object. The displacement mapping boundary is now spherical in shape, and if the Smooth Mesh option is still active, the displaced object will acquire a spherical curvature (Figure 6.35). The number of displacements will depend upon the Horizontal Tiling and Vertical Tiling values. Note that both are now specified in degrees. You might have to change them independently of each other, for which you need to set the Lock Size To option to None.

■ Again, there are a lot of options which you should explore in detail, including different tile sizes, number of times the displacement is tiled both vertically and horizontally, different axes orientations, and so on. Do so before moving on to the next exercise.

EXERCISE 4

Controlled Curves and Meshes

In this exercise, we will first learn how to create controlled curves from straight vector lines. Then, we will move on to work with controlled meshes and explore the various options associated with creating and editing these objects.

WORKSHOP 6

4.1 2D Controlled Curves

▣ Move to a new layer, and change to the Top view. Set the object generation mode to 2D Surface Object and create two shapes using the Vector Lines tool—one open and one closed. Then use one of the Copy modes to make multiple copies of these two objects. You will use them to parade through the different types of controlled curves that are available in form•Z.

▣ Select the C-Curve tool (M-Tool:7a,1) and invoke its dialog (Figure 6.36). It contains various options that determine the shape of the curve and how it will be generated. Select the Construct Directly option instead of the default Edit option. Notice that the type of curve is set to the Quadratic option in the Quick Curves group, and that the Smoothing Interval has been specified as 2'-0".

Figure 6.36

The dialog of the C-Curve tool.

```
Controlled Curve Options
☐ Construct Plain Curve       ☑ Adjust To New Parameters
◯ Construct Directly   ● Edit  ☐ Hide Controls      ☐ Snap
Splines
   ◯ NURBS
   ◯ B-Spline                 Degree      2
   ◯ Bezier
   ◯ Broken Bezier            # Of Points  40
   ◯ Continuous Bezier
Quick Curves
   ◯ Cubic                    Smooth Interval  2'-0"
   ● Quadratic
   ◯ Shallow Tangent
   ◯ Normal Tangent
   ◯ Deep Tangent                    Cancel      OK
```

▣ Make sure the topographical level is set to Object. With the C-Curve tool still selected, click on one of the 2D objects you have created. It will be transformed into a curve. Click on the second object as well, and see the similarity in curvature to the first curve. Zoom in close to any of the two curves and notice that the curve is actually segmented, just like the curves you created in Workshop 1 with the drawing tools on Row 3. The Smoothing Interval value, as usual, determines the resolution of the curve. For a smoother curve, reduce its value from the default of 2'-0".

▣ Invoke the C-Curve Options dialog again and select Cubic from the Quick Curves group instead of Quadratic. Apply it now to another copy of the pair of objects you had created. You will see a definite difference in curvature from the first set of objects. Repeat this operation for some of the other curve types available in the dialog and observe the differences in the curves that are generated. Three of these are illustrated in Figure 6.37.

We will not get into the mathematical differences between the various types of curves here, or even into the differences between the two basic groups—Splines and Quick Curves. There is a whole body of mathematical theory dealing with the equations that constitute various kinds of curves, which can be left to those who are interested to explore on their own. For the rest of us, it is sufficient to know that Splines are more powerful and complex (and therefore slower) than Quick Curves and should be used only when you know exactly what you want in terms of the curvature, and how to go about getting it by drawing the appropriate initial shape. For a more intuitive and visual approach, settle for one of the Quick Curves.

Figure 6.37

Different types of controlled curves generated from the same set of objects.

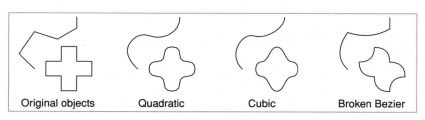

Original objects   Quadratic   Cubic   Broken Bezier

Figure 6.38

Creating a c-curve in the Edit mode.

■ Curves can also be generated in the Edit mode. Invoke the C-Curve Options dialog and select the Edit option instead of Construct Directly. Note the curve type selected in the dialog or pick a new one.

■ Apply the C-Curve tool to a 2D object that hasn't yet been converted to a curve. You will see a somewhat different picture now than what you saw earlier (Figure 6.38). The curve is indeed generated; however, you also see the original line and two types of circular marks, one on the midpoints and the other on the endpoints of all the constituent line segments. The line itself is called the *control line,* the points on it, *control points*, and the segments it is made up of, *control segments*. The points in the middle of the segments are called *knots*. The curves themselves are referred to as *controlled curves* because they are internally stored with all of these controls.

■ Notice also that all the other tools in the modeling tool palette have been grayed out, indicating that you are now in the *c-curve edit* mode. As usual, you can exit this mode by double-clicking the mouse or by clicking on any of the modeling tools. However, don't do that just yet. Instead, move your mouse around the controls, and you will find the cursor changing its appearance depending upon the type of control—point, segment, or knot. Try moving some controls and see how the shape of the curve changes interactively as you do so. Notice that a point or segment can be moved in any direction (provided direction snapping is off), but a knot can only be moved along the control segment that it is a part of. Exit the c-curve mode once you are satisfied with the adjustments to the curve. Thus, you can see how easily a curve can be fine-tuned after generating it from an initial configuration of control segments—it is here that the real power of a controlled object lies!

■ You can also apply the C-Curve tool in Edit mode to any of the curves you created earlier when the mode was set to Construct Directly. Try it. You will again enter the c-curve edit mode and can modify the original controls to change the shape of the curve. If you have modified any of the settings in the C-Curve Options dialog, these will also be applied to the selected curve. To edit the controls of a curve but retain the settings with which it was created, deselect the Adjust To New Parameters option which is checked by default. Thus, if you now click on a Bezier curve, the Edit mode will show the curve with the Bezier settings rather than those of the currently selected curve type in the dialog.

■ Move on to explore the remaining options in the C-Curve Options dialog. The Construct Plain Curve option is off by default, indicating that only controlled curves will be generated with the C-Curve tool. If, however, you wish to create a curve without storing its controls, select the Construct Plain Curve option. A plain curve cannot be edited once it has been created, so use this only when you are absolutely sure you've got the right curve.

WORKSHOP 6

Figure 6.39

Using the controlled curves generated to derive other 2D and 3D objects.

▪ The next two options—Hide Controls and Snap—are activated only in the Edit mode. Hide Controls, in turn, applies only to the Quick Curves group. Go ahead and select it. All the controls in the Edit mode will now be hidden, allowing you to modify the curve seemingly by moving the curve itself rather than its controls. The Snap option, on the other hand, is useful when you are working with control points that need to be coincident. Turning this option on will facilitate the process of snapping to existing control points. The tolerance for this Snap is the same as that for object snapping and can be changed in the Object Snaps dialog.

▪ You must have, by now, a number of curved objects in your window. Well, what can you do with these objects? The answer is: everything that you can do with regular 2D objects. Switch to a non-planar view and apply various kinds of derivative tools from Row 5 to these curves. Figure 6.39 shows a sampling. Be careful, however—once you derive another object from a controlled curve, it loses its controls and cannot be reshaped.

▪ So far, we have generated curves from 2D shapes that lie completely on one plane. It is also possible to generate curves from 2D shapes that are non-planar. To see how this works, create a closed 2D shape on the XY plane made up of at least 10 individual segments (Figure 6.40-a). Then set the topological level to Segment, turn on the Perpendicular lock, and move a few segments of this object in the Z direction. You now have a 2D object that is non-planar (Figure 6.40-b). Convert it to a curve using the C-Curve tool—you will get a non-planar 3D curve (Figure 6.40-c). This can be treated like any other object, for instance, it can be extruded to create a 3D curved solid (Figure 6.40-d). It would have been difficult to create this object using other tools, but you saw how easy it was using the C-Curve tool.

Figure 6.40

The sequence of steps for creating a non-planar curved object, involving the use of the C-Curve tool.

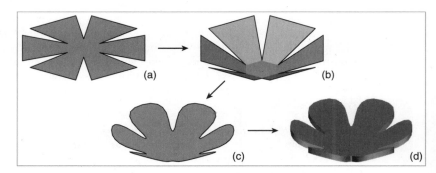

4.2 3D Controlled Meshes

Let us move on to look at 3D meshes. A mesh is essentially a surface that is subdivided into many smaller faces, allowing the mesh to easily take on any curved form. Controlled meshes are created in form•Z with the help of control lines positioned appropriately in 3D space, and are similar to controlled curves in that their controls are stored along with the objects, enabling them to be modified later. They are called *c-meshes* for short, and involve the use of the C-Mesh tool, located just after the C-Curve tool on Row 7.

▣ Clear all the objects in your window or move to a different layer. Use the Vector Lines tool in 2D Surface Object mode to draw a sequence of shapes on the XY plane. Ensure that their starting points and directions are synchronized, as shown in Figure 6.41-a. (This is very important!) Then turn on the Perpendicular Lock and move each shape in the Z direction to a different height. Switch to the Front view, if necessary, to adjust the heights more precisely. The objective is to get a sequence of shapes at different heights, as shown in Figure 6.41-b. You will use these shapes as control lines to generate a 3D mesh that spans across them.

▣ Next, activate the Pick tool and select all these lines sequentially, either from top to bottom or vice versa. It is important to pick them in the correct sequence. Finally, select the C-Mesh tool (M-Tool:7a,2) and click anywhere in the graphics window. A 3D mesh will be generated. At the same time, you will enter the *c-mesh edit* mode which is identical to the c-curve edit mode you saw in the last section. The various control points and lines are indicated in a similar fashion. Move these around and observe the corresponding changes in the meshed object. Keep in mind that you are now moving in 3D, so depending upon whether the Perpendicular Lock is on or off, you will move in a direction perpendicular to, or on the reference plane itself. Double-click or select any other tool to exit the c-mesh edit mode after you have finished sculpting your mesh as desired (Figure 6.41-c)

Figure 6.41

Creating a controlled mesh. (a) The control lines created on a plane. (b) Adjusting the heights of the control lines. (c) The resultant 3D mesh.

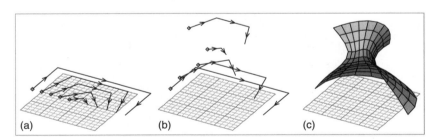

(a) (b) (c)

You might want to give a thickness to the meshed object you have created. You cannot use the Extrusion tool for this purpose, since it operates at the level of individual faces rather than entire objects and will break up the mesh into several smaller objects, one for each surface. Creating the original control lines using the 2D Enclosure mode as double-lined rather than as single-lined also does not work very well. You can, however, use the Parallel tool (M-Tool:5a,6) with the Double Parallel (Solid) option for this task, as you learned in Workshop 4.

4.3 Controlled Mesh Options

▣ The mesh shown in Figure 6.41 was generated with the default settings of the C-Mesh tool. To explore what the other options are, double-click to access its dialog (Figure 6.42). Don't be overwhelmed by the number of options and buttons—we will work through each one of them gradually.

WORKSHOP 6

Figure 6.42

The dialog of the C-Mesh tool.

■ Rather than testing all the controlled mesh options on different sets of control lines, or undoing and reapplying the C-Mesh tool to the same set of lines but with different options, you can make use of the Adjust To New Parameters option (as you did for c-curves) to regenerate the same mesh but with different settings. This option is not activated by default, so go ahead and select it in the C-Mesh Options dialog. The other options at the top of the dialog are the same as those in the C-Curve Options dialog, which were covered in the last section.

■ Skip the Length Of Net and Depth Of Net options for now, and turn your attention to the options for Mesh Length and Mesh Depth in the lower half of the dialog. The *length* of the mesh is the direction along a control line, and the *depth* is the direction across the control lines, shown in Figure 6.43-a. This should also be clear from the mesh illustrated in Figure 6.43-d, which has different values for its length and depth. You have three options for determining both the length and the depth subdivision of the mesh. You can specify the actual mesh interval numerically by using the At Intervals option, or the # Of Segments into which the mesh should be divided. The third option, At Control Points, will use the actual control line intervals for the subdivision. For the Mesh Depth, there is an additional sub-option for # Of Segments, the Per Segment switch, which, when checked, will apply the number of segments specified between each pair of control lines rather than across the entire depth of the mesh. Experiment with all these options and with different values for the first two, applying the C-Mesh tool to the same object to see the resulting changes.

Figure 6.43

Different mesh length and depth settings for the same mesh.

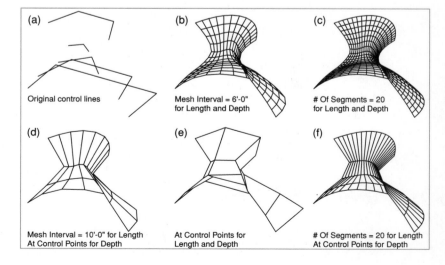

Figure 6.43 shows various length and depth variations for the same mesh shown earlier in Figure 6.41. Note that the length and depth options do not have to be the same. Notice also that a smaller mesh interval or a larger number of segments leads to a denser mesh, which will render more smoothly but take more time. So strive for the least density you can get away with.

■ There is also a Smooth option associated with both Mesh Length and Mesh Depth in the C-Mesh Options dialog, which is checked by default. Deselect it first for the length and then for the depth, and see how it affects the resultant mesh. You will find that the mesh now strictly follows the contours of the control lines rather than being "smoothened out" for a better curvature. This is useful when you draw your control lines very precisely and want your mesh to pass exactly through them.

■ Check both the Smooth boxes once again and click on the Smoothing button at the base of the dialog. This invokes the Smoothing Options dialog, which contains a variety of different curve types for specifying the curvature of the control lines when they are smoothened. These are the same curve types that you encountered in the C-Curve Options dialog in the last section. Experiment with a few different kinds of curves, both for Length and Depth, and see how they affect the curvature of the mesh.

Let us now turn to the Length Of Net and Depth Of Net options that we had skipped earlier. The control "net" here refers to the surface created by joining all the control lines, over which the mesh is then created. It is what you see in thick black lines when you are in the c-mesh edit mode. The difference between the control net and the mesh itself is illustrated in Figure 6.44.

■ Start with the two Depth Of Net options that are contrasted in Figures 6.44-a and 6.44-b. The Use Control Line Intervals option, which is checked by default, gives you as many control lines along the depth of the net as there originally are, and in the same position. Try it on a set of control lines. Then undo the operation and apply the C-Mesh tool again, but with the Use Mesh Intervals option selected this time. You will have a new set of control lines along the depth of the net which coincides with the Mesh Depth specification. This option is useful because you now have more control lines that you can manipulate for re-shaping the mesh—assuming that your mesh depth specification is greater than your original control line specification.

■ The Length Of Net options apply only to those sets of control lines which do not have the same number of points. To see how these work, create a new set of control lines, ensuring that all of them have a varying number of points. Turn on the Show Points option for the Wire Frame display mode in order to see these points. A sample set is shown in Figure 6.45-a. As before, you must also ensure that the starting points and directions of the control lines are in sync.

WORKSHOP 6

Figure 6.44

The same mesh of Figure 6.43-b in edit mode, but with different options for Depth of Net.

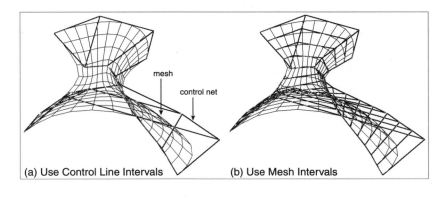

(a) Use Control Line Intervals   (b) Use Mesh Intervals

Figure 6.45

Exploring the various Length Of Net options. The Points display was turned on in the Wire Frame mode.

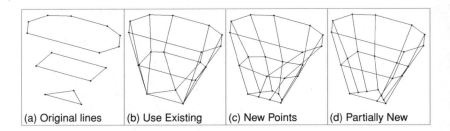

(a) Original lines   (b) Use Existing   (c) New Points   (d) Partially New

◾ In the C-Mesh Options dialog, set the At Control Points option for both Mesh Length and Mesh Depth, since it is with this option that the results of the various Length Of Net options are seen most clearly. Also set the Length Of Net to its first option, Same Points. Then prepick the control lines in the correct sequence and apply the C-Mesh tool. You will be greeted with an error message saying that the mesh cannot be generated, as the control lines do not have the same number of points. The most accurate way of generating a c-mesh is to have control lines with the same number of points; therefore, it is useful to have an option that carries out this check.

◾ Go back to the dialog and select the next Length Of Net option, Use Existing, which is the default selection. Then apply the C-Mesh tool. Watch the control net carefully in the edit mode, and after you've exited that mode, the points on the resultant mesh. You will see that only the existing points of the control lines are used, both in the net and in the resultant mesh (Figure 6.45-b).

◾ Undo the operation, go back to the dialog, and check the third option, New Points. Then reapply the C-Mesh tool. Now, new points will automatically be inserted on all the control lines until they are equal to the maximum number of points on any control line. Not only that, the points will be evenly distributed along the length of each control line, often changing its original shape by discarding its earlier points. The configuration of the mesh naturally changes as well. (Figure 6.45-c).

◾ Finally, repeat the process with the last option, Partially New. You will find that new points are inserted here as well, but the original points are retained, preserving the shape of the original control lines to a greater extent (Figure 6.45-d).

The intention of having so many options is not to confuse you needlessly, but simply to provide you with more control over creating and sculpting your meshes as desired. You will, in all likelihood, use these options extensively only if you do a lot of organic modeling. If you use meshes only sparingly, you can almost always use the default options. It is important, however, to be aware of how to do things differently when necessary.

Let us move on to look at the final set of options for the C-Mesh tool. This involves defining the type of meshed object that will be created by the operation.

◾ In the C-Mesh Options dialog, click on the Type Of Object button, located towards the base. This will open up a dialog in which you can specify the type of c-mesh object you want (Figure 6.46-a). Explore all the available options using the same set of control lines (Figure 6.46-b) and compare the results. The Open Ends option creates a simple meshed surface (Figure 6.46-c). This is the default selection, which is why all the meshes you have created so far have been surfaces. The Closed Ends option closes the two ends of the mesh. For control lines that are closed, this will create a solid object (Figure 6.46-d), whereas for control lines that are open, this will add the ends by connecting the endpoints of the first and last lines, but still remain a surface. The All Closed option works in the same manner as Closed Ends for closed control lines, but for open control lines, it adds an additional face to completely close the object, converting it to a solid. Finally, the Ring option curves the mesh along its depth by connecting the first and last control lines. For closed lines, this will again produce a solid (Figure 6.46-e) while for open lines, the mesh remains a surface object.

■ Try out also the additional options located on the right side of the Type Of C-Mesh Object dialog, which can be used to make other adjustments to the meshed object. The Round Front and Round Back options can be checked to round the ends of all types of meshed objects except Ring (Figure 6.46-f). The size of the rounding is determined by the value specified in the Ratio box. The Two Sided option can be checked to make all surface meshed objects two-sided (i.e., surface solids) rather than one-sided (i.e., surface objects). The Triangulate option can be used to create a mesh with all planar faces. The last Adjust Direction option, on by default, ensures that "inside-out meshes" are not created. It is advisable to keep this option always checked.

Figure 6.46

Exploring various types of c-mesh objects.

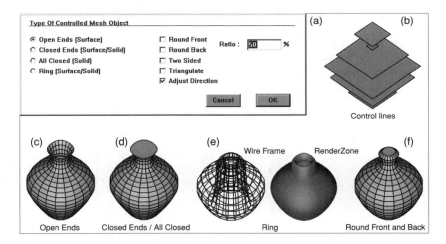

■ End this section by revisiting the Place tool with macro transformations to create multiple placements of a 2D object along a path, as you learned in Section 9.4 of Workshop 4. Turn on the Create C-Mesh option in the Place dialog, and see how the mesh that is generated is governed by the settings in the C-Mesh Options dialog. The meshed object created by the Place tool can also be edited by the C-Mesh tool, just like any regular c-mesh object.

EXERCISE 5

Nurbz and Patch Objects

In Section 2.3 of Workshop 1, you were briefly acquainted with the nurbz and patch personalities, both of which are parametric in nature. In this exercise, we will learn how to work with objects having these personalities. This includes the processes of creation as well as modification, using tools spread out across Rows 4, 7, and 10 of the modeling tool palette.

5.1   Nurbz Objects

Let us review the nurbz personality once again. A nurbz object internally has a NURBS (Non Uniform Rational B-Splines) based representation, consisting of control lines with parameters such as degree, knots, and weights from which curved surfaces can be generated. These control parameters can be modified to smoothly reshape the object.

You know from Workshop 1 that an analytic primitive can be converted to a nurbz object using various tools such as Edit Controls (M-Tool:4b,2), Edit Surface (M-Tool:4b,3), or Drop Controls (M-Tool:10b,5), all of which we will look at in detail later on in this exercise. Also in Workshop 4, you learned how to create derivative nurbz objects using the Revolve, Helix, Sweep, and Skin tools by selecting the Nurbz option in their dialogs. Let us now see how to create more *generic* objects with the nurbz personality from a set of open or closed control lines, in a manner similar to the creation of a c-mesh object. The process involves the use of the Nurbz tool, located just after the C-Mesh tool in the left column of the seventh row.

◻ On a new layer, create a set of at least three appropriately spaced open or closed control shapes, just as you created for the C-Mesh tool (Figure 6.47-a). Take the usual precaution of ensuring that their first points and directions are synchronized. After creating the shapes, prepick them in the correct sequence using the Pick tool.

◻ Select the Nurbz tool (M-Tool:7a,3) and click anywhere in the graphics window. A nurbz object will be generated from the selected controls (see Figure 6.47-b). Unlike the C-Mesh tool, you are not transported into an edit mode for reshaping the object immediately after creation. This graphical editing process is done separately by the Edit Controls and Edit Surface tools, located after the Pick tool on Row 4, which we will study in detail in a later section. For now, verify that the object you have created is actually a nurbz object by applying the Query tool (M-Tool:11b,1) to it. The Object Type in the Query dialog will be listed as Nurbz Object.

◻ Let us now explore the options associated with the Nurbz tool, accessible through its dialog (Figure 6.47-c). The values of the Length Degree and Depth Degree parameters determine the degree of curvature of the nurbz object *along* and *across* the control lines respectively. (Thus, the meaning of the terms "length" and "depth" is the same as that for a c-mesh object.) Both these values must be greater than 0 and less than the number of control shapes. The default value is 2, which is why at least 3 control shapes were needed for us to perform the operation we just did. This default value should be adequate for most modeling operations.

Figure 6.47

Creating a surface and solid nurbz object from the same set of closed control lines. The Nurbz Options dialog is also shown.

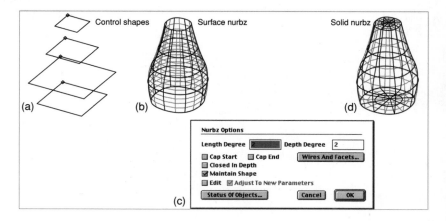

▣ If closed control shapes are used to create the nurbz object, the ends of the object are open by default, making it a surface object. The Cap Start and Cap End options can be selected to close one or both ends of the object. If both ends are capped, a solid nurbz object is created, as shown in Figure 6.47-d.

▣ The Closed In Depth option, on the other hand, applies to control shapes that are arranged in a circular fashion. When this option is selected, the last control shape will be connected to the first, producing a form like a ring.

▣ By default, the Edit option in the Nurbz Options dialog is deselected. Activating this option will invoke the familiar preview dialog when a new nurbz object is created or an existing one selected with the Nurbz tool. The Maintain Shape option also becomes relevant then. If an existing nurbz object is edited by reapplying the Nurbz tool and its degree values are increased, the shape of the object will change unless the Maintain Shape option is activated.

▣ The remaining options in the Nurbz Options dialog are all familiar ones. Adjust To New Parameters has its usual meaning, and so does Status Of Objects. The Wires And Facets button invokes the same dialog for specifying the density of the wires and facets that you explored in Section 2.4 of Workshop 1, when working with the analytic primitives. You can use the options in this dialog to control the density of the nurbz objects you are creating.

▣ The Nurbz tool can also be used to directly convert analytic primitives, as well as objects created with the Revolve, Helix, Sweep, and Skin tools to nurbz objects by simply clicking on them. Try it.

You have seen that nurbz objects can be numerically edited in a preview dialog by the Nurbz tool itself, when its Edit option is activated. The Query tool provides you with the same numerical editing option. Nurbz objects can be graphically modified using the Edit Controls and Edit Surface tools, a process we will explore a little later on in this exercise.

Now that we know how to create generic objects with the *nurbz* personality, let us look at how to create generic objects with the *patch* personality.

5.2   Patch Objects

You know from Workshop 1 that an object with the patch personality is internally represented by a set of patches. A single patch is a rectangular or triangular tile, whose sides are control lines from which curved surfaces can be generated. The patches which make up an object do not have to be all of the same size, enabling them to effectively model curved objects with widely varying surface detail.

The last four tools in the left column of the seventh row are devoted to creating and modifying objects with the patch personality. We will work with the first two of these in this section, and the remaining two in the next section.

▣ The process for creating a patch object is different from creating a c-mesh or nurbz object, in the sense that no control shapes are drawn which define the shape of the desired object. Instead, you simply apply the Patch Derive operator (M-Tool:7a,4) to a solid object or a closed surface, and it is transformed into a patch. A solid patch object will be created from the former, while a surface patch object will be created from the latter, as shown in Figure 6.48. When a surface patch is derived from the face of an object by applying the tool at the Face topological level, the original object is ghosted by default.

Figure 6.48

Applying the Patch Derive tool at the object and face topological level.

Original object　　　Solid patch　　　Surface patch

◼ The Patch Derive tool has a number of options associated with it, as you can see in its dialog (Figure 6.49-a). The density of the patch object is specified using the familiar Wires And Facets option. Two different types of patches can be created: Bezier and Coons. We will not get into the mathematical differences between these two types here—it is sufficient to know that a Bezier patch has a larger number of control points with which the surface can be manipulated using the Edit Controls tool, as we will see in Section 5.4.

◼ There are some additional options which apply to both types of patches. The Maintain 4-Sided Patches option, when activated, ensures that only 4-sided shapes are used to construct the patches. Otherwise patches will be created with 4 as well as 3-sided shapes. The Subdivide option can be used to subdivide each patch at the time of creation with lines that start from its center and end at the midpoints of its boundary segments. This subdivision effect is demonstrated in Figure 6.49-b.

◼ By default, the flatness of a surface is maintained while constructing a patch on it. You can activate the Smooth option if you want the object to be smoothened in addition to being converted to a patch. The In and Out sub-options apply the smoothing towards the inside and outside of the patch object respectively, as shown in Figure 6.49-c. The degree of smoothness is set using the accompanying slider bar. Higher smoothness values will produce more curvature around the centers and edges of the original faces than lower values.

◼ Move on to the next tool on the same row, Patch Grow. Activate this tool, make sure that the topological level is set to Object, and click on an existing surface patch object like the one shown in Figure 6.50-b. It is important for the selected patch to have at least one open edge, i.e., an edge that is not connected to another patch. The effect of the operation will be the construction of new patches on every *open* edge of the existing patch, with dimensions that match the corresponding edges.

Figure 6.49

Exploring the options of the Patch Derive tool.

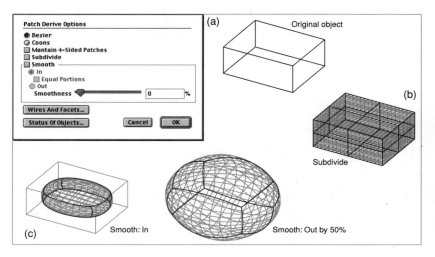

Figure 6.50

Exploring the options of the Patch Grow tool on a patch inclined with respect to the XY plane.

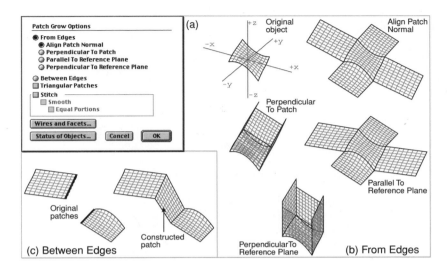

■ Explore the options in the dialog of the Patch Grow tool (Figure 6.50-a). The default option is From Edges, under which four different types of alignments are possible. All these are demonstrated in Figure 6.50-b, derived from the same patch object. Go ahead and explore each one of them—the difference should be quite obvious. The From Edges patch grow method can also be applied with the topological level set to Face or Segment. When a face is selected, a new patch is constructed using every open edge of the face. For a segment, the patch is constructed only if the segment is an open edge.

■ The second patch grow method, Between Edges, can only be applied at the Segment topological level. It is used to construct patches *between* sets of two, three, or four segments, as shown in Figure 6.50-c. If the number of edges is three or four, the edges need to have coincident endpoints, otherwise the operation cannot be performed.

■ The remaining Patch Grow options are fairly straightforward. The Triangular Patches option creates 3-sided rather than 4-sided patches. The Stitch option stitches the new patches to the existing patch selected for the operation, connecting them into one object rather than letting them remain as separate entities. The Smooth sub-option under Stitch smoothes out the edges of the stitch. Finally, there are the usual Wires And Facets and Status Of Objects buttons, as for the Patch Derive tool.

5.3   Dividing and Attaching Patches

■ Activate the Patch Divide tool (M-Tool:7a,6) and apply it to a patch object with the topological level set to Object. You will find that each patch of the object gets subdivided into smaller patches (see Figure 6.51). This subdivision can be useful when the object has to be graphically edited—a process we shall soon look at—as it increases the number of control points and the density of the surface. The greater the subdivision, the smoother the reshaping of the object. The Patch Divide tool can be repeatedly applied to the same object to increase the number of subdivisions.

■ You can also apply this tool at the face or segment level by setting the appropriate topological level. Try it. For a selected face, only that face will be subdivided, whereas for a selected segment, the two faces adjacent to that segment will be subdivided (Figure 6.51)

Figure 6.51

Using the Patch Divide tool at the object, face, and segment levels.

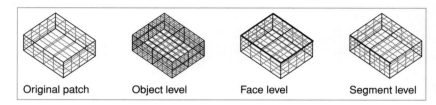

Original patch   Object level   Face level   Segment level

▪ The Patch Divide tool has a small number of associated options, which we can quickly go over. By default, an existing patch is subdivided into 2 parts along both directions. The number of subdivisions can be changed to a higher value, if a greater degree of subdivision is required in one application of the tool. The Lock Edge Points option locks the control points on both sides of the edges that are subdivided, thereby preventing them from being moved when the object is graphically modified. This helps avoid fractures along the shared edges of a patch object. The last option, Undivide Patch, can be activated to remove the subdivisions in a previously subdivided patch object or face.

▪ Move on to the next tool on the same row, Patch Attach. The function of this tool is to attach an open edge of one patch to the open edge of another patch. It is thus somewhat similar to the Attach tool (M-Tool:12b,1) but has more capabilities that are relevant to the patch objects on which it operates. For instance, the "source" patch object can get reshaped like a piece of paper in the process of being attached to the "destination" patch object, as shown in Figure 6.52. Try it. Keep in mind that the two open edges can belong to the same or to different objects.

▪ Let us now look at the options of the Patch Attach tool that are available in its dialog (Figure 6.52-a). There are four main operations possible, of which Attach is the default. Within the Attach mode, the Move Edge sub-option is active by default. This causes the source edge to be moved and scaled to correspond with the dimensions of the destination edge. The second sub-option, Move Patch, causes the patch face of the source edge to be moved to the location of the destination edge. The third sub-option, Move Object, causes the entire object to be moved and attached to the destination edge. All three sub-options are illustrated in Figure 6.52-b.

Figure 6.52

Using the Patch Attach tool in the Attach mode with each of its three sub-options. The dialog of the tool is also shown.

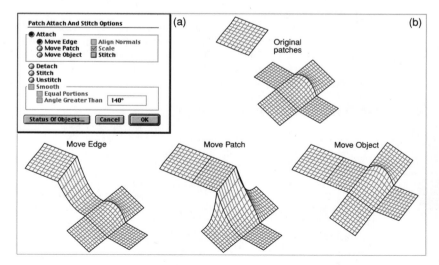

▣ For the Attach operation, there are three additional options in the form of checkboxes that are applicable to all these sub-options. All three are off by default. The Align Normals option, when activated, performs the operation in such a way that the normals of the source and destination patches get aligned. The Scale option, which is active only for the Move Patch and Move Object sub-options, is used to scale the source edge based on the dimensions of the destination edge. And finally, the Stitch option is used to unite the two patches involved in the operation into one object. When necessary, it also modifies the geometry of the source edge according to the geometry of the destination edge in order to maintain continuity between the stitched patches.

▣ Let us quickly look at the other three modes of the Patch Attach tool. The Detach operation is the reverse of the Attach operation—it separates all the patches of an object into separate objects. When applied at the face level, it detaches only the selected face or faces from the original object. The Stitch option can be used to unite two patch edges that are lined up and coincident into one edge. The last option, Unstitch, performs a partial detachment, breaking up stitched edges but making the control points at their ends remain coincident. Explore each one of these modes, applying them to various patch objects.

5.4 Editing Controls and Surfaces

In Section 4.7 of Workshop 2, you used both the Edit Controls and Edit Surface tools, located after the Pick tool in the right column of Row 4, to graphically edit the parameters of analytic primitives. However, these changes were limited only to the options afforded by the primitive creation dialogs. Thus, the only settings that can be graphically modified for a primitive sphere are those that are available in the Sphere tool dialog to begin with, and they apply to the object as a whole. What if you want to reshape, for instance, only a portion of the sphere? For this, the sphere needs to be converted to a nurbz or patch object and then graphically manipulated using the same Edit Controls and Edit Surface tools. Let us actually go about doing this.

▣ Create a primitive sphere using the Sphere tool (M-Tool:1a,4) and make an additional copy of it. We will convert one of these spheres into a nurbz object and the other into a patch object. You already know from the previous sections that you can use the Nurbz and Patch Derive tools to perform this conversion. Let us, however, use another method.

▣ Select the Edit Controls tool (M-Tool:4b,2) and invoke its dialog (Figure 6.53-a). Activate the Convert To option for Parametric Primitives, and let Nurbz Objects remain the selected sub-option. Now apply the tool to one of the spheres. It will get converted to a nurbz object. At the same time, it is taken into a graphical edit mode, where the nurbz controls are displayed in the form of tiny boxes (Figure 6.53-b).

▣ Now modify portions of the sphere by manipulating these controls. A control is selected by clicking on it. Multiple controls can be selected by clicking on them individually while holding down the Shift key, or by holding the mouse down and enclosing them in a frame. (The procedure is similar to how multiple entities are selected using the Pick tool.) All the selected controls are highlighted in the selection color. The shape of the object can now be changed by clicking on one of the selected controls and moving the mouse. All the selected controls get repositioned following the mouse movement, reshaping the object in the process (see Figure 6.53-c). Keep in mind that the setting of the Perpendicular Lock (W-Tool:2,1) will determine whether the movement takes place along the active plane or perpendicular to it.

▣ To deselect picked controls, click on an area of the window with no controls. A second click (after deselecting all controls) will terminate the editing operation. Pressing the Esc key will also have the same effect.

Figure 6.53

Converting two primitive spheres to nurbz and patch objects, and editing their controls to modify their shape. The dialog of the Edit Controls tool is also shown.

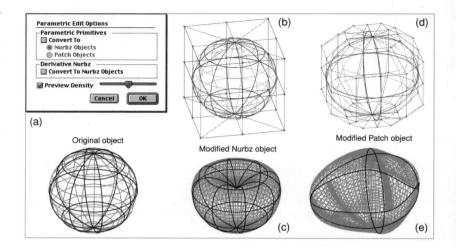

(a)

Original object

(b)

(d)

Modified Nurbz object

Modified Patch object

(c)

(e)

■ Now go back to the dialog of the Edit Controls tool and select the Patch Objects sub-option under the Convert To option. Apply the tool to the other primitive sphere. It will get converted to a patch object, and enter the graphical edit mode where its controls are displayed (Figure 6.53-d). You can see that these are distinctly different from the controls of the nurbz sphere. Despite having different controls, the reshaping of the patch object proceeds in a similar fashion. Try it out. Figure 6.53-e shows one such shape modification.

■ The Edit Controls tool also has a number of other options for reshaping nurbz and patch objects. To access these options, first select the object with the tool, so that its controls are displayed (as in Figures 6.53-b and 6.53-d). Then click anywhere in the modeling window while holding down the option key (Mac) or Ctrl+Shift keys (PC). This invokes the Controls Edit menu at the click point, which is slightly different depending upon whether the selected object is a nurbz or patch object. The menus for both types of objects are shown in Figure 6.54.

■ Let us first look at the options that are common to both menus. The first three options determine how the cursor is mapped when the object is being edited with the Edit Controls tool. The default Reference Plane option, as obvious from its name, maps the cursor to the current reference plane. The Local Normal option maps the cursor to the normal of the control that is nearest to where the mouse is clicked. And finally, the Average Normal option maps the cursor to the average normal of the selected controls.

■ The Move, Rotate, Scale, and Uniform Scale options determine the type of transformation that is applied to the selected controls when they are manipulated with the mouse. The default is Move, as you have seen. Try out the other three transformations as well.

■ A patch object has eight additional editing options which are not available for a nurbz object. These options are activated only when one or more controls of the object are selected; otherwise, they are grayed out. Go ahead and highlight some of the controls of the sphere with the patch personality, then try out all these options. The Locked option, when checked, locks the selected controls and prevents them from being moved. To unlock the controls, simply select this option again. The Corner option causes the selected controls to lose any smoothing that may have been assigned to them. The remaining six options apply various kinds of smoothing at the selected controls. Try out all of them and see how they differ.

Figure 6.54

The Controls Edit menu, for a nurbz object and for a patch object.

 Nurbz object

 Patch object

 ▣ Let us now turn to the **Edit Surface** tool, located immediately after the **Edit Controls** tool. You have applied this tool to an analytic primitive in Workshop 2. Go ahead and apply it to the nurbz as well as the patch object. You will find that you can now manipulate the object directly by clicking on its surface and moving the mouse in the desired direction. This might seem a more intuitive method of editing than having to activate and move individual controls.

▣ If while using the **Edit Surface** tool, you click in the graphics window while holding down the option key (Mac) or Ctrl+Shift keys (PC), a menu is invoked in a similar fashion to what you saw for the **Edit Controls** tool. However, this **Surface Edit** menu—which is the same for both nurbz and patch objects—contains just two items: **Reference Plane** and **Surface Normal**. The first maps the cursor to the current reference plane, while the second option maps the cursor to the surface normal at the click point.

▣ In all other respects, the **Edit Surface** tool is identical to the **Edit Controls** tool. It has the same dialog associated with it that you saw in Figure 6.53-a, and can thus be used to convert analytic primitives to nurbz or patch objects. Both tools can also be used to convert *derivative nurbz* objects—which, as you will recall, are nurbz objects created with the **Revolve**, **Helix**, **Sweep**, and **Skin** tools—to regular nurbz objects by selecting that option in the dialog. These objects will then be edited by manipulating their controls and surfaces rather than their creation parameters.

5.5   Dropping Controls

We will end this exercise by looking at a very simple tool—Drop Controls—that is relevant to all the various object personalities.

Figure 6.55

The conversion capabilities provided by the Drop Controls tool.

▣ Select the **Drop Controls** tool (M-Tool:10b,5) and invoke its dialog (Figure 6.55). You can apply this tool to an analytic primitive to convert it to a facetted, nurbz, or patch object, by selecting the appropriate option. You can also apply it to a derivative nurbz object created by the Revolve, Helix, Sweep, and Skin tools to convert it to a facetted object, or to a regular nurbz object. All of the conversion abilities provided by the Drop Controls tool also come with the other tools you have explored in this exercise, except the conversion to facetted objects.

Cutting and Gluing Meshes

The ability to create and modify individual meshed objects, as you have done so far, might not always be sufficient for your modeling purposes. You might occasionally need to unite two or more meshed objects, subtract one from the other, split two of them against each other, and so on. In short, you might need to perform the same kind of boolean operations on meshed objects that you performed on "regular" unmeshed objects using the Union, Intersection, Difference, and Split tools in Workshop 1. Since most meshed objects have non-planar faces, you cannot apply the regular boolean tools to them. This is why form•Z provides you with a special tool, the Trim/Split operator, to carry out boolean operations on such objects.

6.1   Trimming and Splitting Objects

■ On a new layer, create two meshed objects with non-planar faces, using the C-Mesh tool, or the Smooth Mesh tool with the Smooth option selected. You can also apply the Mesh tool to an unmeshed object and then deform or displace it in some manner. After creating the objects, position them so that they intersect each other. If the line of intersection is open, it should cut the surface of one object from end to end, otherwise the Trim/Split tool will not work. If there are two intersecting solids, as shown in Figure 6.56-a, the line of intersection will be closed, so the Trim/Split tool will always work.

■ Try applying any of the four regular boolean tools—Union, Intersection, Difference, and Split—on these intersecting objects. As expected, you will be greeted with an error message telling you that the boolean operation could not be carried out because the objects have non-planar faces. You can, of course, Triangulate the objects first, but after all, it *is* an additional step, and you cannot "un-triangulate" the objects after the boolean tool has been applied. Also, the process of triangulation does introduce additional faces in an object, increasing its size—not physically, but in terms of the stored information needed to describe it—and slowing down operations. Thus, using the Triangulate tool might not always be desirable.

■ Select the Trim/Split tool (M-Tool:8a,5) and invoke its dialog (Figure 6.56-b). It contains a number of options arranged in a matrix-like fashion. The default selection is Trim under the First Object column, indicating that a trimming operation will be applied to the first of the two objects selected by the tool.

■ Exit the dialog and apply the tool to your two meshed objects, following the instructions in the Prompts palette. Select the larger object first, and do so by clicking on that part of it which is to be retained. As a result of the operation, the second object will disappear, leaving behind the trimmed portion of the first object. (Figure 6.56-c).

Figure 6.56

Trimming an object with the Trim/Split tool. The tool dialog is also shown.

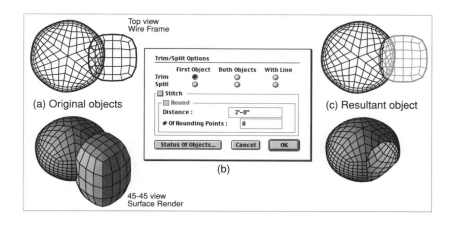

Top view
Wire Frame

Trim/Split Options

	First Object	**Both Objects**	**With Line**
Trim	●	○	○
Split	○	○	○

☐ Stitch
☐ Round
Distance : 2'-0"
Of Rounding Points : 8

[Status Of Objects...] [Cancel] [OK]

(a) Original objects

(b)

(c) Resultant object

45-45 view
Surface Render

For all the Trim/Split operators, the part of the object you click on to select it will affect the result of the operation.

■ The operation you just performed is equivalent to what the Difference tool does for regular objects, except that this leaves a "hole" in the object making its insides visible. Thus, a solid object will get converted to a surface object by this operation. This might not be desirable, in which case you should select the Stitch option in the dialog of the Trim/Split tool. Undo and reapply the tool in this mode, and you will find that not only is the second object subtracted from the first, it also "stitches" up the resulting hole that is created. Which part of the second object gets stitched depends upon where you click on it to select it, so do this carefully based on the result you want. Change to the front or side views, if necessary, to make the selection correctly. As you can see from Figure 6.57, different results are possible—equivalent to the Union, Difference, and Intersection operations—depending upon how both the objects are selected.

■ Get back to the Trim/Split dialog and notice that the Stitch option has a Round sub-option. By selecting this, you can give a rounding effect to the stitch. You can also specify the distance and the resolution of the rounding. Activate this option and experiment with different rounding values for the same operation.

Figure 6.57

Activating the Stitch option for a Trim operation. Different results are obtained, depending upon where the two objects are selected.

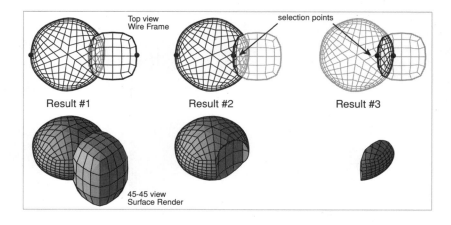

Top view
Wire Frame

selection points

Result #1

Result #2

Result #3

45-45 view
Surface Render

WORKSHOP 6

■   Next, select the Split mode, still under the First Object column, in the dialog of the Trim/Split tool. Undo the previous operation and reapply the tool, and you will get the first object split into two parts by the second object. Move the resulting pieces apart to see how the operation actually worked.

■   In a similar fashion, explore both operators—Trim and Split—for the Both Objects mode as well. Move parts of meshes around to see the results better when you are working in this mode. These are straightforward operations and very similar to their counterparts in the First Object mode.

6.2   Trimming with Lines

It might seem as though the Trim/Split tool can only be applied to meshed objects with non-planar faces. However, try and apply it to regular unmeshed objects having planar faces, and you will find that you can! The only condition is that the objects should not have overlapping faces that lie on the same plane, a condition easy enough to fulfil. But since you have the regular boolean tools for working with these objects, it is advisable to use them rather than the Trim/Split tool. There is, however, one exception to this rule, which has to do with the last Trim/Split mode, intriguingly called With Line. This is a fascinating concept in which you can use simple 2D shapes to perform boolean operations on all kinds of objects.

■   On a new layer, create a meshed solid and a regular solid on the XY plane, positioned next to each other. Then switch to the Front view and draw two open shapes using the 2D Surface Object mode, in such a way that each of the two solids is completely cut through by a 2D shape (see Figure 6.58-a).

■   Invoke the dialog of the Trim/Split tool and select the Trim option under the With Line column. Also activate the Stitch option. Exit the dialog and follow the instructions in the Prompts palette. Select one of the solid objects first, and then the 2D shape which intersects it as the trimming line, taking care to remain in the Front view. You will find that your solid object has been trimmed along the line of the 2D shape, retaining the portion you clicked on while selecting it. The direction of the cut is perpendicular to the active plane, which is ZX in Front view. In a Wire Frame display with the Hide Ghosted option deselected, you should be able to see this clearly. Verify the result by switching to a non-planar view and a paint display (Figure 6.58-b). Then repeat the operation for the other object-line pair.

Figure 6.58

Applying the Trim operation in the With Line mode. The Stitch option was also activated.

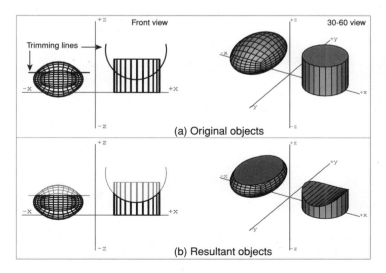

(a) Original objects

(b) Resultant objects

As you can see, this is an amazingly simple way to perform boolean operations on all kinds of objects. It is indispensable for meshed objects, of course, but is also useful for regular objects, as shown in Figure 6.58. Keep in mind that the Section tool (M-Tool:8a,8) can be used to cut a regular object with planar faces, but it can only do so along a straight line, not along a curve or any other non-linear shape. For that, the With Line option of the Trim/Split tool is the most convenient operator.

■ Explore the With Line mode some more, trying out the Split option as well. The Stitch option can be used to connect the split parts back together, etching the lines of intersection on the surface of the object. Remember that the cutting action will always be executed with respect to the active reference plane, i.e., it is the projection of the 2D shape on the plane that is actually making the cut. You will get unexpected results if a different plane is active instead of the one you intended to be. That is why it is always best to execute the operation in the same planar view as the one in which you draw the 2D cutting shape.

6.3 Deriving Lines of Intersection

■ Proceed to select the next tool on Row 8, Line Of Intersection (M-Tool:8a,6). As evident from its name, this simply gives you the line of intersection of any two intersecting objects. These can be any kind of objects—meshed or regular. Try it out on some object pairs.

■ Figure 6.59 shows a simple application of this option. From two intersecting objects (a), a trimmed portion of one object was derived using the Trim option of the Trim/Split tool (b). The Status Of Objects was set to Keep, so as to retain the original objects, whose line of intersection was then derived with the Status Of Objects set back to Ghost (c). The Convergence tool was applied to the intersection shape, converting it to a 3D object (d). Finally, using Endpoint snap and the Move tool, the converged object was positioned on top of the trimmed half of the first object, where it is an exact fit (e).

Figure 6.59

Demonstrating the use of the Line Of Intersection tool.

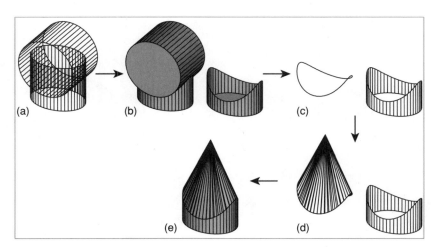

6.4 Stitching Surface Objects

The next tool in the left column of Row 8, Stitch, allows you to create a number of surfaces individually and then "stitch" them together to create a solid object. Of course, you have to ensure that the ends of

WORKSHOP 6

the surfaces indeed all match up and there are no gaps anywhere. The surfaces can be meshed or unmeshed closed shapes. This is useful when the individual surfaces of an object are meaningful in their own right and need to be carefully and precisely shaped, which is difficult to achieve when the object itself is the focus of creation and is shaped first. Let us carry out one such Stitch operation.

◼ Create a square using the 2D Surface Object mode. Mesh it and then apply a mesh move operation to it, but in such a way that its boundary is not disturbed, i.e., it should still be a square (Figure 6.60-a). Then, using the Rotate and Mirror tools in a Copy mode, make copies of this meshed surface until you have all six sides of a cube touching each other, with the same side facing outwards (see Figures 6.60-b and 6.60-c). It is important that the edges of adjacent faces should be completely coincident.

◼ Select all these six meshed surfaces with the Pick tool. Then activate the Stitch tool (M-Tool:8a,7) and click anywhere in the graphics window. The stitching operation will be applied, one surface at a time. As soon as the last surface is stitched and the object is closed, it automatically gets converted to a solid.

◼ To verify that the object is indeed a solid and not "hollow" inside, use the Query tool to check the status of the object. It should say Solid; if it continues to say Meshed Surface, it means that the surfaces were not positioned correctly. You can also triangulate the object and then apply the Section tool to it, as shown in Figure 6.60-d. The results will clearly indicate that the object is a solid.

◼ Invoke the dialog of the Stitch tool to examine its options. The default option is Stitch Multiple Parts, which is the operation you just applied. The alternate option, Stitch Object Parts, can be used to connect open ends within a single object. For both types of operations, the Round option can additionally be selected, allowing you to give a rounding effect to the stitched line. Try it.

With this, we come to the end of the exercises for this workshop. You should have become a "master of the mesh" by now. You will have the opportunity to test your newly acquired skills in mesh modeling in the workshop assignment, coming up next.

Figure 6.60

Using the Stitch tool to stitch six surfaces into a solid, and verifying the result with the Section tool.

ASSIGNMENT
6

A Curved Roof Structure for a Stadium

■ *Model a roof covering for the stadium shown below. You need not go into full detail; it will be sufficient to model the basic components of the structure, conveying a good idea of its configuration and load distribution.*

The steps for modeling the roof structure shown here will now be demonstrated step by step. You can refer to the form•Z files for each step of the assignment in the accompanying CD-ROM, under the folder Assignments > Workshop 6. A rendered image of the model is in the Assignment6.tif file in the same location.

Setup

Open a new form•Z project. In the Working Units dialog, set Unit Type to English, Base Unit to Feet, Numeric Accuracy to 6", and Angle Accuracy to 1°. In the Window Setup dialog, change the module size to 10'-0" with 2 subdivisions. The default Display Scale of 1/32" = 1'-0" is fine. As usual, you can also turn off the display of the default light in the Lights palette.

Step 1

In this exercise, only the roof of the stadium will be modeled, since it illustrates the use of some of the tools covered in this workshop. The body of the stadium is relatively straightforward and can be modeled with the basic modeling tools covered in the earlier workshops. You can copy the stadium body to your project from the "stadium-body.fmz" file, located in the Assignments > Workshop 6 folder on the accompanying CD-ROM. The layer stadium-body containing these objects will be added to your project as well.

◁ Step 2

We need a base slab to situate the body as well as the roof of the stadium. Create a block with absolute coordinates of [-200,-100,0] and [200,280,0], and height [-1]. Rename the layer on which this is created as base plane. Then make the stadium-body layer invisible so that it does not interfere with the modeling of the roof.

Step 3

We will start by modeling the twin central supports located on one side of the roof. (We will first model all the supports on one side and then simply use the Mirror tool in a Copy mode to make copies for the other side.) Activate a new layer, central support, and turn off the base plane layer. Use the Vector Lines tool in 2D Surface Object mode to draw a closed shape at the origin with the following coordinates:

      Pt #1: [0, -48, 0] absolute
      Pt #2: [0, 0, 0] absolute
      Pt #3: [0, 0, 118] absolute
      Pt #4: [0, -4, 0] relative
      Pt #5: [c] or triple-click to close

Extrude this 2D shape by a distance of 1' perpendicular to the surface. Create a copy of it and space out both objects so that they are located 7' apart, centered on either side of the origin as shown.

◁ Step 4

The next step is to model the curved shape cutting through these supports. Switch to the Right view. Use the Vector Lines tool to create an approximate 2D open shape following the shape of the support, starting and ending at its base. Then use the C-Curve tool to convert it to a smoothly curved shape as shown. You can stick with the default curve settings of the C-Curve tool. Make sure that the start and end points of the new curve are still at the same level as the base of the support.

Step 5

Switch back to a non-planar view and apply the 3D Enclosure tool to this curve to extrude it, again in a direction perpendicular to the surface. The enclosure should have the default width of 1'. The extrusion height should be greater than the total width of the twin supports—a value of about 15' should be fine. After the shape has been extruded, position it midway between the supports so that it intersects both of them.

Step 6

Use the Join tool to join the two separate volumes of the twin supports into one object. Then select the Split tool and set Status Of Objects for it to Keep. Use the default One Way mode to split the joined volume with the curved 3D enclosure you just created.

Delete the original joined support as well as all its split portions until you are left with just the outer portions. Do not delete the curved 3D enclosure since we still need that.

Step 7

Switch to the Top view and zoom in close to the supports. Draw two lines coinciding with the outside ends of the supports; these will be used to trim the parts of the curved enclosure that extend beyond the supports. Use the Trim/Split tool with the mode set to Trim under With Line and the Stitch option activated for carrying out this task.

You should be left with the supports having the hole going through them and the curved extrusion spanning the hole. Unite all these separate parts into one object using the Union tool. This will be referred to as the "central support."

◀ **Step 8**

Use the Mirror tool in a Copy mode to create a mirror image of the central support, located at a distance of 176' along the Y axis from the original.

We will now model the cabled truss spanning across these two central supports. Switch to the Right view. Invoke the Object Snaps dialog and activate the Project Onto Reference Plane option under Projection Views. Then use Endpoint snap to draw a 2D horizontal line connecting the inner base points of the two supports. Move it vertically by a distance of 80'. Draw another line of length 5' starting from the midpoint of this line, oriented in the Z direction.

Select either of the last two Arc tools located in Row 3 and activate the option, By Max Sides Of Segments, in its dialog. Change the segment length to 8'-0". Then draw an arc whose endpoints coincide with the top of the central supports and whose midpoint touches the top of the 5' line.

Step 9

Using the 8' segment interval of the arc, the Ortho direction snap, and the Endpoint and Segment object snaps, draw a sequence of vertical lines connecting the arc and the horizontal line. Do it for one side of the central line and mirror them to the other side. You should still be in the Right view.

◀ **Step 10**

Now switch to a non-planar view. All the 2D lines you just drew should be in the same vertical plane coincident with the Y axis, since the Project Onto Reference Plane option was activated for object snapping. Change the active reference plane to YZ. Use the 3D Enclosure tool, with the wall width set to 1'-0", to extrude the horizontal line by a distance of 1' in the +X direction. Change the wall width to 6", set the Heights menu to a custom value of 6", and extrude all the vertical lines in the same manner.

To give a similar thickness and height to the arc, it is better to use the Sweep tool rather than the 3D Enclosure tool. Draw a 1' by 1' square and sweep it along the arc. Then move the resultant object by 6" in the +X direction so that it is aligned with the horizontal band. Also move all the vertical line extrusions by 3" in the same direction, so that they are centered between the other two components of the cabled truss. Finally, use the Union tool to combine all the individual components of this truss into a single object. Move it to a new layer called central truss.

Step 11

Switch to the Top view. Use the Move tool in a Copy mode, with Ortho and Endpoint snaps activated, to make two copies of the truss on either side of the original, touching the two columns of the central support. Delete the original after verifying in a non-planar view that the copies have been correctly positioned.

Use the Extend and Move tools to flush the ends of the central supports and the truss where they meet at the top.

Step 12

We have to complete the central truss by creating 6" by 6" horizontal bands connecting the two separate trusses at their base. First, create one band in Top view on the XY plane, aligned with one of the vertical bands of the truss, and move it to the required height. Then use the Move tool in a Copy mode to create a copy of the horizontal band, aligned with every other vertical band. Use Endpoint snapping for accuracy. The objective is to have the horizontal band spacing of the truss match its vertical band spacing.

Step 13

We will now proceed to model the "middle" support located midway between the central support and the end support. There are two such supports, located on either side of the central support. We will model one on the +X side and make a copy of it for the opposite side.

Ghost the central support and central truss layers. Activate a new layer called middle support and switch to the Right view. Use the last Arc tool on Row 3 in 2D Surface Object mode to draw an arc whose endpoints coincide with the outer ends of the base of the central supports, and whose midpoint lies 100' above the base plane in the +Z direction. The resolution of the arc should still be set to a segment length of 8'-0".

Switch to a non-planar view. The arc should be coincident with the Y axis because the object snapping option is still set to Project Onto Reference Plane. Move it by a distance of 55' in the +X direction.

Step 14

Make a copy of the arc at a distance of 20' in the +X direction.

Select the **3D Enclosure** tool and set the **Enclosure Wall Width** in its dialog to 1'-6". Switch to the YZ reference plane and extrude the first arc by a distance of 40' in the +X direction.

Step 15

Switch to the **Top** view. Draw a line parallel to the Y axis, located 16' inside from the left end of the arched enclosure. Use the midpoint of this line to draw a 2D arc spanning the endpoints of the extruded arc as shown. Make a copy of it 1' away in the +X direction.

Use the **Trim/Split** tool in the **With Line** mode twice to trim the extruded arc with the 2D arcs you just created. Be careful to select the extrusion in the appropriate spot—what is required is the 1' thick slice of the extrusion between the two arcs. Then use the **Mirror** tool in a **Copy** mode to make a mirror image of it about the central 2D arc. You can use the extremities of the ghosted extrusion as a guide for the operation.

Step 16

Make the **central support** and **central truss** layers completely invisible now; they will no longer be needed as a reference. Also delete the straight line you created for drawing the arc in the last step. Use the **Unghost** tool to unghost the inner 2D arc created on the XY plane. Hide the display of ghosted objects for now.

Create a strut of dimensions 60' by 1' by 6" on the XY plane and move it so that it sits on top of the highest point of the 2D arc that runs between the two arched slices. Use the **Move** tool in a **Copy** mode to make copies of it at each point of the arc on one side, except the last two. Then mirror them to the other side. Ideally, the **Rotate** tool should be used, but this requires locating the center of the arc to specify as the center of rotation; so we are using the **Move** tool for a quick approximation.

Step 17

Select all the struts and apply the Join tool to them. Make a mirror copy of the 2D arc on the XY plane (which you retrieved using the Unghost tool in the last step) about the central axis of the support.

Use the Trim/Split tool in the With Line mode again to trim the ends of the joined volume with the two arcs. Make sure the reference plane is set to XY if you are in a non-planar view, so that the trimming action happens in the Z direction. If you encounter any error messages and the tool does not work as expected, separate the joined struts with the Separate tool and apply the Trim/Split tool to each one of them individually. Then delete the 2D arc running through the center of the support.

◀ Step 18

All the middle support now needs is a triangular buttress at each end. Create a block of dimensions 40' by 4'-6" and a height of 8' at one end of the support. Use the Extend tool to trim its sides against those of the support as shown.

Create a mirror copy of the buttress for the other end. Then use the Union tool to unite the buttresses with the arched supports. This completes the middle support. Simple create a copy of it at a distance of 150' in the –X direction to position it on the other side of the central support.

Step 19

It is time to move on to the end support which is relatively simpler than the other supports. Again, we will model the one on the +X side of the central support first, then make a copy of it for the opposite side. Activate a new layer, end support, and turn off the visibility of all the other layers. Using the Vector Lines tool in 2D Surface Object mode to create a closed 2D shape with the following coordinates:

 Pt #1: [182, 0, 0] absolute
 Pt #2: [-25, 0, 0] relative
 Pt #3: [0, 0, 63] relative
 Pt #4: [5, 0, 0] relative
 Pt #5: [c] for close

After drawing the shape, switch to the ZX plane and extrude it in the –Y direction by a distance of 3'. Make a mirror copy of this extrusion in the +Y direction, leaving a gap of 176' between the two extrusions.

Step 20

Create a block of 5' width and 3' depth running between the two supports. Unite all three entities into one object.

Switch to the Front view, and create a 2D curve cutting through the triangular body of the support. Then apply the Trim/Split tool in the With Line mode to carve this area out of the support.

Finally, make a mirror copy of the support in the –X direction, at the same distance from the Y axis as the original. There should be a gap of 314' between the two supports. With this step, the two end supports are also complete.

Step 21

All that remains is to model the meshed roof covering spanning across all the supports. This is actually divided into four parts: an identical pair spanning the end and middle supports, and a similar pair spanning the middle and central supports. As usual, we will model the spans on one side of the central support and copy them to the other side.

Let us start with the roof covering spanning the end and middle support. Activate a new layer, roof1. Ghost the end support and middle support layers and turn off all the others. Switch to the Right view and draw three control lines as shown. They will be used to generate a c-mesh, so make sure their directions are in sync.

Step 22

Switch to a non-planar view, turn on the Ortho direction snap, and move the control lines along the X axis as shown. The straight line should coincide with the left side of the end support, the large arc with the right side of the middle support, and the smaller arc should be positioned approximately midway between the first two.

Step 23

Invoke the dialog of the C-Mesh tool and set the mesh length and depth to 20 segments. Prepick the control lines in the right sequence and apply the C-Mesh tool. A meshed surface following the shape and location of the control lines will be created.

We need to give a 2" thickness to the meshed surface for which we will use the Parallel tool. However, to specify such a small value, the Numeric Accuracy in the Working Units dialog has to be temporarily decreased. Set this value to 1". Then invoke the dialog of the Parallel tool, set the option to Double Parallel with the Center option, and change all the offset values to 1". Then apply this tool to the meshed surface and it will acquire a thickness of 2". Set the Numeric Accuracy back to 6" after this is done.

◁ Step 24

This meshed covering correctly connects to the end support but needs to be trimmed where it overlaps with the middle support. To do this, retrieve the ghosted arc that you used in Step 17 for trimming the struts of the middle support on the right side, using the Unghost tool.

After retrieving the arc, move it by 1' in the +X direction so that it is aligned with the other side of the middle support. Then trim the meshed object with it using the Trim/Split tool. Check to see that it is correctly trimmed against the middle support.

Finally, make a mirror copy of this meshed covering for the other pair of middle and end supports.

Step 25

Let us move on to the second roof covering spanning the middle and central supports. This also happens to be the last object we have to model. Activate a new roof2 layer, ghost the middle support and central support layers, and turn off all the other layers. As you did for roof1 in Step 21, create three control lines in the Right view as shown. These lines must start and end at the same Y coordinate values as the control lines you created for roof1.

Step 26

Position the control lines appropriately and generate the mesh using the same parameters you used for roof1. As in Step 23, use the **Parallel** tool to give a 2" thickness to the meshed surface after you have created it. You will again have to reduce the **Numeric Accuracy** value to 1" to be able to do this. Change it back to 6" after you are done.

Step 27

The meshed roof needs to be trimmed against the middle support, just like the earlier roof. As you did in Step 24, retrieve the ghosted arc that was used for trimming the struts of the middle support on the left side, and move it by 1' in the –X direction. Use it to trim the meshed roof so that it properly connects to the middle support.

As before, make a mirror copy of it for the other side of the central support.

Step 28

With that, your model is complete. Turn all the layers on and color the objects appropriately. Your stadium now has a structurally stable and exciting roof over its head!

Ending with More

This workshop marks the last step of our long and exciting foray into the 3D world of form•Z. Most of the "difficult" tools and operations have already been covered, so you can look forward to a relatively easy time as you make your way through this workshop.

Exercise 1 will introduce you to the amazing realm of 3D text, with which you can populate your models. Then, you will learn to create and use "symbols," or object libraries as they are more commonly referred to. You will venture further into the realm of organic modeling using the sophisticated capabilities of metaformz. Exercise 4 will show you how the Panoramic view type can be used to generate QuickTime VR movies. You will conclude the workshop by learning how to generate and play animation sequences of your modeling world.

Writing in 3D

Very often, you might need to label or annotate different parts of your model. The most obvious solution to this problem, one that you may already have implemented, is to save a rendering of the model as an image file and then take it to any other drawing, painting, or image-editing program to add the text.

There is, however, another option. You can create this text as a 3D object within the modeling environment of form•Z itself, where it will be treated just like any other object and can be moved, scaled, copied, rendered, and so on. At times, you could use such 3D text with the intention of enhancing the overall visual quality and graphic design content of the image. At other times, such text objects could become the focal points of your model, for instance, in the design of logos, banners, book covers such as the one for this book, and so on. In this exercise, you will see how to create and manipulate various kinds of text objects.

1.1 Placing Text

◾ Open a new form•Z project. We will start putting text in it right away. Select the Place Text tool (M-Tool:9a,1) and watch the instructions in the Prompts palette. You will be asked to specify the *text origin*, or where the text should be placed. Select or key in [0,0,0]—selecting the origin will give you a good reference point for the text placement. After this, the program takes a few seconds to load various kinds of fonts. (This will be done only once during a form•Z session.) You are then presented with the 3D Text Editor dialog shown in Figure 7.1-a.

◾ In this dialog, you can write over the highlighted <Text> with the actual text you want. For multiple lines of text, use the return (Mac) or Enter (PC) keys. Go easy, however, on too much text, since these objects do take up space and slow down processing. There are a lot of other options in the dialog that determine the size and placement of the text object, and we will be studying them in due course. For now, simply change the text and click OK to exit the dialog. You should see your text object laid out on the current reference plane, as shown in Figure 7.1-b.

Figure 7.1

Using the Place Text tool.
(a) The 3D Text Editor dialog.
(b) Text placement using the default options in the dialog.

Not terribly attractive, is it? Probably, you would like to use a different font or have text with a different height and thickness. Also, how do you make the text "stand up" on the reference plane? All these options and more are available in the 3D Text Editor dialog you just saw. Let us see how to get back to it.

1.2   Editing Text

To change the settings for a text object you have already created, you need to use the Edit Text tool, located immediately after the Place Text tool.

- ▣ Select the Edit Text tool (M-Tool:9a,2) and apply it to the text object. The same 3D Text Editor dialog you saw earlier will open up, showing the settings for that object.

- ▣ Look at these settings more closely now. In the top right corner of the dialog, you can choose between TrueType and PostScript fonts. Depending upon the choice you make, the fonts available on your computer for that category will show up in the Font popup list. (Just as with any other application program, take care to ensure that the same fonts are available on other machines when you move your work between computers.) Highlight the text—don't forget to do this!—and choose a different font for it from the list. You also have the usual Size, Style, and Justification settings for formatting the text. Make the appropriate choices, depending upon how you want your text object to look.

- ▣ Move on to the Object Type popup menu. This gives you three choices for the kind of object the text should be. The default is Solid, which is why the text object you created had a thickness. If you do not need your text to have this "depth" effect, you can go in for the Surface or Surface Solid options. You know the difference between the two by now.

- ▣ The height of the text object is determined by the Height and Height Base specifications rather than by the font size specified. Keep this in mind as it is often a source of confusion. The value specified in the Height field determines the actual size of the text object. You can also choose between three justification options—Top, Center, and Bottom—which respectively determine if the object is placed below, at the center, or above the reference line passing through the text origin you selected. The Height Base option determines which part of the text object the Height specifications are applied to. You can choose between an uppercase character (the default), a lowercase character, the actual font height, any character that you specify, or the maximum height of that entire string of text.

- ▣ Move on to the next three options. If you have specified your text object type as Solid, you can specify a numeric value for the Depth or thickness of your object. It is accompanied by three additional justification options—Front, Middle, and Back—which are analogous to those you saw for the Height. The Width and Leading percentage values respectively control the width of a character and the space between multiple lines, if any.

- ▣ Next comes the Type of Solid button, which is active only when the Object Type is set to Solid. Click on this button and a second dialog will open up in which you can choose to round or bevel the edges of your text. You have a choice of applying this effect on one or both sides of the text object. Experiment with different values for both rounding and beveling. Keep in mind that the extent to which these operations can be applied is proportionate to the height and depth of the text, and you will be warned if the specified values are not within the range of what is feasible. If it consistently refuses to work, try using a different font—that usually does the trick. Figure 7.2-a shows both the beveling and rounding effects at close range by zooming in on a single character of the text object. Its font and size were also changed from those shown in Figure 7.1.

Figure 7.2

Various 3D Text editing options. (a) The three different Type Of Solid options applied to a single character. (b) Converting the text object to a plain surface object with the Per Character sub-option, and extruding some of the individual characters. (c) Various Angle options applied to a Standing text object.

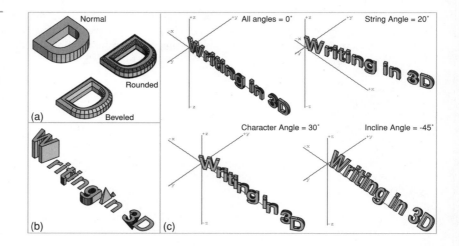

▪ Back in the 3D Text Editor dialog, the Path Options button, next to the Type Of Solid button, is grayed out for now, so move on to look at the remaining options in the right side of the dialog. The Outline Smoothness slider bar lets you increase the curvature resolution of your text object. Experiment with both the minimum and maximum values for this and follow the usual policy of settling for the lowest you can get away with, in order to reduce the complexity of the object.

▪ Change your text object type to Surface and check the Plain Object option. Check also the Per Character sub-option that comes with this option. Then click OK to exit the dialog. You will find that you can no longer apply the Edit Text tool to this text object—it has been converted to a "plain" object which cannot be edited. What's more, each character of the text is now a separate object, and since they are all surface objects, you can derive different kinds of objects from them. This is demonstrated in Figure 7.2-b. Keep in mind that 3D text can also be separated later using the Separate tool (M-Tool:8b,2).

▪ Undo what you just did and get back to the 3D Text Editor dialog by using the Edit Text tool. Check the Standing (Perp To Plane) option, and you will find that your text object is now positioned standing up rather than lying flat on the reference plane. Experiment also with the following three angle options. With String Angle, you can specify at what angle the text object should be placed about the Z axis at the placement point. The default is 0°, which is the +X direction. The angle is, as usual, measured anticlockwise, unless otherwise specified in your Angle Options dialog. Character Angle will rotate each character about the specified angle rather than the entire text object. And finally, Incline Angle lets you rotate the text object about the line of placement itself. Figure 7.2-c shows examples of all three angle options, applied to a "standing up" text object.

The Plot/Print Setup dialog under the File menu has an option related to how text objects are printed—Print Text As Paths—which is off by default. This makes the printer use its own native graphics while printing text, so it usually gives better results. But it might not exactly match what you see on the screen. If that is crucial, you should activate the Print Text As Paths option. Then the outline of each character of the text object is sent to the printer or plotter, eliminating any discrepancy between what you see on the screen and the printed output.

We have finished looking at all the options in the 3D Text Editor dialog, and you might think that this is the end of the story as far as 3D text is concerned. Not so! In fact, we still have to look at the most interesting aspect of 3D text—how to twist and mold and curve it in 3D space. You might want, for instance, your text objects to meander gently along a path, or maybe fly out of a box! Let us see how to go about achieving such effects.

1.3 Other Options for Text Placement

■ Go back to the Place Text tool and open its dialog (Figure 7.3). You will see that it contains many options for text placement, of which you have been working with the Text At Point option under the Text As Object section. Let us see how the other options differ from this default.

Figure 7.3

The dialog of the Place Text tool.

■ Change the text placement option to Text Between Points under the same Text As Object section. When you now use the Place Text tool, you will find that the program expects you to input two points rather than just one. The first point selected determines, as before, the starting point for the text. The second point determines the direction of the text. After you finish specifying both points, the 3D Text Editor dialog will open up in the usual manner. Notice that the only difference is that the String Angle option is grayed out, since this angle has already been determined by the two points. Verify this by entering some text and observing its location in the window when you exit the 3D Text Editor dialog.

■ Get back to the Place Text dialog and choose the Text At Point option, but this time under the Plain Text section. Apply the Place Text tool. Now, you will find quite a few options grayed out in the 3D Text Editor dialog—Object Type, Depth, and so on. Type some text and exit the dialog. You will find that your text appears as a surface object without any thickness. However, you cannot perform extrusions and other operations on it as you could on the surface text objects you created earlier using the Plain Object option in the 3D Text Editor dialog (shown in Figure 7.2-b). Recall that you could not edit those text objects with the Edit Text tool, but text objects created with the Plain Text option can be edited. It is important to remember this distinction between the two types of objects. "Plain text" is useful for labeling or annotating parts of your model, since it is the least complex type of text.

■ The Plain Text section also has the same Text Between Points option you saw earlier for the Text As Object section. It works in the same way. Try it out.

  There are a number of settings in the Wire Frame Options dialog related to how plain text objects will be displayed in that mode. They are very simple and you can explore them on your own.

WORKSHOP 7

1.4 Placing Text Along Paths

▣ We will now move on to the most interesting type of text placement in the Place Text dialog, which is Text As Object Along Path. This lets you place text along a path of *any* shape, rather than just along a straight line. There are three options for this type of text placement. Select the first option, On Line. This has additional sub-options, but let the default of Scale Height & Width prevail for now. Exit the Place Text dialog to get back to the graphics window.

▣ Create a 2D curved shape as shown in Figure 7.4-a. Then select the Place Text tool and watch the Prompts palette. You will be asked to select the path along which the text is to be placed. Select the 2D shape you just drew. The 3D Text Editor dialog opens up in the usual manner. Type some text and change other settings as desired. When you exit the dialog, you will find that your text is now curved along the path, its direction matching the direction of the path. Moreover, the text has been scaled both in height and width to match the start and end points of the path shape (Figure 7.4-b).

▣ Undo and place the same text along the same path, but with the On Line option set to Scale Width Only in the Place Text dialog. You will find that the text is now scaled to fit the endpoints in width only. The height remains true to what was specified in the 3D Text Editor dialog. This might end up making your text object look somewhat disproportionate (Figure 7.4-c).

▣ Finally, try the last sub-option, Preserve Height & Width. This preserves all the text size settings and doesn't worry about matching the endpoints of the path shape (Figure 7.4-d). You would use this if the size specification was crucial and had to be followed. Make sure that the path is large enough for the text to fit when you work with this option.

▣ Move on to the next text placement option, Between Parallel Lines. This is almost similar to the Scale Width Only sub-option for the On Line placement, in the sense that the height remains true to what was specified in the dialog. However, there is a subtle difference in the result which is illustrated in Figure 7.5. When you select the Between Parallel Lines option, you still select a single control line. But the program automatically generates a line parallel to this at a distance equal to the text height specified and creates a bounding box for each character between the lines. This ensures that individual characters do not touch or overlap even when the path is curved. The Standing (Perp To Plane) option in the 3D Text Editor dialog is deactivated for this type of placement.

▣ Placing text on a line or between parallel lines seems simple enough. But what if you want to place text between paths that are not parallel and want the text to be adjusted appropriately? We will now work on such a problem. Let's say, for instance, that you would like to have your text object flying out of a box, getting larger as it emerges. Model the box and then create two 2D shapes that will define the flow of the text, as shown in Figure 7.6. Make sure that the two paths are drawn in the same direction, from the inside to the outside of the box.

Figure 7.4

Using the On Line sub-options of text placement along a path. The first point and direction of the path are indicated.

(a) Path shape

(b) Scale Height & Width

(c) Scale Width Only

(d) Preserve Height & Width

Figure 7.5

Placing the same text on the same control line but using different placement methods.

(a) On Line method: Scale Width Only   (b) Between Parallel Lines method

▣ In the Place Text dialog, select the last option, Between Lines. When you apply the Place Text tool now, you will be asked to select two paths. Select first the 2D shape that will determine the base of the text. Then select the second shape which will determine the upper boundary of the text. You will now see your text placed between the two shapes, appropriately sized and curved (Figure 7.6-a).

▣ The Between Lines method does not even require the path shapes to be on the same plane. In short, there are no restrictions whatsoever, enabling you to create some really "funky" text placements. To see how this works, undo the last text placement operation and rotate one of the paths about the vertical axis, so that it is no longer in the same plane as the other path. Then reapply the Place Text tool to see the result (Figure 7.6-b).

▣ There are two additional options that come with the Text As Object Along Path mode. They can be seen in the Place Text dialog (Figure 7.3), and can also be accessed by clicking on the Path Options button in the 3D Text Editor dialog. (This option is only activated for text placed using paths.) The first of these is the Bezier Smooth Line option. When it is checked, the 2D shape selected as the path is automatically given a curvature, the smoothness of which depends upon the value specified in the accompanying Interval field. To see how this works, create a path made up of a sequence of straight lines. Place text on it, with and without selecting the Bezier Smooth Line option. The contrast in results makes the usefulness of this option obvious.

▣ The Adjusted To Line/Curve option, on the other hand, has to do with the shape of the individual text characters. By default, this option is not checked, so all the characters retain their basic rectangular shapes. Check this option and generate some new text objects on polylines or curves. You will find that the shape of the individual characters is now adjusted according to the angles and curvature of the polyline and curve respectively. Use this feature as scarcely as possible, since it adds enormously to the complexity of the resultant object.

Figure 7.6

Placing Text using the Between Lines method. (a) Using two non-parallel paths that lie on the same plane. (b) Using two non-parallel paths that are not on the same plane.

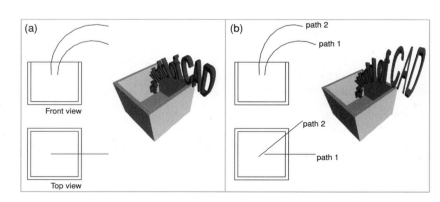

1.5   Editing Text Placement Lines

form•Z not only gives you the ability to place text along paths in many interesting ways, but goes a step further and lets you edit these paths long after the text has been placed. When you modify a path or paths, the text object is resized and reoriented to match the new configuration.

■   Select the Text Line Edit tool (M-Tool:9a,3), and apply it to any text object that was placed along a path. You will now be in the *text line edit mode*, in which all other tools in the modeling and window tool palettes are grayed out. The original path or paths used for the text placement also become visible. Click on a path, and its points become visible. Each of these points can now be moved to give a new shape to the path (Figure 7.7-a). Double-click when you have finished modifying the path to exit the edit mode. You will find that the selected text object has changed its shape to realign itself with the new path shape (Figure 7.7-b). In this manner, you can interactively fine-tune your text object to give it the desired shape.

Figure 7.7

Using the Text Line Edit tool to edit the path of the text object shown in Figure 7.5-b.

(a) Original object   (b) Reshaped object

If you convert a text object to a plain object using the Plain Object option in the 3D Text Editor dialog, you can no longer edit its path.

EXERCISE 2

The Power of Symbols

The concept of an object library must be familiar to you. There are many objects in any design field that are used very frequently across projects. In architecture and interior design, for instance, doors, windows, furniture, fixtures, trees, and so on will almost always be needed. In graphic design, you might create a 3D logo or banner which has to be used repeatedly. There are many such examples in other fields as well. You would obviously not want to remodel these objects every time. You could, of course, model them once and then copy and paste them wherever they are needed. But what if you make a change to the original? You would like all the copies to automatically update themselves, which would not be possible using the copy-and-paste method.

This is where a "library" of objects comes in useful. All frequently used objects can be created once and then stored in the library. If you need a library object for any project, you simply link to it and place the object in the desired position. One advantage of this already mentioned is the automatic updating ability. The other important advantage is that it reduces the file size of the project, since the object description sits only once in the library and does not have to be repeated each time it is used.

In form•Z, an object stored in a library is referred to as a *symbol*, and the library, consequently, is called a *symbol library*. You can create many symbol libraries containing different categories of objects. All that you need to do to use a particular library for a form•Z project is to "load" it. Then you can "reference" any symbol from that library and "place" it as an "instance" into your project. Let us see how it all works.

2.1   Creating Symbols from Objects

▣   Find a suitable object in any of your earlier projects that you need to use frequently in other projects, e.g., a chair, window, 3D logo, and so on. The object itself can be made up of several component objects, i.e., you are not restricted to a single form•Z object. If you do not have such an object, create a configuration of objects in a new file and use that instead.

▣   Use the Pick tool to select all the individual components of this object that has to be stored as a symbol. Then activate the Create Symbol tool (M-Tool:9b,1). You will be prompted to click to create a symbol definition from the picked object. Do so but don't just click anywhere in the window, since the selected point will function as the point of placement for the symbol when you recall it in other projects. Instead, click by snapping to an appropriate reference point, for instance, an endpoint, the center of a face, the center of the base of the object, and so on.

▣   You will now be greeted with a message telling you that a symbol definition cannot be created since no symbol library has been loaded. You are given two options for dealing with the situation. Since you have not yet created any library, Load Existing Library is not an option you can use now. (Remember, however, that you could use it in future sessions when you want to create a new symbol in an existing library.) Therefore, click on the Create New Library button. The familiar file save dialog will open up, allowing you to create a new file with an extension of ".zlb," indicating that it is a form•Z library file. Give the file an appropriate name and change its location if necessary.

▣   Once you have completed the process of creating a new library file, you will be prompted to enter a *definition name* for the symbol. Since a library can contain many symbols, it is important for each one to have its own identifying name. Type in a suitable name, and click OK. You have now completed the process of creating a symbol from the selected object.

▣   How do we know that it worked? There is no visible change in the graphics window. However, go to Options > Symbol Libraries and a dialog will open up, showing you the new library you just created as the active library, along with the object you just created as a symbol in this library (Figure 7.8). So you can be assured that it did work.

Figure 7.8

The Symbol Libraries dialog, showing the new library with the symbol that was created in it.

Figure 7.9

The Symbol Definition dialog for the created symbol.

◼ Spend some time at this stage going through the various buttons and options in the Symbol Libraries dialog. You can create a new library (New), make copies of libraries (Save As) as well as symbols (Duplicate), Load and Unload libraries from the project, get a brief Info as well as a detailed Overview of a particular library, Edit and Delete symbols, and perform an Alphabetical Sorting. Compact Library gives you a couple of options for the memory management of libraries, for which you can stick with the default selections.

◼ Turn to the actual object symbol displayed in the preview window of the dialog. It is highlighted, indicating that it is the active symbol. Double-click on it or hit the Edit button and a second dialog will open up, showing more information about the symbol (Figure 7.9).

◼ Explore the various options available in the Symbol Definition dialog. You can change the origin— the placement point indicated by the intersection of the red axes—by moving it graphically with the Pointer tool in the preview area, or numerically through the Move Origin option. You can do the same to what is called the Handle, indicated by a ghosted cross mark in the preview window. How the handle gets created and what it is used for, we shall look at very soon. Any information for reference can be entered in the Notes area. You can use the icon tools located below the preview window to get a different view of the symbol; then, by clicking on the Camera button, the new view can be registered for display in the main Symbol Libraries dialog. The Color Preview options are relevant when a symbol is placed into a project rather than when it is created, so pass these for now.

◼ Exit both dialogs and get back to the graphics window. Let us see what has happened to the original object that was transformed into a symbol. Use the Pick tool on it and you will find that you can no longer select the individual parts of the object—you can only select it as a single entity. Apply the Query tool to this object, and you will find that its Object Type is seen as a Symbol. What has happened is that the original object has been transformed into an instance of the symbol that was created from it. If you want to retrieve the object, undo the Create Symbol operation you just performed. This will not affect the creation of your symbol library—it still has the object as a symbol. Thus, you can transform any object to a symbol and still get back the object in its original form.

◼ Let us now look at what options the Create Symbol tool comes with. Double-click to open its dialog. You have four choices for Origin/Handle Definition, which are self-explanatory. The default of Pick Origin is the most commonly used one. However, if the handle position is important (and we shall soon see when that might happen), you should opt for Pick Origin And Handle. In addition to the placement point, this will ask you to select an additional point for the handle while creating a symbol.

▣ The Status Of Picked Objects in the Create Symbol dialog is set to Replace With Instance by default, which explains why your object was transformed to an instance when a symbol was created from it. You can choose the Status Of Objects option instead and set the Status to Keep. The object will now be retained in its original state, saving you from having to use Undo to get it back.

2.2 Creating Multiple Definitions of a Symbol

▣ You will now create one more symbol in the same library. Find a suitable object and apply the Create Symbol tool to it. (Remember to prepick its individual parts first.) If this object is in a different project file, you will have to take the additional step of loading the library into that project. Give the new symbol an appropriate name. Then open the Symbol Libraries dialog to verify that the library now has two symbols stored in it. Check out also the Symbol Definition for the new symbol to see how the origin and handle have been positioned.

▣ Back in the Symbol Libraries dialog, look more closely at the iconic tools at the base of the preview window. The first three of these are for different ways of displaying the symbols in the preview window. Try them out. Then turn to the icons marked 1, 2, and 3. These stand for different levels of a symbol. Each symbol can have up to three definitions associated with it. This is useful for storing symbols at different levels of detail. For instance, a window can be stored at one level with its frame, glass and mullions, and on another level as just a flat vertical slab. The level you use will depend upon how closely that object is to be seen in a particular view.

▣ Notice that level 1 is highlighted, indicating that it is the active level in which symbols will be created and from which they will be placed. Select 2, and you will find that while there are still two placeholders for the two symbols you have created so far, they are grayed out, indicating that no definitions for these two symbols have been created at level 2.

▣ Let us create these definitions right away. Ensure that level 2 is still active and get back to the graphics window. Create two simple objects of approximately the shape and size as your two symbols, and apply the Create Symbol tool to each of them in turn. Give them the same names as your first two symbols. If you now look in the Symbol Libraries dialog, you will have definitions for the two symbols at both levels, 1 and 2.

2.3 Placing Symbol Instances into Projects

▣ We will now see how the stored symbols can be placed in a different project. Open a new form•Z project file, or continue with the one you used for Exercise 1. To be able to place a symbol from your saved library in this project, remember that you need to load that library file first. You know that you can do this through the Symbol Libraries dialog, which can be accessed by going to Options > Symbol Libraries. Let us, however, use an alternate and more convenient method. Go to the Palettes menu and open the Symbols palette. It is currently blank since no library is loaded (Figure 7.10-a). Click inside the palette in the top row where the word "Library" appears. This will invoke the same Symbol Libraries dialog you saw earlier.

Figure 7.10

The Symbols palette, before and after loading the symbol library created earlier.

 (a) (b)

◼ No library has been loaded, so the symbols preview area in the dialog is blank. Click on the Load button and select the library you had saved. It gets loaded into the project and the two symbols it contains appear in the preview area. The first symbol is highlighted by default, indicating that it is the active symbol. Click OK to exit the Symbol Libraries dialog. In the Symbols palette, you will now see the same symbols preview that you saw in the dialog (Figure 7.10-b). Double-clicking on a symbol in the palette invokes the same Symbol Definition dialog for the symbol you saw in Figure 7.9. The Symbols palette is thus a very convenient interface to the symbol libraries.

◼ Let us now get down to the business of placing an "instance" of the active symbol into the project. Select the Place Symbol tool (M-Tool:9b,2). You will be asked to pick the *instance origin*, or, in other words, the placement point for the symbol. Select a point in the window and watch your first symbol appear there. Keep clicking at different points and see how easily and quickly you can populate your model with instances of the symbol. Switch to the other symbol in the Symbols palette and place instances of that as well into your project. You should have something similar to what is shown in Figure 7.11.

◼ Notice that the orientation and size of all the instances of a particular symbol are exactly the same as they were when you created the symbol. What if you wanted some instances to be oriented and sized differently? For this, access the dialog of the Place Symbol tool (Figure 7.12), and change the scaling factors and rotation values for symbol placement. Deselect the Scale Lock box to specify different scaling factors for the 3 directions. Reapply the Place Symbol tool and you will see that the symbol instances now being placed follow your specifications rather than the original values.

◼ The default placement option, as you can see in the Place Symbol dialog, is Pick Origin. There are two other options—Pick Origin And Uniform Scale and Pick Origin And X, Y, and Z Scale—which let you dynamically rotate and scale a symbol instance while placing it. Activate each of them in turn. When you now use the Place Symbol tool, the first point you select is the placement point as usual. But you also go on to select additional points that will determine the orientation and size of the instance, which is rubber-banded as you move the mouse. For both these options, the location of the *handle* in the symbol definition affects this dynamic positioning of the instance. Test this by executing the Place Symbol operation for different handle locations of the symbol.

Figure 7.11

Placing instances of the symbols shown in Figure 7.10-b in a project.

Figure 7.12

The dialog of the Place Symbol tool, with the default placement values.

- By default, the Color Display of a symbol instance is set to its Definition Colors in the Place Symbol dialog, which are the colors in which it was created. This option will import the colors if they do not exist in the project. You could opt for Best Matching Colors, which will instead find the closest match to the colors from those existing in the Surface Styles palette. The third option, Active Color, colors the symbol instance in the active color of the project and also lets you change its color freely later, which the other two options do not.

- Similarly, you can also change the layer settings of the symbol instance in the Layer Display popup menu, but it is a good idea to stick with the default of Active Layer. The other option, Definition Layers, will import all the layers used to define the symbol in its project file into the current project, increasing your layer list unnecessarily.

 The colors and layers used by a symbol in a project get locked and cannot be modified. Such colors and layers will appear in a read-only mode in their respective palettes.

2.4 Editing and Exploding Symbol Instances

- What if you want to change the scale, position, or orientation of a symbol instance *after* you have already placed it? Try applying the Move, Rotate, or Mirror tools to any of the instances you created and you will find that you can move or rotate them just like any regular object. However, you will find that both the Scale tools on Row 12 refuse to work on symbol instances.

- For scaling, you will have to resort to the special tool reserved for editing symbol instances which is Edit Symbol (M-Tool:9b,3). Select this tool and apply it to one of your symbol instances. A dialog will open up showing the various parameters for that instance (Figure 7.13).

- Edit some of your symbol instances in different ways using the options in this dialog, as shown in Figure 7.14. You can change the origin or placement point of an instance, rotate it, or scale it. To rotate or scale along all 3 axes independently, deselect the Lock icon. You can change the Color Display and Layer Display settings, which are similar to what you saw earlier in the Place Symbol dialog. You can switch to a different level definition of the same symbol by selecting the desired level from the Detail popup menu. You can also go to the extent of placing another symbol altogether at the same placement point by changing the Symbol Definition. If necessary, you can choose a symbol from another library—if it has been loaded into that project—from the Library popup menu.

Figure 7.13

Applying the Edit Symbol tool to a symbol brings up the Symbol Instance Parameters dialog.

◼ It is also possible to edit multiple symbol instances at the same time. This is useful when you have to apply the same transformation to many symbol instances. Invoke the dialog of the Edit Symbol tool and select the Edit Simultaneously option. You can now preselect with the Pick tool all the symbol instances you want to modify, then apply the Edit Symbol tool to them.

◼ If you want to transform only one of the individual parts that make up a symbol instance, you cannot do it using the Edit Symbol tool, since that treats the symbol instance as one composite entity. In such a situation, apply the Explode Symbol tool (M-Tool:9b,4) to the instance. This will break the instance down into each one of its constituent parts, and they can now be treated as regular objects—moved, rotated, scaled, colored, and so on, independently of the other parts of the instance.

◼ When you apply the Explode Symbol tool to a symbol instance to break it down into its constituent parts, it no longer remains a symbol. Test this by trying to apply the Edit Symbol tool to a symbol instance after you have applied the Explode Symbol tool to it—you will find that you cannot. You have thus lost the advantage of using a symbol for that particular object, including the automatic updating facility. Therefore use the Explode Symbol tool judiciously, only when you have to.

Figure 7.14

Editing the symbol instances shown in Figure 7.11 in various ways.

2.5 Updating Symbols Dynamically

Suppose that you need to modify in some manner an original symbol you had created, and would like the change to automatically take place wherever instances of that symbol are used. Let us see how to do this.

Figure 7.15

Modifying the original symbol automatically updates the symbol instances shown in Figure 7.14. The new Symbols palette is also shown.

■ Use File > Open to open the library file which contains the symbol you want to modify. (Remember that a library file can be identified by the ".zlb" extension.) Open the Symbols palette if it is closed, and select the symbol that is to be modified. It will appear in the graphics window, where you can now use the regular modeling tools of form•Z to transform it as desired. To save the changes to the symbol, click on another symbol in the palette. If the symbol you are modifying needs to have another symbol from the palette placed *within* it, switch the Mode at the top of the Symbols palette temporarily to Place Instance instead of Edit Definition in order to do this. To save the changes to the library file as a whole, you must select Save from the File menu before you close the file.

■ Now switch back to the project in which you placed instances of the symbol you just edited. You will immediately be informed that the library has been modified and will be reloaded. And voila!— your project will be automatically updated, with the changes that you made to the symbol showing up in each one of the instances, even in their edited versions (Figure 7.15). Only the exploded symbol instances will remain unaffected.

■ End this exercise on symbols by checking to see if your version of form•Z came with some predefined libraries. If so, these should be located in the form•Z Libraries folder under the main application program folder. Open these libraries and explore the various symbols they contain, keeping them in mind for future use.

EXERCISE 3

The Metaphysics of Metaformz

In the last workshop, you worked with all the mesh-related tools that greatly enhanced your ability to do organic modeling. In this exercise, we will look at another set of tools that makes the task of organic modeling much easier. These are the three "metaformz" tools, located in Rows 1 and 7 of the modeling tool palette.

Metaformz refers to objects that have the ability to blend seamlessly with each other when they overlap. Each object has a *sphere of influence* that determines how much it merges with or repels another such object. The base objects for generating metaformz are of two kinds: *metaballs*, that are created directly by the Create Metaballs tool; and *metaforms*, that can be derived from regular form•Z

WORKSHOP 7

objects by the Derive/Edit Metaformz tool. Both metaballs and metaforms can be converted to *metaformz* by the Metaformz Evaluate tool, so called because the process of conversion is referred to as "evaluation." Thus, metaballs and metaforms can be regarded as "unevaluated metaformz."

To generate a smooth metaformz from a number of metaballs and metaforms, they need first, to overlap with each other, and second, to be collected into a group. A metaformz is a controlled object in the sense that the original metaballs and metaforms are retained and can be modified to change the shape of the resultant metaformz. This enables you to very easily fine-tune the metaformz after creating it, until it takes on the desired form.

Let us proceed to work with this fascinating concept.

3.1 Creating and Evaluating Metaballs

◼ Open a new form•Z project or move to a fresh layer, and set the display mode to Wire Frame. Select the Create Metaballs tool (M-Tool:1b,2) and follow the prompts. You will be asked to select an *origin point* for the metaball. Click to select a point in the window or type in some coordinate value. You will now be prompted for the *radius*. Move the cursor and you will see a spherical shape being rubber-banded. Click to specify the radius, or type in a suitable value. You should have a spherical metaball, as shown in Figure 7.16-a.

◼ This metaball, as discussed, represents an unevaluated metaformz. Rather than an object of specified dimensions, it represents a *region of influence* which can interact with the regions of other objects of the same kind. This region is indicated by two sets of lines: the inner set in the active color, and the outer set in ghosted mode. (Make sure that the Hide Ghosted option under the Edit menu is not selected, so that you can see the ghosted lines.) Switch to each of the planar views and you will find that both sets of lines are circular, indicating that this is a perfectly spherical metaball.

◼ Try and see the metaball in a different display mode and you will find that you cannot. Some displays such as Hidden Line and Surface Render revert back to Wire Frame, while the others show a blank screen. This gives us our first inkling that metaballs are not like regular objects. To confirm this, try to select a point, segment, or face of the metaball by setting the topological level appropriately, and you will find that you cannot.

Figure 7.16

A metaball generated by the Create Metaballs tool with the default settings, and the resulting evaluated metaformz.

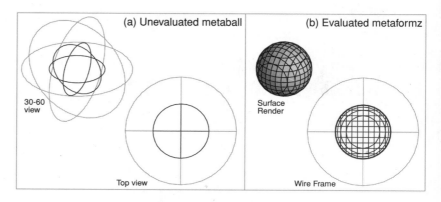

◼ Thus, an unevaluated metaformz such as the metaball you have created is of no practical use until it is evaluated into metaformz. Let us, therefore, do this right away. First, ensure that the topological

level is set to Object. Then select the Metaformz Evaluate tool (M-Tool:7b,2) and apply it to the
metaball. A dialog will be invoked showing various evaluation parameters (Figure 7.19-a). We
will look at these in detail later. For now, stick with the defaults and click OK to exit the dialog.
Your metaball will be evaluated to metaformz, as shown in Figure 7.16-b. This is a meshed spherical
object following the shape of the metaball, and it behaves in a "regular" fashion—it can be rendered
in different display modes and its individual points, segments, and faces can be selected for various
operations.

3.2   Metaballs and Metaformz Options

▣ It is possible to create three other kinds of metaballs—stretched ball, ellipsoid, and stretched
ellipsoid—in addition to the perfectly spherical one you just created and evaluated. Double-click
on the Create Metaballs tool to open its dialog (Figure 7.17). You will see these four types listed as
options, with the default being Ball, the spherical metaball. Select each of the other three types in
turn and apply the Create Metaballs tool. You should now have a metaball of each type. Notice
that both the Ellipsoid and Stretched Ellipsoid types have two options which determine the way
they are created. Experiment with both techniques.

▣ Notice that there is also a Weight parameter associated with a metaball, which is set to 1 by default
in the dialog of the Create Metaballs tool. This parameter controls the extent of a metaball that is
converted to metaformz. A weight of 0 would lead to a metaformz of zero volume, which would
not be seen at all. Weight can also be negative, which is useful when metaformz is derived from a
group of metaballs. We will look at this aspect more closely in the next section. For now, apply the
Metaformz Evaluate tool to each unevaluated metaball as you did before, sticking with the default
options. The difference between the various metaball types is much more evident now.

▣ Let us now try to create a blend of two or more metaballs. Clear the window and create a fresh set
of metaballs, say one of each type. This time, take care to create them so that they overlap with
each other, as shown in Figure 7.18-a. Switch to a planar view to adjust the overlaps better, and
use the Move tool if necessary.

▣ You would think that by prepicking all the metaballs with the Pick tool and then applying the
Metaformz Evaluate tool to the whole selection, the desired blend should be produced. Try it. You
will find that each metaball gets evaluated individually, leading to separate metaformz objects that
are not aware of any overlaps (Figure 7.18-b). Obviously, this is not the way to go about blending
metaballs with each other.

Figure 7.17

The dialog of the Create
Metaballs tool.

Figure 7.18

Evaluating a set of intersecting metaballs into
metaformz, individually
and collectively.

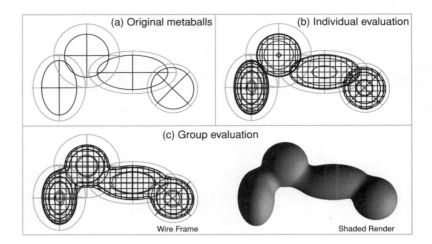

◼ Undo the Metaformz Evaluate operation you just performed to get back to the state shown in Figure 7.18-a. Prepick all the metaballs again with the Pick tool. Then select the Group tool (M-Tool:8b,3). This will automatically invoke the Metaformz Evaluation Parameters dialog you encountered earlier. The difference, however, is that this dialog is invoked only once for the entire group and will determine the characteristics of the resultant metaformz. Stick with the defaults and exit the dialog, and you will now see a single metaformz blending across the individual metaballs (Figure 7.18-c).

◼ Let us now look at the options contained in the Metaformz Evaluation Parameters dialog (Figure 7.19-a) to see how they affect the metaformz you just created. Since the metaformz is a controlled object, there is no need to undo and reapply the operation with different settings. Simply select the final metaformz or any of the original metaballs with the Metaformz Evaluate tool and the same dialog is invoked again, allowing you to change the settings. (Notice that the original metaballs do not get deleted or ghosted after the evaluation. There is a good reason for this which we shall soon see.)

◼ The first parameter in the Metaformz Evaluation Parameters dialog is the Threshold value. This can range from 0.1 to 99% and determines the extent of the metaformz by controlling its region of influence. Experiment with both the highest and lowest values and watch the metaformz expand and shrink respectively.

◼ Next, you can change the Mesh Resolution of the metaformz mesh. This concept is already familiar to you from all the mesh tools you covered in the last workshop. Smaller mesh values will give you smoother surfaces but add to the complexity of the object.

◼ The Metaform Operation parameter determines how the metaformz of the individual metaballs are joined. It has two options, Blend and Join. When Blend is selected, the metaformz will be blended even if the individual metaballs do not fully intersect. Join, on the other hand, will not blend or even touch the metaformz if the metaballs do not intersect. The difference is illustrated in Figure 7.19-b for a new set of metaballs.

◼ The last option, Optimize Surface, can be checked to obtain smoother renderings of the metaformz. This results from an optimization process applied to the mesh which positions its points more accurately on the surface of the metaformz.

Figure 7.19

The Metaformz Evaluation Parameters dialog, and the difference between its Blend and Join operations.

3.3 **Editing Metaballs**

You have seen that the metaformz is a controlled object whose parameters can be modified at any time using the Metaformz Evaluate tool. You can go a step further and modify the *original* metaballs in various ways—the metaformz will be automatically recalculated! Let us see how.

▣ Use the Move tool to move any one of the original metaballs in the group to a different position. Ensure that it still overlaps with one of the other metaballs in the group. You will find that the metaformz is automatically recalculated, blending the moved metaball in its new position with the others. In the same way, apply some of the other transformation tools to the metaballs, and see how you can fine-tune the shape of the resultant metaformz.

▣ If your metaformz is very complex, it is inefficient for the metaformz to be automatically recalculated for every slight change you make—it might be preferable to withhold the recalculation until you have made the desired changes to *all* the metaballs. In that case, double-click on the Metaformz Evaluate tool and select the third option, Evaluate Only When Selected, instead of the default, Automatic Evaluation. (The remaining option, Prompt For Evaluation, will prompt you each time a change is made, and is useful only when you want to prevent accidental modification of your metaformz.) Now you can make various modifications to the metaballs without affecting the metaformz. When you are ready to recalculate it, simply apply the Metaformz Evaluate tool to it.

▣ The original metaballs can be modified in another way in addition to using the transformation tools as you just did. This involves changing the parameters with which they were created. Select the Derive/Edit Metaformz tool (M-Tool:7b,1) which you haven't used so far and apply it to one of the metaballs. This will invoke the Metaformz Parameters dialog, showing the original parameters of the metaball (Figure 7.20).

▣ At the top of the dialog, the Metaform Type shows the metaball as a Stretched Ball. You can change its position by entering different values for Center X, Center Y, and Center Z, although it is more convenient to do this graphically with the Move tool. You can set the size of the metaball more precisely by modifying the three radius values. You can go further and even change the Metaform Type itself to another type from the popup menu. In the case of Stretched Ball, all other options are grayed out except Ball. Switch to this type and see how the Radius 2 and Radius 3 values get deactivated, since the Ball type can have only a single radius. A Ball can similarly be changed to a Stretched Ball; however, the Ellipsoid and Stretched Ellipsoid types cannot be changed to any other type.

Figure 7.20

The dialog invoked when the Derive/Edit Metaformz tool is applied to a metaball.

> Metaformz Parameters
>
> Metaform Type : [Stretched Ball ▾]
>
> Weight : -5.0 ――――――○――― 5.0 [4]
>
> **Parameters**
>
> Radius 1 : [15'-4"]   Center X : [0'-0"]
>
> Radius 2 : [26'-0"]   Center Y : [-18'-0"]
>
> Radius 3 : [20'-0"]   Center Z : [0'-0"]
>
> **Chain**
>
> ⦿ At Existing Points   ☐ Scale Radius : [   ]
>
> ○ By # Of Primitives : [   ]   ☐ Scale Weight : [   ]
>
> ○ By Distance : [   ]   ☐ Random % : [   ]
>
> [Cancel]   [OK]

◼ Let us now examine the Weight parameter which we had bypassed earlier. Change this to 0, and then to the positive and negative extremes of 5 and –5 respectively, and see how the shape of the metaformz responds to the change. You will find that decreasing the weight decreases the amount by which that metaball contributes to the metaform. Thus, a positive value has an additive effect, a weight of 0 is equivalent to the metaball not being there at all, and a negative value has a subtractive effect. All three are illustrated in Figure 7.21. Thus, you can adjust the weights of the metaballs depending upon the form you wish to achieve.

Figure 7.21

The effect of modifying the weight of a metaball from 5 to 0 to –5.

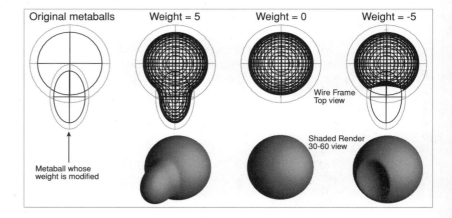

Original metaballs   Weight = 5   Weight = 0   Weight = -5

Wire Frame Top view

Shaded Render 30-60 view

Metaball whose weight is modified

3.4   Deriving Metaforms from Regular Objects

So far, we have worked with only the four predefined metaball types available in the dialog of the Create Metaball tool. While you can group these four basic types in many different ways to achieve a large variety of metaformz shapes, form•Z goes a step further and lets you derive various kinds of metaforms from *regular* objects. These metaforms then behave just like metaballs and can be grouped to create metaformz.

▣ Move to a different layer and create a number of regular form•Z objects, as shown in Figure 7.22-a. Apply the Derive/Edit Metaformz tool to all of them, selecting a different type from the Metaform Type popup menu for each object. The choices available will depend upon what the original object is. Thus, a solid object can only be converted to a Polyhedron type of metaform, whereas a surface object has many other options which we will soon discuss. For now, notice that you can modify the weight, radius, and location values for each type of metaform, as you did before for the metaballs.

▣ After you have finished deriving different metaforms from all your objects, apply the Metaformz Evaluate tool to them in the usual manner (Figure 7.22-b). You can see that a much larger variety of metaformz can be created in this manner, giving you an enormous range of forms to play with. As before, you can group the metaforms before evaluating them to create the aggregated metaformz shape as desired (Figure 7.22-c).

▣ Apply the Derive/Edit Metaformz tool to a new open or closed 2D surface object (as shown in Figure 7.23) and look at the large number of choices you have for Metaform Type. Try out the Tube and Conic Tube options, as well as the Sheet option which applies to closed surfaces only. Remember to apply the Metaformz Evaluate tool to actually see the resultant metaformz.

▣ For the surface object, you can also choose from among the four familiar metaball options—Ball, Stretched Ball, Ellipsoid, and Stretched Ellipsoid—for the Metaform Type. Go ahead and select one of these. These four metaball options are generated as *chains* of metaballs when applied to a regular object. Notice that the Chain options in the Metaformz Parameters dialog (shown in Figure 7.20) now get activated. You can specify the location of each ball of the chain in three ways: using the actual points of the object; the actual number of balls, which will then be uniformly distributed along the length of the object; or the distance between the balls. You can also uniformly vary the size and weight of the balls by applying a scaling factor, or else, specify a random percentage factor for applying to the radius, which will make all the balls look different in size. A couple of these options are illustrated in Figure 7.23.

Figure 7.22

Deriving metaforms from regular objects and then evaluating them to produce metaformz. If they are grouped and then evaluated, a single metaformz object is produced.

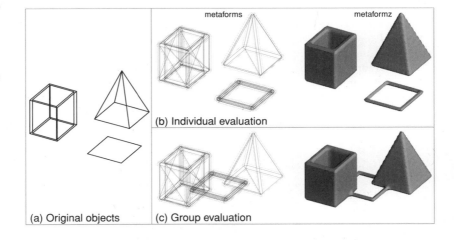

(a) Original objects

(b) Individual evaluation

(c) Group evaluation

Figure 7.23

Creating chained metaformz, with and without changing the radius.

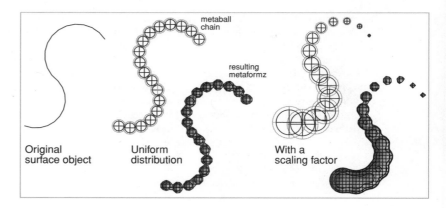

A metaform, once created, can be modified in the same way as a metaball. You can apply any of the transformation tools such as Move, Rotate, and so on to it, or you can select it with the Derive/ Edit Metaformz tool and modify its various parameters. If it has already been evaluated, the resulting metaformz can be updated either automatically or by selecting it, depending upon what option is active for the Metaformz Evaluate tool. A metaform can also be converted back to the original object from which it was derived by setting its Metaform Type to None in the Metaform Parameters dialog.

We have covered all the tools and options related to metaballs, metaforms, and metaformz. Have some more fun with this feature before moving on to the next exercise.

Panoramic Views and QuickTime VR

EXERCISE 4

You were briefly introduced to the Panoramic view type in Workshop 3, when you worked with all the different options under the View menu. You saw that this is not an interactive view in which you can carry out modeling operations, which is why all the tools are grayed out when you are in this mode. Panoramic views, however, can be saved as image files and can make for very interesting presentations of design concepts. You can go further and use them for generating QuickTime VR movies, if your computer has that capability. For more information about QuickTime (which is available under both platforms, Mac and PC), refer to your operating system Help functions.

In this exercise, we will look at how QuickTime VR works. But first, let us explore the Panoramic view options in some more detail.

4.1   Panoramic Views

Open one of your completed form•Z projects and switch to the Panoramic view under the View menu. You should see a 360° view of your model, centered by default in a position where you can see the most of the model. The view point can be changed, if required, either numerically through the View Parameters dialog, or graphically using Edit Cone Of Vision.

■ Let us explore the graphical option first. Go to Edit Cone Of Vision under the View menu, and you should see something similar to what is shown in Figure 7.24. The grid and axes display was turned off by going to the Window Setup option under the Cone Of Vision menu. All the lights in the project were also made invisible before entering this environment. Notice that the Top view (upper left modification window) shows the area of vision as a circle, while the Front and Right views (lower windows) show it as a rectangle. The actual volume of vision is therefore a *cylinder* rather than a cone, as you have encountered for the other view types. At the center of the cylinder is the eye point, and it is connected to the center of interest located at the circumference of the cylinder by a heavy line, which represents the line of sight. This line also indicates the center of the view.

■ Try and modify the panoramic cylinder in the modification windows in various ways, and see the result of the changes in the preview area. The process is similar to the manner in which the cone of vision is modified for other views. Figure 7.24 shows some modifications made to the default panoramic cylinder and the resultant view.

■ Some of the modifications can also be fine-tuned numerically. Select View Parameters from the Cone Of Vision menu. You have already explored this dialog in Section 5.7 of Workshop 3 and are familiar with the Eye Point and Center Of Interest options. There are three additional parameters here for the Panoramic view type: Spin, Angle, and Smoothness. The Spin value indicates the tilt of the panoramic cylinder, while the Angle value defines the extent of the panoramic view. The default value of 360° for Angle shows a full panorama, but you can reduce this value depending upon what you would like to see in your view.

■ The third parameter, Smoothness, determines the "resolution" of the view. Unlike the other views, a panoramic view is composed of a sequence of vertical bands, whose width is set by the Smoothness value. Increase this value from the default of 5 pixels to say 50 pixels, and you will see that all the curved lines appear more segmented (Figure 7.25). For final renderings, you can set a very small Smoothness value to get extremely smooth curves. Naturally, the smaller the value, the greater the rendering time.

Figure 7.24

Modifying the panoramic cylinder graphically in the Edit Cone Of Vision environment for a Panoramic view.

Figure 7.25

The same panoramic view, but with different Smoothness values.

■ Modify the parameters of your panoramic view until you are satisfied with the result; then exit the Cone Of Vision environment. Change the display to RenderZone to generate a rendered version of your panoramic view. You can save this as an image file for a presentation, as you learned to do in Section 1.2 of Workshop 5. You can also go on to generate a QuickTime VR movie from this view, which is what we will look at next.

4.2   Generating Panoramic Movies

■ To save your rendered panoramic view as a QuickTime VR movie, go to File > Save QuickTime VR. If your computer does not have this capability, the option will be grayed out and you can skip the rest of this exercise. Don't forget to come back to it though, when you acquire this extension. (Note that on the PC, you need QuickTime 3.0 or a later version for this option to work.)

■ Selecting Save QuickTime VR brings up the QuickTime VR Movie Options dialog shown in Figure 7.26-a. You can see that you have two main options, of which Generate Panoramic Movie is selected by default. Let us look at this first. It has two sub-options, letting you create a movie of the current panoramic view, if there is one, or of a new view which it will first create. Since you have a panoramic view currently in the window, stick with the first option, Use Current Panoramic View.

■ The two Movie Size values will determine the dimensions of the movie window. You can settle for the default size of 200 by 200 pixels for now, so that the generation process does not take too long. However, for final presentation movies, you can specify window sizes as large as the size of your monitor, if necessary.

■ Finally, notice the option, View Movie When Complete, which is checked by default. Leave it on so that you can see the movie as soon as it is generated. Then click OK to begin the generation process. You will be prompted for a file name for the movie. Specify a suitable name and location. The movie generation process will now be set in motion. It might take quite a bit of time, depending upon the movie size specified and the complexity of the project.

■ When the process is complete, the movie player application on your system will automatically be invoked—for instance, MoviePlayer on both the Mac and the PC—showing one frame of the newly created movie (Figure 7.26-b). To navigate through the movie, use the controls at the base of the window. Refer to the application's Help facility for detailed instructions on how to use the navigation options.

■ The newly created file is automatically given a ".mov" extension. You can play it outside form•Z by double-clicking on it, or opening it in your movie player program. Within form•Z, you can also view the same file at any time by using the File > View File command.

Figure 7.26

Generating a QuickTime VR movie from the panoramic view shown in Figure 7.25. (a) The QuickTime VR Movie Options dialog. (b) One frame of the movie, seen in the Mac's MoviePlayer application window.

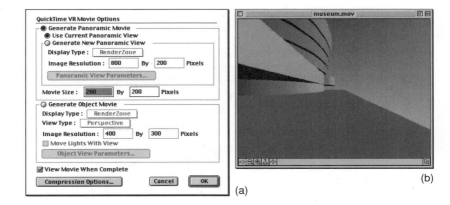

(a)

(b)

■ Back in the QuickTime VR Movie Options dialog, note the second option in the Generate Panoramic Movie section called Generate New Panoramic View. This lets you generate a new panoramic view for the movie, whose settings you can numerically specify by clicking on the Panoramic View Parameters button. Additionally, you can specify the type of display and the resolution of the image. Needless to say, this option is not that useful since it would always be preferable to generate a view first, and then decide if you would like to make a movie out of it.

Movies are useful as stand-alone presentations. They can also be embedded in Web pages and can then be viewed by anyone with an Internet connection, a Web browser, and the QuickTime VR plug-in. In a world that is increasingly going online, this might conceivably become the dominant mode of presentation of design concepts very soon.

4.3 Generating Object Movies

The second type of QuickTime VR movie that you can generate is an *object* movie. This kind of movie comprises views of the modeling world from all sides. You can think of it as a large sphere surrounding the objects, with you standing *outside* the sphere and being able to view the objects through any facet of the sphere. In contrast, in a panoramic view, you stand *inside* a cylinder and can only see the objects as they are mapped to the vertical sides of the cylinder; you cannot see what is above and below the cylinder.

Since a panoramic view consists of a continuous sequence of vertical strips, it can be "unfolded" in a single piece; this is why you can generate a panoramic view without necessarily making a movie out of it. However, the individual facets of the spherical object view cannot be unfolded in one piece; thus, you do not have the option of generating an object view independent of QuickTime VR. Also, the object movie deals with more information than a panoramic movie, therefore it takes much more time to generate.

■ Select Save QuickTime VR once again from the File menu. This time, select the second main option in its dialog, Generate Object Movie. Since this kind of movie is independent of the current display and image settings on your screen, it has an extensive set of options to specify these settings (see the dialog in Figure 7.26-a). Let us go through these options in brief.

■ The first three options are very simple. For the Display Type, you can choose between the six main display types in form•Z. You can opt for an Axonometric or a Perspective type of view. The two

Image Resolution values will determine the width and height of the object movie. Go ahead and make the desired selections for these options.

▣ Move Lights With View is an interesting option. When it is selected, lights are moved as the view changes, which means that the lighting on the objects keeps changing, depending upon where they are viewed from. It gives the illusion of the lights being fixed while the objects themselves are moving. When this option is deselected, lights remain in a fixed position like the objects, therefore the lighting on the objects also remains constant. You should generate two identical object movies, one with this option turned on and the other with it turned off, and compare the results.

▣ Next, click on the Object View Parameters button. This brings up a dialog in which you can make more detailed specifications about the movie (Figure 7.27-a). The first two options, # Of Pan Steps and # Of Tilt Steps, determine the number of facets of the viewing sphere in the horizontal and vertical directions respectively. The names come from *panning* (which refers to the horizontal rotation of the view about the vertical axis) and *tilting* (which refers to the vertical rotation of the view about the horizontal axis). Higher values will lead to more views in the movie, making the navigation through it less "jerky." Naturally, the generation time for the movie will also take longer.

▣ The Center Of Interest option has the usual meaning, and it can be set to desired coordinate values. You can also choose to automatically place it at the center of the scene by clicking on that button. Alternately, you can hit the Current button, which will position it at the point that is the center of interest in the currently active view.

▣ The field of view settings are used to determine the extent of the view. The default is the whole sphere (Use Complete Field Of View), but you can opt for Custom Field of View and specify the starting and ending angles along both the horizontal and vertical directions.

▣ The horizontal and vertical axes for panning and tilting are always defined with respect to a reference plane, for which you have four choices grouped under Rotate Relative To. The default is XY Plane, which makes horizontal movement take place on the XY plane and vertical movement along the Z axis. You can opt for the other two predefined planes or settle for the currently active plane, which could also be an arbitrary plane.

▣ Finally, you can choose between two zoom options. Zoom To Fit Scene will adjust the zoom level to include all visible objects in the views, while Use Current Zoom will use the current zoom setting of the active window.

Figure 7.27

Generating a QuickTime VR object movie. (a) The dialog for specifying the detailed parameters of the movie. (b) One frame of the movie, seen in the Mac's Movie-Player application window.

(a)   (b)

■ After making any desired modifications to the parameters, exit the Object Movie View Parameters dialog by clicking OK. Back in the QuickTime VR Movie Options dialog, make sure that the View Movie When Complete option is selected. Then click OK, and the generation of the object movie will begin. It might take a long time, depending upon the complexity of the model, the type of rendering, and the number of pan and tilt steps specified. When it is complete, the movie will open up in a movie player application window as before (Figure 7.27-b).

■ Navigate through this movie and see how it is different from the panoramic movie you created earlier. In this movie, you can move anywhere and see the scene from all sides, whereas in the panoramic movie, your position is fixed and you can only turn around and see what is immediately visible before you. Of course, you can also zoom in and out in a panoramic view which gives you the illusion that you are moving, but the viewpoint is actually fixed at the position you saw in the Edit Cone Of Vision environment in Figure 7.24.

■ End this exercise by exploring the Compression Options for QuickTime VR, the button for which is located at the base of the QuickTime VR Movie Options dialog. This is a standard operating system dialog, in which you can choose a compression method and the associated color depth and picture quality for the movie. Refer to your operating system manual for more information on the various compression techniques to determine which one is best suited to your needs.

EXERCISE 5

Animating Your World

Starting with version 3.0, form•Z has introduced the capability of generating and viewing animations from a 3D modeling project. The process involves a number of steps, all of which we will go through in this concluding exercise. Let us use a completed project to experiment with, for instance, the stadium roof structure we modeled as the Assignment for the last workshop. We will start by looking at the Cage tool, which is not strictly a part of the animation process, but can be useful in temporarily substituting low resolution objects for high resolution objects to speed up the animation.

5.1   Using the Cage Tool

■ Make a copy of the modeling project containing the Assignment for Workshop 6, and open it. Turn off all layers except the one which has the meshed roof covering. Of the four separate pieces comprising the covering, move one to a separate layer and turn off the original. We will focus on this single meshed object (see Figure 7.28-a), and use it to study the resolution-reducing capability of the Cage tool.

■ Select the Cage tool (M-Tool:8a,10) and apply it to the meshed object. You will find that it gets replaced by a low resolution object that approximates the shape of the original along two of the three orthogonal world axes: XY and ZX. Switch to all three planar views to verify this (see Figure 7.28-b). Look at the new object more carefully, and you will find that it has been derived by a threefold process: first, the perimeter of the original object is projected on the XY and ZX planes; then, each of the two projections is extruded in the perpendicular direction, i.e., along the Z and Y axes respectively, starting from and ending at heights corresponding to the other projection; finally, the boolean intersection of the two extrusions is obtained, yielding the final "cage." The last step explains why the Cage tool is grouped along with the other boolean tools.

WORKSHOP 7

Figure 7.28

Deriving a low resolution object from a high resolution object using the Cage tool.

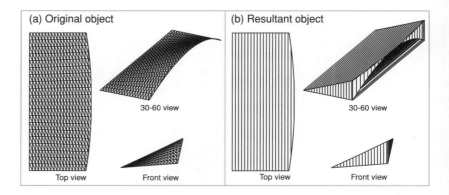

Invoke the dialog of the Cage tool to look at its options (Figure 7.29-a). You will find that the default selection for Extrusion Directions is Y & Z, which is why the low resolution object you just derived is created by the intersection of the projected extrusions along the Y and Z axes. Change the selection to X & Y, and undo and reapply the Cage operation (see Figure 7.29-b). The result is now much more in sync with the original object. Thus, your choice of Extrusions Directions from among the three options available will depend upon the form and orientation of the original object, and usually the reference plane with respect to which it was created. Our meshed roof covering was created with respect to the XY plane, so the X & Y option works best. This is not, however, a hard and fast rule, and you might have to explore all three options before you get it right.

If the original, high-resolution object was created with respect to an arbitrary plane, you can check the **Relative To Reference Plane** option. This will create the low-resolution cage by projecting and extruding with respect to the axes of that arbitrary plane rather than the world axes. Just make sure that the right reference plane is activated before applying the Cage tool.

The last option in the dialog of the Cage tool is used to determine the resolution of the resultant object. When activated, the initial projections are generated such that they do not contain segments larger than the specified value. Thus, the larger the **Filter Segments Shorter Than** value, the lower the resolution of the derived cage. Test it out.

The Cage tool can only produce objects with a single volume. So if the original object has holes, they will not be included in the resultant cage.

Figure 7.29

The dialog of the Cage tool, and using the X & Y option for Extrusion Directions on the same object shown in Figure 7.28-a.

52 Creating an Animation from Key Frame

An animation sequence, as you know, is essentially made up of a large number of separate images, each one of which is slightly different from the previous image in the sequence. The animation is played by changing the image sequence rapidly, conveying the impression of movement due to the "persistence of vision" facility that the human eye is endowed with. Each one of these separate images of the animation sequence is referred to as a "frame."

Before the age of computers, animators had no choice but to manually create each and every one of the frames required for an animation. With the help of computers, however, the animation process has been accelerated and made a lot less tedious. Now, only the critical or "key" frames of the animation are actually created; the remaining intermediate frames, capturing the movement from one key frame to the next, are generated automatically by the computer using interpolation.

The same procedure is followed in form•Z as well. Once your 3D model is ready for animation, the first step that you need to undertake is set up the key frames. These are basically views of the modeling world that are created and saved in the Views palette. form•Z then generates all the intermediate frames by interpolation to create the desired animation sequence. Let us see how it works for the sample project we have chosen.

▣ Go to View > Edit Cone Of Vision. In this environment, create a sequence of different views that will define the path of your animation. Each subsequent view should differ from the previous view in the sequence in the location of its eye point, or its center of interest, or both. Save each view as you create it by using the Save View option from the Cone Of Vision menu. While you can define as many views as you want, at least two are needed for generating the animation sequence. Exit the Cone Of Vision mode when you have completed this task.

▣ Back in the regular modeling environment, the views you just saved will be listed in the Views palette. The next step is to identify these views as the key frames of your animation. In order to do so, first make each one of these views visible by activating the corresponding visibility icons in the palette. Then select these views in the sequence in which the animation has to be generated, either graphically by using the Pick tool, or by clicking in the first column of the Views palette.

▣ Once the key frames are selected in the right sequence, the animation can be generated. To do this, go to View > Animation From Key Frames. This will invoke the familiar View Parameters dialog where you can modify the default parameters of the animation (see Figure 7.30). If necessary, change the View Name, which here stands for the name of the animation sequence. All the other options on the left side of the dialog apply to the individual key frames rather than to the entire animation. These are already familiar to you from Section 5.6 of Workshop 3, so we need not go over them again.

▣ Turn your attention to the options on the right side of the View Parameters dialog. Notice that both the Camera View and Animated Camera options are selected by default for the animation. Be careful not to deactivate them, otherwise the animation will no longer be recognized as an animation. You have already studied the Standard and Custom options under Camera View, when applicable to a regular view, in Section 5.6 of Workshop 3. They work in the same fashion for defining the camera settings of an animation.

▣ All the options under the Animated Camera section are really what we have to focus on for defining our animation, so let us go over them one by one. We begin with three interrelated parameters: Duration, Frames, and Frames Per Second. The Duration is the total time period required for playing the animation, specified in the format, *hours* : *minutes* : *seconds* : *frames (within last second)*. The last number must obviously be less than the value specified for Frames Per Second. The value of Frames represents the total number of frames in the animation, and has to be equal to the Frames Per Second value multiplied by the Duration in seconds. Thus, changing the Frames Per Second or Duration value automatically changes the number of Frames, while changing the Frames value automatically adjusts the Duration value.

The higher the Frames Per Second value, the smoother the animation. However, more frames will be required for the specified duration, so more time will be required to generate the animation. A Frames Per Second value of 30 is sufficient for the human eye to experience a non-jerky, flicker-free animation.

Figure 7.30

The View Parameters dialog, showing the default parameters for generating an animation from the selected key frames.

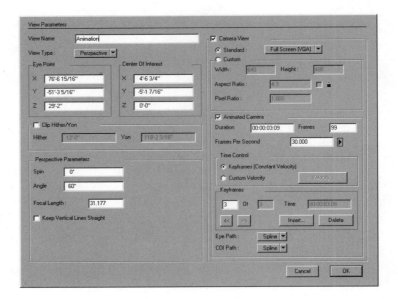

▣   The next parameter, Time Control, determines the rate of change or "velocity" of the animation—how the camera moves from the first to the last key frame in the specified duration. This velocity can be specified in two ways, the first of which, Key Frame (Constant Velocity), is active by default. Using this method, the time at which the camera arrives at each key frame is specified under the Key Frames subsection (which we will soon study). The camera then moves at a constant velocity between one key frame to the next. In contrast, the second option, Custom Velocity, is far more sophisticated, letting you specify the velocity by means of a time-distance curve. To see and manipulate this curve, activate the Custom Velocity option and click on the accompanying Velocity button. This will bring up the Velocity Control dialog shown in Figure 7.31-a.

▣   The velocity curve in the Velocity Control dialog is in the form of a graph with the number of frames and the time represented along the horizontal axis, and the distance along the vertical axis. The default curve, as you can see in Figure 7.31-a, is almost linear, representing a constant velocity. It can be reshaped by manipulating the accompanying *controls*—indicated by the unshaded circles—to apply different velocities to different portions of the curve. This is illustrated in Figure 7.31-b. A gentler slope (more horizontal) represents a slower speed, while a steeper slope (more vertical) represents a faster speed. At any time, you can click on the Constant button at the base of the dialog to revert back to a linear curve representing a constant velocity.

Figure 7.31

The Velocity Control dialog that can be invoked by activating the Custom Velocity option. (a) The default velocity curve. (b) The modified curve.

(a)   (b)

■ Notice that the curve initially has two *points* indicated by shaded circles, one at each end, to which the controls you just manipulated are attached. A new point can be inserted on the curve, if further adjustments are desired, by clicking on the Insert button next to the Constant button. Try it. If a point is no longer needed, you can get rid of it by selecting it and clicking on the Delete button.

■ Notice that intermediate points inserted on the curve are accompanied by their own controls. While moving a control reshapes the curve without changing the position of the point it belongs to, a point itself can also be selected and moved. The two endpoints can be moved along the vertical axis only, while the intermediate points can be moved in any direction. How exactly the selected point gets edited depends upon which Curve Type is selected from the popup menu above the graph. Additionally, the editing can be done in five different ways, depending upon which icon is selected in the upper left corner of the Velocity Control dialog. These icons get activated only when a point on the curve is selected, and are dimmed out when a control is being manipulated. Experiment with each one of these five icons and see how it affects the movement of the selected point.

■ .The only options remaining in the Velocity Control dialog for us to explore are Universal, and its alternate, Per Track, located at the top of the dialog. The default selection is Universal, which means that a single velocity curve exists which controls *all* aspects of the animation. The curves shown in Figure 7.31 are universal curves. In contrast, when you select the Per Track option, you will see a number of curves displayed in the graph, one controlling each *separate* aspect of the animation such as the eye point, center of interest, view angle, and so on. All these aspects are listed in the popup menu accompanying the Per Track option. Selecting an aspect activates the respective curve, which can then be edited in the same fashion as the universal curve we saw. Essentially, selecting the Per Track option as opposed to the Universal option is useful when you want to incorporate complex effects in your animation, such as moving the eye point very slowly but the center of interest very rapidly, and other interesting variations.

■ Now that we have finished exploring all the options in the Velocity Control dialog, exit it to get back to the View Parameters dialog, where we need to explore the remaining parameters of the animation.

■ Turn your attention to the Key Frames subsection. Here, you can navigate through each key frame of the animation by using the << and >> arrow keys, and edit its parameters listed on the left side of the dialog, if necessary. (Remember that a key frame is nothing but a view.) Additionally, you can specify the time at which the camera should arrive at the current key frame, if the Time Control in the previous subsection has been set to Key Frames (Custom Velocity). Needless to say, the time for the first and the last key frame cannot be changed, as the animation must finish within the specified Duration. For an intermediate key frame, you also cannot go beyond the time of its previous or next key frame.

■ It is possible to insert a new key frame into the animation sequence, before or after the current key frame, by clicking on the Insert button in the Key Frames subsection. The location and parameters of this new key frame are interpreted automatically between the two key frames it is inserted within, but you can edit them as required in the left side of the dialog. New frames cannot be inserted before and after the first and last key frames respectively. The Insert button is accompanied by a Delete button, which can be used to delete the current key frame if it is not required.

■ The final set of parameters in the View Parameters dialog, Eye Path and COI Path (COI stands for "center of interest"), determine how the frames that are automatically generated between successive pairs of key frames are actually interpolated, in terms of the paths of the eye point and the center of interest from one key frame to the next. There are six choices for each path parameter, available in the accompanying popup menu: Point (Fixed) causes the path to remain static rather than change over time; Line causes the path to be linear from one key frame to the next; Line (Closed) is the same as Line except that the line loops back to the first key frame after the last; Spline curves the path in the form of a spline between key frames, leading to a smoother transition, and is the default option; Spline (Closed) loops the curved path back to the first key frame; and finally, Use Object is similar to Point except that it uses the local origin of an existing object, which is selected from the accompanying dialog, to fix the path.

If you are a design professional whose primary interest lies in the modeling of the design, and animation is just one more presentation medium you use out of many, you should find that the default settings for an animation in the View Parameters dialog work just fine for you. In that case, you don't really need to explore these parameters in great detail to make any modifications. But if you are a professional animator, you will almost always need to modify the basic settings to achieve the creative and special effects you are aiming for. If so, you should spend a lot of time experimenting with all the animation parameters and see how they affect the final output.

Figure 7.32

Making the animation visible in the graphics window by turning on its visibility icon in the Views palette.

■ After making any desired modifications, exit the View Parameters dialog to return to the modeling environment. You will find the animation you just created listed as a view in the Views palette.

Turn on its visibility icon and switch to a view, preferably a planar one, in which you can clearly see all the individual views or key frames of the animation. You will find the path of the animation also illustrated if you have used the default of Spline for the Path parameters (see Figure 7.32). Just like any other entry in the Views palette, the View Parameters dialog for the animation can be invoked by double-clicking on its name in the palette. You can create as many animations as you want in the same project file; just give them different names and they will all be accessible from the Views palette.

5.3   Previewing Animations Using the Animation Palette

In the last section, you accomplished the task of setting up key frames and generating an animation sequence from them. You still have to render the animation frame by frame, and finally, play it in order to view it. We will look at both these tasks in the next section. In this section, we will explore the Animation palette and see how it can be useful in previewing an animation to verify that it is satisfactory. This is an extremely important step and should be undertaken, so that the time-consuming task of rendering the animation is executed only when you are reasonably sure that it will turn out the way you want.

■   Open the Animation palette, if it is closed, using the Palettes menu. Notice that the palette is blank when a regular view is activated in the Views palette. Go ahead and activate the animation you saved in the last section by clicking in the first column before its name in the Views palette. The Animation palette will now be activated and will display the animation controls of the selected animation. The function of each of these controls is illustrated in Figure 7.33.

■   The Animation palette essentially displays the *time line* of the animation and the corresponding frames in the form of a ruler. The red marker on this ruler stands for the current time. Initially, it is positioned at the beginning, i.e., at the first key frame, but you can move it to any frame of the animation by clicking on its position along the time line. The view in the graphics window gets updated to show the current frame. You can also click and drag the current time marker along the time line, which causes the view to be rapidly updated to show each passing frame, giving you the actual effect of an animation. Thus, you can preview your animation in any manner, forwards or backwards, through a portion of the frames or through the entire time line, by manipulating the current time marker. Just make sure that you are in the Wire Frame display mode, otherwise the view cannot be updated very rapidly and the preview will not be very useful.

 Keeping the Shift key pressed while moving the current time marker will delay the redrawing of the view until the key is released. This can be useful when the animation is complex.

Figure 7.33

The Animation palette, showing the controls of the animation that is activated in the Views palette.

▣ Instead of dragging the current time marker along the time line yourself, you can also use the VCR-like controls located in the lower left corner of the Animation palette to preview the animation. You can play the animation forwards or backwards, or move through it one frame at a time. Try out all these controls to preview your animation.

▣ Look closely at the markings along the time line in the palette again. If you had selected the Key Frames (Constant Velocity) option in the View Parameters dialog, you will find that the start and end key frames of the animation are represented by solid diamond markers. These are fixed and cannot be moved. However, intermediate key frames, which are represented by hollow diamond markers, can be moved to a different location along the time line by clicking on and dragging their markers. You can also make a copy of a key frame at a different location by holding down the option key (Mac) or Ctrl+Shift keys (PC) as you move it. If you had selected the Custom Velocity option, all the key frames would be represented by numbers on the time line. Their positions are fixed and cannot be changed.

▣ You will have already noticed the two convenient time and frame display boxes located at the base of the Animation palette, which get updated to show the current time and frame of the animation. Next to these are two Zoom buttons that you can use for zooming in and out of the time line, when necessary. Try them out. If you are zoomed in, you will be able to scroll horizontally through the time line by using the control key (Mac) or Ctrl+Alt keys (PC).

5.4 Generating and Playing Animation Files

After creating an animation sequence from key frames and previewing it to make sure that it is satisfactory, the next step is to actually render each frame of the animation and store the results in an animation file. The animation can then be viewed by opening and playing that file. Let us see how both these steps are performed.

▣ In the Views palette, activate the animation sequence you had saved earlier and which you previewed in the last section. Then go to Display > Generate Animation. This brings up the dialog shown in Figure 7.34, containing a number of options for rendering and storing the animation.

▣ The rendering options in the Animation Generation dialog are fairly straightforward. You can make your choice of the type of rendering for the animation at the top of the dialog, and access its Options dialog using the accompanying Options button. There are some additional rendering options you can choose to apply: Super Sampling will lead to improved antialiasing; Motion Blur reduces flickering and jerkiness by blurring objects that move fast in the animation; and Blur Filter applies an overall blur which reduces flickering caused by areas of high contrast. The Statistics button takes you to a dialog which provides useful information about the resolution and frames—both actual and sampled—in the animation.

▣ As far as which frames are actually rendered, you have two basic options. If you were generating the final animation, you would naturally choose to render all the frames. For prefinal previews, you could choose to render only some critical frames of the animation. This can be done in two ways. The Frame Range method lets you specify the starting and ending frames, with the option of setting any one of them to the current frame in the Animation palette. Additionally, you can specify an interval for skipping frames between Start and End. In contrast, the Frame List method lets you specify a variable list of frames which can contain single frames as well as a range—for example, 20, 45-60, 89.

WORKSHOP 7

Figure 7.34

The Animation Generation dialog, showing the settings for rendering and saving an animation.

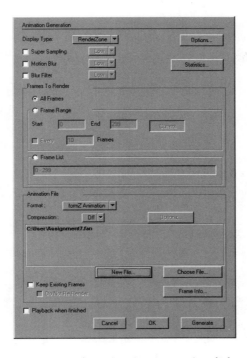

■   The Animation File section in the Animation Generation dialog contains the options for saving the file that will be generated. The default file name and location is listed in the box; it can be changed by clicking on the New File button. An extension of ".fan," standing for "form•Z animation," is automatically appended to the file name. The Choose File button allows you to open an existing form•Z animation for generation.

■   There are a number of options associated with saving the animation file. You can choose to Compress it if you are short on disk space; this, however, will make the playback slower. The Keep Existing Frames option can be checked if you would like to retain frames that were rendered in a previous version of the same animation file, and substitute only certain frames with new ones. This can be useful if only minor adjustments are made to the animation and you do not want to spend time and resources re-rendering all the frames. Finally, there is a Frame Info button, which gives you information on the total number of frames in the file and those still remaining to be rendered.

■   The final option in the Animation Generation dialog, Playback when Finished, can be selected to play the animation as soon as it is generated. There is, however, a separate command for playing the animation which we shall soon look at, so don't bother with this option for now. Instead, go over your selected parameters for generating the animation once again; then exit the dialog by clicking on the OK button. As soon as you do this, the rendering of the selected frames begins, with a progress bar showing the status of the rendering. The graphics window gets periodically refreshed to show the current frame; the Animation palette is also updated to show the corresponding time and frame number. All the rendered frames are stored in the specified animation file.

■   The animation you just saved is in a format native to form•Z, as indicated by the ".fan" extension to the file name. You can export this to a different file format using the Export Animation command under the File menu. The supported file formats fall into two basic categories: QuickTime Movie (Mac and PC) and AVI (PC only) are animation files; the others such as EPS, JPEG, etc., are

WORKSHOP 7

image files. In the first case, the form•Z animation file is converted to another animation file like itself, while in the second case, it is converted to a set of independent image files, one for each frame of the animation.

■ To play the form•Z animation file you just generated, select the Play Animation command, located just below the Generate Animation command under the Display menu. This will invoke the standard File Open dialog from which you can select the ".fan" file that is to be played. Once you do this, the Animation Playback dialog is invoked, containing a number of playback options (see Figure 7.35).

■ There are two options for Playback Method; the one you choose will depend upon the memory that is available to play the animation. If you opt for the Play All Frames method and all the frames of the animation do not fit into the available memory, only the frames that fit will be played; the animation will then pause to load the next set of frames. This can make the playback jerky. The situation can be somewhat improved by selecting the associated Load Frames During Playback sub-option, which loads the frames into memory *while* the animation is playing, slowing it down a little but avoiding the jerkiness at intervals. On the other hand, if you opt for the Play Only Frames That Fit In Memory method, playback is good without being jerky, but the entire animation may not be played.

■ The additional option, Enable Frame Skipping, which applies to both playback methods is used to ensure that the playback remains on schedule, even if that means skipping frames which take too long to load. If this option is turned off and your hardware cannot process the frames at the required rate, every frame will nevertheless be shown, increasing the duration of the animation. For a final animation, you should disable this option at least once in order to see all the frames.

■ The final playback option is Loop, which is used to make the animation go back to the beginning when it reaches the end frame, rather than come to a stop. The Palindrome sub-option for Loop makes the animation play back in reverse from the end frame to the start frame when the end is reached, rather than always loop back to the beginning.

■ After selecting the required options in the Animation Playback dialog, click OK to exit it. This sets the animation playback in motion, clearing everything else from the screen. How long the animation will play depends upon the playback options you have selected. There are several key combinations you can use to control the playback: the Esc (Mac and PC), command+period (Mac), or Ctrl+period (PC) keys to stop the playback and restore the screen to its previous status; the space bar to pause the playback, and again, to resume the playback; and, the left and right arrow keys to move backwards and forwards by one frame respectively when the playback is paused. Try out all of them while you play your animation.

■ Another way to play form•Z animation files is by using the familiar View File command under the File menu. You can also use it to play animation files saved in the QuickTime Movie format. QuickTime Movie and AVI files, can of course, also be opened and played by other animation programs which recognize these formats.

WORKSHOP 7

Figure 7.35

The Animation Playback dialog, showing the settings for playing a form•Z animation file.

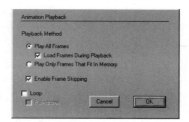

With that, we come to the end of the exercises for this last workshop. Let us proceed to see what is in store for us in the Assignment for this workshop.

ASSIGNMENT 7

Book Cover Design

■ *Design a cover image for this book using form•Z. The objective should be to convey as many capabilities of the program as possible, but in a simple and elegant fashion, without overcrowding.*

The steps for modeling the actual image seen on the front cover of this book will now be demonstrated step by step. You can refer to the form•Z files for each step of the assignment in the accompanying CD-ROM, under the folder Assignments > Workshop 7. A rendered image is in the Assignment7.tif file in the same location. The only Workshop 7 tool really covered here is the Place Text tool; the rest are all tools covered in earlier workshops.

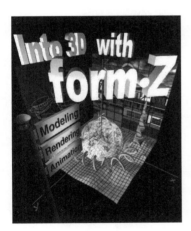

Setup

Open a new form•Z project and save it by an appropriate file name. In the Working Units dialog, set Unit Type to English, Base Unit to Feet, Numeric Accuracy to 1", and Angle Accuracy to 1°. Leave the window setup to the default module size of 8'-0" with 4 subdivisions. As usual, also turn off the display of the default light in the Lights palette.

The setup for this assignment involves an extra step: specifying the image dimensions. Being a graphic design project, the final output is a single image rather than a series of images of the model. Therefore, it is important to specify the dimensions of this image upfront. Go to Display > Image Options and choose the Use Custom Size option for Image Size. Disable the Maintain Proportions option, then specify the Width and Height of the image as 7.375" and 9.25" respectively. For now, stick with the default Resolution of 72 pixels/inch. You will have to increase this when you are ready to print your image.

As usual, create each object on a separate layer. For the sake of brevity, layer-related instructions will not be described in this exercise.

◀ Step 1

Set the object generation mode to **2D Surface Object**. Draw a 64' by 64' square on the XY plane, centered about the origin. You can use **Grid Snap** to do this in a jiffy. This object will form the "base" of our design.

Then switch to the YZ and ZX planes and draw similar squares on these two planes as well. These two squares will be referred to as "grid1" and "grid2" respectively.

Step 2

Apply the **Mesh** tool to grid1 and grid2 to subdivide them into 8' squares. Then move these two objects in the +Y and –X directions respectively, so that they touch the base square rather than intersect it. After this is done, move both of them vertically upwards by 24'.

◀ Step 3

Turn on the **Perpendicular Lock** and move the base object vertically downwards by a distance of 4'. Change the subdivision value in the dialog of the **Mesh** tool to 2' and apply it to the base. Then use the **Move Mesh** tool to move different portions of this meshed surface in various ways, using different profiles.

Step 4

Select the Spheroid tool from the right column of Row 1 and invoke its dialog. Set the option to Revolved Sphere and change both the accompanying Resolution values to 32. Use these settings to create a spherical solid of radius 16', whose center lies at the origin.

◁ **Step 5**

Switch to the Top view and create a 2D curve spanning across the surface of the base mesh. You can use the Curve tools in the right column of Row 3, or create a sequence of lines first and then apply the C-Curve tool to it.

Select the Helix tool, invoke its dialog, and set the mode to Wire Helix Along Path. Specify the Radius value as 4', and the # Of Cycles value as 20. Use these specifications to generate a wire helix along the 2D curve.

Step 6

Create a 1' by 1' 2D square. Then use the Sweep tool to sweep this shape about the wire helix you just created. This will yield a solid spiral object.

WORKSHOP 7

◀ Step 7

Use the 3D Converged Solid mode to create a pyramidal solid of dimensions 8' by 8' by 40' on the base. Apply the Mesh tool to it, using the same settings you used to mesh the base in Step 3. Then apply the Deform tool, with the mode set to Twist, to apply a twisting effect to the pyramidal block as shown.

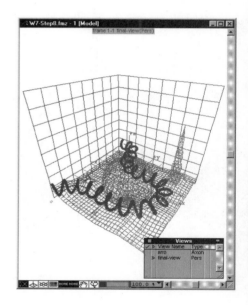

Step 8

The remaining objects of our cover design can be better modeled after finalizing the view in which the project will be displayed. Go to the Edit Cone Of Vision environment and adjust the various view parameters so that you get a perspective view of the entire project as shown.

▷

◀ Step 9

We will now model the title text, "Into 3D with form•Z." Turn off all layers except those containing the base and grids. Switch to the Top view and create two lines on the XY plane touching the base as shown. Then switch to the Front or Right views and move these lines in the +Z direction so that they are aligned with the top of grid1 and grid2. Temporarily ghost the layer containing the grids in order to see them better.

Step 10

Invoke the dialog of the Place Text tool and set the option to On Line with the Scale Width Only sub-option, under the Text As Object Along Path section. Then apply this tool first to the longer line on the left. Change the highlighted text to the words "Into 3D," make the desired font specifications, set the Height and Depth to 15' and 3' respectively, and check the Standing (Perp To Plane) option.

Repeat the same process, placing the word "with" on the shorter line. After this, turn the visibility of the layer with the grids back on.

Step 11

Next, draw a 2D line on the XY plane across the base, oriented diagonally as shown. Move it vertically upwards by a distance of approximately 38'.

Place the word "form•Z" on this line using the Place Text tool. Model the bullet as a period for now. Set the Height and Depth values to 23' and 8' respectively. Also, check the Plain Object option and the Per Character sub-option, since we have to change the period to a proper bullet. Each character of this text will now be a separate object.

Step 12

Delete the period in the text you created in the last step. Define an arbitrary plane passing through the front face of this text. Switch to View > Plane Projection > Front, and draw a circle for the bullet between the characters "m" and "Z" of "form•Z." Back in a non-planar view, extrude this circle so that its depth is the same as that of the remaining text. With this, the modeling of the title text is complete.

Note that in the final design of this book cover, a sphere was used for the bullet instead of a cylinder.

WORKSHOP **7**

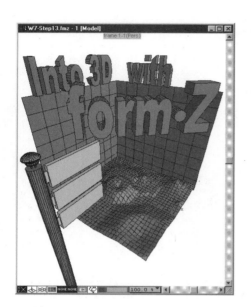

◀ Step 13

We will now model the words of the subtitle which are etched on a signpost, facing the remaining objects. Model the signpost object first, located at the X and Y coordinates of 16' and −56' respectively. Let the base of the signpost extend substantially in the −Z direction so that it extends beyond the lower frame of the image, as seen in the final view.

Step 14

Turn off the layers containing the title text. Create three separate text objects with the words "Modeling," "Rendering," and "Animation," using identical specifications, sized according to the dimensions of the signpost boards. The depth should be comparable to the height of the text. Place each one of them against the three boards, such that they are partially embedded into the board objects. We will eventually Difference them from the boards, but only after applying the desired surface styles.

▷

◀ Step 15

Finally, we come to the last set of objects that has to be modeled for the cover: the three axes and the accompanying labels. Use the 3D Enclosure tool to create three 100' long bands, with a 3" by 3" cross-section, along all three axes. The bands should be centered at the origin. Then with the Ortho direction snap activated, move their end faces to adjust their lengths, so that their ends are prominently visible in the final view.

Invoke the dialog of the Place Text tool and switch to the Text At Point option under the Text As Object section. Use this to create three labels—x, y, and z—near the ends of the three axis bands. The Height and Width of the text should be 4' and 6" respectively. For the y label, the String Angle should be set to 90° rather than 0°. After creating these text objects, position them precisely using the Move tool.

So far, we have what seems like a fairly unimpressive set of objects forming a fairly interesting composition. What will really bring this project to life is the rendering and lighting. We will attend to the rendering first.

◁ **Step 16**

Turn on all the layers. Let us start with grid1 and grid2. Locate two image files that can be mapped to these grids. The width of the image should be equal to its height, so that the proportions match those of the 64' by 64' grid. Also, ensure that the files are of a sufficiently high resolution, so that the mapping is smooth and the individual pixels of the image cannot be seen. You can generate these images from any of your other form•Z projects; just make sure to specify an appropriate size and resolution in the Image Options dialog before you save the image file.

Once you have your images ready, create a surface style using each of them with the Color option set to Image Map in the Surface Style Parameters dialog. Also, deselect the RenderZone Average option under the Simple section and change the Color in that section to the same red color for both surface styles, as shown.

Apply these two styles with the Color tool, one to each of the two vertical grids. Then use the Texture Map tool (as you learned in Section 4.2 of Workshop 5) to adjust the mapping so that the image fits exactly on the entire gridded surface.

Step 17

▷

Invoke the Rendering Attributes tool and select both options, Object Renders As Wireframe and Object Renders As Shaded Surface. In addition, change the associated Line Width to 2 pixels. Then apply this tool to the two vertical grids you just mapped the images to. The grid subdivisions themselves will now be visible in the RenderZone display, colored in the red color you specified under the Simple section of the Surface Styles Parameters dialog.

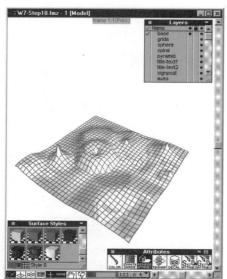

◀ Step 18

Next, turn to the base mesh to which you applied the **Move Mesh** operation. For this object, create a new surface style with the **Color** attribute set to the default of plain white. However, change the **Reflection** attribute to Chrome. Also, deselect the **RenderZone Average** option under the **Simple** section and change the **Color** to the same red color as you did for the two image-mapped styles in Step 15.

After creating the style, apply it to the base mesh. Also apply the **Rendering Attributes** tool to it, but with the **Line Width** for the **Object Renders As Wireframe** option reduced to 1 pixel.

Step 19

Next, create a new surface style with the **Color** attribute set to Marble, Textured and the **Transparency** set to Simple with a value of 50% in the accompanying **Options** dialog. Apply this style to the spherical ball in the center.

We also need to increase the scale of this texture with respect to the object so that it can be distinctly seen. For this, apply the **Texture Map** tool to it. Since the selected style is a solid rather than a wrapped texture, the **Solid Textures Size** value needs to be changed. Increase this from the default value of 1' to 10'.

▷

◀ Step 20

Create two new surface styles. For the first, go to the **Predefined** option in the **Surface Style Parameters** dialog and select the **Polished Gold** style from the **Metal** category. For the second, select the same predefined style, then change its **Color** attribute from orange to red.

Apply these two styles to the signpost. The boards, in particular, should be colored in gold. Apply the contrasting reddish gold color to the three text objects protruding from the boards. Then subtract these objects from the boards, conveying the effect of letters etched into the surface of the boards.

Step 21

Only a few remaining objects need to be colored. For the book title text objects, use the default white color for a new style in the Surface Styles Parameters dialog, but change the **Reflection** attribute to Plastic.

For the axis bands and the accompanying labels, create and apply a bright color that is distinct from the colors of all the other objects. To increase the brightness of the color, invoke the **Options** dialog for the **Matte** reflection attribute in its **Surface Style Parameters** dialog and increase the **Glow** factor to 15%.

For the spiral and twisted pyramid, create two different surface styles, both of which match some color in the images mapped on to the vertical grids. For some variation, increase the **Glow** factor for the surface style applied to the spiral; for the pyramid, choose the **Streaks** option for the **Color** attribute rather than **Plain Color**.

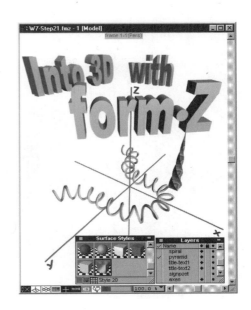

Step 22

All that remains is to adjust the background color and the lighting. Go to **Options > Project Colors** and set the **Background** color to black. Turn off the shining attribute of the default light in the **Lights** palette.

Create a new point light and change its radius to 50'. Also, deactivate the **Shadows** option. Change its name if you like and exit the **Light Parameters** dialog. Back in the graphics window, use the **Move** tool to position it in front of the configuration, sitting on the XY plane.

Create two more identical point lights of radius 30'. Reduce the **Basic Intensity** value to 60%, set **Falloff** to **Square**, and turn off the **Shadows** option. Position them so that they light up the title text objects.

◀ Step 23

Create three identical cone lights with a Basic Intensity of 60%, a Falloff of Square, and no Shadows. Position them so that each one lights up one of the subtitled boards of the signpost. Reduce the light spread so that only the boards are illuminated with these lights.

Create one last cone light with the default values but the Shadows option deactivated. Position this so that it lights up the whole signpost.

Finally, increase the overall brightness of the lighting by invoking the Lights dialog through the Lights palette and increasing the Intensity value of the Ambient Light from 10% to 30%.

Step 24

With that, your cover design is complete. Display it in RenderZone, save it as an image file, and you are in business! Remember to increase the resolution to at least 300 pixels/inch for a copy you can print. For this, you should also activate the Scale By option for Wireframe Width in the RenderZone Options dialog and set it to a value of 4 (the whole number obtained by dividing 300 by the default resolution of 72) so that your wireframe displays are not lost in the printed image.

▷

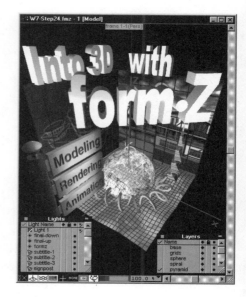

Brief Overview of the Drafting Module

The drafting module of form•Z is provided mainly in support of its modeling environment. After 3D models have been created, they, may need to be communicated to others for presentation or construction. For this, you might need to add text and dimensions to the images derived from 3D models, use a variety of line types and line thicknesses, apply hatch patterns, and so on. All of these tasks can be done in the drafting environment of form•Z, which basically emulates a traditional 2D CAD program like AutoCAD.

You can also draw directly in the drafting module. These drawings can serve as the base objects for the generation of 3D solids by transporting them to the modeling environment. This is useful on those occasions when the base 2D object is quite complex and you would like to create it accurately before proceeding to 3D modeling. The modeling environment, of course, does provide you with all the tools for creating 2D shapes, but you will find that the drafting module has a few extra tools which just might make the task a little simpler.

This appendix will give you a brief overview of the drafting module of form•Z. Since it has lots of similarities with the modeling environment, mastering the drafting module should not be a difficult task, and you should be able to go beyond the information provided here quite comfortably.

1. From Modeling to Drafting

Let us start by going through the process of how objects—or their 2D plans, sections, and elevations—can be transported from the modeling to the drafting environment.

Opening a Drafting Window

For every project in form•Z, just as you can open up one or more associated modeling windows using Windows > New Model Window, similarly, you can open up one or more associated drafting windows using Windows > New Draft Window. Such draft windows can be used to contain all the drafting work related to that modeling project and will automatically be saved when the project is saved. Don't expect, however, these associated drafting windows to automatically display 2D views of the objects that exist in the 3D modeling component of the project; there is no such correspondence between the two.

You can also simply open up a new drafting project using File > New[Draft] for creating the work related to one or more modeling projects. This will now be an independent project that has to be saved separately, just like any other modeling project that you have worked with so far.

The advantage of using an associated drafting window is that all the relevant settings such as working units, window setup, colors, and so on, that you specified for the modeling project will be automatically applied to the associated drafting windows. If you use a new drafting project, on the other hand, you will have to specify the settings again if they are different from the defaults.

Whatever method you choose, a draft window will switch you to the drafting environment when it is activated. This environment looks similar to the modeling environment, except that some of the tools and palettes are different. A draft window will also have the label [Draft] or [Draft Layout] appearing in the window title bar next to the project name, so there should be no confusion about which environment—drafting or modeling—you are currently in.

Copying Modeling Objects into the Drafting Module

Transferring objects between the modeling and drafting modules is a simple process. Simply select all that you want to transfer, go to Edit > Copy, open up a drafting window by either one of the two methods described in the last section, and select Edit > Paste From Modeling. The selected objects will now be "pasted" into the draft window, in the same position with respect to the origin as in the original model. (For copying objects from drafting to modeling, the corresponding paste option is Edit > Paste From Drafting.)

Notice from the asterisk * sign that the Paste From Modeling item under the Edit menu has a dialog associated with it. This can be opened in the usual manner—select this item while holding down the option key (Mac) or Ctrl+Shift keys (PC). You can see that by default, the Remove Duplicate And Overlapping Lines option is selected. This is helpful in getting rid of the many coincident segments that can exist in a planar view of a 3D object. However, this option also removes segment connectivity information, which means that a rectangle will be imported as four separate segments rather than as a rectangle. Thus, you cannot apply a hatch operation to this set of segments in the draft module until you reconnect them with the Join tool into a closed rectangle.

If you deselect the Remove Duplicate And Overlapping Lines option as shown in Figure A.1, the other two options in the dialog get activated. Segment connectivity information can be retained by selecting the Each Face/Outline As A Polyline option. The alternative, Each 3D Segment As A Single Line, is not very useful since connectivity information will be lost again. For both these options, keep in mind that duplicates are not removed, so you will have to remove them yourself step-by-step. It is not absolutely essential to remove duplicates unless the number of objects is very large, in which case it would be better to go for the default Remove Duplicate And Overlapping Lines option.

3D objects can be transferred from the modeling to the drafting environment looking at them either in planar or in non-planar views. The first is essential if you want to dimension your objects correctly, such as for plans, sections, etc. Of the non-planar views, recall that only in an Isometric or Oblique view do objects retain their actual dimensions, and that too only along the direction of the axes. In an Axonometric or Perspective non-planar view, none of the object dimensions will be correct. Since the 3D model is being "projected" on to a flat 2D surface, the dimensions of the original and the projection will only match for planar views such as Top, Front, etc. Thus, non-planar views are generally used for annotating rather than dimensioning when copied across to the drafting module.

Figure A.1

The Paste From Modeling dialog, with the Remove Duplicate And Overlapping Lines option deselected.

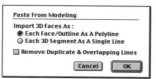

Generating Sections of Modeling Objects for Drafting

You have already seen how you can use the Section tool (M-Tool:8a,8), in either the 2D mode or the 3D mode, to generate sections of objects along a cutting plane. Once the Section operation is complete, those parts of the objects that should not appear in the desired planar view can be temporarily deleted. You can then switch to the view, and copy and paste the objects in a draft window. These "plans" and "sections" can now be annotated, dimensioned, and so on.

If some of the objects in your modeling project have non-planar faces, the Section tool will not be able to operate on them. In this case, you can make use of the Edit Cone Of Vision option to generate the desired sections by following the procedure described below. In fact, you might even find this method more convenient than using the Section tool.

■ Depending upon the plan or section you are trying to generate, switch to the appropriate planar view in your modeling project. Then go to View > Edit Cone Of Vision. Here, adjust both the front and back clipping planes so that you see only the required portion of the model for the given plan or section. To actually see how this would look, go to the Cone Of Vision menu (remember that you can click anywhere on the title bar of the window to access it) and select the Clip Hither/Yon option to activate it. You should now see only the "clipped" portion of your model in the preview window, as shown in Figure A.2. Save this view, and generate more, if necessary, following the same sequence of steps. Exit the Cone Of Vision environment when you are done.

Figure A.2

Adjusting the clipping planes in the Cone Of Vision environment to see only the desired section of a model.

■ Back in the graphics window, you will find that you see the complete object in Wire Frame rather than the clipped portion. Change to Quick Paint but it is still the same. Only when you switch to Hidden Line, Surface Render, and the higher rendering modes, is the view restricted to the clipped portion. Settle for the Hidden Line or Surface Render modes of display.

■ Now that you have obtained a result similar to what you would have if you had used the Section tool, you might think of simply copying and pasting the clipped modeling objects into the draft module. This, however, will not work, since the clipping is just a visual effect rather than an actual cut. Thus, you will be copying and pasting the complete objects and not just the cut portions. Try it. Obviously, we need to do something else in order to transfer these clipped images to the drafting environment.

◼ The solution is simple—you can save what you have into a 2D file format and then *import* that into a drafting window. Before saving it, there is a crucial step you must not forget to perform. Go to Windows > Window Setup and turn off the displays of all the axes and grids. This will leave only the modeling objects in the window, without all the background objects.

◼ Now go to File > Save As and save what you have in the PICT (Mac) or Metafile (PC) file formats. These are the only formats, common to both the modeling and drafting environments, that can save objects as polygons (vector-based) rather than as bitmaps. Bitmaps will be useless since you want to transport the objects in a form that you can also dimension, which you cannot do for a bitmapped image. Stick with the default options for the file format when you save the file.

◼ After saving the file, open a new draft window and use File > Import to choose the file you just saved. You will be presented with a dialog containing some import options. Settle for the default Import As Drafting Elements option. Your objects will be transported, clipped just the way they were in the modeling view that you had saved. The only catch is that the dimensions of what you now have in the draft window will no longer match the actual dimensions of the objects in the original model.

◼ Getting around this problem is relatively simple. Find out the dimension of a particular segment using the Query tool in both the draft and model windows, divide the modeling dimension by the drafting dimension to get a scaling factor, and use the Uniform Scale tool in the draft window to scale all the objects by this factor. You will now have an accurate sectioned drawing of your model in a draft window. This additional step of scaling is, of course, not needed when the Copy command is used to transfer objects from modeling to drafting.

Now that you know how to transfer sections of objects from the modeling to the drafting environment, let us look at the components of this environment and how they differ from the modeling environment that we know so well from all the workshops.

2. Differences Between the Drafting and Modeling Environments

The drafting environment of form•Z has an interface similar to the modeling environment. It is comprised of the main pulldown menu, the drafting tool palette on the left, the window tool palette at the bottom, a number of floating palettes, and of course, the graphics window. Most of the commands and tools are identical to what you have already seen for the modeling environment. However, there are some differences. Let us see what they are.

Main Menu and Graphics Window

In the main pulldown menu, you will notice that the Heights menu is completely grayed out. Since the drafting module contains only 2D objects, the concept of "heights" does not exist. The View menu, likewise, has most of its options deactivated. There is no concept of seeing the objects from different angles—you can see 2D objects only head-on. Thus the graphics window always looks the same. You can choose to rotate it using the different rotation angles in the View menu, or zoom and scroll through it using the various window tools, but you will always be looking at it in exactly the same "view."

Also notice that under the Display menu, all the various display modes are deactivated, except for a Replot command. Since there are no 3D objects, there is nothing to render. All that you might want to do is refresh the screen occasionally, which is what the Replot command does.

Tool Palettes

The drafting tool palette located on the left of the graphics window is revised to meet the requirements for drafting, and we will briefly go through each row of tools of the drafting palette in Section 4.

The window tool palette is essentially the same as in the modeling environment, except that the tools which are not applicable to drafting—Reference Planes, Perpendicular Lock, and so on—are grayed out. The Grid Snap and Direction Snap, as well as the Zoom & Pan tools remain the same. The Object Snap options are almost the same, except for the introduction of a new option called Tangent, which constrains the mouse movement along the tangent to a circle, arc, or ellipse.

Floating Palettes

The drafting module has eleven floating palettes as opposed to the thirteen that exist for the modeling environment. Of these, four are unique to the drafting module (see Figure A.3). These are Colors, Hatch Patterns, Line Weights, and Line Styles. The remaining six are identical to the corresponding palettes in the modeling environment. Notice that you also have a Views palette, although you cannot really have different views, as such, of 2D objects. But you can zoom the graphics window in and out, rotate it, and scroll through it—each of these can be saved as a separate view in the Views palette.

The Colors palette for drafting corresponds to the Surface Styles palette for modeling. Since there is no concept of rendering in 2D, there can obviously be no concept of textures and texture mapping. But you can apply different colors to 2D objects by highlighting different colors in the Colors palette. You can create new colors or delete existing ones in the same manner as you did for surface styles.

The other three palettes are self-explanatory. Hatch Patterns contains various kinds of patterns that you can apply to the interior of an object using the Hatch tool. Line Weights and Line Styles allow you to choose between various line thicknesses and styles an object can be drawn in. Appropriate tools for modifying all these attributes of an object exist in the drafting tool palette, which we shall soon look at.

Figure A.3

The four palettes unique to the drafting environment of form•Z.

3. Draft Space Versus Layout Space

In its drafting module, form•Z gives you the option of working in two different modes. The one you see as soon you open a new draft window is the *draft space* mode. This is the regular working mode, in which you have a graphics window where you create various entities, just as in the modeling environment. Any change made to the view, layer settings, and so on affects the entire window.

The alternate mode, *layout space*, is useful for composing a set of drawings for printing. One *pane* can be created for each drawing. A number of such panes can be composed, in combination with text and other graphic elements, as shown in Figure A.4. A pane is essentially a *window* into the draft space. You can create your separate drawings in different parts of the draft space, or on different layers. Then, in the layout space, each pane can be set to "see" a different part of the draft space or a different layer, so as to have different drawings visible in different panes. Keep in mind that a "drawing" does not have to be something necessarily created within the drafting environment; it can also be a set of modeling objects or even a rendered image imported into the drafting environment. Examples of panes containing different kinds of drawings are shown in Figure A.4.

By default, you are in the draft space mode, as you can see. To enter into the layout space mode, go to Display > Draft Layout Mode. The only visible change is that all your drafting elements will disappear, presenting you with a blank window. Look carefully and you will notice that the word "Draft" has been replaced by the words "Draft Layout" in the title bar of the window.

The next step is to add panes in the window for the number of drawings you want to compose. This is done by setting the object generation mode in the drafting tool palette to Pane—the second tool in the right column of the first row—and using the regular drawing tools. Panes can be of any shape and size. As soon as a pane is drawn, the elements in the draft space will be visible through it.

To manipulate what you see through this pane, activate it by selecting it with the Pick Pane tool—the second tool in the right column of the fourth row. It gets highlighted in gray. You can now change its view, layer, and display settings to compose your drawing properly within it. You can even create or modify entities in the draft space *through* this pane, although it is better to be in the draft space mode to do this.

Figure A.4

Panes in the layout space of the drafting environment, showing various aspects of the project composed for printing.

When no pane is activated, changes in the view and display settings are applied to the entire layout space window. Any entities that you draw or text that you place now are created in the layout space and will not be visible in the draft space. Thus you can format the layout window for printing in any manner, maintaining a clear separation between the entities in the project and the elements added only for printing.

Once created, panes can be moved, resized, deleted, and so on like regular drafting elements by selecting them with the Pick tool (*not* the Pick Pane tool) and applying the desired operation.

To exit the layout space mode, select the same command, Draft Layout Mode, from the Display menu.

4.   The Drafting Tool Palette

The layout of the drafting tool palette is similar to that of the modeling tool palette. The different rows of tools are shown in Figure A.5. This section will provide you with a brief overview of these tools. Many of these are identical to the modeling tools covered in the seven workshops. So we will concentrate only on where and how the drafting palette differs from the modeling palette. Note that a similar notation will be used to refer to the tools. Thus, D-Tool:1a,1 refers to the first tool in the left column of the first row of the drafting tool palette, and so on.

Figure A.5

The thirteen rows of tools, arranged in two columns, of the drafting tool palette.

Row 1: Element Generation Modes

These tools determine the type of element that will be generated by the drawing operators located in the next two rows. (Note that the term "element" in the drafting environment corresponds to "object" in the modeling environment.) The tools in the left column are the familiar single-line and double-line modes. Of the two tools in the right column, we have already looked at Pane in Section 3. The remaining tool is the Area Generation mode, which will be discussed now. It is used for creating a special element unique to the drafting environment known as an *area*. This is a temporary element, used not for creating entities, but for the identification of other drafting elements to which some operation can subsequently be applied.

An area element is generated through the same set of drawing operators on Rows 2 and 3 as the other element types. It can be of any shape, but is required to always be *closed*. Thus, polylines are automatically closed in the area mode, while open arcs are not acceptable at all. The area is displayed on the screen with a gray fill, which clearly distinguishes it from other drafting elements (see Figure A.7-a). It plays an auxiliary role only and does not appear in the final drawing. Also, there can only be a *single* area element in a project at any given time. Generating a new area element replaces the previous one, if any.

Once created, an area element can be moved or modified just like any other shape. The boundary of the area splits the drawing into two portions: the *inside* and the *outside*, forming two separate groups. The area's main function is to *pick* other drafting elements in this manner, identifying them for a particular operation such as move, rotate, copy, etc. This operation can be applied to either the inside or the outside group, the choice of which is made in the dialog of the Area tool, under the Area Type section (Figure A.6).

Figure A.6

The dialog of the Area element generation tool.

There is an additional section in the dialog called Boundary Type, which has three options. The first, In/Out Only, will select only those elements that lie completely inside or completely outside the boundary of the area (for Area Type settings of Inside and Outside respectively). The second, On/Crossing, will also select elements that touch or cross the boundary of the area. The third option, Clip To Area, enables the area to be used as a clipping tool. With this option, elements that cross the boundaries of the area are broken at their points of intersection when an area is picked.

To actually select the elements thus designated or clipped by an area, the topological level on Row 4 needs to be set to Area (D-Tool:4a,6). Any transformation such as Move will now be applied to the elements selected by the area. This is illustrated in Figure A.7-b, where the Clip To Area and Inside options were selected in the Area dialog, and the Move tool was applied with the topological level set to Area. (Note that if the topological level is set to Element, the area *itself* will be moved, rather than the elements it selects.)

Figure A.7

Working with an "area" element. (a) A rectangular area created in a drawing. (b) Moving the area along with its enclosing elements.

Rows 2 and 3: Drafting Operators

These tools can be used to draw polygons of any type, circles, ellipses, lines, curves, points, and arcs. They are identical to those found in the modeling environment and work in the same fashion.

Notice that there are two seemingly identical sets of Arc tools, located on Row 2 as well as Row 3. The difference between the two sets is that the ones on Row 3 are *elemental arcs*, i.e., they are not comprised of a series of segments that can be selected by setting the topological level to Segment. (However, these arcs still appear to be segmented, based on the resolution specified in the Arc/Circle/Ellipse Resolution dialog.) On the other hand, the Arc tools on Row 2 create *polyarcs*, i.e., arcs comprised of a sequence of segments which can be individually selected.

Row 4: Topological Levels and Picking

The tools in the left column establish the topological level at which the subsequently executed operators will be applied, just as in the modeling environment. You are already familiar with Point, Segment, and Auto. Element corresponds to Object of the modeling environment. Compound is similar to Group of the modeling environment—it acts on elements that have been linked into a compound element using the Make Compound tool on Row 6. And finally, Area, as we have seen, refers to the area element that can be drawn using D-Tool:1b,1.

The tools in the right column are Pick, which is identical to its counterpart in modeling, and Pick Pane, which was discussed earlier in Section 3.

Row 5: Deriving Enclosures and Parallel Offsets

The Enclosure tool in the left column generates a double-line element out of a single-line element. The thickness of the double line is specified in its dialog.

The Parallel tool on the right creates a new element that is parallel to the selected element. The offset—the distance of the new element from the original—can be graphically specified by a mouse click. Alternately, a specific offset distance can be set in the tool dialog.

Row 6: Booleans and Compounding

The four boolean operators in the left column—Union, Intersection, Difference, and Split—work identically to their modeling counterparts. In the right column, there is the Make Compound tool, which works on the same principle as the Group tool of the modeling environment. Compounded elements can be restored to their original "ungrouped" status by using the Explode tool on Row 8.

Row 7: Line Editing

Both the left and right columns contain a number of tools for the manipulation and editing of lines in various ways. They are practically identical to the line editing tools in the modeling environment that you worked with in Section 4.6 of Workshop 2. The only difference is that the various options in the dialogs of those tools appear as separate tools in the drafting environment. So, for instance, the six options and sub-options of the Trim tool (M-Tool:10a,3) in the modeling tool palette appear as six separate tools—Trim Open, Trim Join, Trim Fillet, Trim Bevel, Trim Lines, and Trim With Lines—in the drafting tool palette.

Row 8: Placing Text and Symbols

Here are the operators for placing and editing text and creating and placing symbols. They work identically to the text and symbol tools in the modeling environment. The text, of course, will not be 3D text but regular 2D text, which you can place at a point or between two points. The choice is made in the dialog of the Place Text tool. There are a number of options related to text display in the Drafting Display Options dialog, invoked by going to Display > Display Options. Be sure to check them out. One useful option is to use a *stick font* for the text, which helps to speed up screen regeneration while working in the drafting module.

The symbols that you place using the Place Symbol tool have to be drafting symbols, i.e., they must be created in the drafting module and then transformed to symbols using the Create Symbol tool. Both drafting and modeling symbols, however, can be placed in the same library. Only the drafting symbols will show up in the Symbols palette when such a library is loaded in the drafting module. If a library contains only modeling objects, it will be of no use when you are working in the drafting environment.

The Explode tool accompanying the other symbol tools in the right column does not work just on symbols in the drafting environment, as in the modeling environment. It also operates on other drafting elements, reducing their structure by one level. Thus polylines, polycurves, and polyarcs get broken down into their constituent segments, rectangles and arcs into polylines, dimensions into their constituent lines and text, and leader lines into their constituent segments. (Dimensions and leader lines will be covered next.) The most elementary entities are single segments and text, which cannot be exploded further.

Row 9: Dimensions

This row contains all the tools needed for placing and editing dimensions and leader lines. It is unique to the drafting module, since there is no concept of dimensioning in 3D modeling. The first six tools in the left column allow you to apply different kinds of dimensioning on elements: horizontal and vertical, parallel, angular, radial, diametric, and circular. An example of each one of these is shown in Figure A.8.

To create a dimension using the first two tools, you can select any number of points and double-click after you have finished making the selection. A dimension line will be rubber-banded. Click to position it where you want it to be. The distances between all the selected points will appear as dimensions. The Parallel dimension tool creates dimensions parallel to the segments between the selected points, in contrast to the Horizontal/Vertical tool which marks horizontal and vertical dimensions only.

The Angle dimension tool is used by selecting any three points. This will dimension the angle subtended by the first and third points at the second point. The Radius, Diameter, and Arc dimension tools work on circles and arcs only, giving you their radius, diameter, and length respectively. Keep in mind that these three tools will not work on the polyarcs created using the drawing tools on Row 2, only on the arcs created with the tools on Row 3.

Figure A.8

The six kinds of dimensions that have dedicated dimension tools in form•Z.

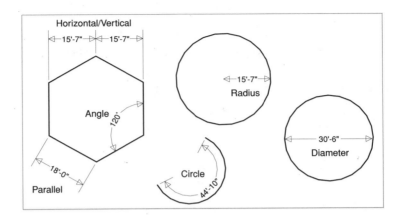

Once a dimension is created, it gets attached to the element it is dimensioning. Thus, it moves when the element is moved, gets deleted when the element is deleted, is updated automatically when the element is resized, and so on. This makes dimensions very simple and convenient to use.

Dimensions can also be placed that do not reference any particular element. These are referred to as non-attached or *non-associative* dimensions. To place such dimensions, simply select the required points in the graphics window. Such points are known as non-associative points, and are displayed by default. They can be selected for repositioning by setting the topological level to Point—the dimension will be automatically updated. The display of such points can be turned off in the Dimension Display section of the Display Options dialog.

Very often, you will find that the overall appearance of a dimension may not be quite what you had in mind. There are many components to a dimension, which are illustrated in Figure A.9-a. Each one of these components has its own dialog, which is accessed by clicking on the respective button in the dialogs of the dimension tools (Figure A.9-b). You can explore each one of these component attributes and see how it affects the appearance of the dimension. For instance, you can change the size and font of the text (using the same Text Editor dialog that comes with the Text tools), use dots or slashes instead of arrows as the dimension terminators, and so on.

In addition to the buttons for invoking the component dialogs, the dialog of each dimension tool comes with its own set of options, as shown in Figure A.9-b. You should take the time to explore these before doing any serious work with dimensions.

Figure A.9

The various components of a dimension element, and one of the dimension tool dialogs through which they can be modified.

Note that you cannot change the attributes of dimensions that have already been created by modifying them through the tool dialogs. You have to take the additional step of applying the Set Dimension Attributes tool (D-Tool:9b,2) to these dimensions. As you would expect, the attribute buttons in the dialog shown in Figure A.9-b are also provided in the dialog of the Set Dimension Attributes tool.

You can also conveniently copy the attributes of one dimension element to another dimension element. First, select the dimension whose attributes are to be copied with the Get Dimension Attributes tool (D-Tool:9b,1). What this effectively does is change all the dimension attribute settings based on the attributes of the selected dimension. This combination of attributes can now be applied to any other dimension element by selecting it with the Set Dimension Attributes tool.

There are two remaining tools on Row 9, one in the left column and one in the right. The Leader tool, located in the left column, is simply used to draw lines that have an arrow or some other kind of terminator at one or both ends. Such lines are often used for annotating various parts of a drawing. The choice of terminator, as well as the end on which the terminator should appear, is made in the dialog of the Leader tool. The Reposition Dimension tool in the right column is used to reposition the dimension line of a dimension element. This is contrast to the Move tool, which when applied to a dimension element, moves the whole element.

Finally, keep in mind that dimensions and leader lines are elements just like any other drawing element, and can be deleted, colored, etc. in the usual fashion.

Row 10: Self-Copy Modifiers and Query

These sets of tools are exactly identical to those found in the modeling environment. There is no Define Macro tool, however, since macro transformations are not provided in the drafting environment.

Row 11: Geometric Transformations

The tools in the left column execute translations, rotations, scalings, and reflections, operating directly on the original element or in creating one or more copies of it, depending upon the setting of the self-copy modifier. These tools are already familiar to you from the modeling environment.

In the right column are the Align, Extend, and Place tools, with similar abilities and functions as their counterparts in modeling. Note that the Extend tool works with polylines and arcs only. It extends or shrinks them, retaining the original orientation of the polyline or the radius of the arc.

Row 12: Attribute Assignment

These tools are used to modify various element attributes such as line weight, line type, color, layer, and ghosting. All of these operators can be applied at the Element level only.

The desired line type and line weight have to be set in the Line Styles and Line Weights palettes respectively. They can then be applied to any element using the first two tools on Row 12: Set Line Type and Set Line Weight. You are already familiar with the Color tool. The fourth tool in the left column, Set All, simultaneously changes the line type, line weight, color, and layer of the selected element to the current settings of these attributes.

Ghost, Unghost, and Set Layer in the right column work in an identical fashion as in the modeling environment.

Row 13: Delete and Hatch

The Delete tool in the left column of this last row deletes entities, prepicked or postpicked, just as in the modeling environment.

The Hatch tool in the right column, however, is unique to the drafting module. This lets you apply a selected pattern from the Hatch Patterns palette to an element. The element can also be an open shape, as shown in Figure A.10, as long as it encloses some amount of area. Obviously, you will not be able to apply a hatch pattern to a straight line. Once a hatch is created, it can be selected with the Pick tool independently of the element to which it has been applied. This makes it possible to select it and delete it if required, which is useful because there is no "un-hatch" command. You should take care to delete old hatch patterns before applying new ones to an element, since the Hatch tool does not do this automatically. If you are not able to select the hatch (which can sometimes happen for open shapes) but want to delete it, try applying the white hatch pattern to the element as a short-term solution.

Figure A.10

Different kinds of hatch patterns applied to various elements. The line weight of the elements has also been increased.

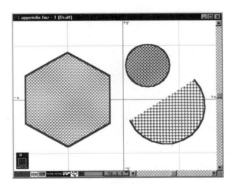

This concludes our brief overview of the drafting module of form•Z.

Index

About the Author

Lachmi Khemlani teaches CAD courses at the University of California, Berkeley, where she is also working toward her Ph.D., specializing in computer applications in architecture. In particular, she has been teaching form•Z workshops there for over four years. Her credentials include a professional B.Arch. (Hons) degree from I.I.T Kharagpur, India, and an M.Phil. in Architecture from the University of Cambridge, UK. She has also worked on several design projects as a practicing architect.

SOFTWARE AND INFORMATION LICENSE

The software and information on this diskette (collectively referred to as the "Product") are the property of The McGraw-Hill Companies, Inc. ("McGraw-Hill") and are protected by both United States copyright law and international copyright treaty provision. You must treat this Product just like a book, except that you may copy it into a computer to be used and you may make archival copies of the Products for the sole purpose of backing up our software and protecting your investment from loss.

By saying "just like a book," McGraw-Hill means, for example, that the Product may be used by any number of people and may be freely moved from one computer location to another, so long as there is no possibility of the Product (or any part of the Product) being used at one location or on one computer while it is being used at another. Just as a book cannot be read by two different people in two different places at the same time, neither can the Product be used by two different people in two different places at the same time (unless, of course, McGraw-Hill's rights are being violated).

McGraw-Hill reserves the right to alter or modify the contents of the Product at any time.

This agreement is effective until terminated. The Agreement will terminate automatically without notice if you fail to comply with any provisions of this Agreement. In the event of termination by reason of your breach, you will destroy or erase all copies of the Product installed on any computer system or made for backup purposes and shall expunge the Product from your data storage facilities.

LIMITED WARRANTY

McGraw-Hill warrants the physical diskette(s) enclosed herein to be free of defects in materials and workmanship for a period of sixty days from the purchase date. If McGraw-Hill receives written notification within the warranty period of defects in materials or workmanship, and such notification is determined by McGraw-Hill to be correct, McGraw-Hill will replace the defective diskette(s). Send request to:

Customer Service
McGraw-Hill
Gahanna Industrial Park
860 Taylor Station Road
Blacklick, OH 43004-9615

The entire and exclusive liability and remedy for breach of this Limited Warranty shall be limited to replacement of defective diskette(s) and shall not include or extend to any claim for or right to cover any other damages, including but not limited to, loss of profit, data, or use of the software, or special, incidental, or consequential damages or other similar claims, even if McGraw-Hill has been specifically advised as to the possibility of such damages. In no event will McGraw-Hill's liability for any damages to you or any other person ever exceed the lower of suggested list price or actual price paid for the license to use the Product, regardless of any form of the claim.

THE McGRAW-HILL COMPANIES, INC. SPECIFICALLY DISCLAIMS ALL OTHER WARRANTIES, EXPRESS OR IMPLIED, INCLUDING BUT NOT LIMITED TO, ANY IMPLIED WARRANTY OF MERCHANTABILITY OR FITNESS FOR A PARTICULAR PURPOSE. Specifically, McGraw-Hill makes no representation or warranty that the Product is fit for any particular purpose and any implied warranty of merchantability is limited to the sixty day duration of the Limited Warranty covering the physical diskette(s) only (and not the software or in-formation) and is otherwise expressly and specifically disclaimed.

This Limited Warranty gives you specific legal rights; you may have others which may vary from state to state. Some states do not allow the exclusion of incidental or consequential damages, or the limitation on how long an implied warranty lasts, so some of the above may not apply to you.

This Agreement constitutes the entire agreement between the parties relating to use of the Product. The terms of any purchase order shall have no effect on the terms of this Agreement. Failure of McGraw-Hill to insist at any time on strict compliance with this Agreement shall not constitute a waiver of any rights under this Agreement. This Agreement shall be construed and governed in accordance with the laws of New York. If any provision of this Agreement is held to be contrary to law, that provision will be enforced to the maximum extent permissible and the remaining provisions will remain in force and effect.